WASTE SIEGE

Stanford Studies *in* Middle Eastern
and Islamic Societies *and* Cultures

WASTE SIEGE

The Life of Infrastructure in Palestine

Sophia Stamatopoulou-Robbins

STANFORD UNIVERSITY PRESS

Stanford, California

STANFORD UNIVERSITY PRESS
Stanford, California

© 2020 by the Board of Trustees of the Leland Stanford Junior University.
All rights reserved.

Printed in the United States of America on acid-free, archival-quality paper

Library of Congress Cataloging-in-Publication Data available upon request.

ISBN 978-1-5036-0730-9 (cloth)
ISBN 978-1-5036-1089-7 (paperback)
ISBN 978-1-5036-1090-3 (electronic)

Cover design: Kevin Barrett Kane

Cover photo credit: Peggy Ahwesh

Text design: Kevin Barrett Kane

Typeset at Stanford University Press in 10/14.4 Brill

For Themis

Contents

Preface

Waste is one of the most universal aspects of human life. Yet humans experience waste in very different ways. The cultural significance of waste changes across time and space, and so does the material form that waste takes. In the twenty-first century some populations live in greater proximity to waste than others. Some are inundated by it, others not. Palestinians in the Israeli-occupied West Bank, whose work and lives this book depicts, are surrounded by unprecedented types and volumes of waste that they are unable to escape, and they must therefore divide their attention between pursuing life under a brutal military occupation that has entered its sixth decade and the need to address a new form of siege, a siege made of discards: a waste siege.[1]

My premise here is that this emergent, yet overlooked, form of siege shapes politics and ethics for Palestinians in unexpected ways. Unwanted things are increasingly important, unaccounted-for actors in Palestine, mediating and complicating life at multiple scales.[2] Those of us outside Palestine thus need new language to position ourselves ethically and politically vis-à-vis ongoing injustices there, injustices that demand consideration of the mundane and seemingly apolitical. This new language will be useful for other areas of study as well.

Palestine is not often at the forefront of anthropological understandings of contemporary phenomena. It tends to capture people's attention precisely because of its purported uniqueness. There are several reasons for this. One is that it seems to be out of step with history. It houses a people some of whose members are still seeking statehood in a moment when the supply of available statehood "cards" seems to have been depleted. Another is that Israel's association with the Holocaust, arguably the most iconic genocide of the twentieth century, merits the treatment of Israel/Palestine as a special, separate case for many observers. The length of Palestine's occupation often exempts it from comparison with other war zones. Yet the occupation also sets Palestinians' experience of everyday life apart from the everyday experiences of people in other contemporary contexts perceived to be in peacetime. Palestine's jurisdictional complexities—that its borders are undefined, that it is under six different legal regimes, including those of a foreign occupier and an "interim" Palestinian Authority—also distinguish it from a twenty-first-century global landscape populated by nation-states with internationally recognized borders and central governments.[3] This book tries to bring Palestine back into the general conversation about the state of the world by looking at it from the viewpoint of waste.

As I understand it, waste in Palestine constitutes a siege whose lifting remains difficult to imagine. Inundation by waste seems inescapable (Nash 2006) as it is experienced by Palestinians today. Any attempt to address the ethical, political, or practical dilemmas that waste generates or, equally, to capitalize on the opportunities it opens up, results in the redistribution and reformulation of waste's dilemmas rather than in their eradication. The phrase *waste siege* is meant to convey a sense of surroundedness: a sense that life without being surrounded by wastes is increasingly inconceivable. My formulation complicates the definition of waste as "matter out of place," as some have defined it following anthropologist Mary Douglas's (2005, 44) definition of dirt, which renewed the argument of philosopher and psychologist William James (1929, 131) that dirt was a matter of classification. For Palestinians, waste has become *matter with no place to go*. It is always present even when it changes form. Unable to export or to incinerate wastes in waste-to-energy incineration plants, for instance, many communities burn household trash and agricultural waste inside or at the edges of residential areas. Refuse reenters their lives through their lungs as dioxins carried by the smoke.

In prioritizing this view of waste, the book builds on recent studies on waste and its management in the emergent field of discard studies that challenge long-standing arguments in anthropology that waste is a cultural category applied to inert matter (e.g., Bowler 1998; Chalfin 2014; Fredericks 2014, 2018; Gille

2010; Gregson et al. 2009; Gregson and Crang 2010; Lepawsky and Mather 2011; Lepawsky and McNabb 2010; Lippert 2011; Magnani 2012; S. Moore 2012; Nagle 2013; Neyland and Simakova 2012; Reno 2015b). It challenges arguments that waste is rejected matter that offends ideas of social order because matter is *perceived* to be offensive, while at the same time giving meaning to ideas about order by contrast with it. *Waste Siege* highlights the material inescapability of dwelling in waste as a material environment. Waste requires people to adapt to it, as people do to forms of violence and humiliation that become routine under occupation (e.g., Allen 2008; A. Bishara 2015; Peteet 2017). Waste acts upon the social. It is political not only as a product of political *processes* but also as a political actor. It is what Sarah Moore (2012, 781), drawing on Slavoj Zizek's work, has called a "parallax object: 'that which objects, that which disturbs the smooth running of things.'" But by emphasizing Palestinians' experiences of waste as everything from odor and illness to the tendency of commodities to break quickly to the ethical burden of having no one to whom one can give still-usable goods, it also builds on scholarship that complicates the idea that waste is a nonhuman actor with an agency independent of humans (see Gille 2007).[4] Waste siege is shaped by cultural and social experiences of risk, but it is also an ontologically manifest threat (Parkhill et al. 2009).

Like any siege, waste siege is productive; living in proximity to waste generates new life-forms and lifeways.[5] In Palestine, as in general, waste is a shifting terrain upon which modern social and political life is built. Waste exerts pressure on one's priorities and one's sense of self, a pressure that results in its own set of responses. People respond to waste siege by improvising, making creative use of the already available. In the closed system of a siege, that includes waste itself. The term *waste siege* describes the necessity of continuing to engage with that which is unwanted or cast off in one's effort to escape it. The infrastructures that must be erected in order to deal with the dilemmas of waste provide sites and occasions for potential improvisation but can themselves also create material and ethical dilemmas. If waste siege is an infinity loop whose texture is constantly shifting but whose components somehow remain the same, it also produces creative engagement with the waste that besieges.

Yet if *waste siege* describes the state of stateless Palestine, it is also a metaphor for a dying planet. As the site of an extreme social experiment, Palestine is helpful for comparison with, and is also a symptom of, what is afoot in the rest of the world. This book joins a growing body of work that attempts to show the ways in which, despite the undeniably singular features of the Palestinian condition, those interested in other places in the world will benefit from thinking about Palestine, and indeed would be unwise not to.[6] This book offers a way to think as much about Palestinian life as about the fact, for example, that radioactive materials are leaking out of nuclear power plants in Japan, France, and New York and that such leakages, like other waste types that humans produce, are outpacing the technologies for minimizing their negative effects.[7] After the 1986 explosion at Chernobyl, the USSR constructed a sarcophagus of concrete and steel to contain contamination leaking from Chernobyl's reactor, which, without a cover, could explode and destroy parts of Europe. But the sarcophagus lost its capacity to contain radioactive leaks and expired by 2016, thirty years after its construction. A similar fate awaits the shield just installed as its replacement, as the shield will, over time, also become radioactive. The sarcophagus and shield are improvised infrastructures whose invention was occasioned by the explosion and whose capacity to contain radioactive outflow is dwarfed by the hundreds of thousands of years radioactive materials take to become less radioactive (Johnston 2007).

Palestinians in the West Bank are overrun by largely less glamorous forms of waste, including household trash, sewage, food scraps, disposable goods, and medical, factory, construction, and demolition waste. Yet the principle of excess holds just as much for these waste types as it does for an oil spill: whether old tires are used to border a new landfill or are burned in a demonstration, and even when wastewater is filtered to the highest possible level of decontamination, something—a material remnant—is always left over. Waste siege is a matter of proportions in finite space. When a Palestinian construction company dumps building materials in a Ramallah neighborhood, it exacerbates a claustrophobia Palestinians already experience as Israel confiscates more of their land and as the Palestinian population grows. The proportion of wastes to habitable earth is similarly growing.

Like efforts to address radioactive materials, oceanic oil spills, or nonbio-degradable plastic bags that fill landfills and animals' stomachs, the way Palestinians experience and deal with the discards that surround them is useful for thinking about the temporal sensibility of humans' relationship to contemporary waste. It is a conscious, reactive relationship where the problem always seems to precede preparation for its solution while the solution always seems to reach into a future shorter than the problem's duration. Waste in the West Bank contributes to a feeling of stuckness in time—for example, between the point in the past when construction companies began piling debris in neighborhoods and the point in an unknown future when the Palestinian Authority might create a place for debris disposal.

A focus on waste also pulls our view of Israel, the most important structuring force in Palestine's waste siege, into a global context. The Israeli state has long held planetary-universalizing ambitions. Many of these have been realized as it has made a name for itself as a global leader that exports ideas such as the kibbutz movement and technologies from wastewater treatment to drones and walls in global securitization projects. The fact that, like disenfranchised people across the world, the people in Israel's occupied territories live in a dilemma-ridden relation, and inescapable proximity, to waste is another side, an underside, of Israel's globality.

By bringing together different kinds of waste—trash, used goods, medical and industrial wastes, bread, and sewage—the book works at the intersection of anthropological investigations of waste, infrastructure, and environment to think about capitalism's material excesses and where they converge with contemporary colonial processes and statecraft, as I describe in the Introduction. It also builds on recent anthropological studies of the environment in the Middle East and North Africa (e.g., Alatout 2006, 2008; Barnes 2014; D. Davis and Burke III 2011; Farmer and Barnes 2018; Guarasci 2018; Günel 2019; L. Harris 2011; Jones 2010; McKee 2016; Mikhail 2011, 2013a, 2013b; Popperl 2018; Rubaii 2018; Scaramelli 2013; Sowers 2011; Stamatopoulou-Robbins 2014, 2018; Tesdell 2015, 2017; Touhouliotis 2018) to incorporate an analysis of environments and their logics into the study of a region more often framed by concerns about violence, kinship, and religion—all concerns, as this book shows, that intersect with environment but that are too often thought independently of it. Doing so in a moment when populations in the Middle East and North Africa, and worldwide, are struggling to come to terms with challenges posed by the refuse left in the wake of war, industry, and consumption makes the case that waste and consumption (for example, of food and cheap goods) are two sides of the same coin. We should think of trade in used goods and recirculation of unwanted bread alongside wastewater treatment, shopping, and landfilling. I wish to encourage questions about how particular contexts of stuckness are formed from the dynamics between waste and political formations such as war, occupation, and statehood.[8]

The book's unusual focus on waste was born out of my thinking about infrastructure in general, and its relationship to waste in particular was sparked by a moment when both came into special focus. During the days leading up to the victory of Hamas, a Palestinian Islamist movement, in the 2006 Palestinian Legislative Council elections, observers in the northern West Bank city of Jenin reported that while factions of the older, secular party, Fatah, clashed, Hamas members walked the streets delivering sermons and collecting garbage with their hands. This type of scene was picked up by commentators in North America and Europe following Hamas's landslide win. They argued that infrastructure was a tool for popular mobilization because it was an object around which public expectations of government revolved. They proposed that occupied Palestinians viewed infrastructural failures, such as that of waste disposal, as a reflection of the Fatah-led Authority's failure to govern. For many commentators, especially those committed to secular Palestinian nationalism, this explained why so many Palestinians had voted for Hamas after ten years of being governed by a Fatah-led Authority.[9]

The argument that bad or missing infrastructures determined voting patterns was based on the assumption that waste and its infrastructures have a stable set of meanings wherever, and whenever, they may be (Stamatopoulou-Robbins 2008). An assumption this book hopes to investigate, it has been reserved for countries deemed in need of development, where foreign states and agencies sponsoring infrastructural and service provision reforms expect their support to achieve specific political outcomes (e.g., Escobar 1995; Ferguson 1990; T. Mitchell 2002). Roads, bridges, and landfills become vehicles for quashing "radicalism" and "insurgency." International governments and aid agencies, Israel, and even the Authority have promoted multi-million-dollar sanitation infrastructures in the hopes that they will win Palestinians' hearts and minds by giving them a sense of being taken care of (N. Gordon 2008).

How, I wondered, could anyone assume that Palestinians—who have lived without a state of their own and under six different political systems—Ottoman, British, Jordanian, Egyptian, Israeli, and Palestinian—in just over a century and who currently live under as many legal systems, would have a predictable relationship to infrastructure and would predictably hold certain actors accountable when sanitary infrastructures failed? Absent that predictability, what is the relationship between waste, politics, and ethics in Palestine? I set out to answer this question in 2007.

Since then prime ministers have risen and fallen. The Authority has been territorially split, with Hamas running it in Gaza since 2007 and Fatah, backed by the United States and Europe, running it in the West Bank. Diplomatic negotiations between these two Palestinian parties and between them and Israel have faltered. Journalists have covered the destruction of Palestinian protest camps and marches demanding that Palestinian refugees be allowed to return to their homes, and media are abuzz about a Palestinian call to boycott companies supporting occupation. Palestinians have begun and suspended hunger strikes in Israeli prisons.

Journalists, scholars, and activists who cover such events tend to frame them as steps closer to, or further away from, realizing the goals either of the Israeli or Palestinian national movements or of specific political parties. The Palestinian everyday, as well as the constant remaking of those goals and movements, disappears under the weight of grand narratives about nation and state. A focus on daily experiences of waste like trash and sewage offers one of the most powerful ways to render that process of disappearance visible and to provide a window onto that which is disappeared. Waste is a mundane material matrix through which we can view Palestinian life outside the usual state- and nation-centered frameworks for thinking about Palestine. And, at the same time, through waste Palestinians engage with one another and articulate ideas of nation and state, among other important ideas.

If Palestinians' experiences of waste siege help shed light on changing planetary conditions because of the universality of the challenge of waste inundation, that same universality offers a new window onto Palestinian life. *Waste Siege* presents an unconventional view of Palestinian experiences by decentering the spectacular violence, nationalist claims, and high politics that tend to animate discussions of this place usually thought of as a holy land suffering from protracted conflict. *Waste Siege* is, then, a situated, object-oriented, and phenomenologically concerned ethnography of *Palestinians'* everyday experiences of waste in their rich variation. It places at the center of analysis the aesthetically and environmentally obtrusive material context in which Palestinians are obliged to forge their lives, one often presented as the background for politics among disenfranchised populations. It seeks to reveal what is made possible, and what other ways of being are foreclosed, by decades of struggle to live livable life in the rubble, debris, and infrastructural fallout of waste siege.

Acknowledgments

My greatest thanks go to the people who shared their insights, homes, work, and lives with me in Palestine. I could not have written this book without them. Knowing many must remain anonymous, I wish to thank those I can by name: Yousef, Sora, Ahmad, Karmel, Khaled, Majd, Im Mujahid, Tahreer, Munadil, Muhammad, Rasha, Qais, Sadeq, Thikra, 'Abeer, Latifah, Rawand, Arij, Dana, Deena, Abdullah, Abu Qais, Abu Mahmoud, Sami, Bashar, Fadi, Fathi, Abu Ayoub, Dawood, 'Imad, Maha, Mai, Mona, Mahmoud, Samia, Faisal Abu AlHayjaa, Marwan Abu Hani, Sa'ed Abu Hijleh, Fahd Abu Saymeh, Muhammad Abu Surour, Iyad Aburdeineh, Abdelafo Aker, Ahmad al-'Araj, Ramadan al-Masri, Ahmad al-Nimer, Iyad al-Riyahi, Mohammad al-Sa'adi, Hani al-Shawahneh, Ayman and Ghassan al-Shaka'a, Shaddad Attili, Fuad Bateh, Firas Batran, Lara el-Jaza'iri, Nasr Etyani, Walid Halayqa, Waddah Hamdallah, Ayat Hamdan, Ahmad Hindi, Muhammad Said Hmeidi, Isaac Jad, Ahmad Jaradat, Munir Jaradat, Penny Johnson, Musa Jwayed, Reem Khalil, Rassem Khamaisi, Saed Khayat, Nameer and Dima Khayyat, Azzam Mansour, Clemens Messerschmid, Misyef Misyef, Sreemati Mitter, Taghreed Mohammad, Mira Mukarker, Qadoura Musa, Reem Musleh, Adnan Naghnaghiye, Manar al-Natsha, Khalil Nijim, David Philips, Hadeel Qazzaz, Khaled Rajab, Abdul Jawad Saleh, Zaghloul Samhan, Vivien Sansour, Hafez Shaheen, Mustafa Shita, Raja Shehadeh, Mustafa Sheta, Abdelkarim Sidir, Mo'min Swaitat, Michael Talhami, Salim Tamari, Lisa Taraki, Rabbah Thabata, Sami Thabet, Munif Treish, and 'Adel Yassin. I thank Brian Boyd and Hamed Salem for introducing me to Shuqba and the employees of Jenin, al-Bireh, and Nablus municipalities, only some of whose names I ever learned but who were exceptionally generous with their time. Raja Khalidi and Etienne Balibar were each more helpful than they probably know in opening the first few doors for me in Ramallah and Jenin.

Numerous others in Palestine also offered me emotional and intellectual sustenance, hospitality, adventures, and nourishment, including Hussein Aamar, Salim Abu Jabal, Nasser Abourahme, Ala Alazzah, Samer al-Saber, Ryvka Barnard, Lisa Bhungalia, Morgan Cooper, Nisreen Farid, Tawfiq Haddad, Sarah Hegland, Neil Hertz, Suha Jarrar, Rania Jawwad, Juliano Meir Khamis, Peter Lagerquist, Ava Leone, Aisha Mansour, Micaela Miranda, JJ Mitchell, Penelope Mitchell, Rima Othman and her family, Nora Parr, Tom Perry, Nicola Perugini, Alessandro Petti, Kareem Rabie, Nabeel Raee, Laura Ribeiro Rodrigues Pereira, Habib Sima'an, Mustafa Staiti, Omar Jabary Salamanca, Omar and Elizabeth Tesdell, Salah Totah, Reem Wahdan, and Dina Zbidat and her family.

Several Israelis were indispensable to my understanding of the Israeli institutional landscape as it has related to waste in the West Bank: Ilan Alleson, Micha Blum, Shmuel Brenner, Gidon Bromberg, Neve Gordon, Jeff Halper, Amira Hass, Shir Hever, Sarah Ozacky-Lazar, Richard Laster, Nitsan Levy, Hillel Shuval, Ayelet Tapiro, and Assaf Yazdi. Orly Lubin and Roni Gilboa and her family took a leap of faith and have been welcoming me ever since.

I am indebted for the inception of this project to faculty at Columbia University. The idea to consider the relationship between infrastructure and politics in Palestine was sparked by conversations with Partha Chatterjee and gained wings through guidance from Nadia Abu El-Haj, Lila Abu-Lughod, and Brinkley Messick. Nadia, who introduced me to the marrying of science and technology studies with the study of the Middle East, also brought a rigor in parsing terms that was invaluable to the sharpening of my questions. Lila's indefatigable and meticulous readings of the many early iterations of this text gave me the consistent sense of what it means to be in conversation about politics and anthropology at the same time. Brink's propensity to see the magic in life's details helped attune me to the value of studying culture as life practice. I gained immensely from working with Claudio Lomnitz, who asked hard questions about sovereignty, the state, and the political stakes of this project. For opening my eyes to the worlds of environmental anthropology and the anthropology of infrastructure respectively, I thank Paige

West and Brian Larkin. Timothy Mitchell, Severin Fowles, and Zoë Crossland convinced me of the imperative to consider the lives of nonhuman things.

I have had the fortune to belong to two long-term writing groups on the environment in the Middle East, each of which has had a monumental impact on how I think, write, read, and research and has given me the gift of deepening friendships based on mutual inspiration and support. I am grateful for conversations with Sarah al-Kazzaz, Jessica Barnes, Tessa Farmer, Bridget Guarasci, Gökçe Günel, Simone Popperl, Kali Rubaii, and Caterina Scaramelli.

For commenting on earlier versions of these chapters, and for offering insights to which I hope to have done some justice, I wish to thank Nikhil Anand, Elizabeth Angell, Rafı Arefın, Sa'ed Atshan, Elif Babül, Waseem-Ahmed Bin-Kasim, Amahl Bishara, Brenda Chalfın, Yinon Cohen, Robyn d'Avignon, Beshara Doumani, Catherine Fennell, Islah Jad, James Ferguson, Denise Gill, Toby Jones, Rashid Khalidi, Colin McFarlane, Elizabeth Povinelli, Jenny Price, Anne Rademacher, Susanne Schneider, Sherene Seikaly, Kirstin Scheid, Paul Silverstein, Rebecca Stein, Audra Simpson, Antina Von Schnitzler, and Amy Zhang. I thank Joseph Masco for bringing out the way this project speaks to questions about the securitization of the environment and for producing work on nuclear America that has been fundamental to how I ask questions about waste in Palestine.

To Robin Nagle and Rozy Fredericks I am indebted for interpellating me into the Discard Studies Collective at New York University and giving this project its most profoundly interdisciplinary home. Thanks to Anne-Marie McManus, Nancy Reynolds, and Vasiliki Touhouliotis for bringing me into the "Wastelands" fold at Washington University in St. Louis.

For infusing my interest in anthropology with renewed effervescence, including through reading and commenting on this research, I want to extend special thanks to my colleagues in the anthropology program at Bard College, Diana and Mario Brown, Michèle Dominy, Laura Kunreuther, Duff Morton, and Yuka Suzuki. I have benefited from generous and provocative conversations about this project with additional colleagues across Bard, including Sanjib Baruah, Norton Batkin, Katherine Boivin, Michiel Bot, Omar Cheta, Wout Cornelissen, Rob Culp, Emilio Dabed, Emilio Distretti, Ellen Driscoll, Eli Dueker, Yuval Elmelech, Jennifer Hudson, Elizabeth Holt, Pinar Kemerli, David Kettler, Peter Klein, Allison McKim, Greg Moynahan, Joel Pearlmann, Dina Ramadan, Alice Stroop, Drew Thompson, Olga Touloumi, Dominique Townsend, Marina Van Zuylen, and Robert

Weston. For accepting photography assignments from me and for supporting and humoring my trash-seeking excursions in Palestine, I am grateful to Peggy Ahwesh (whose beautiful photograph adorns the cover of this book), Jonathan Becker, Maria Sachiko Cecire, Rebecca Granato, Tom Keenan, and Gabriel Perron. I owe Jamal Al-Eisheh a special debt of gratitude for doubling as research assistant and co-analyst of publicly abandoned bread and to numerous Bard students who read early versions of chapter 4.

The Wenner Gren Foundation, the Social Science Research Council, the National Science Foundation, Columbia University, and Bard College funded this research. Kate Wahl, Leah Pennywark, and the editorial team at Stanford University Press offered the book their editorial magic, and two anonymous reviewers helped clarify its theoretical stakes.

Conversations, in some cases over many wonderful years, with Samer Alatout, Lori Allen, Seth Anziska, Danielle Dinovelli-Lang, Dahlia Elzein, Leila Farsakh, Ilana Feldman, Michael Fisch, Seth Freed-Wessler, Maura Finkelstein, Seema Golestaneh, Albert Gonzalez, Maggie Grey, Nayrouz Hattoum, Rachel Havrelock, Kaet Heupel, Tarek Ismail, Nicholas Lewis, Zachary Lockman, Kate Lowenstein, Emily McKee, Amir Moosavi, Dina Omar, Mezna Qato, Joshua Reno, Marc Robert, Andrew Ross, Sobhi Samour, Yara Saqfalhait, Anand Vivek Taneja, Miriam Ticktin, Nomi Stone, Matt West, Darryl Wilkinson, Kate Wilson, and Dina Zbidat fueled my drive to write what I hope is a book as committed to creatively depicting the radical contingencies of the world as it is to taking political positions in it.

I thank Chuck Strozier for teaching me about the Fox and the Hedgehog and what it means to write a book, and Laura for leading me to Chuck.

This book was a labor of love a long time coming. And it took the love of my family on both sides of the Atlantic to bring it to fruition. I thank my late grandmother, Sophia (Fifi) Stamatopoulou, for being a column of wisdom and support throughout the first years of research and writing. I thank my grandmother, Lynne Robbins, for reminding me to dance. My father, Bruce Robbins, has had a greater imprint on what lies in these pages than I can possibly describe here. He introduced me to Palestine as a place and as a politically urgent reality, transmitting an imperative he had learned from, among other people, the late Edward Said. He has been my closest and most challenging interlocutor, not least because of his reluctance to accept tenets an anthropologist easily takes for granted. I learned to listen to how different people give meaning to their lives and their surroundings from my mother, Elsa Stamatopoulou-Robbins, and I continue to be inspired by the rigor with which she fights for indigenous rights. I would like to think that this book's most creative moments owe their playfulness to the spirit of my late brother, Andreas Robbins. His love of poetry and compassionate curiosity about the world, like the playful way we enjoyed sharing music, animate the sensibility I hope this book expresses. Andreas visiting me in Palestine is one of my fondest memories. To Kaet my gratitude is boundless. The sparkle of her unmatched brainstorming sessions and her ability to make everything work smoothly around us while I wrote are matched only by that of the laughter and companionship she brings to my life. Themis, named after the ancient goddess of order in the service of justice, was born into the crescendo of my revisions and has given the process of their completion a sweetness and an urgency that only new life can give.

Note on Transliteration and Translation

I have transliterated most Arabic terms using the simplified system recommended by the *International Journal of Middle East Studies*, with the exception of a few technical terms without English translations, for which I supply *IJMES*'s formal transliteration (with diacritics and long vowel markers). Unless otherwise noted, translations are my own.

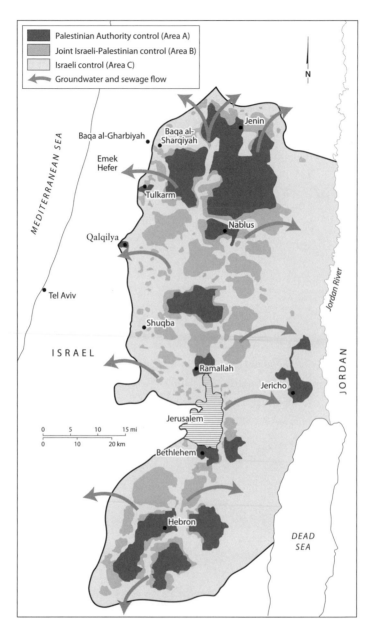

FIGURE 1. Oslo–West Bank Areas A, B, and C. In accordance with the Oslo II Accords of 1995, the West Bank was divided into Area A (where the Palestinian Authority has civilian control), Area B (where the Palestinian Authority has partial civilian control and Israel has security control), and Area C (where Israel has civilian and security control). Israel has full effective military control over all three areas. Arrows indicate the downhill direction of groundwater and sewage flows pulled across the territory by gravity.

INTRODUCTION

ON MARCH 27, 2007, A SEWAGE TANK COLLAPSED IN THE GAZA STRIP, submerging the Palestinian village of Umm al-Nasir in many tons of raw sewage and killing five people. When the Palestinian Authority's interior minister arrived on the scene a few hours later, he was chased out by the gunfire of angry villagers. Two and a half years later I attended the premiere screening of *Gaza Is Floating*, a documentary featuring the incident. The screening took place in the West Bank in the Quaker-run Ramallah Friends Meetinghouse, a beautiful stone building in Ramallah's heart.[1]

A coalition of sanitation-focused nongovernmental organizations (NGOs), international aid agencies, and Authority ministries had advertised the event, and a mixed Palestinian and expat audience of about thirty people attended. As we sat on white-painted pews, footage of the disaster in Umm al-Nasir rolled: people wore wetsuits to wade chest-deep through sewage, and a boy sat on a door in a lake of shit, paddling through it with a wooden plank.

We knew the odor that the film, as a visual medium, was unable to convey. Most of us had at some point driven through Wadi al-Nar on the road connecting the central West Bank to the south. A river of sewage flows through Wadi al-Nar. It flows across the West Bank, downhill and eastward from Jerusalem to the Dead Sea. Even those expats renting apartments in newly constructed Ramallah neighborhoods had likely smelled sewage backing up in overburdened drainage systems.

I had just moved to the West Bank. Attending the screening was one of my first steps as I tried to piece together how Palestinians manage waste that, during earlier visits, had for me been only a putrid but indistinct backdrop to the occupation. Like other travelers to Palestine, I had casually observed the difference between the spotless sidewalks of West Jerusalem, now a predominantly Jewish-Israeli area, and the debris-strewn road leading to Ramallah, a major Palestinian city, from Qalandiya checkpoint, which separates Jerusalem from the West Bank. I had smelled the odor of rotten eggs—sewage stench—in Tulkarem refugee camp. I had learned that Israeli settlers and soldiers use wastes to harass Palestinians, and in Hebron's Old City I had seen chicken wire fencing above Palestinian shops, placed to catch trash thrown from above by settlers. I knew that Israeli trucks dump wastes on Palestinian farmlands.

But that night on my walk to the screening, I trained my gaze to foreground refuse. I noticed men in vests wheeling carts, picking up litter from the sidewalks in Ramallah's market. I saw plastic bags of bread hanging off dumpster handles and an elderly woman sweeping the sidewalk outside her gate. I remembered seeing empty cardboard boxes stacked atop the makeshift roofs of fruit and vegetable stands in Jenin's fresh produce market (see figure 2). I also recalled notes I had written the night before, following dinner with a friend named Ziad.[2] Ziad grew up in Balata refugee camp in Nablus, a city forty-five minutes north of Ramallah. As we ate, he told the story of his brother's death at the hands of Israeli soldiers. His story, surprisingly, was also about waste.

Ziad's younger brother, Faysal, had been active in the al-Aqsa Martyrs Brigades, a secular coalition of armed Palestinian groups based in the Occupied Territory, during the second Palestinian uprising, or intifada. Palestinians across Israel/Palestine had been participating in years of large-scale demonstrations and strikes.[3] Some had taken up arms to protest Israeli dispossession, violence, and humiliation. The intifada, which lasted from 2000 to 2006, had been characterized by intensified Israeli military violence against Palestinians, including incursions into, and closures of, cities and villages, targeted assassinations, mass arrests, bombings, and demolitions (Baroud 2006; Tabar 2007a, 2007b).

Faysal had gone into hiding after learning the Israeli army wanted him. To intimidate his relatives into informing on him, the army had ransacked his family home three times, demolishing some of its walls (cf. Weizman 2007, 185–220). Soldiers had left Ziad and Faysal's elderly parents to sift through the humiliating rubble all over the floor, the broken tables, and the contents of their cupboards. After news got back to the family that the soldiers had found and killed Faysal, the debris had become a testament to the period during which he had successfully evaded them. Sipping a beer, Ziad explained that his parents had cleaned the house with neighbors' help but had left some bullet holes unrepaired for future visitors to see.[4]

Waste Siege is about waste and waste management in the absence of a state. More precisely, it is about waste in the absence of an indigenous state (Palestine) but in the hostile military presence of another state (Israel). In 1918, as the Ottoman Empire collapsed, the British carved the part of the Ottoman Empire south of what was to become Lebanon, north of Egypt, and west of what was to become Transjordan (and later Jordan) into the British mandate of Palestine. As a result of the violent events of the 1947-49 *nakba*, or catastrophe, through which the Israeli state was established, hundreds of thousands of Palestinians were displaced, between four hundred and six hundred Palestinian villages were razed, and over thirteen thousand Palestinians were killed (al-Aref 2013, 177). British colonial governance of Palestine was replaced by governance by three other states. Egypt came to administer what came to be called the Gaza Strip. The newly formed

FIGURE 2. Used boxes sit atop a fruit and vegetable stand in Jenin, 2010. Photograph by the author.

Israeli state seized the territory now understood as Israel proper along with the western half of Jerusalem. And the Hashemite Kingdom of Jordan annexed eastern Jerusalem and a kidney-shaped piece of land west of the Jordan River, which came to be known as the West Bank (see figure 1).

Approximately 750,000 Palestinians fled or were forced to flee their homes during the *nakba*, taking refuge in neighboring countries like Lebanon, Jordan, and Syria and to other areas of Mandate Palestine. Over the next decade, camps like Balata, where Ziad grew up, came to be established in Lebanon, Jordan, Syria, Gaza, and the West Bank. Refugees receive services there from an agency called the United Nations Relief and Works Agency (UNRWA), which was established in 1950 and which provides basic health care, education, welfare, and infrastructure maintenance like trash collection to over five million Palestinian refugees.[5]

In 1967 there was a second mass displacement, which Palestinians call the *naksa*, or setback, during and following a war between Israel, Egypt, Jordan, and Syria. Displacing another 280,000 to 325,000 people from the West Bank, Gaza, and the Syrian Golan Heights, Israel seized the three territories by force, along with East Jerusalem, and has occupied and administered them since. Over six million Palestinians now live under some form of Israeli rule, and a similar number live in the diaspora, or *shattat*. Though the Palestinian Authority, which is staffed mainly by Palestinians, has functioned alongside UNRWA in parts of the West Bank and Gaza as an interim government since 1995, its control, like its territorial jurisdiction, is fragmentary at best. This book is about how, and with what effect, waste siege emerges from the palimpsestic relation between state absence and presence that results.

Where infrastructures function to make wastes disappear, people need not think much about waste (Nagle 2013; Reno 2015b). Humans' experiences of waste are in this sense inseparable from the infrastructures that manage them. Today, this means they are also inseparable from the state because of the central role states play in establishing and operating infrastructures. Most people's experiences of waste are shaped by their state's allocation of resources to waste management, by the relative evenness with which the state distributes waste infrastructures and services across territory, and by the extent to which different subgroups are perceived as exposable to waste, which is to say disposable. The ways in which and the extent to which a population is exposed to waste can thus be diagnostic of the nature of governance. And populations' relative exposure to waste can be part of how people evaluate everything from state legitimacy to definitions of the public good and their own role in pursuing it.

My postdinner notes sketched my impression of Ramallah: "Litter everywhere. Uninhabited lots with half-built or half-crumbling houses. Scrap metal, fabrics that could've been curtains or duvets." What can these disparate scenes tell us, I wondered, about how waste helps shape forms of sociality, politics, and self-understanding for people living under conditions of nonsovereignty?[6] Before answering this question, I use the following two sections to describe the types of waste that make up waste siege in Palestine and the type of siege they enforce.

WASTES AND SCALES

The waste that surrounds just under three million West Bank Palestinians is both waste the occupying state produces and waste Palestinians produce themselves. Given that subjugated, often indigenous communities tend to become dumping grounds for the discards of those more powerful, including those who have colonized their lands, it is perhaps not surprising that the Israeli-occupied West Bank is a dumpsite for Israeli waste.[7] Israel transfers to the West Bank urban and industrial by-products including sewage sludge, infectious medical waste, used oils, solvents, metals, electronic waste, and batteries. There are at least fifteen formal Israeli waste treatment facilities in the West Bank to which these untreated wastes go with the Israeli state's support, though the Israeli government has not made available to the public information about them or about informal Israeli dumping in the West Bank (B'Tselem 2017a, 5-6).

Indicative of the scale of informal dumping is the fact that in 2014 the Civil Administration, the branch of the Israeli army that has administered civilian affairs in the West Bank since Israel occupied the territory, established an entire unit to monitor Israeli waste smuggling into the West Bank.[8] The administration boasts that the David Unit has "thwarted hundreds of attempts to smuggle waste" (COGAT 2017a). Countless more attempts continue unthwarted.

Israel built its first Jewish-only settlement in the West Bank the same year its occupation began. As of 2017 over 413,000 Israeli settlers lived in the West Bank and over 214,000 in East Jerusalem (Peace Now, n.d.). In addition to extensive, fenced-off housing, settlements feature military bases, schools, malls, universities, factories, and government buildings. Settlements generate 446,000 tons of solid waste annually, most of which they dispose of within the West Bank (ARIJ 2015, 1).

Largely located on hilltops, many settlements also dispose of their raw sewage downhill by spilling it into West Bank valleys. Israeli waste dumping in the West Bank contravenes the Geneva Conventions and binding multilateral environmental agreements such as the Basel Convention on the Control of Transboundary Movements of Hazardous Wastes and Their Disposal, to which both Israel and Palestine (as the Palestinian Authority) are party, and is increasingly coming to light through the work of Israeli, Palestinian, and international NGOs (Abdel-Qader and Roberts-Davis 2018).

Less visible to the outside observer, however, whether from a distance or even from closer up, is how Palestinians dispose of—and think about—their own waste. That includes municipal sewage, over 90 percent of which flows untreated into the ground; household trash composed of materials like paper, glass, plastics, and food; agricultural refuse like pesticide containers and plastic irrigation sheets; commercial waste like butcheries' refuse and shops' cardboard packaging; hazardous materials from hospitals; concrete, steel, and wood debris from construction projects; and sludge from olive oil, soap, and plastic bag factories. Meanwhile, Palestinians today import, buy, and discard goods at unprecedented rates, while worrying that what they buy is a waste of money and that acts of discarding make them wasteful.[9] Earlier modes of reuse and recycling have all but disappeared, and existing wastewater infrastructures cannot sustain increasing volumes of sewage as the occupied population grows.

Waste besieges different people differently and at different scales. Built into the Oslo Accords that established the Authority was the prospect that the Authority would eventually turn into a future Palestinian state, but only if it could demonstrate its "readiness" for statehood to the international community and to Israel (Khan, Giacaman, and Amundsen 2014; N. Brown 2003; Rashid Khalidi 2006; Parsons 2005; Schulz 1999). Readiness, I learned, includes evidence that the Authority can protect the environment. That condition was written into the Accords themselves, which codified waste as a matter of environmental concern and, crucially, framed the West Bank as an environment "shared" between Israel and the Authority. This principle became justification for continued Israeli involvement in Palestinian waste management in the West Bank and generated an urgent need to construct large-scale infrastructures, thereby proving the Authority's ability to govern, as well as a need to account for "leakage" of Palestinians' waste. As the Umm al-Nasir story demonstrates, Authority officials also face siege from "below" in the form of scrutiny from the Palestinians they purportedly represent and govern.[10]

When sewage seeps into the West Bank's aquifers, furthermore, it poses challenges to the farmers whose crops depend on freshwater springs but also to the Palestinian engineers struggling to convince treatment plant donors that Palestinians are capable of handling sophisticated equipment. Many Palestinians live in no-man's-lands where the Israeli military fails to collect trash and the Authority lacks the jurisdiction to do so. When they burn trash piling up in public dumpsters, the flaming garbage diffuses into children's lungs dioxins that are difficult for Palestinian physicians to detect. Israelis and foreign observers may read the smoke as a sign of Palestinians' cultural backwardness and conclude that Palestinians are unfit to govern themselves, hence that an Israeli presence is needed in the West Bank to protect not only the environment but even Palestinians (from) themselves. Meanwhile, the odor of burning trash, for some Palestinians working abroad to support their families in the stifled occupied economy, may be the smell of home.

INVISIBLE SIEGE

Waste siege juxtaposes two words to deepen our understanding of each. It offers a way of understanding siege that differs in some respects from military sieges. Military sieges encircle from without. Seen from the viewpoint of waste, the idea of siege expands to include *emissions from within*, whether from within a territory or a body. Waste siege is constituted as much by movement and flow of waste as it is by encirclement—for example, by inflows of commodities that people discard and by outflows and circulations of refuse from economic and household activities.[11] It is created by the chemicals and particles that waft and leak out of attempts to control those flows. People cannot escape even if they leave the place where the waste first found them. Its toxins follow them in their bodies, and its dilemmas plague their minds as they move.

The study of waste as political material and the study of populations exposed to waste by the state reveal that many of the burdensome experiences of life under occupation in the West Bank offer less overt signs of who is responsible for them.[12] When a Jenin resident smells refuse or stops in the street because her shoe strap breaks days after she purchased the shoes, an array of possible actors is available for blame. She may choose to blame street sweepers, UNRWA, the American government that withdrew its funding for UNRWA (Wong 2018), the political party in charge of the municipality, the Authority, herself for walking that route or buying those shoes, China (where the shoes may have been made), the shopkeeper who sold them to her, or "the situation" (*al-wadiʿ*), a term Palestinians often use to refer to the occupation. She might blame the individualist ethos (*anania*) many see as having replaced the mass, cross-class solidarity that characterized life during the first intifada between 1987 and 1993 (Taraki 2008a, 2008b), an ethos many remember as having inspired them to collectively keep streets clean. Ziad's parents' refusal to repair the bullet holes offers one condensed view of what adjudication of responsibility looks like. That Gazan villagers took up arms against a Palestinian official in Umm al-Nasir offers another.

Waste siege creates this indeterminacy around responsibility as a second-order burden following the first-order burdens (e.g., odor, disease, anxiety) of waste itself.[13] Blame is not predetermined, established, or fixed. People experience waste as a material violation more open to interpretation than other forms of violence like bombings or incursions. Military siege makes a spectacle of the prowess of the besieger. It can be understood as a form of authoritarian governance, top down or outside in, an intensified form of rule that creates its own forms of order and that people can and will attribute to its presence. In the infamous nine-hundred-day blockade of Leningrad by Nazi-led forces, for example, over 1.5 million people died, largely from starvation but also when residents murdered each other to obtain ration cards or to eat human flesh (Reid 2011, 284–87). There could have been little question that those who ate wallpaper paste and shoe leather, and a woman who reportedly fed her eighteen-month-old to her three older children, did so as a result of the siege. Historians of World War II do not hesitate to place events in Leningrad during those nine hundred days under the title of "siege." While there can be debate about who or what may have *provoked* military siege, the siege's perpetrator and the fact of the siege itself appear self-evident.

Waste as siege, by contrast, makes accountability more opaque. Waste siege shares the feature of indeterminacy with other contexts: for example, after industrial disasters, where it is hard to trace or prove the toxic cause of disease (e.g., Fortun 2001; Murphy 2006; Petryna 2003). Part of this has to do with waste as a material type: it indexes the presence of people and processes that produced it without the producers having to be present.[14] Waste's murky indexicality can invite discursive displacement (Ortner 2006) of its burdens onto singular actors, making its adjudication misguided or perpetually incomplete. In Palestine, it was striking that despite the range of possible responsible parties for a given burden of waste, people were quick to select one as their primary focus. They tended to narrow or hyperindividuate responsibility—for example, onto themselves or onto the Authority. Or they tended to open it up enormously by blaming China, for instance. Either way, frames for accountability seldom accounted for multiple actors.[15] The diffuse material processes that lead wastes to besiege were obscured.

Waste siege can of course enact what Rob Nixon (2011) calls "slow violence" on a population by imperceptibly wreaking havoc on bodies (Roberts 2017) and ecologies, as when sewage nitrates percolate into an aquifer, and when even nitrates' casualties are invisible, as when intestinal troubles appear only years later. Yet waste siege differs from slow violence in that the waste that constitutes it is both mystifying and perceptible at the same time. People experience waste siege more acutely than they experience structural violence. Waste siege is always an encounter with sensorily accessible materials. It is there for all to see, smell, and feel. It is its relationship to ethics and politics that is obscure and mystifying.

That waste siege obscures the diffuse reasons for waste's burdens means that waste siege is always a problem whose sources exceed consciousness of them. It also means that the relationship between waste siege and military siege—in this case settler colonial occupation—tends to be obscured as well. Waste siege is not just another feature of occupation. It exceeds occupation. But it also interacts with occupation, distracting people from occupation. This is what reorienting politics means. Waste siege is sensorially obtrusive, yet blame varies too much to stick on anyone or anything in particular. It comes without consensus about responsibility. Even when waste is present in overabundance, the chains of responsibility leading back to occupation and to Palestinians' resultant nonsovereignty tend to be less visible.[16]

Waste siege's obscuring quality means that the people with whom I spent time did not always understand their own uses of techniques for mitigating waste's burdens as political. Like military siege, waste siege requires improvisations in order to navigate the everyday challenges siege poses, like scarcity (Maček 2009). People ration goods, develop barter systems. Rationing may be seen by the besieged as a kind of resistance, as a way of remaining alive. Palestinians usually associate the condition of being political, and politics as a field of action, with encounters with Israel. Yet for them their efforts to manage waste siege are not resistance (*muqawama*) or steadfastness (*sumud*), the term used by Palestinians to connote national endurance in the face of colonial processes (Meari 2014; Peteet 2017, 171). Instead they view practices for ameliorating waste siege as matter-of-fact, mundane avenues for relieving pressures of equally matter-of-fact, if undesirable, materials in their midst. Without agreement on culpability, "resistance," the concept that has dominated many observers' understanding of Palestinian society and history for the past several decades (Zureik 2003), lacks an object and, arguably, is a less relevant analytic.

The section below situates waste siege in Palestine's historical context, arguing that waste siege materialized in the 2000s, phenomenologically displacing direct Israeli violence. It lays the groundwork for the two sections following it, which explain how the particular arrangement of occupation, Authority governance, and Palestinians' dependence on foreign aid together came to form what we can think of as rule by waste siege.

A HISTORICAL DISPLACEMENT

The concept of waste siege is especially helpful for understanding Palestine in a specific moment in time, capturing a cluster of intensifications. Palestinians' relationship to waste hasn't always been like this. It is true that decades of displacement and poverty have left many materially destitute. And much longer-standing tropes about waste have made waste important to Palestinians' experiences of power. For example, the idea that the territory that indigenous populations inhabited was a wasteland prior to colonization of course did its part to animate European settlement in Palestine. Despite the long-standing presence of Christian, Muslim, and Jewish Palestinians there, European Zionists in the late nineteenth century notoriously argued that then Ottoman-administered Palestine was "a land without a people for a people without a land" (Shapira 1999, 42).[17] Zionist leaders and British administrators continued to promote the idea that a desolate Palestine needed the Jews to come save it through settlement. They envisioned Palestine's desolation both as an absence of inhabitants and as variations on the theme of absent or problematic land cultivation. Some depicted Palestine's lands as abandoned, while others depicted them as barely, ineffectively, or even destructively used. Environmental imaginaries are constellations of "ideas that groups of humans develop about a given landscape, usually local or regional, that commonly includes assessments about that environment as well as how it came to be in its current state" (D. Davis 2011, 3). As Jewish colonization continued through the twentieth century, including after Israel's establishment, Zionist "environmental imaginaries" relied on visions of parts of Palestine as alternately empty and uninhabitable, wild, and socially and culturally barren (Kedar, Amara, and Yiftachel 2018).

These depictions mirrored logics of European colonization in the Americas, Africa, and the Pacific. Colonists employed the image of colony-as-wasteland to understand the colony as a *tabula rasa* (blank slate) or as a *terra nullius* (land belonging to no one) (Gandy 2013) onto which European order—and, in cases like North America and Australia, European settlement—could be inscribed, or as territory whose inhabitants had left it to lie in ruins (Cronon 2003; Wolfe 2016). Representing a prospective or existing colony as a wasteland helped legitimize the erasure of extant forms of social and political order in favor of new ones (Ryan 2002, 116).[18]

This complex of perceptions around Palestine continues to bolster the argument that the Zionist movement, and now Israel, have made "the desert bloom," importing environmental conservation—for example, through new agricultural and water production techniques, land use regulations, and afforestation (e.g., A. George 1979). It underpins Israel's ongoing expropriation of Palestinian lands for its Jewish citizens—for instance, through the creation of Israeli-controlled nature reserves in the West Bank—while confining the Palestinian population it occupies to less and less of the territory Israel controls. This push to expropriate natural resources for the colonial population's use and to effectively slate the indigenous population "for removal and replacement," coupled with Israeli representations of Palestine as a wasteland—a landscape ripe for the taking—is part of the broader eliminationist logic (Wolfe 2006) that has animated settler colonial policies in the Americas and the Pacific as well (Abu El-Haj 2001; Allen 2008; Elkins and Pederson 2005; N. Gordon 2008; Gregory 2004; Ochs 2011; Pappe 2006; Pasternak 2014; Pateman and Mills 2007; Rodinson 1973; Salamanca et al. 2012; Shafir 1989; Yiftachel 1998, 2005).[19]

Yet what was once a metaphor of Palestine as wasteland has today become material. While wasteland was a representational fantasy that denied the existence of colonized populations or neglected the ways in which those populations inhabited and experienced their surroundings, this century's waste siege is a set of tangible, material conditions. It is the circumstances in which people actually live, circumstances that in Palestine began to change after Israel occupied the

West Bank but, importantly, did not become the siege this book describes until about four decades after the occupation began.

Between 1967 and 1995, Israel directly controlled how and where Palestinians and Israeli settlers in the Occupied Palestinian Territories dealt with waste. In 1995 Israel transferred responsibility for the management of Palestinians' waste to the nascent Palestinian government, making waste management one of the few fields of Palestinian service provision and infrastructural development under the Authority's official care.[20] Over the past two decades, the flows, floods, and pileups of waste have exceeded the Authority's capacity to create acceptable distances between its constituents and wastes, not least, but also not only, because Israel continues to control, if less directly, how wastes in the West Bank are managed.

During the second intifada Israeli control was especially obvious. Armed jeeps and tanks stopped Palestinian municipal garbage disposal trucks from leaving cities, forcing places like Jenin to dispose of forty thousand residents' worth of garbage in the city center for four years. Israeli jets bombed Palestinian infrastructures and Authority buildings. Armed bulldozers demolished neighborhoods, giving people a choice between living in the debris of their own homes and leaving.

As I write this, thirteen years after the end of the second intifada, Israel's occupation is as entrenched as ever, including in ways this book describes, and yet overt material signs of occupation have receded from many urban areas. The past decade has brought a dramatic decrease in the number of Israeli soldiers stationed inside Palestinian cities. The military has reduced its presence at some checkpoints between Palestinian cities and villages. Movement within the Territory is easier than it was during the intifada, including when I first visited in early 2004. A trip between Ramallah and Jenin took me seven hours by car in 2007. By 2009 the same trip took under two hours. The violent military incursions of the early 2000s have died down. Fighter jets regularly break the sound barrier, flying low, but there have been no aerial bombings of the West Bank since the early 2000s, and the Authority has reestablished governing functions after years of Israeli bombardment.[21] The military now mainly enters Palestinian cities at night, often targeting people in their homes. On a primary, experiential level—as opposed to a structural one—waste has replaced overt military violence both indoors and out.

PRODUCTS OF A MÖBIUS STRIP OF SEPARATION AND CONTROL

The post-Oslo period in which waste siege took hold can be characterized as what I think of as a Möbius strip in which separation and control flow seamlessly into one another in a constant loop. The condition of possibility of waste siege is decisive Israeli military control over the environment, economic life, and infrastructures in, and the movement of people and goods into, out of, and through, the West Bank. In that sense waste siege is part of Palestine's "settler atmospherics," "the normative and necessary violences found in settlement" (Simmons 2017). Continuous with, and a result of, occupation, the experience of everyday life I focus on here also shows, however, how *multiple* institutions and groups govern in the West Bank beyond Israel. These include municipalities, the Authority, international aid organizations, NGOs, and private companies. Together these actors have over the past several years been ruling by waste siege, whether intentionally or not.

Israeli policy since the early 1990s has increasingly separated West Bank Palestinians from Israeli society, making Palestinian-inhabited areas appear relatively autonomous insofar as many Israelis, international commentators, and even Palestinians are concerned. In 1993 Israel began to cut off Palestinian areas of the West Bank from Israel. It built new permanent checkpoints along the temporary 1949 Armistice line demarcating Israel from the West Bank, also known as the Green Line, and made permits for Palestinians to enter Israel more difficult to obtain. In 2002 it began construction of a large-scale wall and fence system (which Palestinians refer to as the Apartheid Wall, or the Wall), whose route stretches for 442.4 miles and which, in addition to cutting deep into the West Bank, also now seals off the West Bank's northern, western, and southern boundaries (B'Tselem 2017b). Most West Bank Palestinians are no longer permitted to work in, travel through, or even visit Jerusalem or Israel. Israel also prohibits Israeli citizens' entry into Authority-run areas of the West Bank.

The Accords also carved the West Bank into three areas, or zones, called Areas A, B, and C (see figure 1). The Authority operates only in Areas A and B. Area A is under both Authority civilian and policing control and constitutes 17.7 percent of the West Bank. Area B, in which the Authority has civilian control and the Israeli military has policing control, constitutes around 22 percent of the West Bank. The Accords thus officially permitted the Authority to operate in only roughly 40 percent of the West Bank. The home of Ziad's parents is in Balata camp, which lies within that 40 percent. As Ziad's story makes plain, even where the Authority operates, in practice it offers Palestinians no protection.

The rest of the West Bank, termed Area C, today constitutes 61 percent and is under Israel's full control. It includes most Palestinian farmland and sits above most of the West Bank's underground water sources. Most Israeli settlements are in Area C, as are Israeli military bases, closed military areas and firing ranges, and nature preserves and parks. Of the over 2.8 million Palestinians living in West Bank, as of 2014 roughly 300,000 lived in Area C (Hass 2014).

Palestinian waste, like Palestinians' bodies, is spatially confined by occupation. Area C is the only place where large-scale waste disposal infrastructures like landfills or incinerators can be built because it is usually outside densely populated areas. And the Oslo Accords require that all Palestinian constructions in Area C be approved by a variety of Israeli actors including ministry and military officials. Increasingly, they must also be approved by Israeli settlers and NGOs.[22] These actors have been preventing Palestinians from constructing waste infrastructures since the 1990s. Israel also prohibits the transfer of West Bank Palestinians' wastes into Israel. And Palestinians produce too little garbage to afford to export it internationally (especially since occupation makes all exports exponentially more expensive for occupied Palestinians than they are for Israelis) or to construct large recycling facilities within the West Bank. Palestinian waste thus remains in the West Bank.

If people's experiences of waste today are inseparable from their experiences of statehood, or the lack thereof, so too are they inseparable from the other actors on a territory who, where the state fails, is hostile, or abrogates certain responsibilities, step in to be state-like (Scott 1998) in its stead. Israeli policies of geographic separation have been accompanied by policies of institutional replacement as Israel has abrogated its responsibility to care for the population it occupies.[23] On the one hand, Authority policies for water and sanitation, imports, municipal governance, and law enforcement now all play a major role in Palestinians' daily experiences of waste. The Authority organizes its waste-related functions across the West Bank and Gaza according to laws the Palestinian Legislative Council has passed regulating local governments and the environment, establishing and then amalgamating hundreds of new municipalities that, among other things, manage the day-to-day workings of trash collection and transport. The Authority has created educational materials about litter, recycling, and the environment for

Palestinian schoolchildren and five-year plans or strategies for wastewater and solid waste management. It has dedicated employees for waste management issues in its now over two-decades-old ministries of environment, local government, planning, and water and has created regional government agencies to manage the operation of multi-million-dollar sanitation projects for regional waste disposal and treatment. The Authority's own police enforces order when, as I discuss in chapter 1, Palestinians obstruct completion of an Authority-run waste project. On the other hand, since the Authority lacks the ability to promote industry or exports so as to sustain the Palestinian economy, it has also depended since its establishment on foreign donors for roughly 95 percent of its budget.[24]

INVESTORS IN "PEACE"

International aid agencies and governments have been involved in supporting Palestinian life since long before Olso. But the establishment of the Authority catalyzed a particular donor fervor (Al-Khazendar 1997; Khan, Giacaman, and Amundsen 2004; Bhungalia 2015; Bocco 2009; Challand 2008; Farsakh 2016; Feldman 2007a, 2007b, 2008, 2017; A. Hamdan 2010; Hever 2006; Lasensky 2004; Le More 2008; Keating, Le More, and Lowe 2006; Roy 1995; Yezid Sayigh 2007; Taghdisi-Rad 2011; Wildeman and Tartir 2014; Zanotti 2016) that was fueled in part by growing international interest in—and securitization of—water, sanitation, and the environment. During the first fifteen years of the Authority's existence donors offered at least $450 million for sewage projects and well over $50 million for garbage collection and disposal alone (Palestinian Water Authority 2010, 6; PNA 2013). Germany, Japan, Spain, Italy, and the World Bank fund garbage projects. France, Germany, the United States, Belgium, the Netherlands, Japan, the World Bank, the United Nations Development Programme, American Near East Refugee Aid, and the European Union fund wastewater projects. Every sanitation project and municipal reform plan I researched was funded internationally. And in every project donors imposed conditions on funding, including technical specifications, hiring, and management, and economic and legal institutions for supporting it.[25]

Donors have pushed solid waste burial and large wastewater treatment plants in particular, privileging waste removal from cities over that in rural areas. Donors' priorities are informed as much by the logic of "economies of scale"—reducing cost by scaling up—as they are by ideas about the proper relationship between politics and infrastructure. Many view waste infrastructures as tools for quieting

Palestinians' political agitation, for example, by making occupied life more livable.[26] The 1993 World Bank report, written during the first intifada and upon which much of the Authority's national policy for waste management was based, tellingly titled its volume on sanitary conditions *Infrastructure: An Investment in Peace* (World Bank 1993). Donors also view waste infrastructures as technologies facilitating regional peace and stability by preventing pollution of groundwaters in a water-scarce region, and some partner with private investors seeking waste infrastructures as preconditions for investing in Palestine—for instance, in industrial zones (Alkhalil and Qasem 2009; J. Isaac 2007; Qumsiyeh 1998).[27]

Palestinians' dependence on foreign aid is an extreme version of how development and humanitarian aid function across the Global South. Like development more broadly, aid-driven environmentalist schemes bring with them their own moral logics, shaping local bureaucratic cultures, relationships between national and local governments, and the possibilities for political authority (Asher 2009; O'Reilly 2017; Walley 2004). Conservation, afforestation, and other environmentalist schemes have transformed communities and economies, leading to new mobilizations, alliances, and frictions (Agrawal 2005; Masco 2010; Matthews 2011; Tousignant 2018; Tsing 2005; West 2006).

Palestine's experience of waste siege suggests we might further consider how today's international development projects conduct politics through discourses of, and governmental orientation toward, environmentalism, including discourse oriented toward climate change (McElwee 2015; Matthews 2015). Humanitarian aid, state building, and "regime-change" interventions, including in the form of austerity measures, increasingly value the language and logics of environmental protection, even while foreign, intervening states often keep protection standards lower in "developing" countries than they do at home. In places like the West Bank, Gaza, Afghanistan, Iraq, Yemen, and South Sudan but also Greece, Portugal, and Spain, the survival of national governing structures implementing state-altering or state-building schemes depends on international actors recognizing and approving a certain orientation toward the environment (e.g., Guarasci 2015, 2018).

To speak of Authority influence over West Bank waste in this time of relative separation from Israel is, then, to speak of the influence of aid. But that influence is chaotic. Donors do not all agree with one another. Each represents the exigencies, including differing environmentalisms, of the actors its institutions include. Donors swoop in with a cacophony of often contradictory demands: for example, that Palestinians take leadership of projects but also bend to donor requests. Yet donors sometimes have little familiarity with the Palestinian context, and their representatives constantly rotate in and out of their local offices, so they rarely hold a monopoly over how wastes are actually, finally, managed. In other words, to speak of the influence of aid is also to speak of the influence of the thousands of Authority bureaucrats who, in small and not-so-small ways, carve out space for reforms that seem sensible to them (see also Babül 2017; Hull 2012; Mosse 2005).

And the relationship between the Authority and donors is more than a dialectic. It must always incorporate the occupation as well. Authority employees and donors must factor occupation into their calculations even while Authority employees try to comply with donors' conditions and donors attempt to cater to Authority desires about particular policies, and even when factoring in Israel means purposely diminishing Israel's significance or Palestinians' experiences of it. Since Oslo, the Authority has attempted to simulate the experience of living in an independent state—for instance, by giving Palestinians normal-seeming consumer experiences of mass-produced goods.

To boost a failing occupied economy, the Palestine Liberation Organization (PLO), a representative body of the Palestinian people and the body that signed the Oslo Accords with Israel, also signed the Paris Protocol with Israel in 1995. The Protocol allowed West Bank Palestinians to import goods directly from anywhere in the world in exchange for various concessions (El-Musa and El-Jaafari 1995; Ahmad 2014; Daoudi and Khalidi 2008). Since the Protocol's signing, the Authority has encouraged the growth of an economic system largely dependent on cheap imports, the only goods most Palestinians, whose economy is crippled by occupation, can afford—or can afford for as long as donors continue disbursing aid to the Authority.[28] Disposable goods have thus proliferated, many so flimsy that, once broken, they cannot be repaired. These are goods already on their way to the dumpsite from the moment they are purchased. These are the same goods Authority employees are mandated to manage, and donors are mandated to write reports about, once they are discarded (cf. Gabrys, Hawkins, and Michael 2013; Liboiron 2013; Strasser 2000).

The wastes that besiege Palestinians are products of Authority policies even while Israel, in its status as military settler colonial system, remains an "obligatory point of passage" (Latour 1988) for most major waste-related decisions, as I show in chapters 1, 3, and 5 especially. Occupation enables these forces and processes together to create waste siege even while disavowing its role. Israel refers to the West Bank as an environment it shares with the Palestinians. But Israeli environmental laws do not apply to the West Bank, and Palestinian lawmakers passed a separate, Palestinian environment law in 1999. Meanwhile, enforcement of the latter law is at once important to what goes into Palestinian school textbooks and affected by what Israeli military and donor officials allow Palestinians to build in the West Bank environment. The fact that Israel is in the midst of what Israeli environmental activists call a "green revolution"—with a focus on recycling, sustainability, and green technology—has consequences for Palestinians' experiences of wastes in the West Bank. Aiming for increased recycling and pressure on industries to produce fewer wastes in the form of packaging, Israel has vowed to close its landfills within the next few years. The Israeli government has raised the prices for landfilling within Israel. As what can only be understood as an indirect result of this, Israeli companies dump their wastes in the West Bank to avoid rising tipping fees at Israeli landfills. The besieging waste featured in this book is a waste product *of a process*. It is political waste (Chalfin 2014), the material remains of settler colonialism in its post-Oslo arrangement, which includes a Palestinian state-building process on the road to nowhere.

WASTE REGIMES, MATTER-OF-FACTNESS, AND THE STATE

This section argues that the fact that multiple actors are involved in managing waste in the West Bank means that multiple logics determine what happens to waste there and why, highlighting the significance of waste siege for thinking about the anthropology of the state, and in particular about so-called "failed" postcolonies.[29] Anthropologist Zsuzsa Gille uses the term *waste regime* to describe a unitary approach to the production, representation, and politics of waste that obtains in a given period. In socialist Hungary between 1948 and 1974, for example, Hungary's waste regime was "metallic," placing a unique emphasis on the paradigm of collecting and reusing waste that characterized the metallurgic industry. As such, Hungary's metallic waste regime can tell us something about socialism during that period. But no single industry or paradigm holds for Palestine. Rather, in a specific time and place, waste siege is the product of several waste regimes combined. I identified so many nodes in the networks of institutions and processes that cause waste siege that the idea of a regime makes sense only if we think of a *waste siege effect* as a regime while thinking of its causes as diffuse.

Centering waste offers two apparently contradictory payoffs for thinking about the state. First, it offers a way to think about how and when people feel governed by something state-like, something singular and distinct from society (T. Mitchell 2006), even while diffuse actors and multiple "regimes" are at work. Second, it privileges the flows, blockages, and pileups of unwanted materials that intersect with, or reveal certain things about, the state but that can also have lives and afterlives that track parallel to it.

Whether a state is considered "strong" or "weak," well established or fragile, its formation is never over once and for all; it is an ongoing process. And it always involves local, and always materially rich, encounters (Coronil 1997; Escobar 1995; I. Evans 1997; Greenhouse, Mertz, and Warren 2002; A. Gupta 1995, 2012; Herzfeld 1992, 2016; Hull 2012; Joseph and Nugent 1994; Nugent 1997; Trouillot 2003)—including with waste. Many analyses of the state that emphasize both institutions of state building and "the governed" bind political authority and civic engagement, which is based on people's perceptions of ethics, rights, and duties, to "the state." Either all-encompassing or "resisted," the state remains central (Appadurai 1996; Borneman 1997; Chatterjee 2010; Escobar 1995; Ferguson 1990). They thus offer limited purchase on the scenario we are increasingly seeing: so-called corruption and inefficiency in "failed" postcolonies. If, as some suggest, state "failure"—that is, corruption or neglect of social welfare infrastructures—can catalyze increased civic engagement, it is necessary to ask how public perceptions of ethics and obligations are reshaped when different institutions and actors act "like a state" (A. Gupta 1995; Mbembé 2001; Wedeen 2003; Scott 1998).[30] In this sense Palestine offers a uniquely valuable perspective on a worldwide phenomenon.

Palestinian-inhabited parts of the West Bank are what I call "hypergoverned" in that multiple actors compete to administer them and their inhabitants. They also have an ungoverned quality in that their inhabitants lack a reliable means of redress and their geography is made up of a disorienting patchwork of military installations, prohibited and restricted roadways, and unpredictable encounters with hostile forces including soldiers and armed settlers (A. Bishara 2015; Makdisi 2008; Peteet 2017; Weizman 2007). Although a Palestinian state has yet to be established and occupied Palestinians are not citizens of the Israeli state, they nevertheless additionally experience something they recognize as governance, including by the internationally *un*recognized (as a state) Authority, whose ineffectiveness and existence as an interim government mark the incompleteness of the Palestinian state-building process. Through their encounters with waste that the Authority attempts to manage, Palestinians experience and articulate a wide range of ambivalences about the Authority as an entity that often feels and looks like a state but is not one.

While Palestinians constantly question the effectiveness of the Authority, they also treat it as what I think of as a matter-of-fact presence in their lives that, whether they perceive it as failed or successful, has material consequences for what their lives cost, smell, and feel like. They "make and believe" (Navaro-Yashin 2012, 6) in the Authority's governance even while, as a political entity, it lacks both legitimacy and the sovereignty it would need to properly govern. The state everyone is waiting for has in some ways arrived. Matter-of-factness, the quality that also characterizes how Palestinians perceive their own improvisations to deal with wastes' dilemmas, reappears in their perception of the waste-managers-in-chief. Matter-of-factness is one form that appearing "like a state" (Scott 1998) assumes in a context in which a monopoly on the use of physical force—if not, as Weber (1958) put it, the *legitimate* monopoly—is possessed by another state (Israel). The object of matter-of-factness is the Authority's agreed-upon role as mediator in matters of waste accumulation. It has come to be within what Stuart Hall (1988, 44) calls "the horizon of the taken-for-granted" that residents can and should appeal to the Authority, for instance, when faced with waste-related problems they are unable to resolve themselves.

The following section elaborates on this book's subtitle: *The Life of Infrastructure in Palestine*. It explains how the book deploys analysis of technologies conventionally thought of as waste infrastructures, such as landfills and wastewater networks, alongside what I call "infrastructural" formations to which Palestinians' improvisations to mitigate waste siege give rise. It thus also introduces the concept of improvisation—what might be understood as the "life" part of the subtitle—as key to understanding the ethical openings and pitfalls involved in engaging waste siege.

INFRASTRUCTURE AND IMPROVISATION

By participating in the daily lives of Palestinians affected by waste siege, I learned that it affords novel ways of being and thinking that are improvisations aimed at living ethically with and in waste siege.[31] Palestinians trade in Israeli discards in attempts to find commodities that will endure. They use public infrastructures to recycle stale bread. Engineers attempt to extend the life spans of landfills they are responsible for managing even while they oppose construction of those landfills. The ways in which Palestinians improvise to attempt to ameliorate their experiences of waste siege exceed the dynamics often associated with state-society relations. They improvise informed by the logics of preserving village harmony, of maintaining donor support, or of cultivating religious piety, for example, articulating moral and intellectual universes not entirely dictated, either, by global or settler colonial processes. Improvisations intersect with bureaucratic, techno-managerial infrastructures, but they also surpass and tinker with them. To better understand and analyze waste siege, then, we must understand how improvisation and infrastructures work in the twenty-first-century West Bank.

Waste siege creates openings out of experiences of precarity, a sense that one is living within what Judith Butler (2009, 25) calls "failing social and economic networks." If precarity means not being able to plan, it also stimulates noticing in the search for the available (Tsing 2015, 278). For many, experiencing waste siege periodizes life under occupation, compelling them to notice and mark the end of one historical period—the second intifada—and the beginning of a new time. It offers opportunities to create value—for example, when a pair of Nabulsi identical twin brothers who had worked as farmers decided to collect and sell plastic bottles to Israeli middlemen upon learning that the nearby Authority landfill would not recycle them. It encourages Authority bureaucrats to practice modes of speech and comportment they hope will prove their concern for the environment in meetings with Israelis and donor representatives. Smoldering trash reorients people in space as they choose alternative routes to get to work and becomes a rubric for comparing Palestinian life to life beyond siege.

The improvisations this book depicts acknowledge their own imperfection.[32] They are powered by the sensibility of the "good-enough," where what is good enough is always under revision (Tsing 2015, 255). They are practices accompanied by critiques, shrugs, and dissatisfaction by those who practice them. Like the empty cardboard boxes that spend the day atop fruit sellers' stands in Jenin (figure 2), they are oriented toward a problematic situation's temporary amelioration. Waiting is embedded within them: for a new political future, a better set of conditions, a better life.[33] In that sense they also signal an acceptance of waste's presence, however reluctant that may be. Improvisations are what Jerome

Whitington (2016, 13) calls "compromised practices": practices that do not function optimally but that function.

The book's focus on improvisations makes it an ethnography of ambivalence as well as an ethnography of waste. Palestinians' improvisations cannot be utopian or idealistic because those who practice them know better. To cite a great Palestinian writer: improvisations are pessoptimistic (Habiby 1985). They reside in a liminal space that sees itself as a middle step in between rather than an end goal. They are flexible, spontaneous acts that occur without much preparation. They are practices for handling the slow, plodding, and often unsuccessful process of bringing infrastructures into being.

Yet improvisation's imperfections should not be mistaken for signs of Palestinians' complacency. Improvisation implies "making do," but we must put the emphasis on *making*.[34] Social formations—organized around specific cultural brokers, collectivities, temporalities, mediators, and affective labor—coalesce when Palestinians improvise to adapt to this emergent form of siege. The Nabulsi twins who sold plastic bottles to Israeli middlemen, for instance, received assistance from the deputy mayor of Nablus, a civil engineer and Hamas affiliate whom the Israeli military periodically harasses by arresting him and his son in the dark of night. The twin men, whose family livelihoods had been destroyed by Israel's stranglehold over Palestinian agriculture, now partnered with a man on the Israeli military's watch list, while trading with members of what is rumored to be the Israeli mafia (criminal gangs have controlled plastics recycling in Israel for years). Conventional categories of state and nation fail to capture the social worlds made up of such connections and exchanges (see also Stamatopoulou-Robbins 2014).

Infrastructures are among Palestinians' improvisations for mitigating waste siege. By *infrastructure* I mean a few different things. In addition to using the popular sense of the term, which evokes large-scale, state-sponsored, technological systems or smaller structures like the steel rotating machine the twins used to churn organic wastes out of municipal trash to separate out plastics and other materials, I examine how things, including waste, become *infrastructural*. Here I draw on important developments in the anthropology of infrastructure to help bring the study of waste, which can be siloed into discussions of consumption, value, and culture, more squarely into it.[35] Valuable research on roadways, railroads, oil and water pipelines, dams, landfills, and electric grids frames infrastructures as materials that make exchange over space possible and that connect faraway spaces to one another (Larkin 2008, 5; 2013). Infrastructures here have three characteristics: they are institutionalized, they are a means of transport, and they are networked in that they connect otherwise disconnected or distant sites (Anand 2017; Angell 2014; Appel, Mason, and Watts 2015; Appel 2012a; Barnes 2014; Björkman 2015; Chalfin 2014; Dalakoglou and Harvey 2016; de Boeck 2011; Desai, McFarlane, and Graham 2015; Elyachar 2010; Fredericks 2018; Graham and Marvin 1996, 2001; Günel 2016; P. Harvey 2012, 2017; P. Harvey and Knox 2015; Larkin 2008, 2013; Mains 2012; Nucho 2016; Shamir 2013; Star 1999; Thomas 2014; Von Schnitzler 2016).

Bearing these characteristics in mind, unwanted and discarded materials we would typically think of as things *managed by* infrastructures can also *be* infrastructural (Liboiron 2014). Waste facilitates processes, affects, and practices, like the politically uncomfortable but economically felicitous collaborations in the twins' Nablus recycling scheme. It acts as an assemblage of things that allows for the organization of a patterned phenomenon or process. That which typically demands order, and is defined by that demand, generates its own order. My proposed understanding of the infrastructural resonates with discussions of the "vibrancy" (Bennett 2010) or agency of nonhuman things. Yet my point is less that waste should be viewed as something possessing its own agency and more that it is infrastructural in that it, too, can facilitate flows, circulations, and distributions of people, goods, and ideas. Waste is an enabler.

The fact that conventional waste infrastructures like landfills and treatment plants do not prevent ordinary Palestinians from experiencing waste's presence, and from needing to improvise to manage its noxious effects, suggests that the normative understanding of waste infrastructures as absential technologies must also be rethought.[36] Such infrastructures can in fact form a part of waste siege, as waste management infrastructures rarely serve one purpose alone. They are rarely just the technologies that make waste disappear, in part because waste—like the total volume of water on earth—never truly disappears. Waste merely changes place and form. Waste in waste siege reveals that waste infrastructures are technologies that *redistribute* waste's burdens rather than making them disappear, sometimes through compression (e.g., landfills) and sometimes through dissemination (e.g., Palestinians' plastic bottles ending up in underground Israeli recycling networks).[37] A single waste infrastructure like a landfill subtracts waste from some spaces and adds it to others. More than polysemic, or productive of many different meanings, a landfill has multiple, possibly contradictory, effects. It can augment the vitality of some human groups while producing precarity for others—for example, when hazardous waste is moved to the outskirts of a village to save the city from its hazards.

The precarity and dilemmas that waste infrastructures present are not limited, furthermore, to the people we tend to think of as most obviously exposed to waste's toxicities. Shifting back and forth between the experiences of those who live near infrastructures like landfills or unmanaged dumpsites and waste managers and planners reveals that even Authority employees designing treatment plants face unexpected dilemmas—for instance, in representing waste siege to foreign audiences or in designing "technical fixes" (Günel 2019) for when construction stalls.[38]

RESEARCH AMID THE SIEGE

This book is based on fieldwork I began in the summer of 2007, on two and a half years of continuous fieldwork between 2009 and 2011, and on return visits between 2012 and 2016. During my longest, continuous stay in Palestine I spent half of each week in Ramallah/al-Bireh, twin cities of over eighty-three thousand, including over sixteen thousand refugees in two camps. Ramallah/al-Bireh is the Authority's de facto political capital and center of government. I interviewed people in the Palestinian ministries of water, local government, environment, and planning and shadowed them as they worked to build sanitary landfills to house Palestinian garbage. I joined them in meetings where they discussed the diameters of pipes for sewage treatment plants with municipal engineers and foreign donors. I accompanied them and the engineers they appointed on visits around the West Bank—for example, to convince landowners to sell their lands for Authority-designed waste infrastructure projects. I also interviewed representatives of foreign aid agencies funding Palestinian waste projects.

During the other half of each week I lived in Jenin, the northernmost West Bank Palestinian city and one of the poorest. About forty thousand people, including over ten thousand refugees, live in Jenin, where unemployment rates have fluctuated between 20 and 80 percent since the early 2000s. Jenin is also one of the places that were hardest hit by Israeli violence during the second intifada. In April 2002, for instance, Israel launched "Operation Defensive Shield," a twelve-day operation that killed dozens of Jenin camp residents and left much of the camp and parts of Jenin city, including four hundred homes, in ruins. Around two thousand people became homeless. Jenin is known for its communities' commitment to armed resistance to occupation, while among Israeli and American commentators in particular it is known as "the suicide bomber capital" (Issacharoff 2015) of Palestine.[39] The latter is one of the reasons Israel, the Authority, and foreign donors, who see Jenin as a "poverty pocket" where low quality of life leads to political unrest, have poured resources into waste infrastructures there.

When I arrived in Jenin, the Authority had just opened its first landfill, called Zahrat al-Finjan, fifteen minutes south of Jenin. I lived in Jenin in order to spend time at the landfill and with municipal employees who coordinated trash collection and transport to the landfill. Yet because Jenin is also, I learned, one of the Palestinian cities with the most well-established markets for used Israeli goods, called the *rabish* (from the English "rubbish"), I spent mornings visiting with *rabish* shopkeepers and inhabiting the rhythms of their market.

Conditions for visitors in Jenin gave me a more intimate experience of life there than I had anticipated. I had decided to teach English to a group of young Palestinian actors at the Freedom Theater to get to know people in the city, which, at the time, had very few foreign visitors and only two places where nonlocals could sleep: the guesthouse associated with Jenin's Cinema, which was under renovation to replace the cinema that had closed in 1987, and the guesthouse above the Freedom Theater in Jenin refugee camp. But Jenin residents were periodically targeting both guesthouses. On the day I first arrived at the Freedom Theater to meet with its director and founder, Juliano Mer-Khamis, for example, a group of young men stormed the theater, pounding on its iron doors. Juliano explained that they were members of an armed group to which the brother of Mona, one of the female acting students, had belonged. The army had killed Mona's brother in 2006, and his comrades were upset that his sister was now performing on stage with men. They wanted Mona to stop acting, claiming it harmed the group's reputation, since her brother had become a symbol of heroic martyrdom. Other community members with similar complaints about gender mixing at the theater or about its political stances (its plays were often critical of local political parties and the Authority) had set fire to the theater's guesthouse door at night. Theater employees had been threatened with death, as had employees of the Cinema Guesthouse (where I spent my first few weeks in Jenin). Rumors circulated that at the guesthouse unmarried men and women slept together. Threats were to become reality two years later when someone murdered Juliano in front of the theater in broad daylight.[40]

Sensitive to the uncertain climate in Jenin when I first arrived, three families connected to the theater—including Mona's family—offered to host me. I came to alternate living with five Jenin families over two years. As a long-term guest I was able to participate in and document household practices around the production and movement of refuse, including how waste was classified, when and how it was reused, and where it was disposed of. The abu-Salameh, Mansour, as-Sanouri, Jarrar, al-Haj, and Mwais families humored questions about their garbage and took me to visit grandparents, who offered stories about how they had managed waste over their lifetimes. I learned about the meanings, materials, and practices of cleanliness and how they affected people's use of spaces in and out of doors. I learned what people considered wasteful behavior and how they taught each other to know and to avoid it. I observed what made the members of the families I lived with feel pride or shame around the objects they purchased and displayed in their homes. I shopped with my host mothers, fathers, and siblings and participated in conversations over family meals about the market, budgets, and dreams of children's futures.

As I followed the movement of waste, my research also brought me into Israel, Jerusalem, and West Bank Israeli settlements. I met with Israelis concerned about waste in—and flowing out of—the West Bank. I interviewed Israeli environmentalists, researchers in environmentalist, human rights, and planning rights NGOs, and environmental lawyers at the forefront of Israel's antipollution efforts, and I attended public conferences organized by research institutes showcasing collaborative Israeli-Palestinian work on environmental issues. I came to know a prominent settler environmental activist who has dedicated his life's work to promoting environmentally sustainable human habitation—as well as Israeli control—in the West Bank. Through him I gained access to employees in the Israeli Civil Administration working on waste. Across Israel and the West Bank I benefited from people's willingness to share documents with me, including unpublished materials. I conducted the majority of my interviews and interactions with my Palestinian interlocutors in Arabic. I spoke with my Israeli interlocutors in English.

AN ORDER FOR DISORDER

The structure of *Waste Siege* does double duty, prioritizing the experiential dimensions of siege as well as tracing the material flows, accumulations, and blockages of waste itself. The book follows the thing, but because the following is not linear and there is not just one thing to follow, the organization of the book's chapters mirrors the decenteredness of waste siege. Focusing on Palestinian engineers' efforts to establish sanitary landfills in the West Bank, chapter 1 shows how landfills generate landfill-specific logics, temporalities, and dilemmas. It argues that, as forms of material and political compression, landfills redistribute wastes and their risks on a territory, putting wastes into play with debates about property, the public good, and temporal and spatial scales of governance and modernity.

Chapter 2 explores how ordinary Palestinians experience the proliferation of the disposable and flimsy commodities whose importation Authority officials have sanctioned and that Authority landfills are mandated to manage. It draws on my fieldwork around Jenin's *rabish* market and argues that, increasingly stuck in place by occupation, people in Jenin experience waste siege as a flooding, or inundation, of unreliable commodities in local Palestinian markets that sell new commodities. In this context *rabish* goods become objects of desire and unlikely tools for articulating longing for a life that separation from Israel has foreclosed—where foreclosure pertains both to Israeli ways of living and to Israeli ways of being governed—while also securing prosthetic access to material aspects of that life.

Chapter 3 asserts that accumulated wastes are unique among infrastructural substrates (e.g., electricity, water) because, in their material indeterminacy, they can embody impossible-to-answer questions of culpability. It proposes that sites of waste accumulation in Palestine are characterized by the twinning of what I call hypo- and hypergovernance, arguing that a specific form of nonsovereignty shapes how council members of Shuqba village—a dumping ground for Palestinian and Israeli wastes—adjudicate the toxic uncertainties of accumulation. Adjudication involves what I call "incomplete interpellation," where repeated appeals to the Authority for help that never comes bring a *shibih dawla*, or phantom state, into being.

Chapter 4 foregrounds the relationship between people's treatment of unwanted bread—which creates a kind of ethical-material siege—and cultivation of an ethical self, pointing to the obligation to keep unwanted bread in circulation rather than allowing it to go to waste. It argues that casting off unwanted bread out of doors is a form of gift giving where the giver, rather than the receiver, is the party to the exchange most burdened by obligations imposed by the bread, contra prevailing anthropological understandings of gift exchange that emphasize the recipient's burden. It proposes that outdoor bread deposits are infrastructural because they facilitate circulation of the idea—and ideal—of an emergent, democratic collectivity, or commons. The chapter proposes that we think of cast-off bread as an "incomplete gift," paralleling the incomplete interpellations that invoke the phantom state.

Chapter 5 moves from the scale of the street to that of Israel/Palestine as a whole, investigating the spatial and discursive arrangement often described as the "shared environment" in which Palestinians and Israelis live. It depicts how the dominance of this incoherent environmental imaginary that frames Palestinians as sovereign, always possibly malicious polluters of their Israeli neighbors through sewage spills, yet also as not-yet-sovereign subjects of Israeli control, renders a kind of Orwellian doublethink necessary for Palestinians seeking Israeli and foreign support for wastewater infrastructures. Tracking a trip with Palestinian Water Authority employees into Israel, where I observed their ambivalence both about the environmental imaginary of the project they sought to promote and about its potential efficacy, I show how Authority employees become sewage representatives, performing what I call "aspirational phatic labor" to help build a sewage system for their would-be state.

Chapters 1, 3, and 5 can be read as their own ethnographic cluster, exploring the work of *governing* waste to examine waste infrastructures in the conventional sense of the term. Chapters 2 and 4 take up two emergent, waste-related dilemmas in the everyday lives of Palestine's *governed*, focusing on unwanted materials that do not fit into governors' normative definition of waste. The latter chapters show how, enrolled in systems of exchange, waste can become infrastructural. In circular fashion, the exchange of discards can help mitigate the ethical dilemmas, anxieties, and material challenges of waste siege. My hope is that the five chapters taken together make a case for thinking of refuse and excreta as animating, culturing environments in which socialities, ethics, and politics come alive.

Chapter 1

COMPRESSION

How to Make Time at an Occupied Landfill

ZAHRAT AL-FINJAN LANDFILL (ARABIC FOR "FLOWER CUP") IS A CRATER
cut into a piece of agricultural land south of Jenin. It is nestled between Ajja and
Arrabah villages, occupies an area of roughly 44.5 acres, and is surrounded by
a fence. An access road leads to an opening in the fence. After a metal gate and
booth the landfill's entrance features a bridge where truck drivers stop to have
the contents of their vehicles weighed and evaluated for quality and type. They
haul the wastes of about one million Palestinians here from across the northern
and central West Bank.

Weighed trucks proceed down a dirt road deep into the site. Men wearing
orange vests stand along the side of the road on hills of trash guiding incoming
trucks to the parts of the landfill designated for filling that day. Drivers offload,
then drive back out. Other men use compactor vehicles to compress new trash,
reducing its mass and spreading it into three-foot layers. Later, workers will cover
the cell with dirt from the site's sides.

Zahrat al-Finjan can hold about 102.4 million cubic feet of waste in four cells.
Beneath piles of garbage the crater is covered with two layers of polyethylene liner (see
figure 3) that create a membrane blocking liquids from seeping downward as organic
refuse rots and combines with air moisture. The membrane catches the liquids, called
leachate, at the bottom of the pile. Plastic pipes channel leachate to a pond at one
edge of the landfill. In the pungent pond aerobic treatment reduces odors.

Zahrat al-Finjan is part of a series of internationally funded, multi-million-dollar projects to bury Palestinian garbage. Palestinians are producing unprecedented volumes of waste per capita while living in the densest ratio of population to land the West Bank has seen. The move aims to compress trash into three sites forming the backbone of the Authority's *National Strategy for Solid Waste Management in the West Bank* (PNA 2010a). The *Strategy* envisions a landfill for the north, in Jenin; one for the center, in Ramallah; and one for the south, in Hebron. The Authority opened the northern and southern landfills in 2007 and 2013 respectively. Plans for Ramallah's are still under way (see Stamatopoulou-Robbins 2014).

Landfills are the infrastructures with which the Authority seeks to replace long-standing garbage management systems, including hundreds of smaller dumpsites that are unlined and open. For roughly 130 years, municipalities had moved refuse horizontally across the land's surface from residential centers to administrative peripheries, covering it with dirt, burning it, or reusing it. In the 1980s and 1990s Israel and its occupied territories saw the emergence of a new object of knowledge and intervention. People called it "the environment" (*al-bi'a* in Arabic). Previously understood primarily as problems of public health (e.g., under the

FIGURE 3. View from atop Zahrat al-Finjan landfill in Jenin, 2010. This view shows the liner (thick dark line on left) and pooling liquid (diamond shape in center) in a cell under preparation. An access road and fence are visible in the top left-hand corner. Photograph by the author.

Jordanian administration, physicians designated dumpsite locations), garbage and sewage were newly cast as environmental pollutants. Recasting was catalyzed by, and came to necessitate, new solutions to the new uncertainties associated with waste. It generated the need for expertise in new spatial and temporal scales for which the human senses and existing medical sciences no longer provided adequate knowledge. A reorientation toward protecting the environment prioritized central-ized control over municipal wastes, required prohibitions on waste burning, and placed material buffers between human-produced waste and the ground.

Earlier waste management systems had allowed residents to claim others' discarded materials, such as cardboard and iron, to repurpose or sell it, and had made it easy for people to burn trash in the open. Authority landfills transferred de facto ownership of garbage within municipal boundaries to the Authority under the aegis of an Authority-appointed administrative body, called a Joint Service Council for Solid Waste Management (JSC). A guard now keeps watch at Zahrat al-Finjan to keep out what JSC employees call "waste pickers" and people who would set fire to the trash, irked as nearby communities are by the greatly increased presence of waste in their midst. He watches for trucks trying to dump there without paying the JSC. The landfill, built on a $9.5 million World Bank loan the JSC will pay back by raising municipal fees, increased the cost of disposal for communities while also making disposal there mandatory. The guard also watches for internal combustion, since air intrusion into compressed wastes at this scale can provide the oxygen necessary for increased biological activity, heating waste to the point of burning it.

A guard is also not a bad idea given how concerned nearby Palestinian commu-nities are about who benefits from the landfill. In the mid-1980s, when the Israeli Civil Administration still governed the occupied population directly, it had com-missioned Tahal, Israel's national water authority, to produce a document entitled *Master-Plan for the Disposal of Solid Waste in the Judea and Samaria Region* (Tahal 1987).[1] The plan provided for seven West Bank landfills designed for joint trash disposal from Israeli West Bank settlements and Palestinian communities. For Israel this was planning at the most expansive national scale, as it produced nearly identical landfilling plans for both sides of the Green Line to protect what planners framed as a singular Israeli environment and its underground water sources. The military issued a military order expropriating the land Zahrat al-Finjan now sits on for the Israeli-planned Jenin landfill in 1986. The plan was met with resistance from local Palestinian communities, and, like another four of the seven landfills for which Tahal drew up detailed designs, the Israeli-planned Jenin landfill was not built by the time the Authority was established. In the 1990s the Authority repurposed four of Tahal's remaining plans—for Jenin, Ramallah, Hebron, and Jericho—making them the four pillars of its scheme to build waste management infrastructures for a future Palestinian state.

Attending to the technical properties and temporal qualities of waste burial, this chapter tracks how landfills' new Palestinian managers understood and engaged the contradictions of choosing this waste infrastructure for Palestine. After an introduction to the landfill managers with whom I spent the most time, the section that follows explains how, despite the landfill plans' colonial origins, the new managers viewed implementing the plans as national work.

NEW MANAGEMENT

Over two years, I spent time at Zahrat al-Finjan with Hamdi, the JSC's executive manager, and Mo'tasem, its technical manager. Both had been trained as engineers at the prestigious Al-Najah University in Nablus, but Hamdi was twenty years older and held a degree in civil engineering, since, he recalled, specializations in waste and environment did not yet exist in the 1980s. Mo'tasem had received a master's in engineering in the 2000s and had written his thesis on Palestinians' recycling options, an increasingly popular subject at Palestinian universities.

Hamdi carried himself with the quiet, busy gravitas of an executive manager. His hunch and gray hair betrayed that he had been with the project since before it was a hole in the ground, overseeing its inception from land negotiations through its opening. He spent his days driving between the administrative building and the landfill cells across the road to monitor compaction and equipment and to check for wild animals. He held forth at visits from municipal, Authority, donor, and Israeli army officials and from students.

Though Hamdi and I saw each other frequently, he maintained a polite distance, especially when we first met. He kept our meetings short, rushing to answer calls while I finished my notes. I felt fortunate to have access to these men's worlds. They were understandably defensive, as Jenin was abuzz with stories of the landfill's bad odors, dangers, and connections to Israel. But Hamdi eventually opened up and was forthcoming with documents, offering copies of the controversial Israeli expropriation order and the agreement for loan repayment.

Mo'tasem showed me the landfill, commandeering a small truck off the administrative building's lot to drive us to the uneven, surprisingly nonodorous surface of trash layers while he yelled explanations of what vehicles were doing over whirring engines and metal clanking. Mo'tasem embodied an energy and enthusiasm that came with the post-Oslo period, when many Palestinians were optimistic that a state could soon be built. He was excited to share plans he had drafted to partner with a Jordanian recycling company he had researched for his thesis, which he hoped I would read. He was ambitious, his fervor and social ease giving off a readiness to one day serve as executive manager himself. Mo'tasem dreamt of strengthening Jenin's role in governing surrounding villages and smaller cities, especially since Jenin had historically played second fiddle to Nablus as the latter's less cosmopolitan, less institutionally developed agricultural hinterland (Doumani 1995). It was thanks in part to Mo'tasem's enthusiasm that much of the Jenin JSC's work involved promoting waste burial for the rest of Palestine. Hamdi and Mo'tasem worked with a media team to make videos promoting the landfill and gave interviews on Palestinian television and radio. They gave the landfill an "open house" feeling, framing it as a living prototype for outsiders to engage with as well as a functioning infrastructure.

In Ramallah, a group of waste professionals works in another JSC planning the Ramallah regional landfill and fashioning themselves as landfill ambassadors. I first met Rana Kassim in 2007 while she coordinated cooperation among the Ramallah, al-Bireh, and Beitunia municipalities. A mutual friend put us in touch, and we began by Skyping while I was still in New York. Rana was the first waste professional I met, and, while our Skype connection was not ideal, her combination of optimism and sarcasm cut through the airwaves and began a friendship between us.

When I reached Ramallah we arranged to meet at Eiffel Sweets. As we ate pastries and drank cappuccinos Rana glowed with some of the same effervescence Mo'tasem was to express about his work. She had obtained her degrees—a BA at Birzeit University and a master's at the University of Michigan—during the Oslo years and, in her thirties when we met, she exuded a visible pleasure at the challenge of bringing progress to Palestine. She spent our first meetings guiding me through some basics. She shot off keywords: *solid waste, leachate, lining.* "The latter can be made out of anything—gravel, polyethylene. A landfill isn't 'sanitary' if it doesn't have a lining."

Rana eagerly practiced her English and sought connections to the US, ordering products from there on Amazon when she could find someone to help her get them into Ramallah from her sister's PO box in Jerusalem. (Her West Bank ID means she needs a permit to enter Jerusalem, and Israel controls international mail to Palestinian addresses in the West Bank and Gaza, which means it arrives delayed, if at all.) Two years after we first met, Rana was hired as executive director of the Ramallah/al-Bireh Governorate JSC to build Ramallah's landfill, which the Authority hoped would house trash from all central West Bank Palestinians. Rana was given the same task Hamdi had been given—to procure land and oversee the landfill's design, construction, and operation. Like Hamdi, she viewed her task as a national contribution.

BURYING WASTE TO BUILD A STATE

Landfills are the most common method of waste disposal worldwide, popular because they make waste absent from certain spaces, allowing large agglomerations of people to live together and making relatively waste-free lives reproducible (Reno 2015b). Along with workers who collect and transport waste (Nagle 2013), landfills allow people not to think about their trash. Landfills in Palestine offer Palestinian government employees like Hamdi, Mo'tasem, and Rana the added opportunity to feel that their collective work produces the appearance of a state. And Authority officials and donors tout Palestine's turn to trash burial as an important step toward making Palestine modern. Modern and state-like, landfills are what waste professionals referred to as "national" (*watani*) work. On a JSC visit to Deir Dibwan village to explain the need for a landfill, for example, Rana opened her discussion with landowners whose land the JSC sought to purchase by describing the landfill as a "national project" (*mashru' watani*).

A year later, in March 2010, I accompanied Rana and about three dozen Ramallah area mayors and village council heads, including some from Deir Dibwan, to Zahrat al-Finjan. Construction and operation of a new landfill require compliance from local governments and communities. Residents must pay fees and use dumpsters rather than burning or selling trash, and municipalities must use the landfill rather than dumping, selling, or burning trash. Our Zahrat al-Finjan visit was a culminating attempt to make a case for Ramallah's landfill using material evidence of the impact of the Jenin landfill.

The visit was an encounter between the old guard and the new. The mayors' constituents opposed a Ramallah landfill. Representing an array of political parties that predated the Authority's establishment, they were members of councils elected in the municipal elections of 2004/5. These mayors and those elected before them had been running trash collection and disposal according to local spatial, political, and labor constraints since Ottoman authorities established municipalities in the mid-nineteenth century. JSCs had only existed since 1997, and the Jenin and Ramallah JSCs were established in 2000 and 2008 respectively, answering to the Authority's ministry of local government under the unelected Fatah-led Authority.[2]

Our bus was the only vehicle turning left at the intersection where a newly paved access road (see figure 3) peeled off Nablus Road toward Jenin's southern villages. The bus wobbled as it slowed to turn. Mayors' heads swayed in unison. Energies were drained after the two-hour drive up half the West Bank. Wearing a pink hijab and a long, geometrically patterned cardigan over jeans and a turtleneck, Rana stood facing them next to the driver. She steadied herself on a seat with one hand and held a wired microphone with the other. "Thank God we have arrived safely," the microphone blared. Considering her relative youth as she rallied the group of older, skeptical men, I wondered whether the microphone's warping of her voice amplified her authority. If it didn't, perhaps something else did: the fact that those awakened by her broadcast heard her repeat words of Rammun's mayor, a rare local supporter of the project and representative of a village on whose lands the Ramallah area landfill was slated to be built: "This is a national project," the microphone crackled. "At the very least, we will benefit from Area C."

"At the very least" was Rana's nod to the mayors' disgruntlement. She could understand, she had also admitted to me privately, that transforming agricultural land into underground trash storage was at best distasteful and at worst disastrous for people whose livelihoods and provisions for future generations were invested in that land. Landfills create sacrifice zones (Broswimmer 2002; Fox 1999; J. Mitchell, Thomas, and Cutter 1999; Purdy 2011; Radford 2010) by rendering land uninhabitable, uncultivable, and environmentally vulnerable. And they extract land, a major form of wealth for Palestinians, from intergenerational wealth transmission. This makes landfills environmental dispossession for communities who have already suffered a century of settler colonial dispossession.

"We can benefit from Area C" referred to the fact that all three landfills had to be built on West Bank land under Israeli control, land upon which Israel does not usually permit Palestinians to build (see figure 1). Months before, Rana had explained that, according to the standards of the Authority, the World Bank (which had also funded the southern landfill), and Germany (Germany was funding Ramallah's landfill), landfills must be on flat terrain at least a few hundred yards away from residential areas. In the West Bank most such lands are agricultural and in Area C. This makes an Authority-run landfill in Area C, sometimes called "the prohibited zone" (Bimkom 2008), a political achievement for the Authority.

But by using the word *we*, Rana included the other mayors and Authority under a single term to signal that the achievement was collective, and nationally so, precisely because the priorities of the Authority and those of local communities were, unsurprisingly, not always aligned. Municipalities and villages outside major cities could ostensibly feel that construction in Area C was a political achievement as rural communities endured Israeli control over Area C in the form of demolitions, land confiscation, and military and settler violence.[3] *Something Palestinian*—albeit garbage—was making it into Area C.

But the loss of property and sustenance that a landfill spelled for surrounding communities was hard to square with the symbolic victory of a Palestinian flag over a new infrastructure. It was one of the more uncomfortable meetings I attended. Polite formalities that had accompanied our arrival at Deir Dibwan's village council building—complete with tiny cups of coffee—frosted over into harsh words and silent faces in response to Rana naming prices for the land.

By playing the national card, Rana was attempting to gloss the project as a public good for which it was worth sacrificing individual interests. Though the card may not have worked on the landowners and their representatives, it made sense for professionals like Rana who deployed it. She and other JSC staff understood their work as national for several reasons. For one, it was "in line with the Palestinian national solid waste strategy," as Yaman, a JSC manager of a different landfill, al-Minya (figure 4), told me in 2014. For him, implementing the Authority's *Strategy* was itself a nationalist act.

When we met, I sat in my usual interview position across the big wooden desk from Yaman, notebook on my knees and recorder on the desk. His office had the familiar JSC setup: fluorescent overhead lights, a large wooden desk, and landfill blueprints taped up. That Yaman sprang from an important landowning Jerusalem family of engineers and academics came through in his confident, jovial, almost overly performative generosity. His carved face suggested he was closer to Hamdi's age, but the pleasure he took in his work echoed Rana and Mo'tasem's youthful exuberance. He liked commanding a large team of workers on-site and thrived

FIGURE 4. Satellite image of al-Minya landfill (upper center). The darkest three spots are leachate pools, and the white rectangle is the JSC's administrative building. For a sense of scale, see the Palestinian village of Kisan, visible in the right-hand corner. Source: US Geological Survey, 2018.

on unexpected challenges posed by running a major infrastructure. He made a lot of my being Greek, like the company he had subcontracted to operate the landfill, to which I return below. What were the odds? He laughed and switched out of Arabic to share Greek words he had learned from Kostas, the company representative. A few colleagues, including ʿItiraf, an old friend who had given me a ride that day, joined us, ʿItiraf sitting on my side of the desk and the others leaning against the wall. Yaman had an audience and played it up, making grand arm gestures to tell his story.

As Yaman's version of al-Minya's story unfolded, it became clear that al-Minya was another grand gesture for him. He wanted me to know how integral it was to the *Strategy*, a document that explicitly connects waste burial to state building: "The Ministerial Cabinet . . . approval [of the *Strategy*] has strengthened our hope for a better future. . . . [It is] a key developmental and political dimension within our national march to ending the occupation and earning our independent Palestinian State, with Holy Jerusalem as its capital" (PNA 2010a, v). The gist: waste management is part of Palestine's future advancement, part of a politics that can end occupation.

Waste burial, as embedded in the *Strategy*'s context, also offers waste professionals the opportunity to work at a national spatial scale, not least because landfills are enormous infrastructures compared to anything else Palestinians are building. Many Palestinians consider the territory now called Israel part of the territory that should make up a future Palestine, in no small part because millions of Palestinians either were displaced themselves from Israel or are offspring of those who were. Although the *Strategy* does not treat Israel as a part of the geography of Authority waste planning, defining the precursor to the "independent Palestinian State" as the much-reduced zone constituted by East Jerusalem, the West Bank, and Gaza, it provides for a single plan for the entire Palestinian population of those territories as if they were contiguous and politically unified.[4]

Landfills are a compression technology. Yet in Palestine compression works to expand imagined governmental reach over contested territory. It invites those who design and manage landfills—like the person who gave me the coordinates to generate the map in figure 4[5]—to imagine the occupied landscape as if they were seeing it, and could manipulate it, from the bird's-eye view of a state (Scott 1998).[6]

Waste burial also offers the promise of bringing order at a national scale to what many Authority employees and residents see as a landscape pockmarked with random (*'ashwa'i*) waste practices like dumping, burning, and scavenging.[7] It offers the possibility of a national cleanup. Zaghloul Samhan, one of the *Strategy*'s authors in the environment ministry, invited me to the *Strategy*'s launch in the summer of 2010. For Samhan the *Strategy* was a means of eradicating arbitrariness on a grand spatial scale: "When municipalities collect and dispose of wastes," he said to convince me to join him, "selection of locations for dumping is random!" Jordanian administration physicians having determined dumpsite locations in the 1950s and 1960s, for example, represented a chaos that both upset him and was illegible as order. He described the pre-Oslo period as a time "without a system" (*bidun nidham*). His muted blue suit and the white-and-gray sterility of his office mirrored the sanitizing he imagined his work brought to Palestine. Circles under his eyes disclosed the sleeplessness that that work required.

Samhan, Rana, and their colleagues were the first generation of Palestinian professionals trained in what is now called waste management (*idarat al-nifayat*). They were conscious of being the first to work on solid waste (*al-nifayat al-salba*) as an object of research and regulation, seeing themselves as pioneers struggling to bring science to waste management in Palestine. The idea that they brought a "system" to communities that had been living without one is connected to how they imagined waste had been overseen by Israeli military officials before Oslo and to their understanding of Palestinian municipalities' inability to author a proper system. Their premise was that the previous regime had left a mess to be cleaned up. That premise echoed ways in which, during other shifts from one political regime to another, representatives of new systems anchor claims to legitimacy in being able to offer a positive contrast (e.g., Petryna 2003).

In Palestine, however, pointing to Israel's mess did something in addition to anchoring legitimacy for Authority employees. It performed a time trick, generating an imagined pastness to the Israeli occupation and a sense of replacement where there was actually none. "Cleaning up" implies there is something after which one cleans, where "after" suggests both a distinct ontological entity (*the* occupation) and a bounded time (*of* occupation) that has ended. Cleanup framed the Authority as an entity separate from the occupation that had replaced it.

Former sanitation workers in Jenin's municipality recall that cleaning the mess Israel left behind when it first transferred governing responsibilities over the Palestinian population to the Authority had been one of the Authority's first commands to municipalities. Jenin's street cleaners remember mayors sending workers from

numerous municipalities to clean Jericho's streets in the days immediately following Jericho's "opening," the term many used to connote Israeli withdrawal. The act
of cleanup had symbolized renewal and erasure. 'Adel, who had been a sanitation
monitor in Jenin, smiled and leaned forward, his elbows on the table in the office
of Jenin's municipal accountant that we had borrowed for our interview in 2011.
Most Palestinians I spoke with lamented that the upward, evolutionary linearity of
state building had turned out to be a sham, acknowledging that a Palestinian state
was no closer to existing now than twenty years ago. Still, like Yaman's narration of
al-Minya as a national achievement, this was a moment of pleasure for 'Adel in the
interview: a happy recollection, leaving me surprised it didn't come with cynicism
about how partial the renewal and erasure had ended up being.

'Adel's work had kept him far from the halls of Authority leadership. But he put
sincere, emotive emphasis into the joy of having contributed to the cleanup as he
reflected on it fifteen years later. His enthusiasm suggested that the Authority's
narrative of cleanup had gained some traction and that, as in other places that
have undergone political shifts, cleaning up the previous regime's mess may also
have served to give working-class people with little reason to feel solidarity with
the elites who came to staff the Authority a terrain where they could nonetheless
feel a connection.

If replacement and renewal circulated as one way of framing what had taken
place in the mid-1990s, continued Israeli obstruction of Palestinian waste management since Oslo made the need for cleanup continuous, thereby also underlining
its nationalist qualities. In the 2000s, municipalities and communities were forced
into what Authority waste professionals deem "disorderly" or "chaotic" management practices. Rana explained that during the second intifada the military prevented municipalities from moving waste out of residential areas. In 2000, the
military closed al-Bireh's municipal dumpsite, leaving the municipality searching
for an alternative site for the garbage of one hundred thousand people. Al-Bireh
and al-'Amari refugee camp began using Ramallah's closed dumpsite, suddenly
dumping 350 tons of garbage there daily. The dumpsite quickly reached a height
of 195 feet and was in danger of collapsing. Two years later Ramallah requested
that al-Bireh find another solution. Unable to dispose of its trash, al-Bireh stopped
collection for two months. Residents burned dumpsters' contents, destroying
dumpsters. Finally, al-Bireh turned to an open dumpsite near houses and a school
in al-Jinan neighborhood and on cultivated land (Al-Khatib and Abu Safieh 2003;

Musleh and Giacaman 2001). Similar sequences ensued across the West Bank and Gaza. By the end of the intifada, the number of open dumpsites in the West Bank had reached over four hundred.

Israeli obstructions upended Authority managers' proposition that they had succeeded in bringing order to the territory. Yet the obstructions also underlined the constant need for the Authority to impose order. Rana shook her head. Open dumpsites are a "catastrophe," she said. She warned that when people burn trash, dioxins are released, increasing the risk of cancer, respiratory and skin diseases, and fertility problems. Unlined dumps allow leachates to seep directly into the ground. Part of the disorder that Authority employees were seeking to correct revolved around biopolitical (Foucault 2008) concerns around threats to public health.

The grand scale of the landfills was not only imagined. They were designed to remove waste from massive swaths of the West Bank, minimizing some of the problems Rana described. Within a year of its opening in 2007, Zahrat al-Finjan had already changed the northern West Bank's physical landscape. It permitted the Authority to close approximately eighty local dumpsites, making some into parks for public use that doubled as sample cleanup sites JSC managers could show visitors to endear them to waste burial. The following two sections examine how managers harnessed landfills' technical specifications to open up a national horizon of modernization.

TECHNOAESTHETICS OF A MODERN LANDFILL

Waste burial offers Palestinian professionals rare opportunities to hone, expand, and advertise their expertise in an emergent field of management and research. It draws significant donor investment to the Authority's waste sector—construction of the three landfills promised over $45 million—which means executing a broad mandate, fulfilling major responsibilities, and handling large budgets, often for the first time.[8] Waste burial offers openings to learn transferrable skills like coordination with donors, NGOs, and Israel and infrastructure management. Mo'tasem boasted that the World Bank promoted Zahrat al-Finjan as one of its most successful Middle East projects. The JSC was on the world map for waste management, and so was he.[9]

Rana's excitement at the prospect of working in the JSC was palpable. She had gotten a big break at an early age, having only recently completed her master's in environmental and water resources engineering in the US. She lit up as she described how she would use her training to create a waste management system from scratch for her native Ramallah. 'Itiraf, who had driven me to al-Minya to meet with Yaman, had also recently returned from America. He was one of the fastest and most energetic talkers I met, though speed did not mean brevity. He turned each conversation into a personalized workshop—a forum for brainstorming ideas and seeking feedback. He worked for the Bethlehem JSC coordinating disposal at al-Minya, having transitioned from being a researcher in a local NGO to managing garbage collection and disposal for Bethlehem Governorate's roughly two hundred thousand residents. When Yaman joined al-Minya in 2006, he went from working as one of a handful of employees in Hebron's municipal engineering department, which serves a population of about 160,500, to managing disposal for the entire southern West Bank, serving between 800,000 and one million people. On our drive through Hebron's tan-colored hills, 'Itiraf said Yaman was referred to as "the godfather of the landfill." The term connoted Yaman's personal investment in the project and his successful custodianship over its many moving parts. It also evoked a respect for Yaman's work that was widely held among colleagues and the communities for which "his" landfill provided removal. Working at these expanded scales allowed people like Rana, 'Itiraf, and Yaman to see themselves as representatives of a state in the making (Navaro-Yashin 2012). That these were spatial, institutional, and temporal scales of government work previously closed off to Palestinians in the Occupied Territory for most of Palestine's modern history added to their sense of achievement at a national scale.

The scales at which these professionals were excited to work materialized through particular aesthetic practices and "evaluative aesthetic categories embedded in . . . expert practices," part of what Joseph Masco (2004, 350) calls a "technoaesthetics of change." These practices included holding and attending conferences, celebratory gatherings, workshops, and visits at landfills or cleanup sites. They also included curated interactions with objects and sensory experiences that delivered the message that change was afoot. When I had the chance to attend the *Strategy*'s launch in July 2010, for instance, attendees received a grainy brown, recycled-looking folder. A sticker of the Authority's eagle emblem and the Palestinian and German flags (the latter partly concealing the former) adorned the front. The glossy cover of the English-Arabic reversible booklet featured photographs of workers laying large, black, polyethylene sheets at Zahrat al-Finjan.

We cut short our leafing through images of dumpsters belching smoke to abandon folders on chairs and stand for an awkwardly loud tape recording of the national anthem. Speeches from several people, including Dr. Ghonim, head of the *Strategy*'s National Team, the minister of local government, and a German Development Bank representative, were followed by a forty-five-minute ode to waste burial by Prime Minister Salam Fayyad. Introducing Dr. Fayyad, Dr. Ghonim called for a celebration of the *Strategy* as "a national product. Not only does it make . . . us feel that we own what we do," he said into the podium microphone, evoking Palestinians' experiences of being deprived of self-rule, but this was the outcome of a "very analytical study." Part of what made the *Strategy* a step toward self-rule was its purported basis in science.

Like the launch, visits to landfill sites were designed to transmit a sense of the landfill as a scientific endeavor. The first stop on the Ramallah mayors' trip with Rana was the landfill's administrative building. It was a four-story structure with a stone facade. Air-conditioned air replaced warm, sweet garbage gusts. These swelled momentarily in our nostrils as we walked between the bus and building: the smell of human mastery over material degradation. Conditioned air offered a contrast for most municipal and village council buildings, which lacked air conditioning and heating, leaving employees to use fans, to open windows, or to wear coats.

Throughout our day at Zahrat al-Finjan, visitors were inundated with messages conveying the depth of landfill managers' expertise. We passed accounting and engineering offices and a table with an open guestbook on it. In the visitors' hall on the top floor, moist hands left fingerprints on the plexiglass encasing a miniature model of the landfill, complete with service roads, mock garbage piles to scale, buildings, a weigh bridge, and fencing. The model highlighted that the landfill was so large and complex as to require miniaturization and a view from above. Another case displayed landfill liners for close-up examination of these materials that, buried under garbage, would normally be the hardest part of the infrastructure to see (figure 5).

Visits were arranged so that our senses of sight, smell, and touch were drawn into the landfill's technical workings, inspiring awe toward these as infrastructures at the height of modernity. Palestine, we were given to understand, was modernizing its way out from under Israel's thumb. Mo'tasem, Hamdi, and Rana all used the technics of the landfill to tell a story that was always in part a story of national achievement in the face of an occupation seeking to prevent it. Hamdi invited us to sit in plastic chairs lined up in front of a plasma screen TV and played a ten-minute video showing how, despite obstacles from the military and from donors, JSC engineers had prevailed in building a modern (*mo'asir*) landfill.

To frame the landfill as modern, Hamdi and his staff presented it as an unmarked, history-less, and timeless technology, echoing the fact that the labels in the display cases were in English (only sometimes with Arabic translations) and used nonspecific temporal and geographic language (e.g., "Geosynthetic Clay Liners Used in Municipal Solid Waste Landfills," figure 5). They also marked the landfill as an import. What the dumping municipalities had been doing for over a century was "local" (*mahalli*), whereas landfills came from a boundless outside. The placelessness and timelessness of landfills was highlighted, in fact, by their not being local, while their global scaling out afforded them an expansive time depth. The *national* quality of Palestinian professionals' position was associated with governing techniques perceived to be both *extraterritorial* and *noncultural*.[10] That Zahrat al-Finjan is a landfill like any other is part of what makes it modern, Hamdi and his staff insisted to their audience. Landfills stand in for, and condense, the application of global science and rationality to a dirty, chaotic, and decidedly local world.

FIGURE 5. Display case in the Zahrat al-Finjan landfill administrative building, 2010. Photograph by the author.

That landfills occupied the most important imaginative space in the work of Palestine's new waste professionals was partly because they saw landfills as the only viable solution to Palestine's waste chaos. "In the end," Hamdi said to the Ramallah mayors after the video, "any method you use, you need a landfill. It's just about how much of the waste is buried there." He made landfills sound inevitable. In doing so he omitted discussion of alternatives like regulating product packaging and consumer habits that minimize waste production, although he and Rana discussed these alternatives with colleagues privately. From the professionals' pragmatic standpoint, it was out of the question that the Authority would intervene at the level of Palestinian imports or industry. They had decided that—at least for the time being—landfilling, and garbage production, were as natural to human life as defecation.

LANDFILLS' TEMPORAL HORIZONS

Portraying landfills as natural made their absence seem unnatural. Without them Palestine was in yet another way unnaturally behind a world of modern states. Landfills simultaneously opened up the *longue durée* of modernization as process and the destination of modernity as a state already formed. In this sense landfills in Palestine were unlikely and unspectacular, utopian infrastructures for an aspiring postcolony.[11]

As national infrastructures that opened up modernization's horizon, landfills could ostensibly be conceived as projects without an expiration date.[12] Commentaries on infrastructural imaginaries linked to statecraft and modernization often assume that the engineers and architects involved are earnestly committed to carrying a given infrastructure or technology into an unlimited future. They are assumed to see the bridge or road, the electric grid or nuclear plant as the solution to end all solutions. Some infrastructural visionaries and operators may indeed be devout advocates of the infrastructures they build and see their work in these temporal terms. But to assume that infrastructure professionals imagine the time frames of their infrastructures only in open-ended, utopian terms may miss more nuanced temporal orientations at play.

Infrastructures are always the material products of compromises at multiple scales, and those who design and operate them are similarly always negotiating multiple identities and commitments and their own awareness of the potential for breakdown, failure, and collapse. If engineers designing a dam that stops functioning after ten years are assumed to have expected it to function forever, we can expect its malfunction to be read both by observers and by affected populations as an engineering failure or as a failure of human mastery over the natural world, with blame for false consciousness, naïveté, or hubris among those committed to that mastery (e.g., Graham 2010). Breakdown can be read as evidence of the "recalcitrance" (Anand 2017; Bennett 2010) of nonhuman forces, as evidence of the anthropocentrism of those who celebrate infrastructure as part of linear development. But among my interlocutors it was more usual for time's finitude to be factored in.

Although they publicly framed landfills as utopian and naturally necessary, JSC engineers also saw them as infrastructures whose time in Palestine was to be limited. The hope, they repeated, a few short breaths after asserting landfills' naturalness, was that waste burial would soon be replaced by more "advanced" technology. They upheld a dual vision of landfills as infrastructures for utopian national progress and as temporary fixes until a better solution could be found.

For Palestine's waste professionals, not only were landfills on the bottom rung of a high ladder of aspirations in relation to waste disposal; they were also anachronistic technologies. During the mayors' visit to Zahrat al-Finjan, staff encouraged us to handle pails made of recycled plastics. Cases beside the miniature model of Zahrat al-Finjan boasted sample bits produced by incineration and recycling imported from Japan. Heads bent down to peer in before being directed to a view of the landfill from wall-to-wall windows. During postfilm discussion, Hamdi picked up an asymmetrical, shiny solid black object. In Japan "they incinerate.... One ton of waste becomes about 40 kilos.... These," he said, knocking the opal-like rock on a table, "are very solid materials.... This dense black, rock-like thing, it can be used for construction." Hamdi holding the black rock echoed the way he and his colleagues turned landfills into sites for expanding communities' imaginative horizons—at least to a point. It was as if Rana, Hamdi, and Mo'tasem could not help but display their professional training, which had taught them landfills' low status in global waste management. They sang the praises of waste burial's basis in science-as-future while simultaneously using landfill visits as opportunities to expose Palestinian audiences to other waste management technologies they viewed as superior. This placed waste burial in—but also behind—a historical and global trajectory.

It was particularly ironic that Hamdi discussed incineration while trying to emphasize the value of landfills given that donors were reluctant to fund high-tech incineration projects. When 'Itiraf and I Skyped in 2017, seven years after Hamdi's speech, incineration was still off the table. Incinerators can cost more than ten times what landfills do. I recalled a local government ministry official saying, "There are new, safe incineration technologies. But in Japan even a small one costs seventy million dollars. The one in Singapore cost eight hundred million!" 'Itiraf's young daughter appeared on screen and waved. Wrapping an arm around her shoulders, he added that the energy that incinerators produce covers only 10 to 30 percent of the running cost. Where would we get the other 70 percent?

Donors are also unwilling to fund infrastructures they think Palestinian communities will not pay for. Fritz was an engineer with a graduate degree in solid waste management from Germany. For years he was head of Berlin municipality's solid waste management division and was responsible for managing a quarter of the city's waste, serving eight hundred thousand people. Between 1995 and 2007 he built landfills and primary collection and recycling systems for Berlin before becoming the German government technical consultant working with Rana on the Ramallah landfill project. I interviewed Fritz at Pronto cafe in a part of Ramallah popular among expats. Fritz gave off an "in-group" vibe, getting comfortable in English over a glass of wine in the presence of another expat. He told me he thought "Palestine is forty to fifty years behind Germany" and that "the best solution for Palestine" was "incineration linked to power-heat coupling." But, he added, "That would cost about one hundred and fifty dollars per ton." His team had determined that twenty to forty dollars per ton was the maximum communities could afford. "After five or six years, the infrastructure should run on its own returns. It must be able to reinvest in machines, etc. Those costs have to be covered by fee collection from residents." Donors assume they will someday soon recede. As a result, he continued, referring to landfills, "We chose a low-tech solution." He flicked his wrist. The world is just like that; some people get the high-tech stuff and others the low tech.

In viewing residents as unwilling or unable to pay a higher price for waste management, donors produce categories of preferred and shunned customers for different types of infrastructures.[13] Donors depend on similar categories when determining whether a country has experts with what they call "capacity" to operate a given infrastructure. Donors view landfills favorably because landfills are considered relatively easy to manage. "All you need is to follow the basic principle. You spread the waste and you cover it every day," 'Itiraf reminded me. His daughter had pulled out a coloring book. "She hears me talk about this all day every day," he chuckled. Incinerators are considered much more complicated to operate and manage, requiring specialized training.

Palestine's waste professionals are subject to a constant flow of messages from donor representatives and Israeli officials indicating that they lack expertise. It is characteristic for Palestinians to receive reports from donors that frame the need for donor intervention as based on Palestinians' supposed incapacity to do their jobs. A 2013 World Bank report that circulated online explained, for example, that "the World Bank and other donors provided the necessary funding for a new sanitary landfill at Al-Minya but deem that *the local capacity to manage it is insufficient.*" It went on to say this was why the JSC sought "an *experienced* private sector partner to manage the new facility" (World Bank 2013, 1; emphasis mine). That was the Greek company Yaman had told me about.

Donors further fear that Palestine's political and economic conditions will make incineration challenging. "Nobody wants to invest because of the political instability," Fritz said. "They do not want to donate large sums to infrastructures that run the risk of breaking down or being destroyed." He was wearing a sports watch on a lanky, tan arm. He looked as if he had spent months in the hot Palestinian sun. We talked about the fact that Palestinians rely almost exclusively on Israel for their electricity generation, which is a problem because incinerators require a stable electricity supply and Israeli policies include cutting off that supply. During the winter of the 2008/2009 Israeli attacks on Gaza, for instance, the UN reported that, because Israel cut or bombed Gaza's electricity supply, "incinerators did not function due to electricity shortages" (Bartlett 2013).

Incinerators also require dry waste and a constant stream of large quantities of it to keep burning. About half of waste in "developing" economies like Palestine's is organic, wet wastes. Donors say that Palestine does not have enough of the right types of waste to properly run incinerators. There is no indication, furthermore, that if donors offer to fund incinerators the Israeli military will permit them. Israel has stymied Palestinian electricity generation and access, usually citing security reasons (Dumper 1993; Li and Lein 2006; Salamanca 2011; Shamir 2013). Finally, donors and investors uphold landfills—and not waste reduction regulations or incinerators—as a condition for investment. In 1996, for example, a German company planned to construct an industrial zone on the lands of Jalameh village north of Jenin. The company made a landfill in Jenin a condition for its opening. That landfill ended up being Zahrat al-Finjan. The material properties of Palestine's garbage and its dependence on foreign aid condensed two opposing temporalities—the out-of-dateness of waste burial and the promise of a prosperous future—in the form of the landfill.

NO LONGER MODERN

Despite knowing of and preferring alternatives, Palestine's waste professionals, like donors and Authority officials, treat waste burial as the only conceivable system around which managing Palestinian wastes can be organized *for the foreseeable future*. This made it all the more surprising to hear JSC professionals discuss incineration so often and in public forums like the Zahrat al-Finjan visit. As Hamdi responded to a question from a mayor, Rana burst forth: "Landfills are *not* actually advanced," she said, her voice more high-pitched than usual. Her pale cheeks flushed as she elaborated: "Right now we see the sanitary landfill as something 'Wow, we've started using sanitary landfills!' But actually, in the developed world, this is something long ended." Calling landfills "not actually advanced" was like discussing incinerators. It provincialized landfills vis-à-vis global alternatives, placing Palestine within the world and framing Palestine as a country that deserved the best available infrastructures.

JSC staff knew well that the Authority had staffed JSCs with people trained as environmental and waste professionals in the spirit of modernizing Palestine's waste management system. These people had the potential for "capacity." Staffing the government with new types of experts has both been a form of "regime change" and an earnest push on the part of Authority policy makers and donors to cultivate particular forms of rule across infrastructural and service provision fields. Regime change is meant both to replace Israeli rule and to reorient the work of local governments like those represented by the Ramallah mayors. For the latter, garbage is a shared purview of municipal departments like public health, transportation, engineering, and accounting staffed by employees with high school, general engineering, or accounting degrees.

Rana and her colleagues, by contrast, held graduate degrees in environmental sciences, waste and water engineering and policy, and natural resource management. Some, like 'Itiraf, had previously worked in internationally funded environmental NGOs and taught environmental issues in Palestinian universities. They were part of new global networks of waste professionals. Sometimes speaking with condescension about the lack of education and experience among munici-pal employees, they framed themselves as more similar to waste managers and environmental professionals abroad than they were to the mayors and residents whom they worked to convince of waste burial's merits.

Many of Palestine's waste professionals draw their ideals about how waste should be managed from time abroad in North America, Europe, Asia, and other parts of the Middle East. 'Itiraf's master's degree in environmental science, en-gineering, and policy came from the University of Virginia; Yaman's bachelor's degree was from the University of Baghdad, and his master's was from Jordan. Reem Musleh, who consulted on major Palestinian waste projects, held a PhD in environmental engineering from Michigan State University. They participated in international conferences and published in international, peer-reviewed journals. Before I left for a short trip back to the US, Rana asked me if she could have Am-azon send a book to my New York address. The book, *Waste Management in the World*, was published by UN Habitat in 2010 and describes how reducing landfilling is a goal across cities of the Global South. At al-Minya I mentioned anthropologist Joshua Reno's (2015b) work on the Michigan landfill to Yaman. He brightened and asked me to share it with him: "I need to search, internationally, for the best practice in that." Such qualifications and sensibilities gave professionals the aura of qualified local partners for donors.

Yet the same sensibilities also positioned professionals to critique the *Strategy*'s assumptions. Not a meeting, interview, or visit went by without someone on the JSC staff, in Authority ministry offices, or among Palestinian waste consultants refer-ring to the superior ways in which other countries managed their wastes. Global comparisons were the language of modernity. All had, in Yaman's words, "visited a lot of countries to see their situations." In hallway chat and meetings people shared stories of clean streets in Singapore and Japan. They laughed, contrasting them with Palestine's filth-filled roadways. It was well known, they mused, that despite their widespread use, landfills were no longer a viable answer to the global problem of waste. Professionals also derived critiques of landfills from work with donors. Japan, Israel, and Germany, considered land-scarce places, were replacing landfills with incinerators. Rana had traveled to Germany and, in Fritz's earshot, often repeated that the Germans had banned landfills in 2005.

Critiques of landfills included that they alter the ecological makeup of land. They emit greenhouse gases and put the ecologies into which they are placed and public health at risk.[14] Landfills are also problematic for manufacturers and individual consumers. By displacing responsibility for waste onto those in charge of its disposal and by allowing disposal to be relatively cheap, these end-of-pipe infrastructures fail to pressure industries to reduce waste outputs during manufacturing. By removing waste from people's lives, landfills encourage overconsumption and discourage alternatives such as reuse, waste-to-energy programs, and recycling.[15]

From Israel JSC professionals received contradictory messages. On the one hand, Israel prevented Palestinian landfills from being the best version of themselves, adding to their status as a technology failing to be modern. Sanitary landfills can be designed to capture methane for electricity generation, but Samhan, Rana, and Hamdi told me separately that Israel would likely make capture difficult, citing security concerns over Palestinians having access to combustion technologies. Scrunching his shoulders, Samhan pointed out that "waste is a resource." It offers "the materials for energy." And that's exactly what would make Israel prohibit Palestinian incineration. He echoed older generations I interviewed in Jenin, recounting how for centuries Palestinians had taken advantage of refuse's energy value, burning household wastes to heat public bathhouse water and as fuel for bakeries. Olive pits had been burned to heat homes.

On the other hand, some Civil Administration departments supported the Authority's attempt to build regional landfills, touting landfills as the *military*'s contribution to Palestinian modernization.[16] Donors presented Israel as a model for Palestine even though many representatives believed like Fritz that Israel was "fifteen to twenty years behind Germany." Fritz explained: "Israel has no real good recycling, no incineration with water coupling, no good solutions for renewable energy, and no biomass." Yet both the World Bank and Germany arranged trips for JSC professionals into Israel to show Palestinians how Israelis operated landfills.

Aware of the irony, Palestinian waste professionals nevertheless also used Israel as a model—for instance, when JSC engineers borrowed specifications from West Bank landfill designs that the Israeli military had made in the 1980s. JSC professionals knew that Israeli policy vis-à-vis wastes was changing and that Israel planned to replace Hiriya landfill in Tel Aviv with the Ariel Sharon Park by 2020. Many Israeli environmentalists, including in the Ministry of Environmental Protection, hoped that in the coming decade Israel would reject landfills altogether. Because landfills were old Israeli infrastructures that many in Israel no longer viewed as environmentally sound, borrowing Israeli plans for Palestinian landfills absorbed another anachronism into Palestinian statecraft.

JSC professionals knew of shifts in Israeli policy through their mandatory interactions with Israeli environmental activists and settlers. The latter sit on the Civil Administration committees determining which Palestinian projects are built. Avi Leshem, a West Bank settler and environmental activist, was one such person. A friend from an Arabic program had put me in touch with Shmuel Brenner, former Israeli chief negotiator on water, coauthor of the Oslo Accords' environment article and cofounder of Israel's environment ministry. As a candidate for Israel's Green Party, Brenner was connected across Israel's environmental movement. When I mentioned I was interested in the West Bank he reached for his phone to give me Avi's number.

Avi agreed to speak with me in Tel Aviv during a water conference. We sat on a bench under a line of palm trees surrounded by fuchsia flowers. Avi held a PhD in environmental management, policy, and planning from Hebrew University. Since the 1990s he had been a leader in the Municipal Environmental Association of Judea, a settlement-based Israeli watchdog organization reporting on West Bank environmental issues to Israel's military.[17] Avi was what is sometimes called an "ideological" or "religious-nationalist" settler (Haklai 2007; Herskovitz 2015; Maidhof 2013, 2016; Weiss 2009). He had moved his family to the West Bank three decades ago because he believed the West Bank was Israeli. Given our disagreement about this, I was struck by his candor.

Avi was generous with his time, meeting me in the West Bank, Tel Aviv, and speaking by phone over the course of five years. He took me on tours of the West Bank as part of his daily work and drove me to settlements like Maale Adumim and Psagot. We drove up the road into al-Bireh's unlined dumpsite and to the unlined dump in Al-'Eizariya, a Palestinian city south of Ramallah where much trash from the central West Bank—including Ramallah's surrounds and Israeli settlements—and Jerusalem is dumped. With him I traversed the occupied landscape as understood through settler eyes.

In Avi's car one day driving through Al-'Eizariya, I noticed the roadsides were lined with used objects, likely settler garbage for sale as part of the Palestinian trade in used Israeli goods I describe in chapter 2. Dust swirled off stone-cutting work along sloping sidewalks, and chemical mists sprayed from car repair shops. Through the thick gray particle-filled air the charred iron dumpsters, plastic bags billowing off metal poles, and piles of rotten fruit rinds in this city that I had passed dozens of times before were amplified by their contrast with the clean, palm tree–lined settlement of Maale Adumim we had just left. Avi saw me staring. "You see all the garbage? You see the enormous difference between Israel and the Palestinian Authority?" he asked. "It's a Third World country!" Avi saw his activism as work aimed at raising the West Bank to Israel's level, opposing landfills for the West Bank because they threatened critical underground water sources he and other Israeli environmentalists perceived as Israeli (Israeli Ministry of Environmental Protection n.d.; Nissim, Shohat, and Inbar 2005; Tal 2002). He saw Israel's plan to ban landfills as a step toward a ban in the West Bank.

Like Avi, 'Itiraf saw himself as committed to environmental protection and called landfills a "really bad" option for Palestine. He had grown up in Bethlehem and was raising his children there, so he was disturbed that landfills seemed to be the only path forward. One hundred thousand settlers surrounded the city. Between the settlements, the roads connecting them, and Israeli military installations, Bethlehem had already been reduced to 13 percent its original size while settlements continued to dump there. For JSC staff like 'Itiraf, to govern through waste burial was to compromise ethical and political commitments to their own communities and to deny themselves the use of hard-earned expertise. Waste burial also risked reaffirming the backwardness—what Avi called the "Third World" status—that the Authority hoped to overcome. The following two sections detail how JSC professionals oriented themselves toward the time during which landfills were to function in Palestine and how landfills' properties in turn shaped professionals' orientation toward time.

EXPIRATION DATES AND LANDFILL TIME

Garbage mirrors human population size and consumption activities. Roughly six million Palestinians live exiled from Palestine. Anyone estimating future waste volume must imagine whether some, none, or all Palestinian refugees will move to the West Bank and Gaza, and when. They must predict when and whether the Authority will become a state and, if it does, whether donors will continue funding it, for how long if so, and whether independence will bring economic growth (see also Stamatopoulou-Robbins 2018).

Authority officials ostensibly imagine refugees returning as part of the package of Palestinians acquiring statehood in the West Bank and Gaza. Full return to a future Palestinian state— whether immediate or gradual—would mean a significant population increase, to say the least. Yet JSC professionals designed and ran each landfill with population projections that did not envision the return of the refugees. Environmental Resources Management (2000, 3.9), the company that conducted the environmental impact assessment for the Ramallah and Jenin landfills, for example, projected a 4.47 percent population increase by 2002 and a 2.21 percent increase in 2021, predicting that the rate would decrease rather than increase over the next twenty years. Mo'tasem's 2009 study of recycling for Zahrat al-Finjan used an average rate of 3 percent over fifteen years, predicting increases in waste quantities due only to what he considered was the expected economic development of the Palestinians already living in Palestine. The 3 percent increase was based on what he and other waste managers called a "natural" population growth rate that imagined the population that currently inhabited the West Bank procreating but not an influx of additional people who would both increase the baseline population and procreate. Assuming the population would only increase "naturally" meant that landfills of the planned size could last twenty to thirty years. Inversely, using landfills of the chosen size meant that refugee return within two to three decades was potentially infeasible because existing sanitary infrastructures would not be able to support it. Return was therefore, in a technical sense, unimaginable.

The landfill's interim time frame legitimized this major act of political negligence vis-à-vis Palestinian calls for repair to the historical injustice of displacement. What we might think of as a "for now" temporality made it arguable that there would not be a political resolution with Israel around the issue of refugee return *during the landfill's time* and allowed JSC managers to limit calculations of work worth doing and achievable goals to the time of a single landfill. A landfill's maximum thirty-year life span offered a limited yet expansive time frame, constituting a stage in a Palestinian development that never arrives at its final, ideal stage—a state.

JSC engineers' public references to landfills' expiration dates were an improvised way of dealing with the unease and cognitive dissonance of promoting inappropriate infrastructures to build Palestine. At Zahrat al-Finjan, Rana raised her voice over the mayors' disaffected murmurs. "I imagine during the next twenty years we will be able to develop ourselves," she said, locating the possibility for constructing incinerators two decades in the future and challenging Hamdi's claim that Palestine would always need landfills. For her, what would replace landfills—recycling and reuse or incinerators—was less important than their replacement. She had the mayors' attention. "After twenty years we will arrive at the ability to have incinerators." Rana's use of the phrase "develop ourselves" qualified landfills' modernity. Echoing donor language, she framed Palestinians as not yet prepared to handle more sophisticated management solutions but was also hopeful, offering a horizon for change. She bracketed out the current moment—what we can think of as landfill time—as a frame for understanding practices for now and made this present continuous, slow waiting period into a time of its own (Reno 2015b, 2016).[18]

Inhabiting landfill time meant speaking and planning in terms of the life span of a single landfill. "Right now," she continued, "in Ramallah we will try through our project. . . . We will then move on to other choices." Rana and her colleagues sought reassurance in the idea that the three landfills' life spans would determine the beginning and end of waste burial. Landfills allowed managers to envision a grander Palestinian future through deep time while operating within "the long now" of nonarrival at liberation.[19]

Extracting a temporal orientation from landfills' materialities had ramifications for the governing practices with which managers sought to accompany them. In much of the world, landfills and other large waste disposal infrastructures come with efforts to shape populations' behaviors such as environmental regulations and recycling campaigns that scrutinize discarding practices. In Palestine, however, because Authority waste professionals insisted that waste burial had an expiration date, managers often saw themselves as waiting to deal with environmental awareness (*wa'i*) raising and waste reduction practices like reuse and home recycling until a future date, perhaps when landfills would be closer to closure.

Landfill time allowed managers to disaggregate the time of the landfill from the longer time frame of discipline familiar to other contexts of what Agrawal (2005) calls "environmentality."[20] Operating according to landfill time facilitated disaggregations of objects of rule in such a way that modifying individuals' behaviors was largely left out of the equation. This is akin to what has occurred elsewhere: for example, in development of multimillennial procedures for US nuclear waste disposal. There, thinking "deep time" has meant looking back in time to draw on ancient legal formulas because those formulas appear to transcend context (Ialenti 2014, 38). The difference in Palestine is that current "context" is illegible from the vantage point of normative political units like the nation-state. Context is the in-between, neither occupation as it was understood until 1995 nor statehood. The deep time that begins to extend beyond this in-between is the point at which things like environmental awareness and recycling might begin in earnest. Anachronistic (rather than time-less) infrastructures like landfills serve as placeholders for state building in the meantime. Bracketing out landfills' present continuous period inversely opens up a temporal frame for waste burial that presents the time of landfills as a period in between underdevelopment and an ideal, developed future.

By comparison with Japanese and European initiatives (comparisons my in-terlocutors made often), which place responsibility on individual subjects to clean and separate household garbage into numerous categories, Palestinian governance practices that accompanied landfills' temporality appeared laisser-faire. But in in-habiting bounded landfill time, Rana made a different kind of effort to shape com-munity sensibilities: she called on mayors to be *patient* with the landfill process. She and her colleagues asked critical publics to join them in deferring assumed shared ideals of development—just as she and her colleagues were forced to defer their own. "Other choices" were on the horizon, on display right there at Zahrat al-Finjan. Rana opened her eyes wide to emphasize the excitement of Palestine's future potential. "We will produce energy and we will become completely auton-omous for electricity." Palestine as a whole was waiting for better infrastructures, cultivating a kind of collective infrastructural steadfastness (*sumud*). Palestine was upwardly mobile at the same time as it was stuck.

Professionals framed landfills as temporary to convince communities to ac-cept landfills on or near their lands because the length of time landfills would be operational was a sticking point for many communities. Mayors asked how long the landfill would last. "If only used for Jenin," Hamdi replied, "it will last thirty years. Now that it serves Jenin, Tubas, Tulkarem, and Nablus, it is set to last about fifteen years. But we're arranging for separation and recycling," he said, referring to a plan for on-site separation, "and this will expand the number of years." Hamdi was in a tricky position. On one hand, the mayors were worried about how long a landfill would mar their area. On the other hand, they were less likely to accept sacrificing land for a landfill that was going to last too short a period to be worth it. They were also concerned about what would happen to the land once the landfill closed.

Professionals' insistence on landfills trapped them in another contradiction. They focused on the temporariness of landfills in part as a tactic to promote their value and to keep landfills running beyond their natural life spans. Mayors didn't like Hamdi's answer. "You said fifteen years? What about after that?" Hamdi explained that with recycling Zahrat al-Finjan's life span could expand back to twenty-five years. "And after twenty-five years?" Hamdi said they would do more burial. But this time they would dig a deeper, narrower pit. At that point they would no longer have the World Bank's conditions on how deep and wide the landfill could be. We can do this, Hamdi said with unusual verve, "because our water is far, 280 meters" below the earth's surface. Hamdi depicted a future in which waste professionals would operate outside donor conditions, where Palestine would be like Israel and Brazil, which used only one layer to block leachates. "And in Brazil they are only four meters above their water!" Hamdi asked mayors to believe that Palestine might be a state by the end of this landfill's time.

But Ramallah area communities remained unconvinced, as did the communities whose lands had initially been slated for al-Minya's construction. Hebron landowners had refused to sell land, forcing the JSC to choose another site. Community members both in Palestine and abroad from Deir Dibwan, at-Taybah, and Rammun had campaigned against a Ramallah landfill for years, and by the time of my fieldwork the Authority was on its third attempt to secure land for a site.

The Ramallah project planned to take roughly 826 dunums (204 acres) of land from 220 families in the three villages. After years of negotiations, the Authority offered up to $10,000 per dunum, the highest approved price and over three times what the Authority had paid in Hebron. The villagers still refused. 'Itiraf got very serious in 2016 when I asked how the Ramallah project was going. "They tried to restart the project this summer. But," he said, "the people started an intifada." For these communities, the project was a land grab. By the time the Authority began designing landfills in the mid-1990s, Israel had already seized land to house 105,000 Israeli settlers in the West Bank. Since then, the government had seized thousands more dunums and housed over 280,000 more settlers (Peace Now n.d.), especially in rural areas.

Dina Omar is a Palestinian American from Rammun. We became friends while studying together at Columbia. Distraught by the Rammun landfill project, in 2013 she published an article in which she compared the Authority's plan to settler colonialism: "In 1948," she wrote, "the emerging state of Israel laid waste to hundreds of Palestinian villages. Today, three Palestinian villages are accusing the Palestinian Authority (PA) of laying waste to their ancestral lands" (Omar 2013). Dina implied that in a place where Zionist colonization confiscates land daily, sacrificing large tracts of Palestinian land for trash burial is national betrayal. Authority employees' attempts to bypass the question of legitimacy by harnessing and bracketing out landfill time thus worked only to a point, partly because of the undeniable pressure that landfills, like most large-scale infrastructures, place on land. As the following section describes, landfill time also works imperfectly because of the insatiability of landfills as what I call "accumulation technologies."

ACCUMULATION TECHNOLOGIES

Landfills are designed to compress wastes that would otherwise be distributed across larger areas. As we were shown at Zahrat al-Finjan's weigh bridge, landfills are also infrastructures financially sustained by use. That they must constantly consume more waste makes them accumulation technologies, distinguishing them from other infrastructures that facilitate flows: landfills are one of the only types of large-scale infrastructure designed to physically grow over time as the garbage volume they house grows. They accumulate waste, and, with waste, they accumulate time into the future and space around them.

Accumulation of trash is land-intensive, sucking territory into the landfill's orbit like a sinkhole, not only by comparison to a technology like incineration, which requires less landmass, but also because landfills occupy more than the amount of land they take for cells, roads, leachate pools, and offices.[21] Landfills make land around them unusable and unsellable, unless for further waste burial. In the West Bank, construction of a landfill presupposes that the area around it will cease to be used for agricultural purposes and will not be used to expand residential areas. Plots on a landfill's outer perimeter are purchased in full even when only part of each will be enclosed within the landfill's fence because landowners will no longer be able to use the part left out. Landfills also often decrease the value of land and real estate in their vicinity. The villages of Fahmeh al-Jadidah, Ajja, and Arrabah are known as "the villages next to the landfill." That is also how their residents experience them when trying to sell land or open windows. Settlers like Avi opposed the Ramallah landfill partly because of fears that the landfill would decrease real estate values for them. Landfills taint a large radius in all directions around them (Hattem 2014a), exceeding their own physical boundaries and remaking ambient ecologies (Goumopoulos and Kameas 2009; Hawk 2018; Papadopoulou et al. 2012). They leak not only when leachates break through lining but also from the moment of construction, inserting themselves into property regimes and aesthetic experiences.[22]

When I sat in the uncomfortable meeting between Rana, the JSC's lawyer, and the Rammun landowners, and when, on Dina's recommendation, I later visited Rammun to interview Rabbah Thabata, a leader of Rammun's opposition to the landfill, I saw that community members' greatest concern was a landfill's potential effect on land ownership, use, and protection. Rammun's five basic objections were the following: One, there was no guarantee the land would be returned to its owners in thirty years. Two, these lands were among the most fertile in the area, and a landfill might make the area unfit for cultivation in the future. Three, the site was currently fertile agricultural land that the landowners had the right to cultivate. Four, this land was part of Rammun's heritage and inheritance. Five, the Authority would be unable to prevent settlers from using the landfill, which would result both in the legitimization of settlements and in the potential for toxic dumping without Authority regulation (see also Stamatopoulou-Robbins 2014).

Landfills can also "leak" from the outside in, provoking political contaminations through their accumulations. Rammun's fifth objection highlighted one negative implication of what Rana had called "benefiting" from Area C. Area C infrastructures expose Palestinians to intensified harm from Israel. Settlements have been dumping in Authority-run landfills, as the Rammun objectors anticipated. By 2016, rumors that Israelis were dumping toxic wastes at Zahrat al-Finjan (Dunia al-Watan 2014) resulted in Hamdi's arrest by Palestinian police. 'Itiraf confirmed that settlers were dumping about thirty tons of garbage at al-Minya daily (Al-Haq 2016). There, settler dumping had begun days after the landfill's opening. After Hebron's JSC submitted an environmental assessment to the Israeli military, "then came the political issue," Yaman recounted, drama in his voice. The army demanded that the landfill also be used for settlements. One argument: the West Bank was a "shared environment," as I discuss in chapter 5. The JSC refused, prompting a yearlong cycle of pressure and refusal. At first it seemed the JSC had won and the landfill would be used only by Palestinians in Bethlehem and Hebron. "We celebrated," Yaman said. They invited Dr. Salam Fayyad and "started digging the land." But after construction the Civil Administration sent the JSC a one-page fax in Hebrew forbidding it to open the landfill unless it accepted settlement waste.

The JSC postponed operation from October 2013 until March 2014, when the JSC's board of directors decided to experiment with opening the landfill, having closed other dumpsites to compel Palestinian communities to use the new landfill. Keeping al-Minya closed would mean a return to "random dumping" and a failure of a key *Strategy* component. The landfill operated without a hitch for fifteen days. Then the settlers arrived. On April 11 they approached with three garbage trucks accompanied by a group of army jeeps. "We tried to close the gate," Yaman said. "But they tried to break it down. We had to let them in." The army threatened to arrest Yaman, a man over six feet tall, elegant and authoritative, whom I tried to imagine facing a group of armed settlers and armored vehicles. Arrest could have meant military court and arbitrary detention or imprisonment, possibly without a hearing (Hajjar 2005). The JSC decided to continue operating the landfill while trying not to subject employees to danger. In the following months, the JSC kept the landfill gate closed to settlers until settlers brought the army. This was merely a delaying tactic: settlers, mainly from Efrat Atzion and Gush Etzion, brought the army every time. They still dump at al-Minya.

The volume of garbage settlers dumped at al-Minya was small compared with what Palestinian communities dumped there. But more garbage, however much it was, would result in the landfill filling up more quickly, leading to questions about what would happen once it filled up prematurely. An accelerated expiration date was one part of what concerned JSC engineers. Political legitimacy was another. One motivation behind Authority-run landfills had been decreasing Israeli control over Palestinian waste infrastructures. Once Psagot settlement and Israeli areas across the Green Line had started using municipal dumpsites like al-Bireh, Avi and other settler activists convinced the Civil Administration that al-Bireh required Israeli monitoring. That settlements had been using al-Minya and Zahrat al-Finjan meant possible settlement intervention in their operations as well, further undermining Authority legitimacy. In Palestine, landfills are in this sense sacrificial zones both for the people who give up lands and for landfill managers.

The Jenin and Hebron landfill stories made convincing residents and land-owners like those in Rammun to give up land doubly difficult. They also framed using force against the Authority's own constituency as a necessary evil. In 2012, after years of failed negotiations with Rammun's landowners, the JSC asked for an Authority presidential decree expropriating Rammun's land without landowners'

consent. But since the plots were in Area C and the Authority lacked the legal authority to expropriate them, the Authority requested that the Civil Administration
expropriate the land on the Authority's behalf. Landowners would be compensated
$10 per ten square feet of expropriated land, a paltry sum compared with the $10,000
initial offer (Hattem 2014a, 2014b). The Civil Administration accepted, and by 2015,
the military had decided to confiscate around 800 dunums. The Authority purchased the first 100 dunums that year. This was the first time Israel had expropriated
privately owned Palestinian lands on the Authority's behalf.

Expropriation exacerbated tensions between Rammun and the Authority.
When the JSC sent construction vehicles to clear the land, enraged groups of
men from Rammun descended on the site to stop the work. In 2016, the Authority
made another unprecedented move. In anticipation of more protests, it received
Israeli permission to send armed Palestinian police to the site, in Area C, to quash
Rammun's dissent. On August 10, Authority police fired live ammunition into the
air while standing in a dense group of Rammun protesters (Lazaroff 2016b). The
incident sparked a parliamentary debate in Israel, where the Knesset called an
urgent meeting demanding the army explain its decision to allow the Authority
to operate in Israeli-controlled areas (Lazaroff 2016a).

The JSC's aggression made sense from the JSC's perspective for a number of
reasons. Protesters were contributing to a national embarrassment: with Zahrat
al-Finjan and al-Minya built, only Ramallah, the Authority's seat, lacked a landfill,
while the military and Avi and his colleagues were closing major regional dumpsites in the central West Bank, including Al-'Eizariya's. Palestinian municipal trash
sites were piling and burning in densely populated residential neighborhoods, as
I describe in chapter 3. Ramallah and al-Bireh had decided to haul their trash to
Zahrat al-Finjan, an expensive arrangement with exorbitant transport costs that
was also causing Zahrat al-Finjan to fill up more quickly than anticipated. JSC
professionals could interpret borrowing colonial force as anticolonial—or at least
as antioccupation. Force could save the nation money and build infrastructures
for a Palestinian state-to-be while helping Palestinians in the central West Bank
to distance themselves from waste.

Yet using force in Area C, which was possible only by partnering with the
Israeli military, further chipped away at the Authority's fragile legitimacy.
Solid waste management is one of the few areas of infrastructure and service
provision in Palestine that have been neither privatized nor taken over by

nongovernmental organizations, making waste management a cornerstone of municipal public service.[23] By creating JSCs, the Authority had attempted to scale up control of the service and translate management's publicness into a national enterprise. But Rammun residents framed their opposition to the landfill as a national duty. "Palestine begins with Rammun," one objector declared on Palestinian television. If opposing the landfill was a patriotic duty, supporting it was betrayal. That the JSC partnered with the military further undermined the JSC's efforts to represent the project as an achievement that was distinct from, and that challenged, settler colonial rule. Fritz observed that the fact that the JSC had obtained a decree to acquire land for the landfill "reminded villagers of Israeli behavior." Hamdi recalled that the Authority's use of Israeli landfill plans in Jenin meant it had taken him "years to convince Jenin landowners this was not a Jewish project."[24]

The Ramallah JSC's use of colonial force also challenged managers' sense of themselves as professionals and patriots. Managers who avoided acts like the presidential decree were happier for it. Yaman recalled that the military had offered to expropriate Hebron lands on the JSC's behalf. "They were eager to give us expropriation!" he remembered. The JSC's refusal cost Yaman over a year of convincing more than three hundred landowners to sell. But he looked satisfied. And faced with landowners' pushback, JSC engineers and Authority officials who had initially supported waste burial shifted their views. Walid Halayqa oversaw JSC activities in the Ministry of Local Government. He had defended the Ramallah landfill project on Palestinian television in debates against Rabbah Thabata of Rammun. Yet when I visited Walid in his office he said there wasn't enough land to continue burying wastes. In his late fifties and balding, he spoke slowly as if tired, asking me to "forget" the demarcation of Areas A, B, and C and inviting me to join his state-like, bird's-eye view of the West Bank. "You have 1,200 square kilometers [296,527 acres] of agricultural lands. That's not very much. We must protect them."

To protect lands not yet given over to waste burial, JSC staff choreographed a delicate dance. Landfills expire but they may also expand, gaining second, third, and fourth life spans, since the easiest place to extend them once they are full is beside them. JSC managers had to operate landfills properly to prevent as much waste as possible from ending up outside them, which meant waste had to continue flowing in. But managers also had to use landfill space efficiently to avoid needing to obtain more land for more burial. Not only were these contradictory efforts; one effort could undo the other. I describe the landfill-specific logics according to which managers improvised to navigate this dilemma in the final section below.

LANDFILL LOGICS

As accumulation technologies, landfills crystallize a web of financial, ecological, and governmental logics. Landfills make waste management more expensive for communities, doubling or tripling disposal costs partly through increased cost of transport. Concerns about the financial viability of waste burial plague municipalities, JSCs, and ministries. JSCs receive revenues for operation and loan repayment from municipalities using the landfill, but many municipalities collect under 30 percent of waste management fees and cannot afford disposal. Jenin families barely able to afford food and health care cannot prioritize fees. Many municipalities lack mechanisms for collection and, already in debt to Authority and Israeli utilities, have stopped paying JSCs in protest. JSCs were distressed. In Jenin the clock started ticking on the JSC's loan repayment to the World Bank in 2010.

Because of the cyclical nature of landfills as accumulation technologies, financial pressures make continued trash accumulation a matter of ecological and governmental concern, a concern with its own contradictions. When settlers forced use of JSC landfills, they exacerbated existing financial challenges. Settlers offered to pay a tipping fee, but the Authority refused, arguing that accepting payment would legitimize the settlements. The Authority has refused to condone what Israel and donors call "joint" infrastructures—used both by Palestinians and Israelis—in the West Bank, as I discuss in chapter 5, even though these arrangements already exist. In al-Bireh, for example, Psagot settlement connected to al-Bireh's sewage line down the hill, forcing al-Bireh to treat Psagot's sewage for free. "This is a red line for us," one Authority water lawyer told me. If infrastructural work is to be national work, it cannot offer material support to settlements. But there are instances when avoiding material connectedness is impossible without incurring ecological harm. Al-Bireh cannot disconnect its pipes from Psagot's. As Munif Treish, a longtime city engineer, explained, that would result in al-Bireh, which is at a lower altitude, flooding with Psagot's sewage.

Jenin JSC managers got some of the trash they needed by closing old dumps. But since communities dumping at Zahrat al-Finjan did not always pay, managers had to choose between accepting unpaid-for disposal at the landfill or allowing unregulated dumping to resume, with the latter threatening the environment and the political currency the Authority was aiming to garner for West Bank cleanup. JSC managers also had to reckon with the fact that if settlements did not dump at JSC landfills they would probably end up dumping in unregulated sites elsewhere in the West Bank. Settler garbage occupied space, and space converted into money, time, and political capital that the Authority did not have to spare.

Yet too little garbage at a landfill—the *inability to accumulate*—had its own material consequences. 'Itiraf explained that it was usually leachate that smelled at landfills and that odors tended to be an index of management failure among critical publics (cf. Reno 2011). For the first months al-Minya received too little garbage to fill the leachate pond to the capacity required for pond treatment. The pond was dug wide and the leachate was only about 0.2 inches deep. This left the leachate pungency strong and no options for mitigating it while Yaman tried to placate angry residents by asking, as Hamdi and Rana had, for patience.

In trying to find the balance between accumulating enough garbage and not accumulating too much of it too quickly, some managers decided against urging residents to separate trash at home or outside. What managers called "separation at the source" would be useful, they said, if JSCs were to focus on recycling wastes they received at landfills. But recycling on site would further raise the price of the landfill's operation. Al-Minya opted not to recycle on site because it didn't make financial sense, Yaman and 'Itiraf told me. Ramallah's JSC decided not to include Mechanical Biological Treatment (MBT) facilities in the Ramallah plans for similar reasons. What can be understood as "landfill logics" dictated that the monetary value of mass wastes as financial fuel for the landfill outweighed JSC experts' goals of reducing the volumes of waste Palestinians produce, for example. Accumulative landfill logic, like landfill time, was something JSC staff found themselves inhabiting, often despite their better judgment or that of communities.

Communities, on the other hand, showed interest in separation at the source. At Zahrat al-Finjan, mayors asked Hamdi, "What if we had dumpsters in the streets where we could put the glass by itself, the plastic by itself, and the organic waste by itself?" Their awareness about that practice did not need to be raised. Yet Hamdi responded: "It would easier . . . and God willing we will have that kind of culture, in Jenin and in Ramallah!" Even while being prompted to consider it by the very communities whose cultural ability to do so he questioned, Hamdi wove together financial landfill logic with landfill time to defer the possibility of source separation. "It requires work, fatigue. It needs a big effort," he continued, making it seem nearly impossible. "You need to convince the citizen of how to separate the glass by itself, the plastic by itself, and then to put them in the dumpsters on the streets and in neighborhoods and markets." He concluded by saying that Jenin would soon see "recycling not at the source but on site," inviting communities to understand themselves as culturally stuck while framing JSC staff as patient, nonaggressive reformers.

Concerns about supplying the landfill with more funds also made accepting waste from additional communities attractive to the JSC. Zahrat al-Finjan was designed to house the garbage of roughly three hundred thousand people in Jenin and Tubas. Soon after opening, it began accepting garbage from the whole northern West Bank, including Nablus, Salfit, Qalqiya, and Tulkarem. In coordination with the Authority's ministry of environment, its managers decided it needed more waste to be economically sustainable. As in Ramallah, Zahrat al-Finjan's economic plans were designed on the assumption that there would be 100 percent "cost recovery" through revenues from municipalities. They were designed assuming the landfill would receive 2.2 pounds per capita per day. But it received only 1.54 pounds because Palestinians' consumption and discarding patterns reflected continued unemployment and poverty, which had not been ameliorated by post-Oslo Authority policies. With the Ramallah landfill project stalled and al-Minya still under construction, Zahrat al-Finjan began accepting trash from the central West Bank as well. It was designed to receive 200 to 250 tons of waste per day, but by 2014, seven years into operation, it was receiving over 1,000 tons daily from around one million people.

This was good for the JSC financially as well as for the landfill's odor issues. But it created new problems, filling the landfill more quickly and creating new technical challenges. The landfill's leachate pool was designed to accommodate the leachate from two hundred tons of garbage per day. Now it received five times that. Yaman recalled how Jenin's JSC had improvised to handle the increased load: "They constructed another pool," he said. But that too was "without enough capacity." Leachate gathered inside the landfill. A British research team found

5,283,441 gallons of leachate, a sewage pool, stored under the waste. In solving one problem the JSC had created another. The managerial, technical, and political exigencies of the landfill brought the JSC to an impasse. "I'm not blaming them," Yaman said, referring to Jenin's JSC. "I am blaming the system."

Landfills are systems. They can feel inescapable, but they can also undo themselves. By 2014 Jenin's JSC had plans for more cells at Zahrat al-Finjan. When I returned in 2016, nine years after its opening and six years before its shortest estimated closure date, Zahrat al-Finjan was full. 'Itiraf said the JSC was "looking to extend the landfill," probably by purchasing the land adjacent to it.

CONCLUSION

A short landfill life span is a problem even for people hoping to inhabit landfill time only temporarily. Until an arrangement like statehood makes alternatives more viable, a short landfill life span means needing to find more land, funding, and colonial permits, and it means filling the land with more trash. JSC engineers seek to avoid being left without a better place to put growing volumes of Palestinian waste. Standards have changed. Going back to open dumping is not an option. Though extending landfill life spans keeps Palestine stuck on a lower tier in the global waste hierarchy and stuck in its accumulative logics, many JSC staff feel that burial is their only option.

Landfills make particular modes of governance thinkable and necessary. Landfill time and landfill logics afford new technologies of coercion, for example. One tactic for extending a landfill's life is to improve revenue collection. In the northern West Bank the JSC did this by partnering with the North Electricity Distribution Company, which installed prepaid electricity meters in thousands of homes. Nabil, Jenin's accountant, was one of the plan's proponents. He explained that the JSC had connected waste management fees to the prepaid electricity card. "When someone goes to pay for more electricity for his home," he said, "a percentage is automatically deducted to pay his waste management fee." By 2014 two-thirds of Palestinian West Bank communities were using prepaid meters for electricity.[25] Rendered automatic, fee payment too is now inescapable. It is a mode of governance premised less on the Authority's powers of persuasion—for example, that waste management is a public good or that individuals should be responsible subjects—than on the idea that technical fixes can bypass governance altogether.

For al-Minya's JSC another way to extend landfill life was to mitigate settler dumping. The JSC put out a tender to hire a private company to manage al-Minya in place of the JSC. The company would work under Yaman's supervision but would operate independently, appearing distinct from the Authority. The Greek consortium that won the tender, W.A.T.T. S.A.-MESOGEOS S.A. & EPEM S.A., signed a five-year contract with the JSC. In 2013 the consortium became responsible for operating and maintaining al-Minya. For a short period, the Greek company quietly accepted settlers' payments on behalf of the JSC. This allowed the Authority to remain on its preferred side of the red line of noncooperation with settlements by creating an institutional buffer between settlers and the Authority. But the Authority and the JSC board of mayors became increasingly uncomfortable with the arrangement and eventually refused settler payments.

Meanwhile, 'Itiraf reported that settlers were continuing to dump at al-Minya daily, enticing the JSC with "up to three times as much [money] as the others who dump at al-Minya." In 2016 Yaman said that, theoretically, the JSC was paying "on behalf of [settlements] to the [Greek] operator." But he added that the JSC hadn't yet paid the Greek company for the settlement dumping. By the time of our meeting, settlers had been dumping for free for three years. The Greek company, which also paid the Authority a 16 percent tax for operating al-Minya, had been eating the cost, increasing the price of waste disposal for everyone, including the JSC. The JSC soon felt the added cost wasn't worth it. With the company's contract expiring in 2017, the JSC decided to resume al-Minya's management. But the Greek company expected payment of the outstanding settler tipping fees before leaving, sending the JSC into a tailspin over who would pay the debt. The issue became such a sticking point that, 'Itiraf said, the Authority put it on the PLO negotiation team's agenda for the next round of diplomatic talks with Israel.

Palestinian waste professionals' experiences of the introduction of waste burial into Palestine demonstrate that landfills must be understood as infrastructures embedded both in historical time and in frictional relations (Tsing 2005) with particular political geographies, and as infrastructures that contribute to, and shape, the meaning of waste siege. Landfills are most often located in proximity to already disenfranchised populations, unequally exposing them to health risks and creating toxic ecologies (Bullard 2000; Pellow 2002; Melosi 2004; Myers 2005). But the dilemmas they occasion can have as much to do with the technical workings of waste burial, and those technical workings in relation to time and space, as they do with the materialities of waste—for example, how waste harms organic life. Landfills may be absential technologies, but they can create new, sometimes useful, and sometimes unwanted presences—in this case through landfill-specific logics, temporalities, and dilemmas—including in the lives of those, such as their managers, whose bodies and properties they distance from wastes' offensive materialities. Landfills redistribute waste and its risks on a territory, putting waste into play with debates about property, the public good, temporal and spatial scales of governance, environmentalism, and technological advancement. They remake the ways in which waste serves as a political actant, and themselves become actants "activated" by their historical and geographical context.[26]

This chapter has traced improvisations to mitigate the inescapability of landfills' "long now" in Palestine. The following chapter homes in on another experience of the inescapable: the consuming of ephemeral objects that seem to have one foot already in the dump. In doing so it opens up the everyday worlds of the people whose garbage JSC staff attempt to manage, showing how the former conceive of Authority governance through their understandings of objects that, like landfills, don't last, and in relation to the Israeli governance to which, since Oslo, they no longer have access.

Chapter 2

INUNDATED

Wanting Used Colonial Goods

AT 2:00 A.M. A CAR WITH WHITE PLATES PICKED UP ME AND KAET, who was visiting me, where we were staying in a hilly Jenin neighborhood. The white indicated the car was licensed only wherever Palestinians with West Bank IDs can drive: on West Bank roads not exclusively designated for Israeli (or foreign) use. Fares, who has a West Bank ID, was driving the car. He drove us down the hill five minutes to a house. A large, white windowless van was parked, engine on. Its yellow plates meant it was licensed in Israel and could be driven in Israel or the West Bank, though not by a West Bank ID–holding Palestinian. We followed Fares into the van. Abu Ahmad sat in the driver's seat adjusting the radio. Abu Ahmad was a Palestinian citizen of Israel married to a woman from Jenin. Her West Bank ID prevented her from living in Israel, so they lived in Jenin with their three children. He ensured we had our passports with Israeli visas and Fares his Israeli permit.

We drove about an hour to Niʿlin checkpoint, one of a handful of Israeli checkpoints separating the West Bank from Israel. Since the Wall's erection these checkpoints have become the only openings between the two territories. West Bank ID–holding Palestinians require an Israeli permit to pass from the West Bank into Israel. Fares stepped out of the van into darkness to cross a "workers' checkpoint" down the road. Fares had a rare three-month permit to work in Israel. Between the late 1960s and the late 1980s hundreds of thousands of Palestinians had worked in Israel. When Israel tightened its permit system in the 1990s, movement into Israel slowed to a trickle. To get a permit Fares had needed an Israeli employer to request him by name, vouching for him to the occupation authorities.

We drove up to what resembled a toll station with armed soldiers. In the past decade Israel has formalized some checkpoints' aesthetics, giving them the appearance of border terminals between any two sovereign states. An armed soldier opened the van, which was empty aside from us. Feeling nervous, we pretended to be asleep, but she ignored us. She slammed the door shut, speaking to Abu Ahmad in Hebrew. She kept us there for fifteen minutes, then let us through. We found Fares after the checkpoint. He handed us bags of steaming falafel he had bought from a truck serving Palestinian workers.[1]

We arrived in Jaffa's old city around 5:00 a.m., parking by an open, cobblestone plaza beside other vehicles. The plaza was covered in mounds of objects, some glimmering from car lights. It was still dark and cold. People in jackets and hats huddled over squares painted on the ground, each designating someone's allotment for selling wares. We were in Jaffa's Shuk Hapishpeshim (flea market), which opened at 9:00 a.m. for the general public. Wholesale purchasers like Fares, however, were able to make purchases early. By 6:00 a.m. it was in its first full swing. Abu Ahmad sat for coffee in a corner shop, half his driving job done for the day.

We followed Fares around the plaza as he browsed. Speaking Hebrew with sellers, who were Israeli, he turned to me in Arabic to explain that shoes and clothes sold most in Jenin. Everything imaginable seemed to be on sale here: clothes, electronics, furniture, paintings, carpets, tools, toys, mantelpieces, kitchenware, hospital beds, and books. He handled objects to inspect them for stains, tears, and brands. We helped him make several trips back to the van with armloads of purchased items. Our next stop was the market's periphery. Municipal dumpsters were arranged at block-long intervals. People stood on tiptoes peering in, using phones as flashlights. Others squatted over objects scattered on the ground around dumpsters, turning items over in their hands, as I was to discover they also did around Haifa's flea market (figure 6). Fares inspected a bit more, telling stories about unusual items he had found, like a set of gold teeth.

By 1:00 p.m. it was time to return to Jenin. The van was full of miscellaneous objects: blankets tied around shoes, blenders with wires stuffed into crevices, stacks of clothes. We drove back through Ni'lin checkpoint, this time without being stopped. By 3:00 p.m. we had entered Jenin's *suq al-rabish* (rubbish market), also called *al-bala* (singular of *balat*, or bales).

The *rabish* is made up of about fifty shops and another thirty or so temporary stands, including blankets on the ground where men sell used Israeli goods. Like many secondhand markets, the *rabish* is located in the interstices of the city. It lies beyond the last produce-sellers' shops in what locals call the *hisba*, or fruit and vegetable market (figure 2), and even further from Jenin's central commercial district along Abu Bakr Street, where most Jenin residents shop. Abu Ahmad drove carefully to avoid crushing objects on blankets on the ground. *Rabish* shopkeepers stepped out of doorways of low, concrete buildings with large openings that gaped like mouths to see what Fares had brought.

When the van stopped in the shade, men approached to comb through the booty, pulling pieces or whole bundles out to perform their own inspections. Some *rabish* shops are variety shops, selling everything from dream catchers,

FIGURE 6. A man from Jenin ties a sheet around objects he has collected from the periphery of Haifa's flea market in Wadi Salib, 2010. Behind him three religious Jews browse. Photograph by the author.

grandfather clocks, tea sets and mobile phones inside to couches and toy cars out on the pavement. Others specialize in one or two categories like shoes. Most shopkeepers depend on the weekly procurement trips of Abu Ahmad, Fares, and a few other unusually mobile men like them to stock their shops.

This chapter explores what Jenin's *rabish* market means to the people who work in it and to the community where it has become an unexpected source of affordable, durable, brand-name goods. By investigating the relationship between the *rabish* and what I call "regular" markets selling new goods adjacent to it, I discovered another feature of waste siege: inundation by new commodities that bring exposure to physical and moral harm as well as a sense of wastefulness.[2]

Since Oslo, Palestinians have been increasingly faced with things aging out— expiring—early, creating a gap between the amount of time consumers hope a commodity will last and its actual life span. That gap generates disappointment: sadness or displeasure caused by the nonfulfillment of expectations. Dismay and despondency often accompany trips to Abu Bakr street's regular market as the promises of style and efficiency that new goods offer are eclipsed by dissatisfaction. People I spent time with who purchased unused products expressed anxiety in the most literal sense: unease oriented toward an imminent event with an uncertain outcome. While bringing things home by shopping in town was a necessary, routinized practice that always held the promise of renewing a household, upgrading its aesthetic, or facilitating maintenance, agitation pervaded the prospect of spending one's hard-earned money on things unlikely to last.

The *rabish*, I discovered, is both diagnostic of, and an improvised response to, this feature of waste siege, a response through which existing discards are catalyzed, transformed from Israeli castoffs into commodities. Like an enzyme catalyzing substrate molecules into new products, the *rabish* catalyzes twice over: once when procurers like Fares revalue discarded Israeli objects by extracting them from their Israeli milieu and transporting them across a boundary, and again when Jenin shoppers purchase *rabish* objects, incorporating them into their homes. Yet this chapter shows that, whereas the *rabish* and other used-goods markets like it give castoffs second and third lives, they create important forms of value in addition to—and through—the objects they revalorize. The *rabish* interrupts cycles of purchase-and-discard in new market exchanges, giving time, labor, and money new value while offering consumers reprieve from obsolescence.

The idea of something lasting is shaped in part by people's experiences of goods on offer in the *rabish*. Evaluating differences between used and new goods is a way of thinking about living in a place where both mobility and political aspirations are constantly curtailed. The *rabish* elicits articulations of experiences of governance, separation from Israel, and class mobility.[3] Lastingness—objects' temporal reliability—metonymizes people's senses of physical and historical location and becomes a commentary on the political present. In addition to being objects through which people think politics, *rabish* goods serve as aesthetic, practical, and pleasureful materials with which people craft lives, allowing them to exchange precarity for a semblance, fantasy, or experience of its opposite. *Rabish* objects are prosthetic access points, like open checkpoints, for modes of life outside waste siege.[4]

PEOPLE AND THINGS UNDER THE RADAR

Markets selling Israeli discards have proliferated in Palestinian-inhabited areas of the West Bank since the early 2000s, and Jenin's *rabish* emerged as a discrete commercial destination for shoppers as the second intifada was ending, around 2006. West Bank ID holders partner with Palestinians with Israeli citizenship to smuggle Israeli rejectamenta into the West Bank. Ironically, these goods travel from Israeli sites of particularly visible Palestinian displacement. The Shuk Hapishpeshim in historically Palestinian Jaffa, for example, which is being absorbed into Tel Aviv, is *rabish* traders' main source of goods. Haifa's market in Wadi Salib (figure 6) has as its backdrop the empty stone houses of tens of thousands of Palestinians who were forced to flee in the *nakba*, and Jerusalem, which is being Judaized at an alarming rate, is an important *rabish* source. By the time I was conducting fieldwork, almost every city, town, and village in the West Bank had a *rabish* market that housed material outputs of Jewish Israeli activity in these cities across the Wall. Some West Bank cities had four or five *rabish* markets. The largest were in Jenin, Hebron, and Qalqilya, bordering Israel. They are part of increasingly global waste flows and exchanges, as sites have proliferated for the production of secondhandedness where used and discarded goods are refurbished, taken apart, and sold (Crang et al. 2012).

Palestinian trade in used Israeli goods is of a piece with Palestinians separating, reusing, and reselling Israeli bulk trash, including trash dumped by Israelis in the West Bank. For at least fifteen years before al-Minya landfill opened, for example, up to two hundred boys and young men lived on the Yatta dumpsite in Hebron, some of whom were still there when I visited in 2011, rummaging through heaps of trash for metal to sell as scrap. West Bank Palestinians also partner with Israeli citizens to transport larger used objects, including stolen cars, from Israel into the West Bank to use or sell them, often for parts, as chapter 3 describes. Yet before arriving in Palestine I had never heard of *rabish* markets. They fly beneath the Authority's regulatory radar and are absent from donor reports, which likely reflects the low social status and political invisibility of the people who run *rabish* markets, the fact that the discards being "managed" are Israeli and therefore not part of the Palestinian waste management schemes Authority officials and donors are focused on creating, and the fact that the goods for sale there are probably perceived as uncategorizable materials resisting interpretation or as consumer flights of fancy.

Getting to know the men of the *rabish* was hence a fortuitous fluke in my research. An American I met when I first moved to Jenin insisted I visit the market. I soon learned that a family I knew from al-'Amari camp in al-Bireh had bought all its living room and bedroom furniture from a *rabish*. The students and teachers at Jenin's Freedom Theater bought costumes and props from the *rabish*, and members of each of my host families had at least visited the *rabish,* some buying furniture, kitchenware, clothes, and shoes.

This chapter draws on stories of the men who worked in one specific corner of Jenin's *rabish*. I came to know them particularly well—better, perhaps because of the slow sitting- and story-based rhythms of the *rabish*, than I got to know almost anyone involved in formal waste management. Five of the men belonged to the al-Sa'di family. Abu Mahmoud, his son Mahmoud, Abu Mahmoud's brother 'Omar, and their nephews Basel and Sari were refugees from the same village of al-Mazar just across the Wall from Jenin. Farooq, who lived in al-Jalamah village, was from Nuris village across the Green Line, which, like its neighbor al-Mazar, had been ethnically cleansed in 1948. Refugees turned hosts, the men of the *rabish* made their corner of the market my corner, integrating me into the cadence of their work. It was slow, unevenly fruitful work that looked a lot like sitting idle but that was productive in more ways than even they perhaps imagined.

Over two and a half years I sat in the *rabish* weekly. Shopkeepers and I spoke freely and intimately about politics, marriage, personal aspirations, and worries. There was mutuality to our interactions. They hosted me elaborately, offering coffee, juice, and frequent gifts like jewelry from their shops. They invited me to their weddings and for meals at their homes. But they also treated my visits as gifts of their own, encouraging me to speak with customers, to share my research, and to tell my own stories.[5] I brought my family and friends from New York and Greece to visit the *rabish*. When I returned to New York, we kept in touch by phone.

It was on the basis of the trust we developed over this period that, a year into knowing me, the men of this corner arranged for me to accompany Fares and Abu Ahmad on a *rabish* run to Jaffa. I couldn't tell if it had taken so long because they had been gauging whether my involvement could risk exposing their fragile, illicit practice to someone—Israel? the Authority?—that might stop it, or whether they preferred to preserve a mystery around the process of procurement to which almost no one in Jenin had access.

The following section shows how the priority Jenin residents placed on maintaining their homes through cleaning and renewal gave *rabish* goods an ambiguous role in mediating their senses of themselves and their homes. It argues that, despite the market's classed connotations and political dubiousness, residents expressed desires for and through *rabish* objects.

MAINTAINING HOME, SUSPECTING THE MARKET

The men's desire for mystery wouldn't have surprised me given that the *rabish* sold "intimate objects" (B. Gordon 2006) whose origins and materialities *rabish* visitors carefully scrutinized, above all for cleanliness. *Rabish* objects are naturally associated with dirt, so it was striking that Jenin residents wore *rabish* goods on their skin, adorning their bodies and homes with them. It was hard if not impossible for my host families to imagine keeping waste or dirt in their homes or physically proximate to them. For many there was a direct, if not exclusive, association between cleanliness and godliness derived, for example, from the imperative to clean oneself before prayer.

As someone who became something like a member of my host families, I was subject to lessons that demonstrated how highly people valued the practice and result of meticulous cleaning. One family with which I stayed lived in Faqu'a, a village of five thousand residents a fifteen-minute drive northeast of Jenin. The abu-Salamehs were farmers who made a modest living selling vegetables at the *hisba*. Like most families, the abu-Salamehs spent much of each Friday at home. During my first few winter Fridays there I was encouraged to sleep in under heavy blankets, lulled by the smell of frying. But I was soon invited to join the women's most important Friday ritual: *shatif*, rinsing or washing with a squeegee, which puts cleaning anywhere else I have lived to shame.

Each Friday, Thikra and her sister Abeer would wear matching sweat suits with pant legs pulled up knee-high, and plastic sandals. I pulled my skinny jeans as high up as they would go around my shins. Thikra would kick off smaller sandals in my direction, slipping into a pair outside the bathroom, a no-shoes area, where cleaning supplies like antibacterial sprays and sponges remained because of frequent use.

The house had a front room, called a *salon*, where the family received guests on formal occasions like engagements or guests of high esteem. The room featured a sofa and armchair set, probably a dowry, made of wood and striped satins in different tints of brown and beige, and a dining table made of carved, lacquered wood with matching dark wood chairs. A wooden case with glass doors protecting decorative objects and photographs of the children on display stood at one wall across from another adorned with heavy wooden calligraphy plaques. Further inside the one-story, concrete house was the family sitting room, where colorful, paisley-covered foam mattresses were stacked on top of one another.

In the living room we pulled rugs and cushions off the floor, plopping them on beds in the girls' room. Two buckets brimming with sudsy water stood on the tiles. In dramatic strokes as if putting out a fire, we tipped them and the water filled the family sitting room. Kitchen, bedrooms, bathroom, and living room flooded as we dumped sudsy bucketfuls. Every room in the house had a fist-sized hole in the floor, called a *masraf*, whose cover was pulled up with a fork on cleaning days. We used squeegees on long wooden broom handles to make waves against the walls. We collected the water back toward us and guided it into each room's *masraf*.

Our goal was to fill each room's corners with force. When water flowed back in the *masraf*'s direction, it carried matter lodged there with it. We squeegeed until only thin streaks of water remained. Then, folding a dry, white clean cloth over the squeegee at its corners, we went over the floor as many times, and through as many cloths, as it took for the cloth to come up white. It felt as if it took forever. "The water must be clear by the end!" Thikra laughed, perhaps because after the floors there was more. In the kitchen Latifa, their mother, asked me to wash the walls, which to me already looked clean. She filled a plastic jug with water, placing it in my left hand. A three-inch nailbrush went in my right. The walls were glazed up to about six feet off the floor, so weekly *shatif* left the paint unscathed. She placed one hand over my right hand and showed me how to brush the wall in circular motions while pouring the water with my left.

For women across the West Bank, Fridays are constituted by versions of this cleaning ritual, an intensified version of daily sweeping, dusting, and mopping. This is in part how it is possible for families to eat on the floor, as we did in the abu-Salameh household and when I visited Abu Mahmoud from the *rabish*, the food laid out on a low table in the center of the sitting room and sometimes on a sheet placed directly on the floor.

Cleaning one's home finds its sumptuary parallel in an ethos of object renewal, whereby people consider frequently outfitting home or body with new objects a significant achievement. This ethos, which favors consumption in general and commodity renewal and abundance in particular, has pervaded the West Bank in the post-Oslo period.[6] Whatever families' financial situations and however much they work outside the home, women in particular spend many hours taking care of their households, often awakening as early as 4:00 a.m. to clean before work. After work and school, especially around holidays, men and women take children to shop for new clothes, accessories, and furniture. My host families spoke of expending large chunks of their incomes on gifts for children during holidays like Ramadan. But clothing renewal took place year-round with much commentary and enthusiasm.

Women and girls in my host families frequently brought home new clothes for each other and for themselves, turning the hours following purchase into almost mandatory ritualized celebrations of the newly arrived spoils. On one occasion in the as-Sanouri home, for instance, the three college-age daughters and I had decided to watch a film and eat chocolate chip cookies I had insisted on baking. No sooner had we pressed play to watch the film, squished against a mountain of pillows on one sister's bed, than several female cousins arrived with bags full of new clothes and high-heeled boots. The film kept playing but the room became a catwalk for the rest of the evening.

A similar emphasis on newness and renewal feeds people's sensibility around household furniture and infrastructures, whether or not a family owns or rents (the Jarrar and Mansour families lived in houses they owned, and the as-Sanouri and al-Haj families rented apartments). Across my host families and families I visited for meals and tea, the well-maintained house was one without the signs of use, repair, or decay. The emphasis was greater in spaces used for hosting like living rooms and bathrooms and for objects like serving dishes. When my father visited me and we ate at the as-Sanouris', the daughters and their mother fussed about which tablecloth—the perfectly pressed golden, gauze-like one or the red, taffeta one, neither of which I had seen before—they would use for the meal.

Signs of domestic infrastructural erosion or breakdown are painful. They are embarrassing and can determine whether one is able to participate in broader social circles, for instance by hosting visitors who are not immediate family, or becomes reclusive. The shape of household infrastructures determines whether a house call remains a quick veranda visit or becomes a longer stay inside, involving food and stronger social enmeshment.[7] The Mansour house stood on the steep hill opposite the as-Sanouris, overlooking Jenin. When the air was clear, one could even see lights of the village of Umm al-Fahm in Israel, beyond the Wall. Im Lutfi, the mother, was partially blind and fed eight children by selling her embroidery through a women's cooperative. Her home was a dark, older house with just one bathroom, while wealthier families and families in newer apartment buildings had a guest water closet and a family bathroom. The bathroom mirror was cracked, and a torn curtain hid the washing machine and a hamper teetering on top of it beside a shower. Plates were chipped, the stove was broken, and the couches had cigarette holes in the seats. While I was there, guests from outside the family were less frequent than they were in my other host homes.

The *rabish* plays an ambiguous role in mediating families' senses of themselves and of their domestic spaces, and there was ambiguity in how people in Jenin perceive the *rabish* as a space itself. For many, there was something filthy about the market, and its filth was physical, moral, classed, and political (cf. Bauman 2004; Jayaraman 2008). Some suspected *rabish* objects of carrying diseases, including AIDS. The *rabish* market itself lacked running water, which meant shopkeepers could not *shatif* and had to relieve themselves at a nearby mosque. The *rabish* was one of the last neighborhoods serviced by daily municipal trash pickup, and I never saw any of the city's nearly hundred street sweepers sweep there.

People's mixed feelings about the *rabish* stemmed also from its classed associations. People were embarrassed to be seen or to have their relatives seen there. "It's just not accepted," Layla, in her forties, told me. She and Malik as-Sanouri rented an apartment in a new building on a hill above Jenin's valley. Malik spoke in low tones and drank Indian tea, which he had learned to love while living in exile in Yemen in the 1970s and 1980s. He worked for the Authority's Ministry of Interior, and Layla had worked for a time at a local cultural organization. Malik lifted a full cup of tea to his mouth. "I don't accept someone, a man, who *might not be respectable, who is less than me*, seeing my wife in the *rabish* market buying shoes for 5 NIS ($1.38). It means she's a poor thing, she is pitiable, that she doesn't have money to buy." In reputation it was a place for the poor—for example, for refugees from the camp and peasants (*fellahin*), who, like my Faqu'a host family, visited Jenin from surrounding villages.

In public, people spoke of the market in whispers. Early on in my time in Jenin, I asked Dana Mansour, one of Im Lutfi's high school-age daughters, if she had news from the *rabish*. She had been looking for a watch there the week before. I raised my voice so she heard me across the front of the theater. She and her friend gasped, "Eeeeeh!," flapping their hands in front of their faces to signal I shouldn't refer to the *rabish* in public. "It's shameful (*'ayb*)," Dana said. "The *rabish* is for, um, poor people." There was something undignified about buying *rabish* goods, even for those who admitted they did it.

Part of the shame had to do with the idea that the *rabish* was Israeli "dumping" on Palestinians. Dana's sister, Amahl, was thirty years old and studying fine arts. She often bought furniture and decorative objects for the family home in the *rabish*. But she reflected on the market with a sigh: "We're taking Israel's garbage. Like the people who collect from the garbage dumpsters," she said. In his sitting room one evening, Malik brought out a pair of leather shoes from his bedroom. They were Italian Martinelli brand shoes he had bought in the *rabish* for 30 NIS ($8). He boasted that normally they would have cost $400. He leaned forward, resting elbows on knees, his voice grumbling under his thick gray mustache. "Israel dumps its garbage on us." He stared with heavy eyes. "They want Palestinians to buy their used stuff and to feel grateful for it, to feel like their own level is lower, like they don't have things that are as good as what Israelis have. It's a way of lowering Palestinians' morale." For him Israelis played off of and affirmed cultural stereotypes about Arabs to get rid of unwanted goods through the *rabish*, humiliating and affirming their superiority to Palestinians.

The *rabish* is part of the productive afterlife of Israeli waste. Yet the fact that the *rabish* carries these classed and politically troubling connotations, while people of all socioeconomic strata nevertheless shop there, makes the *rabish* a phenomenon imbued with rich meanings and the power to shape socialities of its own. As a public secret, something "generally known but [that] cannot be spoken" (Taussig 1999, 50; 2016), it sustains something of local-level sociality while being "by turns confusing and soothing" (Taussig 1999, 121).[8] It is a public secret that people do not so much keep as learn to be kept by.

Understanding how and why people in Jenin not only accept but desire things about and within the *rabish* helps show how this secondhand space is not entirely defined either by market logics or by financial desperation (Reno 2015a, 558).[9] This matters because of how easy it is to read the sale of Israeli discards in the West Bank only as a symptom of structural inequalities between Israeli citizens and Palestinian subjects of the Israeli state.[10] Given the significant income gap between Israelis and West Bank Palestinians, the *rabish* does look like a "North-South" waste stream-cum-trade-network that both benefits from and underscores the differences and inequalities between the two territories' populations.[11] It looks a lot like the end-of-pipe story of how Israel's throwaway society overconsumes and discards.

Yet scholars of global recycling networks have challenged the idea that all North-South movements of discards constitute the moralized and negative practice of "dumping." That gloss, they argue, elides the important role waste traders in the Global South play in recovering and revaluing materials (Furniss 2015; Gregson and Crang 2015; Lepawsky 2015; Lepawsky and Mather 2011; Minter 2013). I want to further suggest that we cannot always assume that northern discards moving southward are, ontologically speaking, waste—valueless or negatively valued matter—and that southerners' revaluation of discards constitutes a kind of redemption from the ashes, both for the materials and for those southerners. While it may offer an opportunity to celebrate southern waste workers' ingenuity, and while many Palestinians legitimately reject Israeli racism and disregard for Palestinians' well-being through *rabish* critiques, to classify the *rabish* only as a waste stream is to present the traded matter only from the perspective of those who discarded it, in this case on the Israeli, "supply" side.[12] I build here on studies highlighting the productive work of revaluing objects by adding that, in revaluing and incorporating *rabish* commodities into their aesthetic and practical lives, Palestinians on the "demand" side of *rabish* exchanges remake not only objects but social and political life.

My point is partly that participating in the *rabish* is a choice, if a compromised one. The market condenses and materializes people's desires, thriving both because of and despite political and aesthetic ambivalences. Many of my interlocutors viewed the fact that *rabish* goods were discards—which could some-times be physically detected on the objects—as a *source* of their value, for exam-ple, rather than as something to be erased in the process of revaluation. And *rabish* objects' origins in what people assumed had been Jewish Israeli households—built on land my interlocutors viewed as stolen—made *rabish* objects attractive. The *rabish* thrives because people's interpretation of it is a worlding practice.

A firewall tends to organize popular thinking about the comparative role of secondhand goods in privileged versus poor or disenfranchised places. In so-called developed countries, repurposing practices take on names like dumpster diving and thrifting, which connote ethical and clever lifestyle *choices* that contribute to personal style while rejecting mass production. People tend to view secondhand markets in so-called developing countries, by contrast, as almost natural by-prod-ucts of economic—if creatively navigated—*necessity*, as if the unavailability of new goods or resources *forces* consumers to purchase secondhand ones. It is need, not desire, that tends to frame understandings of the uptake of used goods in the South, where the meaning of need is attached to poverty or the absence of desirable things and people in need are depicted as passive, economically driven rather than as social, desiring, or political subjects. My friends and host families in Jenin complicated this dichotomy by showing me how they evaluated *rabish* commodities in comparison to the quality and types of commodities available on Jenin's regular market (cf. Steiner 2001). As the following section explains, it was out of a feeling of being flooded by *the wrong kinds of things*—a harmful abundance—that many saw value in *rabish* commodities.[13]

STUCKNESS AND THE CHINESE INVASION

People's sense of being flooded by an abundance of faulty, hazardous commodities results from geographical immobility, or stuckness, which has been the condition of most occupied Palestinians since Oslo. For many I met in Jenin, stuckness was particularly severe. Some were banned from travel altogether, including to Jordan and therefore to the rest of the world. Others suffered from lifetime bans on travel to Jerusalem or Israel, which often meant a ban on making religious pilgrimages or even visiting their ancestral lands.

All members of the al-Haj family, for instance, were banned from entering Israel. Im Munther, head of the al-Haj family and a widow who worked cleaning and assisting for a dentist, supported four children in a rented apartment in a commercial area. To get to her building she crunched over tile shards through a covered alleyway between two stores. Israeli soldiers had broken into her apartment in 2006, shooting and killing Munther, her eldest son, who had been politically active, after chasing him out of his bedroom window and onto a nearby roof. Soon thereafter Im Munther and her other five children discovered they were banned from entering Israel for "security reasons." The ban included 'Aseel, Im Munther's eldest daughter, who was married to a Palestinian with Israeli citizenship. Like Abu Ahmad from the *rabish* and his wife, the couple had to find West Bank housing to live together.

Immobility from closure has exacerbated Palestinian impoverishment, and impoverishment has in turn exacerbated immobility. Financial stresses make it difficult for many to travel even within the West Bank. Amahl, Dana, and members of the Jarrar family frequently traveled to Nablus, a forty-five minute drive south. Amahl went weekly for class, and the Jarrars enjoyed picnics on Jabal Nablus, one of the city's two mountains. But Ramallah, a two-hour drive south, was reserved for rare, special occasions. Some, like Basel, Abu Mahmoud's thirty-five-year-old nephew who sold kitchenware, electronics, and decorations in the *rabish*, had never left Jenin. Since closure, many people's geographical and social worlds have shrunk. Not being able to leave (and being prohibited from entering Jewish settlements) means access to fewer—and to only Authority-regulated—markets. That, in turn, means exposure to objects perceived to be less safe and less helpful for social mobility.

Signs of stuckness are disguised in the form of colorful, synthetic materials and densely located consumption activities. But this is how waste siege works. An outside observer wouldn't know stuckness just by walking through Jenin's urban center. By 2009 Jenin's central commercial district was full of shoppers. Brightly colored objects dangled from awnings over busy restaurants, cafes, banks, pharmacies, and shops selling clothes, cell phones, jewelry, and toys. After the intifada Jenin returned to its status as a shopping destination for Palestinians with Israeli citizenship who come for the lower prices, out of solidarity, and to see friends and family (see A. Bishara 2015). They can drive a mere thirty minutes from cities like Nazareth to spend Saturday, Israel's day off, in Jenin, exporting Israel's commercial rhythms into market life across the Wall.

Yet to the seasoned Jenin shopper this colorful abundance signifies closure, not porosity, and major changes in everyday consumption—in particular, deterioration in quality and shorter-lived commodities. For stuck Jenin residents, it evokes concerns about the devaluation of incomes and consumers' exposure to harm. Suspect goods have become ubiquitous, and shopping, therefore, distressful. I often met Im Munther at work. We had a routine where I picked her up and we would walk home together for lunch, moving through Jenin's central market arm in arm. She sometimes let go to handle things for sale: a toaster, a broom, a blow dryer. The scrutiny with which she handled goods resembled the way Fares had handled things in Jaffa. But they were looking for different things: Im Munther looked for signs that the thing would, in the future, break, tear or fall apart. Fares looked for signs of past use that could either make the object undesirable to consumers or just the opposite, as I discuss below.

Still, both Im Munther and Fares in some sense tried to manage waste. Im Munther tried to manage an item's potential to *become* waste. Fares tried to gauge how the fact that something had been discarded would affect its value. Both used sight and touch. Im Munther was keen to teach me how to inspect objects, to bargain, and to know when to walk out.[14] It was akin to knowing how to maintain a home. This toaster was too light, for example. Or the broom had an extra nub of plastic sticking out of its handle. Was it a factory reject? She clicked her tongue to show disapproval when quality was unsatisfactory. Letting out a dramatic "Let's go!" (*Yallah!*), she pulled me out the door by the elbow.

As Im Munther browned meat for lunch one day I mentioned that I liked to drink fresh local (*baladi*) juices. She lifted her eyebrows, closing her eyelids in disappointment and pulled a wisp of hair out of her face. She only drank Israeli juice, she said. "Because there's no monitoring of Palestinian goods—there are bad chemicals. People get sick. There are cancers." In fact, she continued, "The municipality's health department started monitoring the market more recently." She trailed off to underscore her pessimism. I remembered Malik, who had bought the Martinelli shoes, telling me, "We know shoes from the regular market develop fungus in the feet."

In response to Im Munther's comment, Mona, her daughter, offered a gentle correction as we set the table: "There *are* now two or three stores that bring Turkish stuff," she said. Turkish-made goods were beginning to gain wide appeal as quality commodities and were more expensive. It was also common to hear people describe stores as "bringing" goods. The verb *to bring* implied transport from across borders. It also reflected stuckness. For Mona, who was banned from travel to

Israel, stores "bringing" goods expressed a sense of being forcibly constrained to live entirely in one place, of being hindered in movement by an external obstruction. As people stuck in place, many in Jenin find themselves in a holding pattern hoping, among other things, that stores will bring desirable goods.[15]

They are often disappointed. As in many parts of the world, in Jenin the words "made in China" and "Chinese" (*sini*) have become synonymous with something made cheaply that is potentially harmful. They are synonymous with obsolescence, goods that are dead-end objects (Hawkins and Muecke 2003, xiv). Chinese imports make up under 6 percent of total Palestinian imports. In 2016, for example, they made up 5.7 percent, less than imports from Turkey, which made up 6.2 percent. Occupied Palestinians import 59 percent of their goods from Israel (Observatory of Economic Complexity 2016). Yet discussions of the regular market along Abu Bakr street almost always turned to China because Jenin residents tended to view commodities available in their local markets as Chinese.

And good things were, almost by definition, not Chinese-made. When Nabil, an employee in Jenin's Chamber of Commerce, was explaining that Palestinian businesses had "directed their attention to Chinese imports," the switch to talk of exposure to harm was instantaneous. "Ninety-nine percent of them are not good, even for our health!" he exclaimed. "The shoes stink!" 'Ali was from a wealthy and politically powerful Nablus family. He saw himself as cosmopolitan, speaking with me in English and French. In his high-ceilinged office in Nablus's Old City he spoke of changes in trade as if they were a nuisance. He described the post-2000 Palestinian market as having been "flooded with Chinese products," the same inundation with which I was familiar from Jenin and the dark doppelgänger of goods being "brought" in. Flooding suggested that markets were overwhelmed with things that were burdensome, as much because they were unreliable as because of their excess. Such commodities made shopping particularly uneasy because they were everyday objects expected to facilitate care (Auyero and Swistun 2007, 2008) that they repeatedly failed to provide.

Many in Jenin saw the problem of the central market as a problem of Palestinian regulation. Oslo had transferred authority over markets within Palestinian residential areas from the Israeli military to the Authority. In citing a lack of "monitoring" (*raqabah*), Im Munther was saying that the regular market lacked Palestinian government oversight. Yet this view leaves out of the picture Israeli control over Palestinian imports. The fact that it does underlines the ways in which immobility makes certain forms of knowledge inaccessible to West Bank Palestinians. I learned this firsthand when I visited the Jaffa and Haifa flea markets, where Israeli Jews were represented in large numbers (see figure 6), then returned to Jenin to find that residents rarely imagined Jews as also taking objects discarded by other Israelis. The view that regular West Bank markets suffered under faulty Palestinian regulation also presents foreign (especially Chinese) goods as inherently uncontrollable, displacing concern about control from the occupation to commodities.

Palestinian customs officials have access to imports only once imports enter the West Bank. While Palestinians can import from foreign countries they choose, all imports pass through Israeli ports of entry, either on the Israeli coast (e.g., in Haifa, Tel Aviv, and Ashdod) or by land across the border with Jordan. Palestinian customs officials are not allowed at these ports. And Israeli customs officials do not perform quality controls there for commodities such as clothes, shoes, household appliances, and furniture. They check imports for what they call "security" issues, searching for prohibited products and unlicensed Palestinian imports. Palestinian importers have little power to ensure the quality of imports in what they requested. ʿAli sighed: "What comes through the Authority is not really controlled," and added, in desperation, "We don't control the Chinese goods!"

Majid, Jenin's local historian and a retired school principal (not a businessman), echoed ʿAli's sentiment with a focus on the incapacity of the importer derived from the inaction of the Authority: "Look at this cup," he said, picking up his plastic coffee cup. "It's forbidden!" As he squeezed it easily between two fingers, I realized he meant the cup's quality was beneath a certain standard, though he did not specify whose. "The person who imports will import a certain thing, but when it arrives it will be something different." The importer "can't do anything about it." By then it is too late, and too expensive, to send goods back to manufacturers.

The West Bank's separation from Israel means provisioning life from unreliable global markets—markets allowed to be unreliable by a negligent national government. Geographical separation has brought inundation, or flooding, but has also laid the structural conditions for *rabish* goods to become fetishized colonial objects and material expressions of colonial abandonment, as the section below describes.

COLONIAL FETISH, COLONIAL ABANDONMENT

Critiques of the Authority's lack of monitoring express disappointment at its failure to perform a role, indicting Authority governmental neglect rather than Israeli policy. Yet they gain specificity and force through stories about how things could be otherwise not if Palestine were a state but if occupied Palestinians lived either in Israel (if they could escape the West Bank) or as Israeli citizens rather than subjects where they currently live. Through consumption people articulate images of the lives they feel separation has foreclosed for them, where foreclosure pertains both to other ways of living and to other ways of being governed.

My interlocutors imagined that in Israel merchants imported higher-quality goods, for example. For 'Ali, Israel was where standards ruled. "In Israel you *do* have Chinese stuff," he said. "But fabricated according to certain *standards*." He rested his hand on a digital clock sitting on a bureau. "In China, they can manufacture this clock for 10 NIS ($2.77) or for 200 NIS ($55.36), depending on the specifications you request."

Like Palestinian landfill managers, Jenin residents measured Palestinian governance against the standard of Israeli governance. It was not surprising that Palestinians spent as much time as they did thinking about what Israelis thought and did. Until two decades before, West Bank Palestinians had been intimately familiar with how Israel governed its own citizenry. Abu Mahmoud, who when I met him was in his mid-sixties, had in the 1970s slept in the houses of Jewish Israeli friends in Tel Aviv. My friend's family in al-'Amari camp had for a period received Jewish Israeli houseguests—people they had known before being exiled in 1948—for friendly visits. Those who had been in their teens or older in the 1970s and 1980s also remembered well how different life under direct Israeli administration had been before the Authority's establishment.

For people like them, critiques of Authority neglect and ineffectiveness in regulating Palestinian markets expressed a sense of abandonment by Israel, doubling as critiques of Israel's lack of "care" (*ihtimam*) for West Bank Palestinian consumers.[16] Munadil, a Ramallah-based economist who spent two years in Tel Aviv, told me that "when any products come in for import to the West Bank, the Israelis don't *care* about the standards and the quality. . . . If it's being sold in a Palestinian market they don't *care*." *Ihtimam* in these contexts was "an affective stance," a "mode of action," and a "core ethical value" (Barnes and Taher, forthcoming; Buch 2015; Martin, Myers, and Viseu 2015; Mol, Moser, and Pols 2010).

Ihtimam was an ethically and politically charged term whose invocation claimed the right to care by asserting its violation. It also implied governmental calculation and deliberation (Barnes and Taher, forthcoming), which people viewed as available only to Israelis. When 'Ali highlighted Israel's lack of care, he argued that Israel's indifference was premised on the Israeli government's confidence that Palestinian-imported goods would not reach Israeli consumers. He believed this was "why goods imported by Palestinians or produced by them can be sold only in Palestinian markets." He was both right and wrong, the latter in ways I was able to gauge because of my privilege to move between Israel and the West Bank, a privilege he lacked despite his wealth and high social status. Separation of West Bank Palestinian enclaves from Israel has consolidated a price and quality border, buttressing a more expensive but more reliable zone in Israel and a cheaper, more dubious one in its occupied territories. But the quality border has also created an illicit market for Palestinian-imported goods in Israel. Im Munther's son-in-law, who had Israeli citizenship but lived in Jenin to be with 'Aseel, made a living illegally transporting West Bank–imported goods into Israel. Palestinians with Israeli citizenship then sell them to Jewish Israelis. That, I learned, was why the tiles in the alleyway leading to Im Munther's apartment building were broken. Her son-in-law parked his van in the tiled alley nightly to load goods out of sight of Authority police.

Israeli-made products, by contrast, are available in—indeed forced upon—West Bank Palestinian markets. They include foods like vegetables and milk, household cleaning products and pesticides. In Jenin such products are often deemed better in quality and safer, the idea being that commodities produced for Israeli consumption are of inherently higher quality than are goods Palestinians either produce or import for their own use. Even those who have suffered indescribable horrors at the hands of the Israeli state insist not only that Israeli goods are superior to Palestinian goods but that they seek them out wherever they can find them.

Before lunch one day at Im Munther's house, I went to the guest bathroom off the formal *salon* to wash my hands. I returned singing the praises of the hand soap's jasmine scent. "You see?" she exclaimed, smiling and stirring her pot. "It's *Israeli!*" Members of the Mansour household expressed similar enthusiasm. Over breakfast in the kitchen one morning I sat alone with Amahl. "Israeli goods are better. . . . They've got *really high-quality goods*." Im Munther and Amahl had both experienced Israeli violence. Soldiers had killed Im Munther's son before her eyes and had prevented an ambulance from reaching him in time to stop the bleeding. Amahl had been tortured while in Israeli prison for four years, and then settlers had hit a shared taxi she was in, leading her to need multiple operations for her injuries, one of which left her vocal cords warped and her voice hoarse.

Yet fetishization of (Israeli) colonial commodities is one reason why the Palestinian call for a worldwide boycott of Israeli goods is most challenging for Palestinians who live under occupation and why the call is oriented to people outside Palestine. The common sense that Israeli goods are superior is one of the local "myths" that the Boycott, Divestment and Sanctions (BDS) campaign aims to counter to induce Palestinian participation. Though the campaign is gaining ground in the West Bank, responses like "There is no alternative" (*fish badil*) are common.

For *rabish* traders and shoppers, Israeli discards sold in the *rabish* are valuable *as Israeli commodities*, even if they were not necessarily made in Israel. In one sense, *rabish* objects take on lives of their own, independent of their status as former colonial possessions. But they also gain trustworthiness from the attachment they are perceived to continue to have to the metropole. As the following section describes, they become figures—semiotic objects that make stories possible and that carry political and social weight exceeding their definition as objects for daily use (Rubaii 2018). In this sense Israeli discards are what Anne McClintock (2013, 217) calls "a contradictory image," embodying the hope of progress through reference to Israeli life while simultaneously rendering visible fears of colonial contamination and humiliation. At the same time, Palestinian indictments of Israel for having abrogated its responsibility expressed through engagement with the *rabish* reveal Palestinians' "passionate attachment" (J. Butler 1997) to Israel within the inclusive exclusion (Ophir, Givoni, and Hanafi 2009) that now characterizes their palimpsestic relationship to the Israeli state.

ARTIFACTS OF METROPOLITAN LIFE

Smuggled into the colony in the form of high heels, couches, and candlesticks (figure 7), *rabish* goods are artifacts of Israeli colonial metropolitan life made available again for service (Taussig 2010, 31). They mediate Palestinian experiences of post-Oslo modernity, "inhabiting and mediating uncertain threshold zones between domesticity and industry, metropolis and empire" (McClintock 2013, 210). The circulation of Israeli discards through the West Bank creates "ecologies of comparison" (Choy

2011) between life on the two sides of the Green Line. For Timothy Choy, ecologies of comparison are methods of comparison that "call relations of interdependence, connection, and disjunction into being" (12). *Rabish* narrative forms hold goods across the two sides of the Green Line in comparative evaluation with each other, giving localized meaning to the objects in their midst but also to the midst itself.[17]

Jenin shoppers I knew tended to assume that Israeli-imported *rabish* objects had originally been checked by Israeli customs officials who evaluated them according to Israeli state standards. Yet apart from some trinkets anagrammed with Jewish names (one jewelry box featured "Rebecca Klein" on its lid), or the occasional Israeli Defense Forces memento or menorah, there was no visible evidence that the objects were Israeli. Trappings of state regulation for most *rabish* objects—paperwork, receipt, or labeling—were absent. And no one, not even Fares or Abu Ahmad, had information on where and by whom *rabish* goods had been owned before they arrived in Jenin. Unverifiable through contact with the objects themselves, the certainty with which people believed that Israel had vetted the objects seemed to be connected to ideas about how the Israeli state functioned. Trust in *rabish* goods was part of an albeit emotionally uncomfortable trust in the kind of state Israel was for its own population.

FIGURE 7. Ornamental objects for sale in a Jenin rabish shop, 2010. Photograph by the author.

Rabish procurers, shopkeepers, and consumers also almost always assumed that *rabish* commodities had been initially purchased and discarded by Jewish Israelis, and this assumption added to their value. There was no way to verify this either, especially since the locations, where traders like Fares and Abu Ahmad source what they sell in Jenin, like Jaffa, Haifa, and Jerusalem, are heavily populated by Christian and Muslim Palestinians, who make up about 25 percent of the Israeli population. Those cities are also inhabited by other non-Jewish immigrant populations from Africa and Russia, a diversity elided in *rabish* stories. The words of Ahmad, a Jenin resident in his twenties when I ran into him in his father's optician's shop, capture the Jewish Israeli gloss most in Jenin attached to the *rabish*: "The *rabish*," he said, "is where you find a Jew sick of his stuff and wanting new stuff." It was meaningful that Ahmad conflated the Jew as a person with *rabish* goods as objects. *Rabish* objects carried with them something of the imagined Jew who had possessed them previously. In Jenin, at least, they were *Jewish objects*.

The assumption of *rabish* objects' Jewish origins seems to be based on three other assumptions related to comparison between how occupied Palestinians and Israelis treat objects. One is that Palestinians, including those in Israel, do not throw valuable things away. Prior to the *rabish* boom in the mid-2000s, there was a light trade of used Israeli goods in Jenin, starting in 1968. Abu Mahmoud had been involved on and off in the trade's earlier iteration, moving back and forth between Israel and Jenin while working in Israeli construction. He didn't remember any market of used *Palestinian* goods because, he said, Palestinians couldn't afford to discard prematurely. "We're a poor people," he said. "Someone wears a pair of sneakers . . . until it *has* to be thrown in the dumpster!" Palestinians also did not waste a good thing. "The Jews are different," he said. Basel, Abu Mahmoud's nephew, was sitting with us in Farooq's shop. "Arabs don't throw perfectly good things away," Basel said. *Rabish* objects *had* to be Jewish.

On the one hand, Basel was expressing a pride that Arabs knew a good thing when they saw it. Jews were liable to waste things, and wasting wasn't a good thing, as chapter 4 shows. On the other hand, a second assumption that affirmed *rabish* goods' Jewish origins was that Palestinian Israelis, the other discarding population in Israel, sought out cheaply made goods, contrasting with Jews, who had expensive tastes. Farooq elaborated: "The Chinese is worn by Arab Israelis. Only! By the Jews, no." It was that proclivity for purchasing cheap goods that people who shopped in the *rabish* often sought to dispel about themselves in remaking themselves through *rabish* objects, as I describe below. Jews made good trash—or good trash could be assumed to be Jewish—because Palestinians on both sides of the Green Line inhabited a different class, and aesthetic world, from Jewish Israelis. This made Jewish discards into tools for Palestinian class mobility.

A third assumption upon which the Jewish origins of *rabish* objects rested was that Jewish Israelis' habits and religious rituals led them to discard objects still in excellent shape. *Rabish* goods were in this sense "surplus things" (Gregson 2007; Gregson and Crang 2015) rather than trash. The Israelis who had once possessed the objects and who had discarded them continued to see value in them but were unable or unwilling to keep them. This was one of the first points Abu Mahmoud emphasized when we met. Seeing me place the recorder on his table, he began listing reasons why Jewish Israelis discard. He sounded like an early twentieth-century anthropologist teaching students a cultural system. "The Jews renew," he said, pausing for me to take notes. "More than Arabs. Why? The Jews, they have the holiday. It's called *Pesach* [Passover]." He slowly pronounced the Hebrew he knew from years of working in Israel. "They renew everything in the house. The pots, the cups, the spoons. . . . Stuff here increases during that holiday."

Through the *rabish* Palestinians imagine Israelis' ordinary lives and mundane decisions. In the van on our way to Jaffa, Abu Ahmad had said that Israelis "just throw things away, they renew. Maybe a woman got angry at her husband, she kicked him out of the house and then threw his stuff out." He laughed. "The [Israeli] who dies, they throw out his stuff. The guy who moves, they throw out his stuff. [Israelis] who travel go out and buy gifts, shoes, et cetera, they don't need their own stuff anymore!" There was an intimacy to his mental exercise, an openness to the arbitrariness of what life looked and felt like to his colonizer. It humanized the colonizer, holding open the distinction between an ordinary Israeli citizen's decision to throw away a perfectly good toaster, say, and the Israeli state as a system structuring that citizen's life in other ways.

Rabish valuation of Jewish Israeli life also semiotically erases the visible patina of use marking many *rabish* objects like the shoes Abu Mahmoud sold in chaotic, dusty piles on his tiny shop's floor. It grants patina added value as if the scuff marks and flattened shapes of high-heeled boots are what guard against the dangers and unreliability of siege by unmarked, Palestinian-imported goods.[18] Abu Mahmoud sold shoes that bore faded labels and showed signs of wear, what could be taken as material signifiers of an absence of government monitoring in trade. Yet those very marks make *rabish* shopkeepers like him credible salesmen when they tell customers *rabish* objects are not "Chinese."

Time is another important factor in *rabish* objects' appeal. Commodities in general mediate time, since the length of time a commodity lasts before it is discarded ostensibly determines when a similar commodity must be purchased to replace it.[19] Many of my friends and host family members viewed items sold in Jenin's regular market as knockoffs that lasted too short a time.[20] As Jewish discards, *rabish* goods were assumed to be "original" (*'asli*) and therefore to potentially last longer. "There's a difference between the Chinese and the Moulinex, for example the French one," Abu Mahmoud said in the expository tone of the *rabish*. "The Chinese one, a couple of rounds and it burns out. The French lasts your whole life." To buy unused goods is to set oneself up to have to spend more money on the same type of commodity (e.g., a blender) sooner than one hopes.

The extent to which commodities last also relates to the period of time across which an income extends. This was a serious concern for many in Jenin, including the Mansour and al-Haj families, where very small monthly incomes barely covered basic expenses. Economic stresses are exacerbated and extend to families that are better off, as Israel and international donors often suspend Authority funds and Palestinian incomes grind suddenly to a halt. Money is also connected to labor time, like the countless hours Abu Mahmoud spent sitting next to his pile of shoes and Im Lutfi spent embroidering cell phone cases and wallets. To his customers Abu Mahmoud argued that to buy Chinese, "counterfeit" commodities on Abu Bakr was to waste time and money. *Rabish* goods in this sense are time capsules offering "slow-release" use, and therefore value, to people flooded by commodities that consume time too quickly. They offer reprieve from a war against time similar to that which Authority-run landfill operators have also been waging as they try to extend landfills' life spans as they wait for a state.

Rabish merchants sell leftover colonial time in object form.[21] In other words, *rabish* goods not only contrast with the goods available in Palestinian markets but also make the *rabish* a prosthetic mode for accessing features of Israeli life itself. The following section considers how *rabish* objects contribute to the making of the men who sell them.

MEN WHO SERVE THROUGH THINGS THAT SERVE

Meanings people attribute to the *rabish* help deepen our view of the experience of waste siege as a sense of uncontrollable loss of time, money, and safety derived from unreliable goods flooding regular markets. They also explain why *rabish* shopkeepers express pride in their work as a form of service provision. Though most of Abu Mahmoud's interactions with customers were about prices, the purpose of the *rabish* was about more than money for shopkeepers, who made little of it. Abu Mahmoud expressed satisfaction, for example, that each time he offered a low price to a customer he offered what he called a service (*khidma*).[22] He touched a forefinger to his chest and told me, "They say: 'I buy shoes from Abu Mahmoud for 10, maybe 20 shekels. And they serve me (*bikhdimuni*) for a year, two years! Instead of going to a store and buying them for 100, 120, 180 shekels, and they don't even serve me for a week.'" Objects serving means lasting and functioning. The *rabish* offers an antidote to precarity that takes the form of anticipation of new objects' unreliable temporalities.

"Service" also offers the safety Im Munther sought in warning me about cancerous chemicals circulating in the regular market. "The Chinese product: you wear it and you feel electricity on your body," Abu Mahmoud's son explained on a typically slow afternoon in his shop. "But," he added, contrasting "Chinese" and "foreign" manufacturing, "the foreign manufacturing [in the *rabish*], or the Turkish, the wool is *real* [*haqiqi*]."

Lastingness and safety were functions of "realness," a word used interchangeably with "originality" in the *rabish*. Farooq sold kitchenware and novelty items. His was one of the most delicately curated shops in the *rabish*. He feather-dusted the shelves nightly. As we sat on low stools in the rear in front of a large fan, he downed a shot of coffee and turned its disposable plastic cup he had bought from Abu Bakr street upside down. A number 5 was imprinted into its base. "It's supposed to mean you can use it five times," he said. "But the number 5 is a lie. You use it once, and then if you wash it and use it again it becomes dangerous. Chemicals come out, cancerous ones. Whereas the original china," he pointed to tea sets he had arranged neatly on a shelf, "you use that your whole life. There's no expiration date."

That *rabish* shopkeepers offer the public good of durable commodities matters especially because Abu Mahmoud and the other men who worked in the *rabish* tended to be some of the least educated, poorest, most marginalized men in Jenin. Older men like Abu Mahmoud left school young to work construction in Israel and did well for themselves (Abu Mahmoud sustained two wives with separate households and several children) but then lost their jobs. And younger men like Farooq, Sari, and Bashar missed the opportunity to study when Israel closed schools during the first and second intifadas and struggled to find local work after the Wall went up. These are generations of men whose plight the more educated and resource-rich returning Palestinians of Oslo seem to have forgotten. The *rabish* men's status, like the market's status, means that even those in my host families who frequented the *rabish* voiced discomfort at the fact that I spent time there and preferred I not tell strangers or their guests that I did so. They warned me to protect myself from the *rabish* men's gazes—for example, by wearing high-collared shirts.

Rabish shopkeepers were aware of their classed reputation and seemed to appreciate my lack of suspicion just as they appreciated customers' faith that they offered real goods. They thought of themselves as connoisseurs of quality and sought recognition for it. In the *rabish* they could see themselves not as people eking out a living but as professional service providers for needy customers. They provided doctors, public employees, and lawyers access to a higher standard of living, regulating *rabish* "imports" by selecting for brand names as Fares did in Jaffa and by trading only in objects perceived as Israeli or Israeli-vetted commodities (though the most obviously Israeli objects like menorahs and army paraphernalia did not budge from Farooq's shelves during my time in Jenin).

Men of the *rabish* could be proud to be creators of this trade and market, making otherwise inaccessible experiences and ways of thinking possible for their communities and offering residents opportunities to access a relationship to the Israeli state as prosthetic consumers under its protection. *Rabish* men played a role the Authority abrogated, becoming unlikely providers of a *bottom-up* charitable care to people who had both less and more than they did, a phenomenon I also discuss in chapter 4.[23] Yet while *rabish* men frequently critiqued the Authority and the municipality for failing consumers as well as themselves (for example, by neglecting to extend water networks to the *rabish* for bathrooms), they also attached their work to Authority officialdom.

On a day when I had brought my camera to the market, for example, Sami al-Sa'di, a shopkeeper in his late twenties, insisted I photograph his municipal license (figure 8) stamped by the Authority's local government ministry. He displayed it in true *rabish* style with an antique-looking bronze frame from his shop. The license, which declared he had to display it visibly, located his shop in Na'eem Jarrar's building (which Sami rented) in *suq al-rabish* (the rabish market) and covered the period from February 11, 2010, until December 31, 2010, for twenty-nine Jordanian dinars (roughly forty dollars). That it was issued by the municipal health department—the same department coordinating trash collection and transport to Zahrat al-Finjan landfill—seemed as important to Sami for highlighting that it was a place upon which customers could rely as did the fact that he could demonstrate he was a reliable subject of Palestinian governance by having a current license, even if Authority regulation was often lacking.

Sami's simultaneous connection to smuggling and Authority regulation shows how the *rabish* connects people across space and mediates their relationships to one another. In making the *rabish,* men like Sami have produced an improvised, transboundary infrastructure made up of "networks that facilitate the flow of goods, people, or ideas and allow for their exchange over space" (Larkin 2013, 328). The *rabish* connects these men to the authority of the municipality, to Authority governance, and to Israel, while also connecting consumers to Israeli experiences that are out of reach. Its growth and influence over more than a decade show not

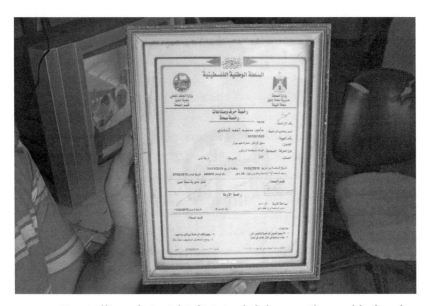

FIGURE 8. Municipal license for Sami al-Sa'di's Jenin rabish shop, 2010. Photograph by the author.

only that markets depend on infrastructures, as scholars of infrastructure studies have helpfully observed, but also that markets can become *infrastructural*.

Rabish traders are both managers of *rabish*-as-infrastructure and constitutive of it.[24] A "waste stream" is the flow of waste from its domestic or industrial source through to its disposal, a flow usually seen to rely on mediation by waste management infrastructures (Reno 2015a). The *rabish* is a by-product of Israeli municipal waste streams originating in Haifa, Tel Aviv, Jerusalem, and their surrounds, but *rabish* goods exist because Palestinian traders *divert* Israeli waste streams into the West Bank. *Rabish* traders, procurers, and shoppers thus manage Israeli waste by separating it out from Israeli municipal management systems.

The *rabish* is an *improvised* infrastructure in that it comes into being through iterative practices of bricolage. *Rabish* traders make use of material and legal tools "at hand" (Lévi-Strauss 1966, 17). They creatively use, and respond to, the Israeli occupation's twenty-first-century features, exploiting aspects of occupation together with cultural capital they have accrued through personal histories that were also often forged out of encounters with settler colonial rule. Fares, for example, had worked in Israel before the West Bank's closure. Years later he mobilized personal and professional connections he had made to secure his role as a *rabish* middleman. Others, mobilizing occupation-imposed legal categories and controls, made use of the fact that Israeli ID holders married to West Bank ID holders had to live in Jenin to keep their families together. *Rabish* work is in this sense political, though its participants do not tend to view it that way. It is insurgent each time it *uses* military siege to *break* that siege by generating alternative flows of goods for a public good denied the occupied population.[25]

Practices of identifying and making use of gaps in regulations or informal support networks are common among waste traders globally. In this sense *rabish* traders are part of a worldwide network of people who fix opportunities for value creation through transboundary trade, thereby doing something to shape their own destinies. Scholars analyzing improvisation in postcolonial cities more broadly tend to do so to suggest that the urban poor have agency, albeit precariously so (de Boeck 2011; Das and Randeria 2015; Desai, McFarlane, and Graham 2015; Mbembé 2001; Simone 2004a). This is an important point borne out in the stories and experiences of *rabish* traders in Jenin, for instance in their feeling of providing a service. Yet depictions of improvisations of the urban poor often isolate an analysis of those improvisations from those of other urban dwellers.

The *rabish* is a collectively constituted infrastructure, as, in the end, is any market. A cross section of people in Palestinian cities and villages across the West Bank seeks it out for the services it offers. Stuck Jenin residents who have *rabish* shops employ Israeli ID holders to drive across the Green Line since they cannot, relying on the probability that Israelis soldiers will not check vehicles entering the West Bank. And *rabish* shopkeepers sometimes pay municipal licensing fees, rent, and utilities for their shops with the help of loans from friends and family.

Through Jenin's *rabish* trade and market, middle-class, elite, and poor residents and refugees thus improvise *together*. Abu Mahmoud and Fares give Jenin's households their aesthetic flair and object reliability in tandem with the imaginations and desires that shoppers like Malik and Amahl bring to their *rabish* encounters, as the following, final section demonstrates. Tandem improvisations may not indicate harmony along class, gendered, or nationalist lines, but they make something more than survival possible for everyone involved.[26]

"THE BEST KINDS OF SHOES IN THE WHOLE WORLD"

The more-than-survival that the *rabish* trade enables in Jenin is based in part on the fact that *rabish* objects can function as a way to positively assert social status. They do so in several ways, two of which I describe below. One, they offer a means for those stuck by enclosure to forge connections to a world beyond Israel's military siege. And two, for those inundated by counterfeits, fakes, and unserving commodities, they offer access to that which is "unique" (*mumayaz*).

Nothing expires in the *rabish*, whose slow pace contrasts sharply with the regular market through which Im Munther and I raced each day after work. Objects for sale in the *rabish* tend not to go out of fashion. The market does not sell food. Nothing goes out of stock because everything is one of a kind. It lacks a sales season; all prices are negotiable. It is a place for lingering, for sitting and sharing stories.[27] Abu Mahmoud opened his shutters at 7:00 a.m. When I would arrive at his shop later in the mornings, I would come upon him sitting behind his desk, a radio and coffee pot in front of him. One or more visitors would be beside him on a couch, discussing the news and plans for lunch.

Many shops are meticulously and often thematically arranged (see figure 7), offering an experience akin to a museum of curiosities, as Farooq's shop did: a display devoted to consumption of life beyond siege. Through creative curation, the *rabish* offers shopkeepers and consumers an "in" to international trade networks between Israel and Europe, the United States and Southeast Asia. These networks' paths differ from those cultivated by the Authority, which, through trade, links the West Bank to Israel, Turkey, and China especially. Abu Mahmoud continually reminded shoppers of the excitingly unusual origins of objects. A woman came in to ask about a pair of shoes she had seen two days before. "Oh, those were nice sneakers," said Abu Mahmoud. "Italian!. . . . You have manufactured in Vietnam. You also have made in Spain, and USA. . . . You also have made in England. Nice! It's sewn over here," he continued, showing me the side of a shoe where the sole met the leather. "These are the best kinds of shoes in the whole world."

Commodities' manufacturing origins are key to *rabish* talk alongside what the commodities help Jenin shoppers know about the place where they were previously bought and discarded, on the one hand, and knowledge they allow *rabish* shopkeepers to show, or to show off, on the other hand. Shopkeepers eagerly put their knowledge of things Jewish and Israeli on display, sometimes throwing Hebrew into their Arabic for effect. "I heard last year or the year before," Abu Mahmoud said, describing how Jewish religious practices affect the *rabish* to a potential customer, "that their *hacham*—their sheikh—told them that they are allowed to eat from their household items another year." He was referring again to Passover practices of renewal. "Their sheikh told them they don't have to renew this year. Because of the economic situation."

Pride at knowing what goes on across the Wall was evident in shopkeepers' words and body language. "Do you know what the Jews do?" Abu Mahmoud asked me, bringing his fist down onto his small, rickety desk. "They take the clothes, they wash them, and they iron them! And put them on the sidewalk. So people walk by and take them." He displayed knowledge about and admiration for Jewish practices. He was taken by Israelis' tendency to iron unwanted clothing. He paused: "He may be my enemy, but I'm telling you what's true."

Through displays of specialized knowledge about Israeli daily life, *rabish* shopkeepers fashion themselves as people positively and intimately connected to the Israeli state. "Every end of the year," Mahmoud said, "they have sales. So we go and buy things from Israel." His father nodded, adding: "We also buy from the *hajiz*. The Jews—you owe taxes, for example, or you owe money. They come to your house and take your TV, your refrigerator. They take the stuff of your house. They collect it all at the police station." Talk of occupation and settler colonialism seemed far from their minds in these moments of self-fashioning. Knowledge about the Israeli economy, Israeli regulations, and Israelis' mundane habits was much more valuable in generating cultural capital.

My friend Mais, Malik and Layla's middle daughter, joined me in the *rabish* several months into my time there. It was her first time in the market, her parents having finally let me bring her after some negotiation. "Why do the police take them?" she asked Abu Mahmoud, following up on the men's story. He lit a cigarette and lowered the radio volume by turning a knob between pointer and thumb, in full storyteller mode. "Listen, in Israel if you owe taxes, or you haven't paid something to the government, they come to your house and take the TV, the fridge, everything, even the car! They take it so the government can retrieve the money owed. The government collects the goods and then sells them." The father-son team was on a roll. Mahmoud, who had only completed high school, seemed to be enjoying that Mais, a younger, university-educated woman from a known, well-to-do Jenin family of Oslo returnees, was listening so attentively to their stories.

A common way for *rabish* shopkeepers to perform authoritative knowledge about Israelis was to describe the Israeli government's treatment of its own citizens and its level of "development" compared to the Authority's. Mahmoud and his father offered unsolicited details about the laws and bureaucratic mechanisms governing Israelis. "The Jew has insurance," said Mahmoud. "The woman gets 2,500 NIS ($690) for her children. If every day you buy sneakers, you take [money] from the state. The Jews are different from us. How? They have insurance for their children. . . . They also get 300 NIS ($83) every month. From the army."

The assumed Jewish origins of *rabish* goods and the visible patina—the chips, scratches, and scuff marks—they sometimes carry allow the objects to serve as ethnographic devices condensing Israeli culture while permitting poor, uneducated, and marginalized men to fashion themselves as cultural brokers of life beyond siege. Mahmoud saw me nodding and "wowing" at his details. But perhaps he felt unsatisfied by the fact that I didn't respond by asking questions with my usual enthusiasm. "I know all of this," he said, as if to get my attention. "I have *a lot* of information about them." It went without saying that by "them" he meant "Israelis." "Why?" he asked. "Because I *lived* with them." Given Palestinians' current lack of contact with Israeli civilians, given their stuckness, he knew this last statement would more likely capture our attention.

Rabish shopkeepers offer imaginative as well as material approximations of the colonial otherwise through particular narrative patterns in their shops. Abu Mahmoud liked to pick up a shoe and repeat things like: "[Jews] all travel abroad." And then, as though he had also recently traveled the world (which he hadn't since the 1980s): "You find them in America, in Spain, in England, Sweden, Norway, and they bring things back with them."

While *rabish* work affords shopkeepers, most of whom cannot enter Israel, a sense of continued connection to it, it also allows people like Abu Mahmoud to reformulate their relationship to the past—a past before occupation had looked like *this* kind of siege. The discards he and other shopkeepers remake as commodities are themselves things with pasts, but it is less the objects' specific pasts than their origins as Israeli that helps the men connect to their own pasts in Israel.

In helping shopkeepers draw their past into their present, the *rabish* also reframes shopkeepers' relationship to Israel now. Mahmoud, too, was banned from entering Israel for what the military called "security reasons." He had been wanted by Israel because of his participation in one of Jenin's militias. "How am I going to go to Israel?" he asked, lifting his hands at his sides. His father had not been there since losing his job in the 1990s. But Mahmoud was adamant that "our life is *there*," in Israel. "[Israel] is our second home." He was depicting a present continuous connection predicated neither on the ability to physically travel to Israel (which he lacked) nor on a political demand to return to his native village of al-Mazaar (which he never mentioned) but rather on a long-distance partnership with unknown people and places forged through transactions around discards.

Just as landfills allow waste to be absent from everyday domestic spaces, so *rabish* goods, by promising real commodities that last, facilitate consumers' efforts to maintain their homes and bodies in a certain aesthetic mode (Reno 2015b, 16; Graeber 2012, 278). As a result, they create opportunities for people to appear upwardly mobile or to "pass" as families that are economically better off than they are. Amahl described her mother's discovery of the *rabish* as a moment that helped her family participate, during hard times, in a socially appropriate aesthetic otherwise beyond their reach for economic and class reasons. With Jenin's curfews and incursions lifted around 2007, formal hosting and visits had begun to take place more regularly. Pressure to make one's home presentable had increased. After the intifada, Amahl said, "People were inviting each other to their houses, and they would see that their houses were very beautiful. Our neighbors—everything in their house was strange (*gharib*). Even the carpet." "Strange" meant unique, unusual, and special. It was hard these days to find strange objects amid the more affordable, Chinese "floods" of objects. "When there are things I like, that I feel are strange, I buy them," she told me as we sat in the bedroom she shared with two sisters. The wardrobe was adorned with stickers of Michael Jackson, Nancy Ajram (a Lebanese singer), and Micky Mouse. "There are things here I brought from the *rabish*. Antiques, like a table. . . . Things that Buddhists use, or people from Africa." She had bought a pair of *rabish* chairs for the family living room. "They were strange. They look old, from another time," she smiled. She said in the *rabish* one could find "things for show: *dekor*." Possessors of strange things can perform mobility and access to one-of-a-kind objects unavailable in the regular market to which people are confined.

Amahl's explanation for how her family had coped with the sudden need to meet a new set of standards framed Abu Mahmoud as something like a doctor or healer for working-class woes:

> Mama asked, "Where did you get this carpet?" They pointed her to Abu Mahmoud. So she went to Abu Mahmoud and found a really nice carpet there, and other things that were really unique. My mother continued going to Abu Mahmoud, and told other people about him. Then I wanted to go, see who this is, what he has. Who is this Abu Mahmoud who brings very unique things?

The *rabish* offered Amahl, also banned from entering Israel, an escape from stuckness via access to positively valued strangeness. Amahl liked "to go and look around" in the *rabish*, which was a space for making finds. The market allowed her a kind of noncorporeal travel in time and space. She momentarily approximated being a citizen of a global city—a cosmopolitan traveler—while her family approximated upward class mobility through *rabish* goods' approximation of geographical mobility.

CONCLUSION

Since separation from Israel, Palestinian consumers have become increasingly inundated by commodities they perceive to be unreliable and ephemeral. By considering *rabish* workers' and consumers' improvisations in remaking value, this chapter has shone a spotlight on an important feature of waste siege: inundation generated out of immobility. We can view this inundation as a version of the compression that Authority waste managers experienced in attempts to bury Palestinian wastes, in no small part because the objects applying pressure are the same, disposable goods.

We see too another way in which the Authority is bound up in the life of West Bank commodities. There is a relationship between people's disappointment at the failure of imported objects to meet their expectations and people's disappointment at the Authority for failing them. When commodities in regular markets fail, so too does the Authority, just as when the Authority fails so too do those commodities. The *rabish* smuggles in Israeli discards as a corrective.

The *rabish* is a phenomenon born out of Palestine's settler colonial condition. The market is not only a sign of poverty and unemployment in Palestine but a symptom of the Möbius strip of separation, autonomy, and dependence that has characterized Israel's relationship to the West Bank since the 1990s. It is a response to colonial control in its most recent form.

The spatial constraints of settler colonialism manifest themselves in the experiences of the *rabish* as they do in landfilling. The *rabish* and landfilling are both characterized by a stuckness, an immobilizing inundation with stuff. Inundation with unreliable stuff contributes to people's sense of their limited, provincial place in the world, even if the materials doing the inundating come from as far away as China. Inundation translates into a sign of low-class status in Jenin, as landfilling translates into scientific and civilizational behindness for Authority waste managers.

Still, *rabish* dynamics are not unique to Palestine. The West Bank's post-Oslo experience of closure with continued control by Israel offers an intensified view of dynamics by offering a window onto how separations and connectedness across political borders are experienced by populations upon whom such arrangements are forced. This points to the importance of considering how *unused* goods—in regular markets—are perceived in parts of the Global South where used goods have wide appeal. It suggests that the idea of a "North-South" separation bridged through discard trading may elide the power-laden relationships of separation, dependence, and autonomy between territories connected (additionally) through used-goods exchanges. Secondhand exchanges are diagnostic of, and creative responses to, inequalities that manifest themselves in the form of firsthand market experiences in the Global South.[28]

In and through the improvised response of the *rabish* to unreliable commodity inundation, Palestinians articulate their experience of one of the less-discussed materialities of settler colonialism in its current form: the materiality of commodities and their afterlives. As a particular response to, and part of, this experience of settler colonial materiality, the *rabish* is both troubling and generative. It provides access to the desired global represented, for example, by Israel and Europe, and an escape from an alternative, treacherous global, represented by China. In doing so, the *rabish* provides something more than imitation of the colonial metropolitan as a way to escape colonized stuckness. It offers physical, sensory, and aesthetic proximity to the world of the former—the world beyond siege. Yet, like building landfills in the twenty-first century, which is both a reminder of Palestine's behindness and provincialness and a way to get onto the linear track toward developed globality represented by Israel, Europe, and Japan, wearing and adorning one's home with *rabish* goods always runs the risk of marking one as potentially insulted, dehumanized, or socioeconomically behind.

In Jenin there is a bittersweet quality to the perception that *rabish* goods are of Jewish Israeli origin and that they have been discarded. The *rabish* offered Amahl the experience of almost-mobility and a reminder of her stuckness at the same time, for example. "In the moment a person will be excited, happy about the piece he's bought," she reflected. "He's not thinking about whether an Israeli used it. But after a bit, when he's sitting at home and looking at it, maybe he'll start thinking that this was in an Israeli house. And maybe he'll start thinking . . . 'How are we taking Israeli things?'" These moments of reckoning with the ethics of the *rabish* are perhaps why it remains a public secret.

As this chapter has demonstrated, *rabish* markets are diagnostic of widespread experiences of consumption and governance in the West Bank. Through them waste siege appears as an effect of the qualities and temporalities of objects *before* they are discarded as much as it appears as an effect of the temporalities of rejected materials and their infrastructures, as we saw in chapter 1, and their being dumped in proximity to communities, as we will see in the following chapter.

Chapter 1 investigated the temporalities of landfills and those temporalities' effects and flexibilities. It investigated landfills' *obsolescence*: their status as infrastructures that are dying out, aging, moribund, and outmoded. This chapter has shone light on the *ephemerality* of the objects that end up in landfills—that is, the fact that they last but a very short time, are disturbingly transitory and fleeting—and details how ordinary people improvise to deal with that fact by turning other commodities into infrastructures. Both chapters explored the desire to extend the time of things, even if the things are imperfect.

As I walked the streets and took taxis around the West Bank between trips to landfills, the *rabish*, and family homes, I observed the material remains of more flows. Valleys and roadsides, especially on the outskirts and outside of cities, were covered in piles of trash. I asked city engineers and local government employees what these were if not materials waiting to be hauled to landfills. They pointed me again to holes in Authority regulation. Neither Zahrat al-Finjan nor al-Minya landfills accepted medical, hospital, construction, and demolition wastes or animal carcasses. Yet Palestinian municipalities did not collect these wastes either, leaving responsibility for their disposal to individuals or companies that produced them. In Bethlehem I asked 'Itiraf why that was. It was a matter of space, he explained, evoking landfill time. Construction and demolition wastes, especially, would take up too much space in al-Minya. Its managers worried that al-Minya would "fill up too quickly."

The following chapter moves to the spaces filling with discards many of which have been rejected twice over—once upon abandonment and again upon rejection from Palestinian waste burial. Crucially, in those spaces Palestinian discards meet, mix, and mingle with more discards crossing the Green Line from Israel into the West Bank. Together these two waste streams flow into and produce Palestinian communities as hyper- and hypogoverned no-man's-lands where toxicity dominates but blame is uncertain.

Chapter 3

ACCUMULATION

Toxicity and Blame in a Phantom State

ANWAR WAS A PALESTINIAN FILMMAKER IN HIS TWENTIES. HE WORE his hair deliberately disheveled. He lived in Jerusalem's Old City on the Israeli side of the Wall. One day he decided to cross Qalandiya checkpoint with his car to visit a friend's new apartment in Kufr 'Aqab, part of the Israeli-run Jerusalem municipality that also governs the Old City. But the Wall has cut Kufr 'Aqab off from the rest of Jerusalem, containing it on the Wall's West Bank side. Like several other parts of Jerusalem populated by Palestinians and similarly cut off by the Wall, it has become a de facto part of the West Bank. Kufr 'Aqab residents must cross a checkpoint to enter the rest of Jerusalem or Israel. And Kufr 'Aqab residents' relatives and friends in Jerusalem must do the same to visit them.

Anwar and his friend had lunch inside and talked about Anwar's latest film project. The balcony, where they would have preferred to sit, was too noisy and dusty. Kufr 'Aqab is a mess. It has come to feel like one big construction site. People live in apartments in unfinished buildings. Piles of concrete and stone, tiles, paint, wood, plastics, buckets, dirt, and rebar seem to be everywhere. The air is thick with dust. Kufr 'Aqab's domestic trash is piled up in large iron dumpsters and on the concrete dividers that separate lanes on the main road between Jerusalem and Ramallah.

In the evening it was time for Anwar to drive home. At Qalandiya checkpoint an Israeli soldier put up her hand to stop him. He was not surprised; leaving the

West Bank to enter Jerusalem is much more difficult than the reverse. Soldiers rarely stop vehicles entering the West Bank from Israel. The soldier told Anwar to exit the car, demanding that Anwar open the trunk. He obliged. The soldier pointed angrily at what she saw: a large, white, turgid plastic bag whose opening was tied in a knot. Anwar recognized it and suppressed a laugh.

This was the kind of moment his films represented. It captured the absurdity of occupation. The bag was his household trash, which he had taken with him on his way out that morning. He had put it in the trunk, anticipating he would drive by a dumpster on his way to Kufr 'Aqab, but had forgotten to stop and dump it. The trunk was hot with the smell of rotting food. It had been sitting in the sun all day.

The soldier beckoned to other soldiers at the checkpoint while cars honked in a long line behind Anwar's. She wouldn't let Anwar back into the Israeli side of Qalandiya with the bag in the car, she told him. Anwar insisted the garbage was his property. Surely someone living on the "Israeli" side of Jerusalem should be able to take his property with him. He held his blue—Jerusalem—ID up in her direction. The trash was also from Jerusalem, he said, but lacked an ID. In fact, it was Jerusalemite trash from the city's historic heart! But the soldiers would not let him pass. They would do so only if he drove back into Kufr 'Aqab and dumped the bag there. Anwar got back in his car. He spent an hour weaving back toward his friend's house through the clog of cars and exhaust. He found a dumpster and tossed the bag atop an already overflowing pile of trash, returning to the checkpoint garbage-free, and was allowed to drive home.[1]

Military siege tends to undermine the relationship between governance and people, which often means undermining the relationship between people and wastes. This is especially true for Palestinian-inhabited areas under direct Israeli military rule. Most of the West Bank and parts of East Jerusalem on the West Bank side of the Wall lie outside Palestinian Authority jurisdiction. These lands are largely administered by the Israeli army. About half a million Palestinians live in, own, or cultivate lands there. Thousands more visit or pass through daily. Some of the communities in these areas live in thick urban conglomerations, as in Kufr 'Aqab.[2] Others live in agricultural villages. Over the past two decades, many of the spaces they call home have become sites for what is arguably the most physically intense form of waste siege experienced by Palestinians in and around the West Bank.

Waste, saturating streets and threatening homes, is a fundamental part of the experience and politics of living in these areas. Waste there is matter that will not go away. It has no place to go. It creates a collective experience of surroundedness, imprisoning bodies in forced and constant proximity to it. Waste besieges from the ground, the water, and the air. Sewage and leachates seep into springs and wells and flood streets. Waste creates an ambient, constantly present ecology, a wastescape in which people dwell and that dwells within them—physically, as toxins that course through bloodstreams. The wastescape also dwells within them as bodies politic, even perversely—for example, when members of communities living in accumulation sites take advantage of wastes in their midst, as I discuss below.[3]

Waste accumulation sites offer iconic images of environmental injustice. Yet the communities around them do not always understand their own problems primarily in terms of something called the environment. Nor do they always channel their energies in the direction of the authorities—in this case Israeli authorities—formally responsible for governing them. Residents of accumulation sites sometimes perceive the relevant party as the Authority, focusing on its failure to care for them. Sometimes they blame themselves, indicting their own community's failure to act ethically vis-à-vis waste and each other. This chapter explores what this means for understanding how toxicity functions in nonsovereign contexts. To do so it tracks local representatives of one accumulation site: the village of Shuqba.

Waste is often associated with toxicity, understood as the degree to which substances can harm an organism (Arnold 2016; Bohme 2014; P. Brown 1997, 2007; Cram 2011; Dillon 2014; Hoffman 2017; Romero 2016; Voyles 2015). As a radiating harm exceeding individual or visible objects (Rubaii 2018), toxicity is difficult to litigate or to ratify scientifically (K. Brown 2016; Murphy 2006; Petryna 2003; Voyles 2015). For this reason, the rhetorical, legal, and sometimes actual wars waged over toxicity in the past few decades have centered on the problem of evidence. Scholarship investigating toxicity's controversies has tended to ask about the politics of evidence in which scientists, activists, and others become embroiled when trying to prove harm or harm's potential, usually to representatives of states (Kimura 2016; Petryna 2003; Rubaii 2018; Touhouliotis 2018). Critics have shown how evidence required to prove toxicity is constantly upset and contested—for example, in debates around the validity of environmental impact assessments in infrastructure projects like the Dakota Access Pipeline and the adjudication of biological harm to populations in war, as in the case of birth defects in post-2003 Iraq (Rubaii 2018). Commentators have tended to think of toxicity in terms of biophysical harm caused by certain substances, analyzing the contested mechanisms for proving toxicity but neglecting the experiences of toxicity themselves. But the experiences of toxicity vary greatly, and their variation needs to be understood as well.

Understanding Palestinians' dilemmas in accumulation sites helps show how toxicity is a culturally and politically specific experience of harm. A confluence of social, political, and material factors makes the inhabitants of Palestinian accumulation sites "sick" with a particularly acute form of waste siege. And Shuqbans interpret the toxicity of waste accumulations so as to improvise ameliorations to it. They perform a local "toxicology" of waste siege, revealing the forms and meaning toxicity assumes for a population under two simultaneous types of siege: one from military rule and the other from waste accumulation.

HYPO-/HYPERGOVERNANCE

Accumulation sites accumulate waste because they are Palestinian-inhabited areas entirely under Israel's military rule while they are subject to minimal actual Israeli governance. The Israeli authorities do not provide basic services there and generally ignore the areas' use as disposal zones by Israeli settlements and companies. Waste builds up and floods in these sites because Israel polices the outward movement of waste, as it did with Anwar's trash, making expelling wastes from them difficult and often dangerous.

Accumulation sites also house waste that Authority infrastructures like Zahrat al-Finjan and al-Minya landfills do not accept. They are no-man's-lands where Palestinians who live under Authority jurisdiction go to get rid of their most difficult-to-manage, unwanted discards. Kufr 'Aqab, for example, is a dumpsite for construction and demolition waste from the greater Ramallah area. Because building in Kufr 'Aqab is unregulated, Kufr 'Aqab's own construction and demolition waste also accumulates there.

The sewage floods and trash fires in accumulation sites give them the appearance of abandoned, ungoverned zones.[4] The Authority generally lacks ministerial or police presence there. But village councils, which are formally under the Authority's aegis but are made up of elected local representatives who can be from political parties other than Fatah, which controls the Authority, do work there. Councils are the only Palestinian government body with a constant phys-ical presence in villages like Shuqba, registering births, deaths, and marriages, and coordinating street cleaning and lighting and cultural activities. However, councils lack the funds and political capital to initiate large infrastructure projects like road building, and they lack police and courts.

In these senses accumulation sites are what I call "hypogoverned," where *hypo-* connotes that people are governed to an extent that is below, and less than, a normal extent defined by Palestinian cities under Authority rule. With the Authority mainly absent and the Israeli army negligent and belligerent, these areas appear to be the epitome of what some, following Giorgio Agamben, call spaces of exception. Like the camp as Agamben (1998, 168–69) describes it, they appear to be "the space opened up when the state of exception begins to become the rule." Yet with respect to both Israeli rule in the Palestinian territories and to governance more broadly, the narrative of abandonment flattens out the textures and complexities of everyday life for these communities.

In Greek *hypo-* also connotes being spatially beneath and subordinate to some-one or something. Places like Shuqba are hypogoverned in these senses as well. Alongside harassment from surrounding hilltop settlements, the Israeli army's surveillance, assassination, and demolition activities in Shuqba mean residents live in unmediated exposure to military brutality in a state of "inclusive exclusion" (Ophir, Givoni, and Hanafi 2009). Residents are excluded from the Israeli political community, as we saw in chapter 2, yet their bodies, properties, and movements are subject to direct Israeli rule more than those of residents in Authority-run cit-ies. The same conditions that make accumulation sites places of hypogovernance, then, also give their residents the experience of its opposite: what I call arbitrary, hostile hypergovernance, where *hyper-* connotes a governance exceeding and at the same time in violation of the normal as defined by life either in Area A or on the Israeli side of the Green Line.

Councils in these areas are the front line and first call when residents appeal for solutions to waste siege as accumulation. They are arbiters of waste crises and controversies. One of the ways life unfolds in these sites is in fact through the fragments of waste problems councils choose to address. Far from sovereign, they can only improvise, chipping away at fragments of the problems waste creates, experimenting with applying money, cultural capital, and rhetorical savvy to those fragments to make their communities less toxic.

Laura Bear and Nayanika Mathur propose the term *precarious citizenship* to name the status of individuals afflicted by what they see as a new global form. Precarious citizenship is "not characterized by the dynamics of absolute inclusion and exclusion associated with the colonial and welfare/developmental state." Instead, they write, "It is shaped by forms of contractually delimited partial inclusion" (Bear and Mathur 2015, 28). Councils' responses to accumulation reveal how ideas about what is worth preserving, what is worth fighting to change, and the time scales at which those priorities are thought about emerge through engagements with waste siege. Those ideas crystallize into assertions about what counts as a public good, or desirable ideals considered universally beneficial for everyone, always constrained by the "restricted contracts" (28)—relationships framed by rules understood by both parties—that councils have with Israel and the Authority.[5]

How councils interpret the dilemmas they face sheds light on the intersections of waste siege with local governance under the most extreme conditions of nonsovereignty, made all the more extreme by the very existence of councils trying to govern (Bonilla 2015). Depicting councils' work in their communities offers a view of what an anthropology of waste management in "failed" or "stateless" contexts can look like, especially if we do not assume that the state is a central, predefined, coordinating force and if we attend instead to the contrasting, competing, and fragmented practices that make up an actual governmental landscape.

SHUQBA

Shuqba is a village of five thousand inhabitants. It is a forty-five-minute drive from Ramallah, cradled by hills on the westernmost boundary of the central West Bank just across the Wall from the Israeli towns of Hamaniyot and Rekavot and from Israel's Ben Gurion airport. It is made up of a cluster of densely packed, mainly concrete houses reaching two to three stories. Many roofs feature black water tanks needed to store water since Israel frequently cuts the village's access to water, especially in summer. Shuqba also features older stone houses built in the nineteenth century.[6] Its built-up area is surrounded by open spaces where crops like tomatoes, beans, and cereals grow. Greenhouses and cows, sheep and goats dot much of the rest of the landscape. Uncultivated areas are covered in low, green shrubs, grasses, and dry, stony patches of land. Ninety-two percent of Shuqba lies in Area C, under total Israeli military jurisdiction. The other 8 percent, in the center of its built-up area, is under the Authority's civilian control but under the exclusive security control of the Israeli army (Area B). None of Shuqba is under the greatest possible Authority control (Area A).

Because of Shuqba's proximity to Ramallah, many residents commute to the city for work. One such person is Marwan, a thirty-seven-year-old when I met him, with a sociology degree from Birzeit University. Marwan owned a cell phone accessories store on Irsal street in Ramallah's central commercial district. I visited his shop one afternoon in 2016. This was the first time I was meeting him, and he put me at ease right away with a lighthearted greeting. He leaned round, tan elbows on a table in the back of his store, while I sat on a chair across the table from him. Sari, one of Marwan's oldest friends and my connection to him, sat on a white plastic stool on my side of the table. Both men had grown up and lived in Shuqba, and Sari was its council's secretary.

Sari had majored in media while studying with Marwan at Birzeit. He had put his degree to use as the village's unofficial public relations representative by posting a constant stream of updates about Shuqba's communal activities on Facebook. He gave hours beyond his paid time to show visitors around the village and to help coordinate archaeological research. He had ambitions to one day continue on to graduate school in sociology.

Shuqba's council, housed in a building in the center of the village, is made up of eleven Authority-appointed members and four employees. It oversees the needs of eight hundred households and Shuqba's two mosques, two public schools, sports club, nine medical facilities, six fruit and vegetable stores, two butchers, two bakeries, twenty professional workshops, four clothing stores, four green-houses, forty household rainwater collection cisterns, and a post office. It is also responsible for Shuqba's trash collection, road maintenance, and street lighting and cleaning. The council's everyday work includes balancing the council budget; reading and addressing letters of complaint from residents; recording births, deaths, weddings, and divorces; and holding meetings about ongoing projects. There was some excitement at the moment around plans for an archaeological museum in partnership with Birzeit and Columbia universities.

Councils are what Authority officials and donors call "local government units." Some, like the larger Ramallah, Nablus, and Jenin municipal councils, have existed since the late Ottoman period. Hundreds of others, Shuqba among them, were established during the Authority's first few years of existence in order to create Palestinian institutional "facts on the ground," as one Local Government Ministry employee put it. Authority leaders felt councils made rural communities visible as part of an official Palestinian presence in the West Bank and helped establish Authority control over taxation and services where its jurisdiction was weakest. Councils were also a way to co-opt existing local political power bases like families. Whether co-optation has succeeded is unclear. Sari was a member of the Shalash family, one of Shuqba's three largest families.

SHUQBA'S ACCUMULATIONS

Shuqba is known internationally as a world heritage site. It is the home of what archaeologists call the Epipaleolithic Natufian culture, which lasted between 12,500 and 9,500 BCE. In 1928, archaeologist Dorothy Garrod found prehistoric human and Neanderthal skeletons in a cave on Shuqba's lands.[7] In 2012, four years before I met Marwan, Columbia archaeologist Brian Boyd and Birzeit archaeologist Hamed Salem had invited me to Shuqba to see the cave where a joint team was beginning the first archaeological fieldwork in Wadi en-Natuf since Garrod's 1928 excavation.

The team had invited me partly to see the debris from prehistoric Neanderthal flint making and partly to show me Shuqba's much more recent waste deposits. There was not enough time to see them all before the heat of the day made us retreat to lunch, but Sari insisted on taking me and a few students through the valley in front of the cave. We witnessed how, penned in by the Israeli Wall to the west, an Israeli-only bypass road and army checkpoints to the east, and an Israeli quarry to the south, tracts of Shuqba's land were caked with yellow dust and piles of trash the size of small buildings.

Factory, Medical, and Construction Wastes

Shuqba has been a dumpsite since at least the year 2000 for construction, hospital, and factory wastes from nearby Israeli settlements like Nili and Ofarim and from across the Green Line (see figure 9).[8] It is also a dumpsite for waste from Authority-run areas around Ramallah. It is where Ramallah area contractors dump construction and demolition debris, especially bulkier or more hazardous materials that cannot go to Kufr 'Aqab's densely packed side streets. It is where Ramallah hospitals send X-ray images to be burned down for their silver. Across both sides of the Green Line, Shuqba is known as a kind of metabolic, digestive space where objects rapidly become materials, where things are taken apart, broken down by fire and human labor.

Past an enormous scrap heap of cars northeast of the cave, we took a winding route, stopping to photograph the mounds of broken plastic pipes, rubber hoses, yellow paint buckets, empty gallons of chemicals, wooden planks filled with crooked nails, computer monitors, broken drawers, mattress innards, and hundreds of plastic bags billowing in the hot summer wind. A gutted, shrub-covered Israeli ambulance crowned one of the piles. We entered the village and my lungs clenched, inhaling air choked with the smoke of trash fires. The smoke hung low over houses, moving slowly with a barely perceptible breeze. Sari explained that residents set fire to the dumps to shrink them. When they do, he said, dumps burn for three or four months on end, even when it rains.

Household Trash

Shuqba is also a place where residents have difficulty getting rid of their own wastes because of a combined lack of Authority infrastructure to house them and Israeli military policing of their movements. We learned that Shuqba's residents also keep their windows closed to keep out the odor of rotting household trash. As it does in other villages, the army periodically confiscates Shuqba's only garbage collection truck.

FIGURE 9. "Israeli wastes dumped illegally, under international law, on Palestinian village lands." Shuqba, 2017. Photograph and caption by Sami Thabet of the Shuqba Village Council.

In his shop four years later, Marwan told me this had happened again just a couple of months before. "You couldn't walk in the streets from the stench of the garbage!" he said. He was wearing a red- and blue-striped, short-sleeved polo shirt over jeans. He was a bit overweight, and the shirt was tight, pulling up at the belly. The army kept the truck for two weeks. Without the truck, trash piles up in Shuqba's narrow streets. Food scraps, which make up roughly 60 percent of Palestinian refuse, and shit-caked toilet paper, which Palestinians do not flush for fear of clogging their sensitive plumbing systems, putrefy as they bake in the sun. The stench can be unbearable. Fed up, people set fire to dumpsters as well.

Carcasses

In Marwan's shop, Sari recounted a story he had just heard. The Authority had recently set up police headquarters in Shuqba, taking over the ground floor of the council building. This was the first time Palestinian police had a stable presence in Shuqba. The night before, the Israeli military had been surveilling an area southwest of Shuqba on the border of Budrus village. They spotted two men walking along a fence carrying what looked like a heavy bag in the middle of the night. The men dumped the bag down the mountainside. Suspecting from afar that the men were Palestinian, an Israeli officer called the Palestinian police headquartered in Shuqba. He informed them that two men had dumped human remains in a bag near Shuqba and commanded that they assess the situation.

The Shuqba-based Palestinian police requested that an ambulance from Ramallah meet them onsite. Palestinian security forces readied themselves in the event that an uncovered murder would disrupt public order. The police searched the hillside for a corpse for over two hours. "At the end," Sari said, "what they found in the bag was the body of a lamb!" The lamb must have died of old age or disease. Marwan and Sari broke out into uncontrollable laughter, slapping their knees and rocking in their chairs. Marwan, who clasped his goatee with glee, was hearing the story for the first time. "I swear, I was expecting something like that!" he said between laughs at the story's absurdity. He seemed to relish this example of the occupation's weakness and the foolishness of Shuqba's new police force.

Sari's story points to the constraints under which West Bank Palestinians must dispose of waste and how their waste is policed. The men carrying the lamb corpse had presumably chosen to dispose of it at night because disposing of it otherwise was risky. About 10 percent of residents in Shuqba keep animals like sheep, cows, and goats. Other communities keep many more. Until the mid-2000s, animal carcasses could be dumped and burned together with domestic waste at the boundaries of villages and towns. But over the past two decades it has become increasingly challenging for Palestinians to dispose of them as centralization of waste disposal into Authority-run landfills made no plans for animal remains.

This means municipalities and village councils, which send household waste to landfills and tend not to separate wastes before doing so, hesitate to collect carcasses and prohibit carcasses from being disposed in municipal dumpsters. Yet neither the Authority nor municipalities provide alternative means for the carcasses' disposal. When animals die from illness, old age, or accident or when carcass parts remain at butcher shops, animal owners are responsible for disposing of them. Concerned with the health risks of disposing of carcasses near houses or agricultural fields, people seek out-of-the-way places for their disposal. But most of those places are in Area C, under army and settler surveillance.

The Israeli army presents itself as custodian of the West Bank's environment (e.g., COGAT 2017a, 2017b, n.d.-a). Though Israel, and Zionism before its establishment, have a long history of coupling settler colonial force with environmentalism and nature preservation in various iterations (Alatout 2006; Deutsch 2011; Tal 2002; Tesdell 2015, 2017), as did the British Mandate, when it established the David Unit in the Civil Administration's environment department, Israel called the unit the first body in charge of environmental protection in the West Bank (Fendel 2014). In doing so the army affirmed the objectification of the environment as a matter of Israeli state security—that is, the environment's securitization—while adding harassment around environmental issues to the army's repertoire. When the army confiscated Shuqba's only garbage truck for two weeks, "they said we were dumping wastes in the wrong place," Sari said. The men carrying the lamb carcass had likely been trying to avoid a fate similar to that of Shuqba's truck, or perhaps worse.

Buildings/Debris

Israel's demolition campaign against Palestinian structures creates special kinds of waste that, like the animal carcasses, medical waste, and *rabish* goods, are ubiquitous while also falling outside the Authority's managerial remit. Shuqba in particular has seen a "fever of house demolitions" (ARIJ 2006) by Israeli armed forces and is further burdened by the accumulation of refuse from demolition of its own buildings.

To learn about the major features of this practice, in the spring of 2010 I interviewed Jeff Halper, an American-Israeli anthropologist and director and founder of the Israeli Committee Against House Demolitions (ICAHD). Jeff cofounded ICAHD in 1997 to organize Israelis and Palestinians around what he saw as the political act of rebuilding demolished Palestinian homes in the occupied territories, including Jerusalem.

We met in Jeff's office in West Jerusalem. The walls were covered in maps and posters of demolition statistics. Jeff reclined, his perfect American English betraying his midwestern upbringing (he had moved to Israel in 1978). ICAHD keeps track of demolitions. On average the military demolishes about 150 homes a year. At the time of writing, Israel had demolished about 48,038 Palestinian structures in the Occupied Territory since 1967, and as of 2008, ICAHD had rebuilt about 190 homes. Jeff's hair had gone white as he had rebuilt homes, some of which have been repeatedly demolished.

The staggering statistics about house demolitions tell silent stories of further accumulation. They tell stories of what I think of as a *dispossession by accumulation*—accumulation of the rubble of demolished structures.[9] Demolition dispossesses Palestinians of land, space, wealth, and peace of mind. Demolitions tend to leave the destroyed house in place, for example, often leaving residents to live amid the rubble of their own homes, factories, and offices (ARIJ 2006). Demolition rubble is bulky. It occupies space, partly because many Palestinian homes are built from cement, which is a space-occupier; there is no way to metabolize it (Rubaii 2016). And with the Authority rejecting construction and demolition waste at its landfills, moving destroyed cement is both expensive and dangerous.

The army usually gives a family ten to fifteen minutes to leave a home before demolition. Families almost never have the chance to remove possessions, leaving with whatever they can salvage in the panic that erupts under the shadow of the bulldozer. A demolition generates piles of concrete, stone, and wood alongside the contents of a home or business, producing a private mountain. Your possessions become waste before your eyes. In some cases, instead of demolishing a house, the army fills one or more rooms with floor-to-ceiling cement. The structure eventually buckles under the weight of the cement and collapses. Then it just sits there.

A demolished house also takes up space where rebuilding could happen. This makes cleanup difficult. Demolition is often a one-off event lasting only a few minutes—enough for cell phones to capture the devastating moment that changes the life of a family forever. But it opens up a painful, present-continuous temporality based on the materiality of demolition. A new, bulky mess slouches on a family's property for the next, unknown period of time.

Homes turn toxic. If demolition produces the hazard of space taking, space taking is its own type of toxicity in a place where the indigenous population is under constantly, spatially squeezed threat of erasure, affirming Danny Hoffman's (2017) argument that toxicity is "ontologically indeterminate." Most structures demolished in Area C and in East Jerusalem are demolished because the Israeli government argues they have been built illegally. In these cases, Jeff says, there is no Authority policy for cleanup. And sometimes the Israeli military demands that home or business owners clean up the rubble themselves.

The order is sometimes followed by visits from the Israeli Civil Administration's building inspector. This is one reason ICAHD tries to prioritize cleanup, which costs between $700 and $1,000. But "it is too expensive for most people," Jeff sighed. They have already lost most possessions. Owners often rebuild next to the rubble of the demolished structure. Or, lacking more land next to their now-wasted house, they do not rebuild at all, leaving the rubble to stand as testimony to destruction (Gordillo 2014; Keenan and Weizman 2012; Weizman 2017).

Sewage

From my earlier visits to Shuqba I had remembered smelling human excrement. Shuqba is fortunate in that all of Shuqba's households are connected to a water network. Residents consume just over 26,417,205 gallons of water annually. This means they produce an estimated 21,397,936 gallons of wastewater per year (ARIJ 2012, 14). Yet Shuqba is less fortunate in that international donors deem villages of its size too small to warrant construction of village-scale wastewater treatment plants. Without such infrastructures, residents have little choice but to let their own excreta flow directly into the ground via cesspits or open street channels.

Some hire wastewater tankers to discharge sewage collected by mostly unlined cesspits into open areas or nearby valleys. This bypasses the need to use sewage tankers by releasing wastewater into the ground. Sewage mixes with groundwater, making it unsuitable for drinking. Mosquitoes feed off pools of raw excrement and proliferate. Fights break out among neighbors as one household channels its sewage too close to another.

Dust

Keeping windows closed in Shuqba is also a way to prevent yellow quarry dust from creating a layer of caked toxins in the interiors of people's homes. In 2007 an Israeli company opened a quarry only 547 yards from the built-up areas of Shuqba and Shabtin, a neighboring village, expropriating lands privately owned by residents of both villages. Israel extracts 25 percent of its construction materials from ten West Bank quarries. At the beginning of 2016, the quarries were producing 2,930 tons of crushed stones, 1,400 tons of gravel base course, and 3,030 tons of rock dust powder (ARIJ 2016).[10]

Quarries emit solid particulate matter referred to as dust that reduces visibility by scattering and absorbing sunlight. It can damage crops, and when small particles are inhaled by human beings it causes respiratory damage (Qumsiyeh and Tushyeh 2000). The quarry is an added threat to Shuqba's structures on top of demolitions. In using dynamite to separate out rock, quarry operators shake the earth around it. This causes cracks in buildings throughout the village. "It destabilizes the land. It has already created problems in the nearby homes," Sari said. "In the long term, it's more dangerous than garbage." People worry the whole village could collapse under the shaking might of the quarry.

The quarry is also an indirect source of construction waste in Shuqba. Companies constructing buildings in Israel and Jewish settlements with stone from the Shuqba quarry truck some of their construction and demolition waste back into the West Bank to dispose of it in places like Shuqba. Israel allowed private Israeli businessmen to confiscate the lands on which the quarry is located on the basis of the argument that the land was not being exploited. Here again we have dispossession by accumulation: the more waste piles up in Shuqba, the less likely people will be to use the land on which the waste is placed, and the easier it becomes for Israel to claim that the land is not being exploited. Meanwhile, Shuqba's environment is turned to waste, then returned to it, like the demolished houses, in the form of bulky rubble.

SHAKĀWĪ

Sari and his colleagues in the council were at the forefront of efforts to deal with Shuqba's accumulations. What struck me most about their response to the challenges they faced was that they focused primarily on the Authority and Shuqba's own residents—not on the Israeli army or government, or international donors. When I first visited Shuqba in 2012, Sari introduced me to Ramadan al-Masri, who had been head of Shuqba's council for years and had served as Shuqba's *mukhtar* for several years before that. The Ottoman government established the position of *mukhtar* ("the chosen") in 1861 as a representative of a village who was chosen or elected by the villagers. For over a century, *mukhtars* condensed the functions of municipalities in the form of a single person, registering births and deaths, signing official documents such as land transfers and bills of sale, and collecting and allocating taxes, but also liaising with central authorities and providing information to them about the village (Baer 1978; Brynen 1995; R. Davis 2010, 216; R. Sayigh 2007).

Mr. al-Masri had become *mukhtar* at the unusually young age of twenty-eight and had served along with two other *mukhtars* from the two other leading families from 1990 to 1997. His position had involved solving problems within or among families and forging connections with Israelis—for example, to help residents with permits for Jerusalem. But in 1997 the Authority had asked all *mukhtars* to give up their stamps. "We gave them up," he said. And, at least officially, the *makhtara* was over. But, he added, now in his fifties, "Being head of the council is basically the same thing." Like Sari, he gave much personal time to his work on the council. For both it was a matter of keeping Shuqba livable.

I asked Mr. al-Masri what Shuqba's response had been to becoming a site for so many waste accumulations. His hair too had gone white. "The people yell," he said. The council "issued letters of complaint to the Health [Ministry], to the Environment [Authority], to the Governorate." Over several visits I learned that Mr. al-Masri and the council had written numerous letters to other Authority offices as well.

The letters Shuqba had written to the Authority are part of an Islamic tradition of writing petitions and letters of appeal to rulers (Stern 1964). The Ottomans continued the tradition of the *shakwa*, which roughly translates into "complaint or petition presented to an official" and was often used for people to write directly to the sultans, including in Palestine (Barkey 1994; Doumani 1995; Gerber 1994; Majer 1984; Messick 1996, 262).[11] The *shakwa* assumes that a direct line of communication is open between subject (or citizen) and ruler. It also implies a degree of optimism on the part of the petitioner that the ruler is both open to and capable of addressing the petitioner's complaint.

Mr. al-Masri read a letter aloud to me during one of our meetings. It followed up on a previous *shakwa* and was addressed to the Authority-appointed governor of Ramallah and al-Bireh on April 8, 2007 (figure 10):

We write to you about Mr. [blacked out], about whom a complaint was issued about the waste, and after his pledge to stop and his being bound by a financial guarantee valuing 3,000 [Jordanian dinars] in front of the leadership of the police. But he has now returned to the practice of doing this, and the council has begun to receive many complaints from the citizens. For this reason we ask you to issue the required directives to stop [the practices], thanking you for participating and for your patience with us, and may you always remain an asset to your homeland.

This was one of two letters he and Sari gave me when I asked about Israeli dumping. I noticed that the words *Israeli, Jewish, settlement, occupation*, and *colony* did not appear in any part of either letter. Instead the letter concerned a Palestinian man from Shuqba who, it seemed, had become a local party to Israeli dumping.

The letter also began in the middle of things, its language presupposing that Authority officials to whom it had been sent had been following the case closely or at least were aware of it. Among the sewage-related letters, the following one sent in 2012 offers evidence the council had of the Authority *not* following up to address its complaints. It lifted an entire paragraph from a 2006 letter, likely because the Authority had done little to mitigate Shuqba's concerns between 2006 and 2012. Six years apart, both letters are addressed to the Ramallah Governorate general director of environmental health, one on August 22, 2006, and the other on July 11, 2012:

We hope that you will do something to present a solution to the problem of the health abomination that is located at the entrance of our village from the side of Shabtin village and that happened after some of the citizens from among the owners of the homes there in the neighborhood moved their private sewage in their homes to a private sewage network in their neighborhood in that direction (near Shabtin) without a license or a consultation from any responsible authority particular to it.

Seeing the Authority had done nothing to fix the sewage problem at its point of origin, in July 2012 the Shuqba council appealed for a solution that would at least address one of its effects. The council sent another letter to Ramallah's general director of environmental health on July 11, 2012, requesting that Shuqba be included in a campaign to spray insecticides on Authority-controlled areas of the governorate. Insects had proliferated as a result of the privately installed

بســـــم الله الرحمن الرحيـــــم

Palestine National Authority
Ministry of Local Government
Shuqba Local Council
Ramallah Government

السلطة الوطنية الفلسطينية
وزارة الحكم المحلي
مجلس قروي شقبا
محافظة رام الله

حضرة عطوفة محافظ رام الله والبيرة المحترم حفظه الله ورعاه ٠

تحية طيبة وبعد :

نحيطكم علما أن السيد؛ ▬▬▬▬▬ والذي كانت بحقه شكوى بخصوص

النفايات وبعد تعهده بوقفها والزامه بكفالة مالية بقيمة ثلاثة آلاف دينار من قبل قادة

الشرطة إلا أنه عاد الآن لمزاولةهذه الأعمال وبدأت ترد المجلس شكاوى كثيرة من قبل

المواطنين ٠ لذا نرجو من حضرتكم إصدار التعليمات اللازمة لوقفها شاكرين لكم

تعاونكم وصبركم علينا،ودمتم ذخرا لوطنكم ٠

رئيس وأعضاء مجلس قروي شقبا

FIGURE 10. Letter from the Shuqba council to the Ramallah Governorate, April 8, 2007. Image by the author.

sewage network that spilled sewage and pooled. The privately moved sewage to which the letter referred was flowing through and pooling in areas of Shuqba's periphery designated Area C, where all issues deemed "environmental" are the responsibility of the Civil Administration as well as two environmentalist settler organizations (APEJS).

In a 2011 conversation at Beit El military base with environmental engineer Assaf Yazdi, I had learned that the Civil Administration in fact had staff for extermination throughout the West Bank, irrespective of Areas A, B, or C. Assaf had told me about Samir, a Palestinian Civil Administration employee who headed a team of six to eight Palestinian workers who exterminated mosquitos every day, year-round. They also handled rodent problems or other issues when, as Assaf put it, "someone complains," which led Samir and his team to "bring the proper cages to catch them." Assaf and I had been joined by a soldier, Joshua, who was of college age and had just moved to Israel from California. His Hebrew was good enough to help translate for us. Samir and his team drove "a big truck with a big tank," Joshua said. "Or a tank on their back and they just go around spraying" using pipes.

Assaf said something to Joshua, and Joshua turned to me: "Samir and his team are all Palestinian, and obviously they don't have a problem going into [Area] A." The military uses Palestinians with West Bank IDs as prostheses for its work to exterminate in Areas A and B—where the Palestinian Authority has nominal jurisdiction and where Israel nominally prohibits Israeli civilians from entering— as well as in Area C. I imagined that sending Israeli Jews to exterminate daily in Areas A and B would risk political provocation, so uncommon has it become for Israeli soldiers and government employees to walk around Palestinian cities (unless they are harassing, arresting, or trying to assassinate someone in particular) since the end of the intifada. Their appearance would shatter the illusion of a line separating Israeli from Palestinian Authority jurisdictions in the West Bank. Given Israel's neglect of accumulation sites like Shuqba, I also imagined that the Civil Administration considered West Bank Palestinian bodies more expendable, exposable to what Assaf called "all those chemicals," the insecticides, with which exterminators come into contact.

According to Assaf and Joshua's description, the area where the insects gathered, at Shuqba's entrance toward Shabtin village, should have been included in the military's insecticide spraying, but it hadn't been. Avi, director of the Municipal Environmental Association of Judea, whom we met in chapter 1, was technically the civilian supervisor for Shuqba's waste-related issues as well. Yet Avi never mentioned Shuqba's case to me. Like Assaf's office, his organization seemed to operate according to an unspoken distinction between ruling the area and governing it.

What concerns me here is the fact that Mr. al-Masri and his colleagues operated according to a similar distinction: Israeli institutions might have the ultimate authority to intervene regarding waste accumulations, but that did not suffice to make them the council's point of address. Shuqba's council had not appealed to either body to resolve the issue. Instead it appealed in the July 11, 2012, letter to be included only in the *Authority's* insecticide spraying campaign despite the Authority's failure to respond to the previous six years of sewage-related complaints.

The Shuqba council treated both infrastructures and the effects of their absence or failure as Authority responsibilities. Yet despite Authority absence, the letters and language the council used were symptomatic of the palpable, if quiet and unsatisfactory, presence of the Authority in residents' everyday lives. The letters are artifacts of bureaucratic encounters that "contain an unresolvable tension between desires for the collective good"—proper Authority governance—"and the reality of inequality"—which precludes that good's realization (Bear and Mathur 2015, 19). In holding the Authority accountable, villagers made the Authority their government, giving it on-the-ground traction despite its failures.

For the Sake of the Blood of the Martyrs

The Shuqba council had sent another letter on May 1, 2010, to the governor of Ramallah and al-Bireh. It requested the help of the governor's office in stopping a Shuqba-based businessman from dumping X-ray images from Ramallah hospitals in Shuqba. He and his business partners had been burning the images in Shuqba to extract silver and sell it. The council's letter closed with an appeal: "We plead for the sake of the blood of the martyrs that this is a severe phenomenon, this situation of waste." It was signed "your brothers in the Shuqba Village Council." Mr. al-Masri and Sari shared two more letters concerning Shuqba landowners who allowed dumping on their land. Both letters closed with another statement similar in tone: *wa dumtum dhikhran lawatankum*, a closing I had found often in correspondence from municipal and village councils to Palestinian ministries. It translates as "May you remain an asset for your homeland," or "May you always stay active, or work for the benefit of your homeland."

When I asked friends to help me translate it, one explained it was "a compliment for somebody who just did a nationalist task." It meant "I wish you to continue being a national resource for your country." Mais, one of my host sisters in Jenin and daughter of an employee in the Authority's Ministry of Information, said it meant "We are proud of you, our Authority, and God willing you will remain an asset for your country." Another friend was more dismissive, calling the line "pretty standard courtesy language when addressing higher officials in a letter."

Yet given Shuqba's repeated pleas for Authority help, inclusion of this kind of language deserves a further reading, one that extends beyond its utility in the service of politically strategic flattery. It can be read as a gesture, its repetition serving as the council's attempt to interpellate ministry and governorate employees into a locally national sense of duty.

The language echoes greetings and opening statements with which linguistic anthropologists and philosophers of language have long engaged. It may appear formulaic or superficial, yet in this instance it both presupposed and entailed relationships and responsibilities. It helped conjure relations of legitimacy and authority out of weak and imperfect governing dynamics. The language was a "performative utterance" or "speech act" that went beyond describing a need, on the one hand, and a relationship to the Authority, on the other; it changed the social reality it appeared merely to reflect or describe. The language and letters in which it was embedded were what J. L. Austin (1962, 1970) called "unhappy" in that they did not bring about the governance they invited. But they nevertheless opened up a space of interpellation between governed and governor.

In this interpellation we also see that the relationship between the Authority and local Palestinian governments is not fixed but unstable and, as such, negotiable. Given its inability to govern in most meaningful senses due to Israel's control over it, the Authority's main presence in Palestinians' everyday lives is enacted through municipalities and councils. But even in a village like Shuqba, whose council was established as part of the Authority's move to establish facts on the ground in the 1990s, the council experienced the boundary between the council and central Authority institutions as a hard one, so hard as to necessitate interpellation across what people like Sari and Mr. al-Masri experienced as a dramatic divide.

The significance of statements like the ones in Shuqba's letters resides less in their expressing belief in the political legitimacy of the Authority as a national(ist) body and more in their enactment *as if* the Authority possessed the legitimate authority that it has not exhibited in any sustained way. In this type of enactment we see compliance, too, though the terms of that compliance are open to and indeed require negotiation. Rather than guaranteeing transparency, knowledge, or rights for officials and citizens, as Annabel Pinker (2015) has argued discussing documents in Peru, the letters provoked "unstable productive relations as flexible as the bureaucracies they are a part of" (Bear and Mathur 2015, 30–31). The letters were "speculative, partial, fluid [social] contracts" that perpetuated "uncertainty and inequality" (30–31). The language of the letters represented some recognition, albeit a cynical one, that the Authority governs in the name of (if not as) the nation as it builds itself a state.

TOXIC UNCERTAINTIES

One of the council's challenges as it grapples with growing waste accumulations in Shuqba and the silences with which its appeals for help are met is the fact that accumulations bring with them what Michelle Murphy (2006, 10, 24–25) calls regimes of imperceptibility. Bodily discomforts and deteriorations imposed by Shuqba's wastes compound painful uncertainties about wastes themselves. Regimes of imperceptibility compound uncertainties about the pathways of risk, toxic harm, and hazard (Adam 1998; Nixon 2011; Petryna 2003; Rubaii 2018; Touhouliotis 2018).

Councillors and council employees share this challenge with the rest of Shuqba. Marwan is married. He and his wife had been trying to have a child for ten years. "The doctors couldn't find what was wrong with me or with my wife," he said. "But I think it was me. I think I am impotent." He paused. Marwan looked at Sari, Sari looked at me. I looked at my notebook. My recorder was on the table, red light on. As we hovered over the blinking light, I sensed that the weight of hope that his family would grow sat like lead on Marwan's shoulders. I worried that our conversation had taken an unexpectedly intimate turn that might be stressful for the two friends. Sari had married three years earlier and already had two children, his fortunate life change showing on his body. He had gained weight since marrying, and Marwan teased him for it.

Marwan's pause was full of unanswered questions. Doctors had told him they couldn't discern the cause of his childlessness. Desperate, he had self-diagnosed, determining his impotence was because of the trash fires. "But now," he continued, having let the long pause sit with us. He smiled weakly and lifted thick arms into the air: "Thank God my wife is pregnant. It is some kind of miracle."

Still, uncertainty lingered because it lingered in Shuqba. Marwan believed anyone's capacity to have a child was compromised. "It is in God's hands," he told us. I stopped taking notes to smile back at him. This wasn't the end of his story—again. "I'm not the only one with impotence issues," he added. "Many men my age in Shuqba are having difficulty having children." Sari cleared his throat, crossing his legs. His thick fingers found each other in a clasp around his knee. "Don't forget how many women miscarry. Much more than they used to." His nails were bitten down. He reminded us that Dr. Mustafa Nimir, supervising doctor at the village health clinic, and Noh Farsa, Shuqba's pharmacist, reported that Shuqba had seen 150 miscarriages in three years. The numbers were increasing. I remembered Sari telling me when I first met him in Shuqba that children in the village had trouble breathing. Some had boils. Their parents took them to Dr. George Masih, supervisor of Shuqba's pediatric medical clinic, who diagnosed them with skin and eye infections. "Shuqba, Shabtin, Rantis, Qibya"—Sari listed the villages neighboring Shuqba. "There is a lot of cancer in the area. Increasing. Blood cancer especially."

When I had first met Sari, he had not wanted me to record our conversations. Now he helped make sure my recorder was placed so as to capture all our voices. He adjusted it as Marwan poured juice from a tall plastic bottle into small plastic cups he had pulled off a stack on the table, indicating he was settling in. I asked if Shuqba residents felt they knew their illnesses stem from waste. Sari shifted from my question to another. "There are other reasons [for the cancers] too," he said. Someone had recently burned down Shuqba's telecommunications tower. He didn't explain why, but he surmised that "this might be why there are cancers."

Marwan gave a dejected look, suggesting that these unspectacular episodes were a normal part of life in Shuqba. Cancers and boils, marking the bodies of Shuqba residents, were among the things slowly chipping away at his resolve to stay there, though he was more fortunate than many. He had his own shop in a commercial center and traveled to China for merchandise. It would be a stretch but by taking out loans or borrowing money from friends he would be able to move his family out of Shuqba and into the city, where, paradoxically, the air might be cleaner.

But uncertainty also makes staying in Shuqba thinkable—*for the time being*. Like landfill time, it opens up its own liminal period during which decisions can remain pending. And uncertainty is especially powerful when it applies not only to the effects of the problem but even to the facts. Uncertainty begins in Shuqba with residents not having a comprehensive sense of what wastes are dumped there. No one in Shuqba keeps track of the fits and starts of dumping. Sari wasn't sure if the X-ray images were still being dumped and burned there. "No one is monitoring the situation." Without that information it was even more difficult to understand waste's effects on people's bodies. I asked if Sari and the council knew how many Israeli factories and companies dumped in Shuqba. "From construction companies and factories," he said. "That's all we know. You would have to go to the exact source." His answer betrayed knowledge gaps. The rest of the waste's origin, as well as the contents of mountains of construction and demolition wastes, remained mysterious.

Two things could help Shuqba residents ascertain what wastes surround them. One would be lab testing of the materials. That would require excavation of the layers that cover the surface of Shuqba's area: an archaeology, or garbology (Rathje and Murphy 2001), of Shuqba's refuse heaps. But since all dumping occurs in Area C, any such work requires Israeli military permission, which is almost always denied (Bimkom 2008).

The other would involve obtaining information about the wastes' origins. Those who dump take pains to conceal the identities of businesses and institutions involved. Wastes arrive in unmarked trucks, often at night. In this sense the situation departs from that which follows exposure to nuclear materials, for example, where the content of the spill is known but proof of its having affected the health of a body requires particular forms of evidence (Kimura 2016; Masco 2006; Petryna 2003). No one in Shuqba knows the names or origins of the Israeli factories whose waste ends up in Shuqba. Residents cannot enter the settlements and factories themselves, since Palestinians are forbidden from entering without an Israeli permit. It is easier for Shuqba residents to travel to 'Amman, which is about a day and an international border away, than it is to travel to Nili settlement or to Israel, five and fifteen minutes away, respectively.

Uncertainties range in severity. The possibility is whispered that Israel is disposing of nuclear wastes in Shuqba, for example. Mr. al-Masri was concerned that Israel was transporting nuclear wastes there from the Negev Nuclear Research Center, which some people refer to as "Dimona." He wasn't alone. As early as 2005, the Authority had reported that Israel had buried eighty tons of nuclear waste 328 yards from Nablus, and more in Hebron. Mr. al-Masri's words and demeanor also revealed the opacity of information held by the Authority on the subject. "There are studies," he said. "They did tests." I asked who. "The Authority," he replied, seeming to find my question redundant. "The Ministry of Health?" I tried to clarify. "Yes," but he sounded unsure. He seemed never to have seen them himself. "They say there are things of this type [nuclear wastes]." I asked if his office had copies of the studies. It didn't.

Mr. al-Masri's tone echoed the uncertainties I myself encountered while spending time in Authority ministries. In 2010, Zaghloul Samhan, the Palestinian Environment Ministry's director general for policies and planning, had told me the Israelis were bringing unknown materials into the West Bank. "If you have a closed container sending tires," he said, "I don't know where they've been used! Maybe in Dimona!" Samhan's language highlighted the impossibility of the Authority enacting or embodying the public good of "transparency" because it lacked the knowledge necessary to do so.

With so many possible vectors of toxicity, there are almost too many sources even to try to name them. It was difficult for Shuqba's council to disaggregate cancers from miscarriages and X-ray burning from nuclear traces and burned telecommunications towers. It was hard to know where—on which toxicity, or which uncertainty—to focus. I remembered telling Sari and Mr. al-Masri that I had come to ask about Israeli dumping. They had quickly turned the conversation to sewage, mosquitoes, and X-rays. One problem had bled into the next.

LOW EXPECTATIONS

Despite how powerful it was in shaping their experience of waste accumulation, as it is in toxic sites outside Palestine, uncertainty was not the primary object of Sari, Marwan, and Mr. al-Masri's upset. For them the fact that Shuqba residents were facilitating dumping was both what pained them most and what they chose, finally, to address. To understand why that was the case, this section addresses how nonsovereignty in general, and military occupation in particular, intersect with toxicity.

We know from uncertainties born from toxicity elsewhere that people seek to combat uncertainty most where they demand change based on evidence of injury (Auyero and Swistun 2008, 2009; Brickman, Jasanoff, and Ilgen 1985; Nixon 2011; Kimura 2016; Murphy 2006; Petryna 2003; Reno 2011; Rubaii 2018). Survivors attempt to demonstrate proof to employers, governments, and courts, for example.

Uncertainty chafes those expecting repair by care-providing actors. Uncertainty as unprovability becomes a focus when there is a reliable *address* to which evidence can be presented toward repair.

In Palestine's waste accumulation sites, finding a reliable address is nearly impossible. And each attempted address comes with complicated consequences. There is no promise of care from the state—Israel—as the state is hostile. The army recently built a road that extends from the nearby Israeli settlements directly into Shuqba, for instance. The road has made it easy for trucks ostensibly driving waste from settlements to disposal sites in Israel to dump it in Shuqba instead. The settlement municipal environmental associations show no interest in rehabilitating Shuqba's dumpsites or in holding those responsible for dumping accountable.

The Israeli legal system, one of the strongest elements of the Israeli state apparatus, is no more reliable. I asked Sari if the council had tried to work with NGOs. Several Israeli environmental and human rights NGOs have taken an interest in the West Bank, sometimes bringing cases to the Israeli courts. Not much, he said. Sari was pessimistic that NGOs could help. The courts have historically played an obstructive role in Shuqba. In 2009 lawyers with Yesh Din, an Israeli human rights NGO, filed a case for the Israeli High Court of Justice to demand the closing of the ten Israeli quarries operating in the West Bank (Yesh Din 2009a, 2009b). The grounds were that quarrying products served neither the local population's needs nor Israel's security needs but rather Israeli government and corporate interests, so quarries violated Article 55 of the Hague Regulations (1907) (Yesh Din 2011, 5).

The Court rejected the case outright in 2011. Among its arguments against the plaintiffs was that the Court was not an appropriate party for involvement in the matter. But the Court also rejected Yesh Din's attempt to act "as an entity arguing on behalf of the Palestinian population's rights." The Palestinian Authority, it said, was the appropriate body for doing so, despite the quarries' Area C locations (Yesh Din 2011, 8). The Israeli legal system thus upheld and simultaneously undermined the Oslo-era jurisdictional carvings marking Shuqba and much of the rest of the West Bank and Jerusalem as outside Palestinian governance, even though by 2000 the Oslo agreements had expired. Like Shuqba residents themselves, the legal system acted as if the Authority had control over Area C. The Court's ruling demonstrates that the state to which Shuqbans could ostensibly appeal to mitigate the toxicities they face is a cause of, rather than the solution to, waste siege there and contributes to a generalized confusion about what entity in fact governs hypo- and hypergoverned areas like Shuqba.

The Authority also fails to mitigate waste accumulations' toxicities in Shuqba. This is partly because it lacked any kind of presence in the village until 2015. By Israeli order, its closest police headquarters was forty-five minutes away in Ramallah, and Palestinian police needed permission from the Israeli army to travel to the village at all. Even if permitted, Palestinian police vehicles were required to be accompanied by Israeli army jeeps. The Authority could operate only in civil matters such as traffic, road maintenance, and building licensing within Area B, all of which it did through the council. But it could not have a physical presence in the village. Authority offices only occasionally responded to the letters asking it to make arrests. When it did perform arrests, the Palestinian police only held the landowners benefiting from the dumping for up to a few weeks. Today the Israeli army continues to control various aspects of the police's work. The army determined where the police could be located in Shuqba, for example. The Authority had asked for its police to be on a bypass road just outside the village where they could presumably have a better vantage point. Forced onto the ground floor of Shuqba's council building instead, they see little more than the house across the street.

The village ostensibly needs the wastes removed from its lands. But the Shuqba council must assume that an Authority-led cleanup is not on its way, or even on the table. For one, were the Authority to try to clean up Shuqba's existing dumps, it would be hard-pressed to find somewhere to dispose of their contents. Authority-run landfills are already filling up faster than Authority officials can handle. Cleanup would require political wrangling with Israel to secure other lands—likely in Area C for distance from high-density communities—for the trash mountains in the West Bank. Exporting waste that Israelis have dumped in Shuqba back to Israel is out of the question. Among other things, it would be nearly impossible to differentiate it from waste heaps dumped by Palestinians, and, as Anwar's story at Qalandiya checkpoint illustrates, Israel prohibits waste movements from the West Bank into Israel.

Nor is the prospect of international donor help realistic. Donors usually pay for infrastructures in more heavily populated areas and tend to avoid Area C projects. They may not want to antagonize Israel, or they may assume that what they build in Area C will be torn down, laying waste to thousands or millions of dollars. "The

Americans won't do projects in Area C without Israeli agreement," Sari said. The council had recently succeeded in getting a wastewater project funded. But "the Israelis didn't agree, so the money was withdrawn."

In other toxic environments, uncertainty can also be the central problem plaguing those exposed to waste hazards when the hope of moving away from the toxic environment is under discussion. Such was the case in Chernobyl and in Fukushima, for instance, where officials designated evacuation zones as part of managing the fallout of nuclear disaster (Akahane et al., 2012; Burrow-Goldhahn 2008; Figueroa 2013; Kimura 2016; Ogawa 2014; Petryna 2003; Tanigawa et al. 2012). But most Shuqba residents cannot or do not want to move from the village. There is no organized option for relocation to a less toxic place within Palestine, just as there is no organized option for moving the toxic wastes themselves. People could move to Ramallah, and some do. But that is too expensive an option for many. To move to Ramallah means paying expensive Ramallah rents and leaving the relatively fewer expenses of living in a home one owns. To move also means losing the ability to work one's land, or losing one's land entirely.

We often hear that those exposed to toxic environments elsewhere develop a sensibility of anger or indignation about their exposure, orienting their efforts toward proving damage to get those responsible to take responsible action to ameliorate it. That desire to prove damage from toxic substances is predicated on the idea that removal of those substances—or movement away from them—is possible. It is predicated on open horizons of possibility.

As the stories of the lamb, the Authority's enforcement constraints, and the mobility constraints of living under settler colonial rule demonstrate, Shuqba's wastes are there to stay, at least for the time being. Sari, Mr. al-Masri, and Marwan all spoke about Shuqba's mountains of wastes rather matter-of-factly. They were devastated by what was happening in the village not least because it touched them intimately, invading their bedrooms at night and their children's breathing patterns. Yet there was a lack of urgency to the way they described the waste. It was as if it were now part of the village, as if it were an installation, a feature like the cave, buildings, and trees. It was as if the men had waste siege *fatigue.*

I showed concern, documenting, returning, bearing witness. But my interlocutors in Shuqba didn't seem to see me as someone who could do anything. Perhaps it was because they were unsure something could be done. I remembered the shock of seeing Shuqba's trash mountains for the first time. For Sari and Marwan the shock had worn off. The wastes are in what I think of as a "present continuous" state of accumulation. Handling their toxicities is a matter not of proving something but of finding what feels *handleable*. It is a matter of identifying what about waste siege, if anything, is within the possible—and ethical—realm of intervention.

INTERMEDIARIES

When I asked Sari to compare the quantities dumped in Shuqba now to those half a decade before, he nodded, saying, "There are huge quantities," but quickly dove into a different discussion. It was a repeat of a discussion I remembered well from four years before. He asked if I remembered the *muqawilin*, or intermediaries, as he and the other men in the council called them. "What do they do?" He boomed, seeming impatient to reach his point. He lifted arms up to answer his own question: "An Israeli truck arrives in coordination with a *muqawil* from the village, in exchange for an amount of money. To hide what he's doing the *muqawil* buries the wastes or covers them with dirt." Sari contorted his face into an exaggerated look of disgust.

Sari was fixated on the *muqawil*. I scribbled what he was saying, though we had discussed it before. He continued: "Maybe each village has its own *muqawil*. We have four or five." "Beyond the health issues," he added, "the actions of the *muqawilin* have created social problems. The *muqawilin* have had problems with other people. Physical fights." He and others in the council had made and posted a video about it on Facebook. The *muqawilin* threatened the council and demanded they take it down. The council's *shakāwī* to the Authority had listed names of the *muqawilin* and asked for their arrest, causing further tension between the council, whose signatures were at the bottom of the letters (see figure 10), and the *muqawilin*.

I asked if the council had thought about going to the Civil Administration. "It's crazy," I admitted, meaning to acknowledge the administration's belligerence toward, and neglect of, Palestinians. Surprisingly, Sari's first response was to dispel my idea that going to the administration would be crazy. "It's not that it's crazy," he said, explaining the council had contacted the administration for other issues like connecting homes to an electric grid and relocating an electric tower away from homes. Because Shuqba's dirt road is in Area C, the Shuqba council is not allowed to pave it, so the council had sent letters via the Authority's office of coordination (*tansiq*) to the administration requesting it be paved. It had also requested Israel's help to establish a wastewater network and to continue building a playground the army had ordered they stop building.

If it wasn't crazy to ask the administration for help, had the council considered bringing Shuqba's many dumpsites to its attention? Sari sighed, seeming frustrated. I let my pen sit on my notebook again. As I gave it one more try—"I'm just saying that the wastes coming in are the problem, no? Not the *muqawilin*?"—I realized my view of Shuqba's challenge with the dumpsite was colored by the other environmental justice stories. I thought of Robert D. Bullard's *Dumping in Dixie* (2000), Elizabeth Hoover's *The River Is in Us* (2017), Joan Martinez-Alier's *The Environmentalism of the Poor* (2003), Rob Nixon's *Slow Violence* (2011), David Pellow's *Garbage Wars* (2002), and Julie Sze's *Noxious New York* (2007), recalling tales of communities dumped on and the battles they have fought against responsible industries. That the waste is the problem—and therefore so are the people who *produced* it—is taken for granted in these stories. That is part of what I had understood it meant to think *environmentally* about waste. Environmentalism is often a politics centered on blaming the original producer-as-polluter.

Accumulation sites like Shuqba *are* sometimes part of environmentalist narratives for NGOS writing about Palestine. Israeli-Palestinian-Jordanian NGO Friends of the Earth Middle East (now Ecopeace) published *A Seeping Time Bomb: Pollution of the Mountain Aquifer by Sewage* (Tagar, Keinan, and Bromberg 2004), for example, and Al-Haq, a Ramallah-based human rights organization, published *Environmental Injustice in Occupied Palestinian Territory* (Pontin, De Lucia, and Rusin 2015). In 2017, Israeli human rights organization B'Tselem published *Made in Israel: Exploiting Palestinian Land for Treatment of Israeli Waste*. These renditions frame both waste producers and those who allow dumping as primary culprits.

But Sari was showing me that people who live in places like Shuqba do not necessarily think in these environmental terms about their own waste-related problems. Rather, it was the social rot of the *muqawilin* benefiting from accumulation that most perturbed him and his colleagues. This *social* toxicity was the feature of Shuqba's waste siege most powerfully shaping how the council felt it could respond. It tied his hands. "With issues of wastes," Sari said, "it has to do with the *muqawil*. He is from the same village. I can, as a 'son' of the village, write a letter against him, or a complaint, to the Authority. That is acceptable (*ma'qul*). But that I would write a letter of complaint against him to the Israeli authority? Then you have *betrayal*."

The fact that the *muqawilin* are such an important part of Shuqba's waste siege excludes the Israeli military from the list of possible addressees for the council's calls for help. "The issue is sensitive," Sari concluded. I realized this was likely why Sari had not let me record our conversation when we first met. I recalled sitting in the municipal council building four years earlier as Sari and Mr. al-Masri had pulled out a stack of *shakāwī*.

Smiling gently, Mr. al-Masri had asked for my patience. Sari was photocopying the letters. As each sheet exited the copier, Sari had blackened some words with a marker (see figure 10). Once Mr. al-Masri had handed me the papers, I saw that Sari had been concealing names of Shuqbans involved in dumping. The men seemed to be in agreement that, while publicizing Shuqba's waste problems and the Authority's negligence was acceptable and even helpful, exposure of the people responsible within the village was not, at least not to outsiders like myself.

In Marwan's shop Sari insisted that, with waste, there is always someone involved. This is a difference, the men said, between electricity and waste, for instance. They expressed a mix of protectiveness toward fellow Shuqbans and fear about revealing the names of the *muqawilin*. They wanted to talk about *muqawilin* but avoided too many details. "At the end even the *muqawil* is my neighbor," said Marwan to support the council's approach. "He is present. There should be privacy in the village. Because we are a village. So many of us are relatives."

Waste, especially when its accumulations are intense, disorderly, and enduring, is unlike other infrastructural substrates such as electricity or water. It contains or embodies questions not only about responsibility—for instance, the responsibility to provide energy or clean water—but also about culpability.[12] Supplementarity both describes that which is external to an object and supplies that which is missing from it. Paradoxically, therefore, the external is always already inscribed within that which is then added (Bernasconi 1990; Derrida 1998, 145; Lévi-Strauss 1969; Rousseau 1999, 2000). People serve as supplements to accumulated waste in the sense that people are external to waste but are in some way part of its formation and thus remain attached to it as long as the waste remains out of order—or toxic. Water, by contrast, may be produced in part through human action (Barnes 2014), but it tends neither to provoke questions about culpability nor, as a resource perceived to be natural, to raise associations with particular humans. Water can stand on its own. Waste cannot.

Sari and Marwan helped me see that out of toxic uncertainties one can elect to focus on any one of a number of supplementary humans. For them it felt clear that who *benefited* from dumping, and produced the local conditions of possibility for it, took—or had to take—precedence over who had produced the waste and transported it to Shuqba. That informed the ethics by which waste controversies could be adjudicated in the village. It effectively made the only party with the power to ameliorate the situation, the Israeli state, off limits to appeals. Today the council, still hoping for change, continues to send *shakāwī* to the Authority. The section below describes what this means about the Authority as a governing body in Palestine.

MATTER-OF-FACTNESS AND THE (PHANTOM) STATE

Residents experience the Authority as a matter-of-fact presence in their lives, but a peculiar one—what some of my interlocutors called a phantom state (*shibih dawla*). The Arabic word *shibih* can mean ghost, shadow, phantom, apparition, shape, specter, spectrum, shade, spook, wraith, spirit, sprite, gremlin, idol, and bogey. It suggests something both present and not. At once material and immaterial, it is something in which only some believe. It can be good, neutral or wicked, beautiful or foul. It can be ghostlike or the image of something ghostlike. A wraith, for instance, can be an image seen shortly before or after death. Wraiths are often pale, thin, and insubstantial. Yet they are traces, indices of something real, whether the real is impending death or a person who once lived. A wraith can be a dead person who appears in life after death. It can be an immaterial or spectral appearance of a living being, frequently regarded as portending that person's death.

The phantom state and toxicity are two sides of a coin. Waste accumulations invite people to call upon the phantom state. For residents of places like Shuqba, the phantom state is one of the faces of toxicity. But toxicity is also what gives shape—matter-of-factness—to the phantom state. The term *phantom state* describes Palestinians' experience of the Authority as the central governing body to which appeals are made even where the Authority fails to act or cannot do so. It also describes the unspoken acknowledgment that Israel remains the sovereign state that must nevertheless be ignored (cf. Simpson 2014, 20).

The term *shibih dawla* suggests a nonsovereign governmental entity that fails to govern both according to its own standards and according to those of the people who seek its care. To it is nevertheless attributed what I think of as "better than" or "good enough" legitimacy rather than legitimacy that is satisfactory according to higher moral or national standards, and a hoped-for authority, though this, too, repeatedly falls short.[13] Lacking authority and viewed as corrupt, the Authority is buoyed by matter-of-factness among Shuqbans and across the West Bank.[14] Waste siege, in turn, comes to index both the Authority's failure to act and its constant potential to claim a position that—in their responses to inundation by waste—Palestinians hold open for it to one day potentially fill.

Toxicity often inspires "whodunit" responses. Recall the fevered investigation to find "Typhoid Mary" in early twentieth-century New York. The goal is to identify an originary and satisfying source of harm (Murphy 2006; Rubaii 2018; Shapiro 2015). But for Palestinians, the question of the original source of harm is often bypassed. There is an alternative sensibility. In Shuqba, the question who or what *caused* waste accumulations is subordinated to a matter-of-fact bearing—to an acceptance, distressed while also numbed, of their presence, and to an articulation of who should do something *about* them. This is a sensibility that operates around the periphery of the problem rather than thinking it can dive straight to its core.

The case of Shuqba's accumulations shows how Palestinians' status as an occupied population under nonsovereign, indigenous governance refracts through their dynamic relations with waste. Nonsovereignty is intermixed with waste just as waste is intermixed with experiences of nonsovereignty. If waste is key to the formation of the modern public and therefore to that of the modern state, it is equally, if differently, key to the experience of that state's absence.

But waste and statehood (or its absence) are not, as might be expected, in a relation of perfectly mirrored "failure" or absence. Rather, their relation takes the form of complex and often unexpected ethical dilemmas that fall on the shoulders of the nonsovereign population. One of the defining characteristics of waste in a nonsovereign context like this one is the population's lack of control over waste's movements. In Shuqba, as in the experience of landfill managers we saw in chapter 1, pathways thinkable for populations trying to solve waste crises under sovereign conditions are out of bounds. And Shuqba's focus on intermediaries forecloses possibilities. It defines a narrow scope of intervention that can neither prevent the problem from continuing nor reverse it. At the same time, it generates opportunities for the articulation of boundaries and relationships between the Authority as a central government, on one side, and local governments it created to carry out its vision, on the other.

Popular thinking on toxicity as a problem of environmental injustice tends to take for granted the ontological status of the parties that either should be, or are, held responsible by those affected. Those parties may be the state, corporations, international agencies, or employers. Yet as Shuqba's case shows, toxic encounters are also moments—what science and technology studies scholars call controversies (Jasanoff et al. 2001; Latour 2005)—in which the boundaries around addressee and addresser coalesce as the people harmed and their representatives focus accusations of responsibility. Toxic encounters occasion the articulation of what constitutes an actor—for example, as the boundaries between governors and governed are (re)drawn.

In Shuqba we see the view of local community representatives who look to the Authority for help with toxic accumulation. We see modes of appeal from occupied subjects to their aspiring state. We follow experiences of the letter never answered, the problem never fixed. In this largely one-sided relation—the beginnings of a (bottom-up) interpellation that is never rounded out to *become* interpellation—we discern a particular mode of political authority that toxicity in this nonsovereign context makes visible. *Shibih dawla* is one name for that mode.

The phantom state is ghostly. It is not a state. But it is and does something. It is world-making. If people in Shuqba act "as if" the Authority were a state, their actions demonstrate layers of "as ifs" *all the way down*.[15] These "as ifs" produce realities that, like waste on land, accumulate and in doing so accumulate matter-of-factness caked, unsatisfactorily, onto political life. The immediate horizon for the generation of matter-of-factness is made from a series of toxic crises while the horizon of actual statehood remains frozen in space.

In chapter 2, inundation by ephemeral commodities indexed the Authority's failure to govern because it failed to regulate local markets. Here its failure to adequately respond to waste accumulations indexes something slightly different. People living in accumulation sites seem willing to hold open the space for the Authority to one day become the state it is not yet. This way of inhabiting a generously open temporality, rich with belief in potential change, suggests, on the one hand, that the phantom state is part of an imaginary that expects the "phantom" part to eventually drop off as statehood finally becomes its real self. On the other hand, the phantom state's workings have become a way for the status quo—separation, dependence, nonsovereignty, and continued settler colonial entrenchment—to be maintained.

That is not to say that the Authority, even in its failures, does nothing. In one sense the Authority is doing something through the very local government units that appeal for its help, making the village council as much a component of the phantom state as are the ministries to which it writes letters. The phantom state has no authority *except for the local level*. The phantom state does govern, then. It just governs in ways typically thought of as failures. It governs through partial interpellations, by building infrastructures (e.g., landfills) that set certain material flows in motion (e.g., animal carcasses, debris). It serves as an address for claims to protection, drawing attention away from the occupying authorities and toward inward work on the collective self.

CONCLUSION

I often heard West Bank Palestinians use words such as *state* (*dawla*) and expressions such as *like a state* or *phantom state* to describe aspects of life there. People used the word *muwatin*, meaning "citizen," to describe themselves, and they referred to Mahmoud Abbas, the Authority's then president, as "president of the state" (*ra'is al-dawla*). Pronouncements such as "There came to be order" (*sar fi nidham*) and "There came to be law" (*sar fi qanun*) were commonplace descriptors for the post-2007 period. It was usual for people to speak of occupation in the past tense, even while sharing stories about occupation today.

Mr. al-Masri and I had an exchange in which, after first explaining the Authority's current nonsovereignty, he referred to the pre-Oslo period as "the time of the Israelis" (*zaman al-'isra'iliin*), implying that that time had passed. If the present can no longer be characterized as the time of the Israelis, what is it, and what is here in its stead? Of what cause is this local periodization an effect?[16] This chapter has argued that what has emerged to fill the place of "here," after "the time of the Israelis," is a phantom state. Experiences of waste governance have allowed residents to experience Authority involvements in waste management—and failures to manage wastes—as something with "the appearance of an abstract, nonmaterial form."[17]

Despite the stubborn presence of critical constituencies and the circulation of critical commentaries in the West Bank, aspects of the Authority's governance have secured the Authority a kind of compliance. Compliance is not based on tradition or on charisma, for the post-Arafat-era bureaucrats with whom I spent time possessed neither. Nor is it based on belief in the rule of law, per Max Weber's (1958) definition of legitimacy. And recognition proffered to the Authority is not consonant with Shuqbans believing that the Authority possesses authority over (i.e., the ability to determine the outcome of) cases pertaining to public waste such as waste dumping. The Authority has proven ineffective in solving residents' waste problems at least for as long as those problems have plagued them. Neither is this a clear-cut case of what Lisa Wedeen (1999, 144) calls utilitarian compliance, or compliance secured through "spectacular display of [government's] imperious presence" or with "dazzling development projects" of colonial and postcolonial statecraft (Coronil 1997, 239; Larkin 2008). As we saw in chapter 1, Authority bureaucrats are themselves ambivalent about the extent to which their rule constitutes something state-like and about the extent to which they seek to enlist residents into Authority reforms at all. The compliance represented by years of letters from Shuqba to Authority ministries is thus not secured through concerted efforts at persuasion either, at least not in the realm of waste management and sanitation.

Residents of accumulation sites seek the most powerful and *appropriate* body to help solve their problems. Though doubt about the Authority's moral authority to rule is strong among many, the Authority remains appropriate and more powerful—at least more than the exposed residents of a municipality.[18] This is how, among residents and their local representatives, the choice to address the Authority is made, seemingly by default. This reiteration of the choice to appeal to, or to expect care from, the Authority may well be contributing to the relative political stability that has characterized Authority rule in the West Bank over nearly two decades.[19]

Palestinians' recognition of the Authority seems to represent a misrecognition both of the Authority's identity and of residents' "own fundamental situation or circumstances" (Markell 2009, 5).[20] But it is a misrecognition of which everyone in Palestine is to some extent aware and in which nearly everyone, sharing that awareness, willingly participates. In the choice between sending *shakāwī* to the Israeli authorities and sending them to Authority ministries, it still goes without saying (Wedeen 1999, 12) that one should do the latter.

The idea of the phantom state implies disruption of law and social order where individuals and institutions act extractively or violently without victims of those acts having recourse to justice. It implies a breakdown of older forms of social order. Yet as the following chapter shows, new forms of collectivity can also emerge in the phantom state. The following chapter develops an analysis of ethics and culpability, this time bringing it down to the scale of the individual and to one particular type of discard. It explores the possibilities opened up by halfway, incomplete interpellations with unwanted bread.

If Palestinians have a sense that they cannot reuse or recirculate their own discards, just as Shuqbans remember a time before dumping, older generations remember a past when what they made and purchased could be recirculated, a time when it was easy to find new ways to keep unwanted objects in circulation—to keep them moving rather than accumulating. The following chapter shows how movement was and remains especially important for objects that Palestinians continue to see as sacred even after they have become unwanted. Both despite and because of their dependence on foreign aid, today the sacred object that Palestinians most commonly end up needing to get rid of is bread.

Chapter 4

GIFTED

Unwanted Bread and Its Stranger Obligations

AS I TRAINED MY EYE TO CAPTURE SCENES IN THE LIFE OF PALESTINIAN discards, one of the most consistent features of city streetscapes was discarded bread. Bread deposits are so pervasive as to be a silent, national marker.[1] Like burning trash fires and rubble piles along West Bank roads in places like Shuqba, they are a material sign you are in Palestinian territory. As I walked and drove through Jenin, Nablus, Ramallah, Jericho, Bethlehem, Hebron, Abu Dis, and Jerusalem, bags of this bread, and sometimes bare bits or whole rounds, were affixed to infrastructures of all sorts out of doors.[2] Bread bags hung off rebar sticking out of concrete walls (see figure 11) and awnings, tree branches and fire hydrants. They rested in stone wall alcoves and were shoved into empty pieces of piping. Some were tied in a bow, others left open. Unbagged, single pieces or short stacks of bread rested on ledges marking private plots' boundaries. Others sat on concrete steps above sidewalks. The most common bread in Palestine, *khubz 'adi* (regular bread), is a white, wheat flour–based, slightly leavened bread. It is round and flat, about ten inches in diameter, and has an opening in the middle so that, if cut into halves, it can create sandwich pockets. This is the kind of bread most often cast off outside.

I walked around Ramallah counting the number of deposits I saw within a ten-minute radius: five in some cases, twenty in others. I attuned myself to the unique rhythms of bread movements. Every morning a woman from al-ʿAmari camp walked out of her house in a turquoise sweat suit to hang a bag of bread on a piece of broken pipe jutting out of a school wall. A bag hung off an iron window grate in the alley outside my hotel in Bethlehem's Old City for three days. I moved it to an electrical box on a street steps away, and in two hours it was gone. One afternoon in Ramallah I spotted a cluster of bread bags hanging off a dumpster handle outside a construction site; the bags hadn't been there that morning.

Returning to New York, I received emails with photographs by students and colleagues in Palestine. I hired Jamal, an undergraduate from Hebron, as my research assistant. He sent stories of bread incidents and scenes he observed in Hebron, where he lived with his family on weekends, and in Abu Dis, where he attended Bard's al-Quds University–based college. We found bread deposits in new real estate developments and old city streets, in shopping districts and industrial zones. The one place we never found bread was on the ground. This chapter asks what cast-off bread's careful vertical placement, its rhythms of appearing and disappearing, and its pervasiveness tell us about waste siege.

FIGURE 11. Bread bags hang off wires above the word "Hamas" graffitied on a concrete wall in Bethlehem, 2016. Photo courtesy of Peggy Ahwesh.

THE GOLD OF THE (GARBAGE) WORLD

Bread left outside is the result of a social act legible to Palestinians across religious and political affiliations, age, gender, and socioeconomic status. Everyone knows what it is. "Oh, *that?*" people asked, surprised I didn't know. "It's because it is a sin to throw away bread." "We don't throw bread away; it is wrong to waste bread." Each answer was a variation on a theme: that it is ethically dubious, if not prohibited, to let bread go to waste, where "waste" is both a condition and a destination. Waste is the condition of not being fruitfully used, and it is a destination as ground, household waste bin, dumpster, or landfill. "We leave it out," people said. "Someone will take it." Some answers were matter-of-fact, signaling a kind of acceptance of the use of urban spaces for depositing unwanted bread similar to that I found in Shuqba about waste accumulations. It was enough that bread was left outside even if they did not know whether it would be taken and used.

Yet others' answers betrayed unease. "When it's time to throw out the garbage, I beg my mother to take out the bread," Lina, a student at al-Quds University, managed to say over the chatter of a group of students I had gathered on campus one afternoon. I had asked students what they did to dispose of bread. "I don't want to be the one sinning!" Lina explained in a feigned panic. She shrugged and let out an awkward giggle. Lina commuted to Abu Dis from Bethlehem, where her father was a pharmacist and her mother was a lawyer. Each evening someone in the family sealed bags of kitchen and bathroom garbage. They tied off a separate bag with yesterday's leftover bread. Lina didn't mind taking out the garbage, she said. But she preferred not to experience the discomfort of carrying the bag of bread out as well. When it was her turn to take out the trash, she insisted she and her mother go together. Lina tossed the kitchen and bathroom trash in the dumpster while her mother hung the bag of bread on the dumpster's handle (e.g., figure 12). Lina's depiction of her daily practice was both funny and serious. It was funny—and perhaps embarrassing—that she needed her mother's help to take out the trash. But it was serious in that she was genuinely apprehensive about how to dispose of bread. Discarding it could make her a sinner, damaging her sense of herself.

Unwanted bread in Palestine is the gold of the garbage world. Bread cannot be discarded because its special status sets it apart from other unwanted objects, including foods.[3] In Jenin parents and children expressed a general desire not to waste food—leftovers went in the fridge or were covered for later—but there was nowhere near the kind of worry about wasting other foods that there was about wasting bread. And while people agreed that other foods should not be discarded, they frequently were, with the result that 50 to 60 percent of Palestinians' municipal solid wastes collected in the West Bank was organic, or food waste. It was also common for people to toss trash out of moving cars or as they walked. I heard stories of residents in high-rise apartment buildings throwing garbage out of windows, and fallen fruits and vegetables lay strewn all over the ground in fresh produce markets.

People referred to bread and sometimes to wheat as sacred, holy, and a blessing. The word *bread* was often used as a metonym for life. Jamal interviewed Sheikh Abu Sneineh in Hebron, where the sheikh is an imam and Islamic judge, and Father Abu Saʿda, a Roman Catholic priest in Bethlehem. Both men used the Egyptian word for bread, *ʿaysh*, highlighting that it connoted not only biological life but also life lived within society.[4] As a material underpinning of society, bread serves as an edible, and ethical, anchor.

Giving bread to those in need is a virtuous act, one that can even result in absolution from sin or restitution for other, ethically problematic acts. On separate

FIGURE 12. Bags of bread on a dumpster in al-Bireh, 2016. Photo courtesy of Peggy Ahwesh.

occasions, two of Jamal's friends had run over cats accidentally with their cars. Feeling guilty, they went to bakeries and mosques, gave money, and asked them to give bread to anyone who came in asking for it. Two or three people came into Saraffandi bakery in al-Bireh daily saying that something bad had happened to them or that they had done something wrong and donating money (three to eight dollars), the amount depending on their means and the gravity of the offense. Khalaf bakery in the Ramallah Tahta neighborhood routinely received donations of 20 to 50 NIS ($5-14) to offer bread to the poor.

Bread is a site for shaping selves and disciplining bodies. It is common for people to scrutinize, comment on, and intervene in each other's practices vis-à-vis bread, especially at home. Sheikh Abu Sneineh described eating with his family at the table where, "if someone leaves a small bite of bread, we tell him or her to eat it." This echoed my experiences with Jenin families. Adults frequently instructed children to eat remaining bits of bread or take bits leftover and throw them into the soup children were eating. When a person tore a piece off a round, the remaining piece was returned to the pile of bread, ready for use by the next person. One of my host mothers, Salwa Jarrar, once told her ten-year-old son to kiss a piece of bread after he dropped it on the floor. If the sheikh saw a person throwing away bread on the street, he stopped to "advise him not to do so."

Unlike other commodities like cheaply made goods that break and lose use and exchange value, bread retains positive value even after its use value has expired. That is why continuing to possess it generates a dilemma. It becomes a sacred, abject object, where *abjection* refers to its having been cast off and to people's uncomfortable but inevitable need to cast it off (Kristeva 1982) to maintain the physical integrity of not being inundated by that which is no longer usable or desirable.[5] Recycling and reuse networks like those that bring Israeli discards into Jenin for resale reveal how objects that lose their use value in one context can retain exchange value, and even use value, through particular forms of labor. Unwanted bread, by contrast, retains, and even develops greater, sacred—religious, spiritual, and emotionally charged—rather than exchange value after its use value has expired. Or, seen through the lens of ethical acts of caring for unwanted bread, it retains exchange value only insofar as it can be used as a moral currency whose possession strengthens the ethical self.[6]

That Lina's mother placed her household's bread on the dumpster handle was a way of breaking out from between the rock and the hard place her family's production of unwanted bread had imposed upon them. It was a way of breaking the siege of unwanted objects. It also offered a way to maintain order at home by preventing the unending pileup of excess bread there. Adam Kendon (2004) argues that a gesture is akin to an utterance because it is a kind of "visible action." Kendon explains that the modern word *gesture* is derived from the Latin root *gerere*, meaning "to bear or carry, to take on oneself, to take charge of, to perform or to accomplish." More recently, the medieval Latin word *gestura* meant "way of carrying" and in its earliest uses in English referred to the "manner of carrying the body, bodily bearing or deportment" (Kendon 1983, 153). Casting bread away is an attempt to carry the moral weight and the physical fact of possessing unwanted bread.

BREAD AND THE ETHICAL SELF

The anxiety Lina recounted experiencing daily is, I learned, a widespread experience that strikes at the core of who people in the West Bank think they are. Doing the right thing with bread is a way of being a good person, a good Muslim or Christian. Some say, as Lina did, that throwing bread away is a sin. Some call wasting it a sin. For Father Abu Sa'da, not wasting bread was a matter of "caring" and of showing "respect." The sheikh told Jamal, "The Qur'an says: 'Those who waste are brothers of devils.'" He added that those who wasted bread were particularly egregious offenders and called it a "religious duty" not to throw away bread and not to insult it. For Sadeq, an East Jerusalemite taxi driver, not wasting bread was a way of showing gratitude for what God had given him.

Ideas about the ways in which placing bread outside makes ethical sense go largely unarticulated in everyday speech. They are woven implicitly into sociality and self-judgment. Though many do what Lina's mother's did, as evidenced by the thousands of bread deposits hovering above the ground, many share Lina's unease: their movements to cast bread away are furtive and quick. Few in my informal team of bread observers witnessed anyone carrying out the act of placing it outside. And, unlike giving unwanted bread to specific other humans or animals, which I discuss below, leaving it out in the city was neither something to brag about nor a sufficient way to secure absolution from the sin of wasting bread.

The injunction against discarding bread puts municipal garbage workers in a particularly tricky situation. Most municipalities have a team of salaried sweepers who walk through the streets with carts and lift trash they find into a container on the back of the cart. When they reach a dumpster they deposit the container's contents inside it. Others drive in collection vehicles, circulating to empty the dumpsters' contents into the back of their truck for transport to a transfer station, dump, or landfill. Their mandate is to keep the streets free of discards, whether discards are on the ground or above it, as in the case of a plastic bag stuck in a tree.

Jamal interviewed four street sweepers, two in Hebron and two in Ramallah. They were puzzled at being asked about bread but forthcoming in their answers. They had never received instructions about how to deal with bread outside. They dealt with the ethical dilemma this produced by straying from the municipal script. Mohammad al-Mohtaseb had been working as a Hebron street sweeper for fifteen years. He often found bread inside or next to dumpsters. "If I see bread," he said with pride, "I collect it. I put it on the side." He kept it out of the dumpster whose contents went to the landfill. Another sweeper told Jamal that he worked "first of all to satisfy God and then for myself." Workers regulate themselves to make up for the fact that, when it comes to bread, the municipality's ethical supervision is lacking. "God sees me all the time, but the instructor might see me for how long? One hour a day?"

Despite years working to rid cities of litter, ostensibly a noble, even nationalist act in that it makes Palestinians' difficult lives more livable, all four sweepers suffered a similar ethical unease around bread disposal, which they managed by remaining vigilant, evaluating their own treatment of bread and that of others. For al-Mohtaseb, someone who prevented bread from being wasted was "someone who wants to be good to other people." Faris Abu Eisheh, another Hebron sweeper, said that removing bread from dumpsters and finding plastic bags to hang it in, his preferred approach to bread, implied "a fear of God."

Doing the right thing with unwanted bread was also about being a good child to one's parents. Jamal's father told Jamal the first thing he thought about when he heard about bread was his own mother. In our group conversation with Lina another student said her mother would "kill [her] if she saw [her] throwing away bread!" A third chimed in: "My father gets *so angry* if anyone throws away bread." It was equally about being a good parent and elder community member. Father Abu Sa'ada told Jamal that "mothers should teach their children not to throw away bread. . . . Mothers should teach them to respect life and bread." The sheikh made a similar point. I remembered seeing a woman with a toddler on a Ramallah sidewalk. When the toddler dropped the sandwich he was eating, his mother swooped down and picked it up, moving it to a plot of earth housing a tree a few feet away.

Abu Eisheh and others described correct treatment of bread as a matter between themselves and God, whether or not their supervisor or parent was watching. Yet people also sought to appear correct in the eyes of others when they dealt with bread. Jamal interviewed Abu Eisheh, municipal street sweeper and a distant relative, in the presence of Jamal's father, Anwar. As Jamal asked Abu Eisheh questions, Anwar interrupted. "Do you know what I do at home when there is moldy bread?" he asked, not waiting for an answer. "I throw it out of the window into the piece of land that is close to us for birds to eat it." Jamal made a note at the bottom of the interview transcript he shared with me in Google Docs. "I have seen my father do it only once or twice all my life," he wrote, seeking to ensure I didn't take his father's statement to mean this was a common household practice.

Jamal had been conducting a two-week home observation and, guarding his own integrity, was committed to giving me the most accurate possible rendition of bread's life cycle. The conversation with his father and Abu Eisheh centered on how the latter helped recirculate bread by helping people with animals reuse it. I took Anwar's interest in making his own claim—based, as Jamal said, on a handful of acts over the course of two decades—as an indication of Anwar's investment in showing his son and cousin that he too had ways to avoid wasting bread. Telling the men about his tossing of bread out the window was a way of calling attention to Anwar's own creativity and moral worth.

THE OBLIGATION TO RECIRCULATE

But, as this section shows, the moral worth one could prove to oneself or others by placing unwanted bread on outdoor infrastructures was never entirely secured. The highest moral value was placed on successfully *recirculating* bread, and placing bread outside did not guarantee that would happen. As Lina's reaction to the idea of placing bread outside suggests, use of public infrastructures to take leave of bread was a compromised practice. It was a tolerated but imperfect solution to bread's ethical dilemma. For her the act was abandonment, whether bread was left inside a dumpster or on its handle.

Lina's response to her mother hanging bread on the dumpster handle resonated with the words of a restaurant owner in Bethlehem. Sitting with colleagues to eat the restaurant's famous hummus down the hill from Nativity Square, I noticed a tall basket near the cash register. Above it a sign in Arabic read, "This bin is for bread. Please do not throw trash here." I asked the owner, Mr. Badir, about the basket's purpose. He explained that all bread left over from tables and all uneaten, excess bread from a day's work was thrown into it.

As a matter of principle and good business, Mr. Badir brought new bread from a nearby bakery each morning no matter how much was left over from the day before. Mr. Lutfi came by each evening to pick up yesterday's bread from the basket. Mr. Badir was a 1948 refugee from Jaffa. A chicken owner in his thirties from a nearby village, Mr. Lutfi replaced Mr. Faisal, another chicken owner, who had picked up Mr. Badir's excess bread since the restaurant's establishment in 1948 until his death the year before. I expressed my admiration for Mr. Badir's system and asked whether neighboring restaurants did something similar with their leftover bread. He shook his head, disappointed. "No, unfortunately not," he answered, slowing down for emphasis. "They leave it on the dumpster handles." His disapproval was clear as his cheeks went slack. For him, as for Lina, leaving bread on a public dumpster handle threw a negative light on one's character.

Mr. Badir left the exact reason for his disappointment in his fellow restaurant owners ambiguous. But the pride he exhibited in telling me about his own restaurant's practice suggested he viewed offering excess bread to specific others who needed or wanted the bread as ethically superior to leaving it out. Out, bread could be ruined, becoming inedible and even unusable for feeding animals. It might be picked up by municipal waste collectors and dumped with the rest of the trash in a dumpsite. For Mr. Badir, unwanted bread needed a destination. It had to be kept in a cycle about which the person who cast it away had explicit and specific knowledge. One was obliged not only to offer bread up for recirculation but also to take responsibility for its recirculation by letting go of the bread only when one was certain it would be consumed at its next destination.

Marcel Mauss (1990) interpreted the principle in gift exchange as the obligation to give, to receive, and to reciprocate a gift.[7] As Mauss's critics have observed, Mauss spent more time thinking about the obligations of the gift's recipient than he did about those of the giver, as if the giver were automatically inclined to give the gift as a result of being in a larger, endless cycle of gifting-receiving-reciprocating. In Mr. Badir's formulation of the ideal way to deal with unwanted bread, however, as in the words most friends and interlocutors used to describe getting rid of unwanted bread, the giver of that bread is the party to the exchange with the most burdensome obligation. The giver continues to be custodian of the gift after letting go of it. The obligation of custodianship after gifting threads through the tripartite system of gift exchange, while the giver is burdened to serve the function of the ever-vigilant custodian. In the Palestinian analysis of gift giving around bread, contra a Maussian reading of gift exchange, it is the initial gift giver who is burdened by the fact that the gift continues to contain something of that giver once the gift has been let go of. Rather than the donor establishing what Jonathan Parry (1986, 457) calls "a lien" on the thing given, the thing retains a lien on him or her—and not necessarily on the recipient of the thing-as-gift. This is a version of what Annette Weiner (1992) refers to as keeping an object while at the same time giving it.

The pressure placed on gift givers in Palestine, which goes beyond what societies based largely on gift giving usually place on them, resonates with Parry's (1986, 467) proposal that we should not be surprised if an "ideology of the 'pure' gift" develops where gifts' "political functions are progressively taken over by state institutions." In Palestine, the Authority as phantom state may be ineffective and neglectful, as we saw in chapter 3, but it has nevertheless contributed to a sense of the existence of a state *out there* that can serve as an address and that lays claim to certain political functions. If policies that have given the Authority the likeness of a state have contributed to a perceived social fragmentation and an ethos whereby people journey through life as atomized individuals, as chapter 2 demonstrated, they also seem to have fostered investments in an ideology of a pure or well-placed gift that lends gifts a particularly voluntaristic character and puts more pressure on the voluntary nature of the giving to be emphasized for others to observe. It suggests that Maurice Godelier's (1999, 3) observation that the 1990s saw an increased call in Western capitalist societies for people to give in order to "reduce the 'social fractures'" perceived to have been left by the state's withdrawal from the economic and social realms may also be relevant to those places we tend to think have not yet been fully formed into the likeness of the Western capitalist—or state—model.

The question of how capitalist Palestine is or isn't invites further questions about the relationship in Palestine between the commodification of objects under capitalism and the social function of gifts. Mauss (1990) argued that it is the fact that the gift is not a commodity—exchanged for money—that allows the gift to contribute to relations of mutual dependence and solidarity. In Palestine, bread is left outside much more often in cities, where bread is a commodity purchased at bakeries and grocery stores, than in villages, where people often bake their own bread. Again contra Mauss, bread's sacredness and ethico-social significance—as a factor of anxieties about where it should go when unwanted—is in this case *intensified* by its commodification as well, perhaps, by the greater consumerism present in cities.

Ascribing sacredness to bread-as-commodity in Palestine is a way of framing a relationship between this commodity and one's own relationship to God. Mr. Badir's concern to find a recipient for the bread started the gift-giving clock when his restaurant purchased bread, one step earlier than the Maussian formulation. As a sacred object, or blessing, bread became a gift from God, and the recipient—now possessor—of bread became its custodian. In this system of gift exchange, the recipient could fulfill the presumed obligation to reciprocate the sacred gift by ensuring that the gift continued to be treated as sacred—by not being wasted—once it left his or her possession, with high stakes. Recirculation of bread was a form of reciprocation to the divine, making bread's sacredness unique among sacred objects that cannot usually be given (Weiner 1992).

Palestinian bread is the sacred object that *must* be given. In this formulation, the bread donor can see herself as giving a gift both to the divine and to unknown recipients. Cast-off bread is a (reciprocated) gift to the divine *because* the donor also makes the gift materially available to nondivine others, and the donor makes the gift available to others *because* she seeks to offer a gift to the divine.[8]

The simultaneity of God's gift being reciprocated through bread's being passed along to a third person is echoed by another simultaneity in bread's status as it moves from wanted to unwanted. Bread is both gift and countergift. Its transformation into almost-discard, or possessed-but-unwanted, allows it to be both. Bread is both the object with which someone reciprocates God's gift of bread and the initial gift itself—that is only, of course, if we take bread's ontological status to be stable throughout this cycle of gifting.

Though much ink has been spilled about whether Maussian and post-Maussian gift analyses correctly understand the extent to which the distinction between persons and things is blurred in gift exchange, little has been said about whether the thing gifted is consistently *itself*. Unwanted bread is a useful site for thinking about this question because both its semiotic and material statuses are constantly in flux. When purchased, the bread ideally starts out fresh and warm.

At home in its plastic bag it breathes. The condensation it generates works on it over the course of a few days on the counter, helping the bread nurture mold growth. It transitions from being the object of a family's desires at a meal to an object of anxiety that must be made to disappear. One can hardly say it is still the self it was on the day it was purchased. Still, as the bread has transitioned to being unwanted, it has also transitioned to being sacred. In this sense, the object that it was when it was purchased no longer exists. Upon finding someone to whom to recirculate bread, one restores it to a semblance of the self it was when initially purchased.

Palestinians define and value different approaches to recirculating bread differently, even as most agree on a few main principles: that one should avoid ending up with excess bread in the first place; that, should one end up with it, one should find a new way to use it in one's own kitchen, for instance by transforming it into another food; and that, failing to eat it, one should find a way to give excess bread to the needy or feed it directly to animals.

Some feel more strongly than others about the need to personally ensure that bread is not wasted. For Mr. Badir the open-endedness of leaving it out was unacceptable. The sheikh was more lenient, though he offered that as a last resort. Were he to give a sermon about bread, he said, he would preach first that people be grateful for the blessing of bread that God had given them. The more grateful they are, the more likely they are to keep and eat it themselves and the less likely they are to waste it, which implies that gratefulness itself, if properly cultivated, can be a form of reciprocation. Second, he would "ask people to be moderate in their use of bread and not to use it excessively, and therefore not to throw it away and to keep it." Limiting consumption of bread limits its waste.

Third, the sheikh said, "If you have too much bread, you have two ways of dealing with it." One is to "reuse it by toasting it and transforming it into another food." In his own house the Sheikh uses leftover bread to make "fatta," a Palestinian dish using small bits of bread. Jamal's own family fried stale bread as a snack. Dishes like fattoush salad, which Palestinians celebrate as a national dish, reuse stale bread by including fried bits of it with lettuce, tomatoes, and onions. Otherwise, the sheikh continued, "you give it to birds and animals if possible, or send it to people who own farms and have animals. You shouldn't, *you shouldn't, you shouldn't*, throw away bread with waste." At the end of his answer the sheikh revealed that he approved of the placement of unwanted bread on outdoor infrastructures with reservations. "If none of the two precedent ways is possible," he concluded, "then we put it in a special receptacle, or a special bag that is different from other trash bags, so that the worker who collects trash can differentiate bread from everything else."

If in Palestine to eat bread is to repay the divine, not to eat it risks not reciprocating the divine's gift. Ensuring that someone else eats it is a second-best option, and casting bread away out of doors is third in line. Destroying bread by eating it is the ideal way to deal with it. Eating bread, or ensuring that others do, is akin to sacrificial destruction as Georges Bataille imagined it. For Bataille, according to Daniel Miller (2005, 92), "Sacrifice is the violent destruction of some otherwise useful resource in an act of expenditure." Sacrifice restores to the sacred world what base use has degraded or rendered profane (Arnould-Bloomfield 2016, 104; Bataille 1988, 1997). Consuming bread, disappearing it from the earth oneself, is in this sense restorative. Casting bread away out of doors is another, lesser kind of destruction, an act whereby bread that could be consumed at home is cast out of the home and distanced from the possibility of consumption as it should properly occur. To fail to consume bread or to fail to ensure that it is eaten by others is to run the risk that reciprocation to the divine may not occur. In this sense one sacrifices the certainty of one's ethical status vis-à-vis the divine in leaving bread out in public, even while one attempts to recirculate the bread by not discarding it in a dumpster.

INFRASTRUCTURAL COLLAPSE

Yet, as this section shows, the ability to recirculate unwanted bread to others about whom one has firsthand knowledge relies as much on structural and material conditions—what we might call infrastructural conditions—as it does on being a good person: for example, by cultivating gratefulness for blessings. Indeed, not being wasteful is almost always contingent on political, economic, and infrastructural conditions.[9] Modern waste management systems in many parts of the world privilege recycling, for example, a process by which commodities are treated, taken apart, and rendered raw materials for reuse. Recycling requires tremendous human labor and infrastructural coordination for separation of objects and transport for treatment as well as separate containers for different materials in households. In such contexts, one's ability to be a dutiful recycling subject, for example, is contingent on having separate containers for different waste types.

In Palestine, bread's circulations to known others were once helped by human labor and infrastructural coordination that allowed unwanted bread to move easily through physical and social space. Urban Palestinians are besieged by unwanted bread because that assemblage of conditions—the social, spatial, and economic infrastructure that once made it much easier for people to keep bread in specific, knowable circulation—has collapsed. The conditions that once helped people avoid wasting bread depended on a complex system that included people, materials used for bread transport, and storage, land cultivation, animal rearing, housing, and migration patterns. People's unease today about disposing of bread derives in part from the collapse, after Oslo and the end of the second intifada, of this set of infrastructural conditions that made it easier to consider oneself a good person.

During my first two years of fieldwork I collected oral histories of how people managed domestic waste prior to the Authority's establishment. Histories of modern Palestine tend not to focus on everyday encounters with refuse, taken up as they very naturally are with the origins of violence, diplomatic events, population movements, large-scale economic activities, and infrastructural developments.[10] Nevertheless, there are good reasons to restore awareness of everyday Palestinian experience. In this effort, I spoke with septuagenarians and octogenarians in Jenin about what they had done with their own households' waste between the 1940s and the 1980s and about what they recalled earlier generations having done during the British Mandate period. Jenin municipal sanitation workers, the head of the city health department, agroeconomists, NGO workers, and Authority bureaucrats also volunteered what they knew of past practices.

Land and Animals

One part of the infrastructure that once allowed for easier bread reuse and that was first to decline was the use of unwanted food to fertilize agricultural lands. Muhammad Abu Surour, a Jenin-born man in his fifties and head of the municipal health department, came to our second of several meetings prepared with a page full of notes from conducting an ad hoc oral history of early twentieth-century waste management in Jenin. He drew his finger down his list of bullet points. "Most people in Jenin city once possessed a bit of garden (*shwayat hadiqa*) beside their houses," he said, where unwanted bread could be thrown beneath plants or to chickens and goats along with other food wastes.

Jenin is an agricultural area. Verdant fields surround a built-up city center, which consists of an old city, whose origins date back to around 1300 CE; a new city built largely after the 1927 earthquake that devastated the area and the old city with it; and Jenin refugee camp, which the United Nations established in 1953. Abu Surour did not offer a specific time period when bits of garden were common but was likely referring to the remembered decades preceding the 1970s, when Jenin city's population had hovered between 2,500 and 4,000 residents. Before Israel occupied Jenin in 1967, the relatively low density of housing allowed people to cultivate land on urban properties, in turn allowing them to keep animals to which they also fed food scraps. Today Jenin's population numbers over 40,000, and its density makes the same practices much more difficult.

Jenin households once kept separate buckets by the door: one for wet food scraps, the other for dry. Bread soiled by other foods or mixed with sauces was thrown into the former. Stale or moldy bread went into the latter. A municipal worker would drive his mule-drawn cart by the household and pick up the contents of the wet bucket (*zibil*, or organic waste) every few weeks. Workers would consolidate their piles and transport them to nearby farmers to use on fields or to feed livestock. Those who cultivated watermelons and olives collected the food remains from city households to fertilize their soil.

After Israel occupied the West Bank, drip irrigation replaced rain-fed agriculture in many parts of the latter. This affected the types of fertilizers Palestinian farmers used, increasing Palestinian farmers' dependence on chemical fertilizers because, unlike rain-fed agriculture, drip irrigation requires chemical fertilizers. Israel also flooded Palestinian markets with chemical fertilizers, making their use irresistible to cash-strapped farmers.

The move to drip irrigation led to changes in the materials used in farming and the overall material ecosystem into which households could dispose of their refuse. Fuad, a Jenin-based agroeconomist working to reintroduce organic compost to northern West Bank farmers, lamented that Palestinian farmers soon shifted from organic, compost fertilizer to purchasing Israeli chemical fertilizer brands. The organic waste that older generations had carried in baskets on their heads, as some recalled, to their lands or to their house's piece of garden was no longer as useful. Not only did the large plastic coverings used for drip irrigation conspire with the need for chemical fertilizers to cut out household refuse as an agricultural input; those same plastic coverings themselves became one of the first unassimilable, synthetic materials—a discarded output—that burdened municipalities like Jenin with larger volumes of waste that had to be buried or burned because they could not be productively or safely recirculated with other refuse.

Plastic bags for everyday use presented the next big challenge, especially after the 1980s. Abu Surour recalled that for a time households that used plastic bags continued to leave them aside for farmers together with other refuse like food. Farmers would dump the unseparated refuse onto their lands, but livestock like cattle would swallow the plastic bags, some of them dying as a result. Plastic-littered, undifferentiated household waste became still less appealing to farmers even as a supplemental source of fertilizer.

The proliferation of disposable consumer goods made of plastics, including nylon packaging and especially, at the outset, plastic bags for daily use, was soon met with a decreased tendency among residents to separate household waste. People began to combine previously separated waste categories and to mix them with newly circulating waste like plastics. This produced a type of *zibala* (garbage) that had to be burned or thrown away. Unwanted bread could either be thrown into that, now dominant, mix or kept aside on its own.

A broader set of ecological relations thus shifted with changes in agricultural production and consumer waste. The shift involved diminishing roles for animals like livestock in the processing of human-produced refuse and the increasingly prominent role of undomesticated animals like wild dogs, cats, and birds, to which piles of waste at the boundaries of municipalities were increasingly relegated. We can see this ecological shift as a kind of "wilding" of waste represented by the shift from the use of refuse by humans and their companion animals to its use by those animals more often perceived as intruders on the human world.[11]

During the same period the opening of the Israeli labor market to occupied Palestinians in the West Bank and Gaza encouraged many farmers to leave their lands in search of more lucrative work in Israel. Many used their newly boosted incomes to build homes or to extend existing ones. Pieces of garden on urban properties shrank. The 1990s closure of the West Bank brought with it renewed urbanization and a further decline in agricultural land use (Peteet 2017). Now unemployed, thousands of workers tried to return to agriculture in the West Bank, but Israeli control over Palestinian exports and Palestinian land use made that expensive or impossible, and new designations of the West Bank into Areas

A, B, and C left most agricultural areas and most natural building growth areas off limits to Palestinians.

Since Oslo, farmers have continued to seek work in cities, and many residents of the West Bank's northern and southern extremities have migrated to Ramallah in search of work in the service industry, which has rapidly replaced traditional economic activities in local industry and agriculture. Meanwhile, the Palestinian West Bank population has increased as roughly 270,000 Palestinians were allowed to return from exile, some chasing the promise of a state and others having lost their jobs in the Gulf during the first Gulf War (Khan, Giacaman, and Amundsen 2004; Isotalo 1997; Lubbad 2007; Maliki and Shalabi 2000). Large numbers of Palestinians have become renters in apartment buildings (Harker 2014) far from where they grew up and far from the land that had supported earlier lifeways, including easy use of unwanted bread.

People

People were also key to the previously robust infrastructure for recirculating unwanted bread. By the late 1980s land and animals were less frequently used for discarding excess food in cities, and other people—extended family, neighbors, and fellow partisans and volunteers—became destinations for each other's unwanted bread. By the late 2000s that too had receded. The end of the second intifada ushered in yet another wave of urbanization and what many view as increased social isolation (Hilal 2010). A greater anonymity pervades urban neighborhoods. As more people move from villages into urban centers, their capacity to know the economic situation of a neighbor's household, for example, or even the right time to bring over bread or extra food, has diminished.

My host families in Jenin had lived there for decades. They knew their neighbors well and felt themselves to be lucky that, with the exception of one daughter in the al-Haj family, only a handful of their extended family members lived in another city or country. My host parents nevertheless lamented a breakdown in older, more intimate forms of sociality, mourning the loss of solidarities based on extrafamilial bonds. Salwa, my host mother in the Jarrar family, was in her forties. She had been a student activist with the Palestinian communist party at Birzeit University during the first intifada and was imprisoned by Israel for four years. Her ethos as a mother, wife, and professional still influenced by her time as a student organizer, today she reads biographies of Che Guevara and is moved to share passages with her husband and children, who sometimes humor her and listen. After the intifada Salwa moved back to Jenin, married, had four children, and became a high school principal. She and her husband Yazid built a large house in Marah as-Saʻd neighborhood. Her siblings built houses there too. When she cooked for her nuclear family of six she usually cooked extra food to bring across the road to her unmarried older sister. Yet she frequently expressed melancholy, saying her social circle had shrunk so much that she barely spent time with nonfamily neighbors.

Others similarly described feelings of disconnection. They contrasted the individualism and political apathy—the anomie—of the present, post–second intifada period with the sense of community in previous periods like late Ottoman and British rule and the first intifada.[12] Many conflated pre-1948 Palestinian experiences with romanticized notions of peasant life, referring to that life as *basit* (simple). *Basit* connoted a life that was pure and harmonious, without many needs and with simple satisfactions, as contrasted with fast-paced, consumption-centered life today.

Many, especially people like Salwa who had spent younger years in the first intifada (1987–93), expressed nostalgia for modes of solidarity and mutual exchange that had organized life. They told stories about how people had helped each other by feeding each other, hiding each other from the military, and running secret schools and home clinics for the wounded. Some were also nostalgic for the mutuality and solidarities that had emerged during the second intifada (2000–2006). They recalled having used bread to help neighbors during the brutal incursions, bombings, and curfews that had characterized the uprising. Those were times, they suggested, when it went without saying that if a household had excess bread someone would knock on the neighbors' door to see if he or she could use it.

No matter the idealized time period to which they contrasted the present, people read the changing times in a set of shared observations. They read change in the fact that there was garbage on the streets, the fact that people hardly knew their neighbors, and the fact that people appeared to no longer extend informal modes of material care to one another. Mr. Badir's disappointment that other restaurant owners left bread on dumpsters can be read through this nostalgia. He critiqued his fellow restaurateurs for not seeking out the needy to give bread to directly and was disappointed that recent social transformations had made it difficult to find new destinations for excess bread. For him, reading the physical and social landscape was a mode of apprehending and articulating the meaning of public life as if the landscape were a tapestry or text.

Ihraj in the Age of Aid

Another important blow to the human infrastructure that until recently had made recirculating unwanted bread easier involved people's changing sensibilities around receiving food aid and extending food aid to one another. West Bank and Gaza Palestinians receive some of the highest per capita amounts of international aid in the world (Hever 2015).[13] Much of that aid comes in the form of, or is transformed into, food and food aid staples, including flour and bread. Food aid is not new in Palestine; Palestinians have been receiving aid since the early twentieth century, and the UN has been distributing food to Palestinian refugees since the 1950s. Thousands continue to receive aid and local charity donations, and commentators in Palestine and abroad have attributed political developments, such as Hamas's victory in the 2006 legislative elections and the movement's continued popularity in the West Bank, to the mobilization of free food to the poor.

Yet over the past two decades Palestinians have become increasingly vocal about their ambivalence toward international aid. There is much debate about the long-term effects of being humanitarian subjects, in no small part because that status clashes with or substitutes for citizenship in a sovereign state (Haddad 2016). Many are embarrassed for it to be known that they accept "handouts" in the form of food, including bread, the staple of their diets, especially outside camps.[14]

People with excess bread increasingly hesitate to offer it to others directly for fear of offending them, and people in need of bread hesitate to ask or, if they do, take pains to find the right kind of person, the right time, and the right way to ask. It is likely due to Mr. Badir's subtle system of bread distribution that the needy feel comfortable coming by to see if he has bread to spare: Mr. Badir instructs waiters to place leftover bread he holds back from Mr. Lutfi in black, opaque plastic bags. This disguises what he gives to those who come by. They shoot him inquisitive looks he interprets as need. Sometimes, a baker told me in Ramallah, people come asking for leftover bread by saying it is for their animals. As I stood across him at the counter, he cocked his head to one side and said: "They actually plan to eat it."

I spent a morning in Saraffandi bakery in al-Bireh and ended up standing next to a cashier while he took a break. We stood together to the side as people lined up to buy bread. In a hushed voice, he said the manager had printed a poster and hung it in a corner of the shop. It announced that all bread on the counter beneath the sign was for the taking for any person in need (*al-mihtaj*), in whatever amount would fulfill their need (*kifayatak/kifayatik*)—no questions asked. But the poster had made those in need visible to other patrons by directing them to the corner of the store under the word *mihtaj*. It had caused embarrassment (*ihraj*), he said. People had stopped coming by for leftover bread. The manager had removed the poster. Saraffandi had also tried offering coupons that patrons could show the person working the counter instead of paying in cash. Saraffandi had stopped that too because of *ihraj*. Now the bakery leaves a stack of leftover bread in a corner, unmarked and unsupervised. People come in and take bread on their own without interacting with the shopkeepers, placing it in plastic bags they have brought with them.

As the need for anonymity in these exchanges suggests, face-to-face modes of recirculating unwanted bread have receded, while more formal institutions like NGOs, bakeries, mosques, and municipalities have not generally stepped in to fill the void left by the new social disconnection.[15] These institutions do not typically accept leftover bread from private individuals for redistribution, probably because there is no way to ensure their quality. By the mid-2000s, a group of construction workers or students who accidentally ordered more bread than they could eat would find unwanted bread a private burden, and a heavy one.[16]

Mold versus Staleness

A final key element of the infrastructure that once allowed bread to recirculate more easily resided in the bread itself and in how it was transported. In one of a number of extended conversations I had with Sadeq, a Jerusalemite taxi driver I have known for years, he alerted me to the importance of bread's changing materialities. *Khubz 'adi* tends to grow mold more quickly and more easily than do older types of bread, he told me. It molds faster than the thin, crepe-like bread called *shrāk* (also called *sāj* or *markuk*), and *ṭabūn* bread, named after the *ṭabūn* oven in which it is baked. *Ṭabūn* is traditionally baked in a hole in the ground on small rocks. It is flat and tends to be larger in diameter.

Mold and staleness are not equal in their effect on the possible (re)uses of bread. They both represent bread having gotten old or gone off. But the "offness" of staleness can be overridden: stale bread can be fried, soaked, crumbled, baked, and reheated over a flame as human food or crushed to feed animals. By contrast, many kinds of mold are harmful to both humans and animals and render bread unreusable.

Sadeq asserted that the sensitivity of *khubz 'adi* was due to its ingredients and use. Regular bread's pocket differentiates it from *shrāk* and *ṭabūn*. As it bakes, it puffs up, filling with hot air in its center. This allows it to be cut in half or sliced at its seam and used as a sandwich shell, making it popular for meals on the go. *Khubz 'adi* has partially replaced *ṭabūn* bread, which is now a kind of specialty commodity.[17] Along with high-rise apartment buildings in places like Ramallah, fast-food restaurants and a tendency to eat meals—usually falafel or chicken sandwiches—while standing or walking characterize the daily rhythms that go along with rapid urbanization in the post-Oslo, state-building period. More people want sandwich-shaped bread, and Sadeq was convinced that bakeries used chemicals to ensure the bread's pockets would open properly.

Plastic bags, including some made in Palestine, are also increasingly used to transport bread. When they get home, many people store bread in the same bags. Taking the bread out would allow it to go stale within hours. Some households keep the bag of bread on the kitchen counter to help make it available for a quick snack or for the next meal, both to eat and as a utensil to pick up other food. However, as Jamal observed at home in Hebron, the bread sweats inside the bag, especially when purchased fresh and still warm. Jamal's father, Anwar, developed a system for staving off the molding process. Upon bringing the bread home, he turned the plastic bag inside out, allowing the moisture that accumulated between the bag and the warm bread to evaporate. But not all households make such techniques common practice, especially since many assume tomorrow they will buy fresh bread. People sometimes knowingly let bread become unwanted or unwantable.

BREAD AS INFRASTRUCTURE AND ITS LATENT COMMONS

Unsurprisingly, given how strongly Palestinians value bread freshness, most pedestrians walk by bread that has been left outside. But some walk over to it, touching it to feel it for softness and shape. Some take it home, others feed it to their chickens. While driving one day through the back streets of al-Bireh, Mustafa, a friend from al-'Amari camp, and I encountered a shepherd. The shepherd had stopped his goats on a stony, open plot of land. I asked about bread. He squinted as if my question were too obvious. *Of course* he took bread he found, he said. As long as it was dry. He broke it into pieces and spread it across a plot like this one. Mohammad al-Mohtaseb and Faris Abu Eisheh, who swept in Ramallah and Hebron, told Jamal that neighbors asked them to bring them bread from their daily routes.

If bread's proliferation out of doors signals the collapse of a *previous* infrastructure for the recirculation of unwanted bread, the widespread use of spaces out of doors has transformed bread into a new kind of infrastructure all its own. Bread deposits are infrastructural in that they mediate urban public life, creating networks that facilitate the flow of people and ideas, allowing for their exchange over space (Larkin 2013, 328).[18] Outdoor bread deposits are able to do this because, left out, bread is endowed with the power to interpellate.

Bread outside can act upon those in whose midst it is placed. It addresses an audience, inviting humans (and other organisms) who want or need it to take it. Because this style of bread-leaving is such a pervasive phenomenon, bread also informs passersby that the person who placed it there shares a sense of moral constraint around treatment of bread with others who might consider doing the same. Cast-off bread creates opportunities for the interpellation of strangers, making public locations like ledges and walls sites for individuals to perform care for an imagined stranger-collectivity. One of the most important ideas that this bread practice helps make circulate is that such a collectivity exists.

The idea that cast-off bread can interpellate returns us to cast-off bread's status as a possible gift that, Godelier (1999, 12) reminds us, both creates and reduces distance between people. Whether casting bread away constitutes initiation of gift giving to anonymous others or reciprocation of God's gift of bread, it is a gift that "attracts an increment" (Parry 1986, 465). In 1925 Mauss (1990, 11–12) described what, following the Maori practice, he called the *hau*, which he translated as the spirit of the gift that bound the gift's giver to its receiver. The moment of placing bread outside produces a *hau*-like effect as Marshall Sahlins (1972, 160), commenting on Mauss's analysis, describes it: cast-off bread produces a yield or product in the form of an aspired-to collectivity to which the giver contributes. The increment the gesture attracts is the collectivity itself. And the gesture does not end there. To cast off bread is to give to that which produces the possibility of sustenance in a social sense. In Sahlins's reading of the *hau*, reciprocation of the initial gift by a third party is the act of rejuvenating the forest, or the space that gives. In post-Oslo Palestine, casting bread away makes visible or public a generalized collective willingness, or mandate, to share.[19]

Among humans, bread outside has the potential to enact a kind of moral interpellation that works both on the person who casts it away and on the person who feels herself addressed by the bread. How one deals with discards imputes one's membership in a social and moral system partly because, as I have argued, casting off bread correctly is key to cultivating an ethical self. Leaving bread out of doors can be read as an ethical response to the unethical privatization of the burden of unwanted bread. It turns the burden public again. Before being cast off, every piece of bread contains the power to interpellate its possessor into one of two imagined groupings: a collectivity of the sinful, wasteful, and ungrateful, and a collectivity of the ethical, socially upright, grateful, and generous. When a possessor of bread chooses to hang the bread on the dumpster handle, she can recognize herself as a member of the latter.

Yet social recognition is not indispensable. A bread taker will likely never know who left it there. In a twist on the unknown origins of toxicity we encountered in chapter 3, placing cast-off bread outside is a gesture toward stranger others whose specific origin (i.e., the person who cast it off) is unknown to those others. Like some forms of graffiti, it indexes a gesture made in public for a public while erasing the person making it.[20] The anonymity of the person who offered unwanted bread to unknown others can be as important to the virtue of casting it off properly as its openness to anyone in need (Parry 1986, 467). It echoes the practice of offering anonymous donations in general—and donations of money for the distribution of bread to the poor in particular—common across the Occupied Territory. When Jamal's two friends, after running over cats, went to a bakery and mosque to donate money for bread distribution to the poor, they concealed their names. Those who donated money to Sarrafandi and Khalif bakeries concealed their names from those who took the prepaid bread.

This kind of anonymity does not of course extend to the intermediaries—the bakery employees and the mosque attendants who receive donations. But the virtue of anonymity vis-à-vis those who receive the bread may come from the idea that the giver does not *seek* to be known by society. Seeking recognition for a virtuous act erodes the act's virtue. The giver can be satisfied by the knowledge that she is good in her own estimation or that of a higher power. And virtue may come from the giver's protection of the receiver from *ihraj* over publicly receiving handouts.

Bread out of doors conjures a collectivity inflected by social class and financial precarity, but also delicate, affective relations of gift exchange. Bread's abandonment places additional constraints on its interpellating call. Picking bread up off the street is not something anyone wants to do in plain sight. This is probably why I only once saw someone *almost* doing it and never actually saw anyone do it. I was walking along a side street toward Ramallah's Clocktower Square and caught a glimpse of a second-long interaction between a man and a bag with two pieces of bread in it. By the time my eye fell upon his hand touching the bread on a waist-high wall, he had lifted his hand again and walked on.

Yet from the perspective of its broad reach, casting bread away can be read as more ethical than giving bread out through establishments. Bakery and restaurant workers whose employers have arrangements with people who pick up excess bread daily told me that others sometimes came by asking for leftover bread. The owners instructed employees to politely turn them away, citing their agreement with a specific person. Casting bread away outside, by contrast, is democratic. It makes bread available to anyone who wants it. Its availability depends only on one's recognition of its continued usefulness. For those for whom an imprisoned husband, debt, a lost job, or confiscated land means income cannot cover basic necessities, it is important that bread bags on the street obviate the need to prove eligibility for aid.

People who cast off bread out of doors attempt to recirculate bread but are unable to guarantee a destination. They never witness a transfer, except to the city writ large. No one I spoke with ever waited to see what happened to the bread once they left it out. Nor did I see anyone linger on the street near an abandoned bread deposit. In the Maussian definition of a gift that privileges receipt and reciprocation, cast-off bread is not a gift at all.[21] It is a *potential* gift without the obligation to reciprocate, an offering that can become a gift but that can also maintain offering status. An offering can be a contribution, a benefaction (which can be a donation or gift but also an act of conferring a benefit or of doing good), a sacrifice, or a token of devotion. The incompleteness of casting off bread as gift giving affirms the argument some have made that reciprocity in gift giving tends to be taken for granted and overemphasized (Godelier 1999, 6; Parry 1986, 466). Perhaps, in other words, a gift not received or reciprocated does not incompleteness make.

It is the open-endedness, or incompleteness, of casting off bread outside that can serve as a corrective to the problematic—because always conditional and increasingly alienating—"gift" of aid (Godelier 1999, 5). As has been widely noted, humanitarian aid, like any gift, easily creates "a relationship of superiority because the one who receives the gift places himself in the debt of the one who has given it, thereby becoming indebted to the giver and to a certain extent becoming his 'dependent'" (Godelier 1999, 12). Even if only symbolically, casting off bread is a social welfare provision that avoids the vestigial moralism that has so often been complained of in welfare programs: there is no need for a giving subject to recognize a recipient who is deserving, and there is no need for the recipient to feel indebted to the giver. This is aid without the need to prove to UNRWA, for example, that one's family is a special or a "hardship" case. It is aid that bypasses the dynamics of what Adriana Petryna (2003) calls "biological citizenship" and what Miriam Ticktin (2011) describes as performances of humanitarian need.[22] In these senses cast-off bread's collectivity is organized around the principle of universal welfare rather than personalized solidarity.

At Saraffandi bakery, the young man taking orders explained that bakery staff knew who was in need "by their faces" (*min wijihhom*) and that those in need knew the bakery's policy: "They just know to come in, take what they need from one of the piles of bread, and go." This shows that semipersonalized networks of material solidarity continue to exist. But it also shows that a bakery worker or restaurant owner maintains the ability to vet who is deserving of aid in the form of bread. The worker keeps a mental database of the people who are in such dire financial straits that they cannot afford to buy bread themselves. Leaving bread out, by contrast, casts a cloak of anonymity over those who would take it.

Finally, leaving bread out of doors is ethical because it cites others who cast off bread in similar ways. A walk along most streets is guaranteed to involve an encounter with others' public bread deposits. It is a practice often learned at home. But, observable as it is outside, it is part of what Clifford Geertz (1973, 6) calls a "public code." In (re)iterating the practice, people who cast off bread make gestures both to others who have done the same and to others who might take an interest in leaving bread out as well. Placing bread out of doors is a Geertzian wink, an act full of meaning, both because it is intended to be understood in a certain way by the placer and because it is discernible by others as such.

On the one hand, the casting off of bread outside represents the breakdown of face-to-face networks of gift exchange that, as Mr. Badir believed, build durable solidarities among known persons. On the other hand, it creates the conditions for the formation of a different form of connection, or at least the conditions for the expression of an aspiration for connectedness. Cast-off bread allows something shared to come into view, even if the exact thing that is shared—godliness? obedience to one's parents? gratefulness? fear? habit?—is not entirely clear.[23]

Casting off bread outside performs investment in something shared in performance's double sense: it produces the effect of, or iterates, that which it appears to reflect. And it performs participation in a moral community through participation in a public code. Cast-off bread has a social life after it is cast off, presupposing the existence of, and generating a sense of opportunity for participation in, the existence of a collectivity, defined neither by state (or state-in-the-making) nor by nation, thereby almost, sort of, bringing that collectivity into being (Appadurai 1988).

One way to describe the collectivity bread makes possible is as a public. Publics in general are usually fleeting and porous, and the provisionality of the socialities that coalesce around bread out of doors echoes the provisionality of the status of the cast-off bread that helps make them coalesce. For, in the words of Oskar Negt (2006, 121), publics are "something, which is in process, which denotes a process, not a state."[24] The fact that cast-off bread's collectivity is one that gathers around the apparently contradictory moves of individuals cultivating ethical selves and individuals investing in an imagined collective also contributes to its fleetingness. Like the phantom state that is neither quite a state nor quite the absence of a state, this collectivity is never entirely centered on the collective or the individual's role in it but rather emerges in between. Publics are also spaces of address and attention constituted by strangers. They are spaces for people who do not necessarily have preexisting common interests, issues, and identities but who are constituted as publics when they are hailed as such, since publics form constantly new relations.

Yet bread out of doors does not quite constitute a public. Passersby may read it as part of their streetscape-as-text. But many do not. Bread outside fails to leave linguistic traces, unlike the media that traditionally underpin the address to publics.[25] Nor does bread index language as a flag can be said to index a national anthem. It also lacks human accompaniment, unlike the placards held at demonstrations and the banners waved from cars celebrating freed Palestinian prisoners. Most importantly, although some people stop to touch or take the bread, most do not.

The collectivity evoked by bread cast away out of doors is not entirely united, in other words, partly because it is never entirely addressed in ways publics tend to be. Like the countless unanswered letters from the Shuqba council to the Authority, the casting off of bread constitutes an incomplete interpellation. This aligns the nature of bread collectivity most closely with what Anna Tsing (2015, 255) calls "latent commons." Latent commons, she writes, "are latent in two senses: first, while ubiquitous, we rarely notice them, and, second, they are undeveloped. They bubble with unrealized possibilities; they are elusive."

Latent commons exclude as much as they include, bringing together human and nonhuman in "mutualist and nonantagonistic entanglements" (255). Bread's collectivity is to some extent national, or closed. One's participation in it is mediated through the lessons one learns growing up in a Palestinian household, hearing parents and grandparents scold younger members for discarding bread. It is likely because most West Bankers would probably assume that foreigners need not be schooled in its ethical rubric that my Airbnb hosts in Ramallah omitted reference to the practice. Airbnb rentals in Palestine are usually used by expats. In English, the welcome booklet made no mention of unwanted bread: "No garbage separation system available. All garbage must be placed in outdoor garbage collection bin across the street."

CONCLUSION

The dynamics of the outdoor casting away of bread show that socialities can be conjured through the leave-taking of possessions. Seen as a form of discard, unwanted bread can be infrastructural, mediating the production of something akin to a latent commons.[26] The movement of discards can thus both index and help to conjure collectivities or their approximations.[27]

In drawing people into effervescent participation in a public code, the casting away of bread conjures in the sense that it invites imaginative play, but also in the sense that it is also norm producing, or iterative. There is an ideal way of performing to which casting-off practices refer. Yet there is also perpetual slippage in the ways in which people actually perform the norm. Those who cast off bread avail themselves of the code's space for creative license. The code provides a small selection of *negative* injunctions: do not place bread on the ground, do not throw bread "away." Beyond that, the number of ways in which bread can be cast off out of doors is as infinite as the opportunities that outdoor urban spaces offer for bread to rest or hang without touching the ground or the inside of a dumpster.

Another slippage within the performance of the norm arises from the flexibility with which the injunction not to throw bread away can be interpreted.

As I was told time and again, "you" cannot be the person to discard bread. But you may be able to accept someone else doing it. Though it is difficult to verify, most of the bread bags suspended from dumpster handles are likely dumped into municipal trucks and hauled to a dump. Most people who leave their bread on dumpster handles may imagine this to be the case even if they spend little time actually thinking about it. The fact that the bread they leave out will probably end up exactly where it wasn't supposed to and at the hands of another person is cut out of one's daily moral calculations.

Herein lies the same flexibility that Lina and Mr. Badir perceived as morally dubious. If all the "you's" could not be the ones to put the bread in the dumpster, and given the fact that cast-off bread is not always, or even often, picked up by individuals in need, such bread would pile up and overwhelm the city. The practice of hanging a bag of bread outside becomes a way to work around the moral absolute of not wasting bread and the moral dilemma of finding oneself to be potentially wasteful. It also helps avoid the impracticality of thousands of tons of old bread piling up on the sidewalk. It sanctions municipal employees to take care of the moral weight of others' leftovers, thereby inclusively excluding them from cast-off bread's collectivity.

To remain ethical, these practices of casting away bread embed unwanted bread within existing urban infrastructures that serve other purposes, transforming the meaning and function of existing infrastructures like telephone poles, walls, and grates. The dumpster handle where Lina's mother placed bread was designed to allow municipal workers and trucks to move, emptying the contents of the dumpster, and the window grate in Bethlehem was designed to provide protection. People's use of walls, rebar, dumpsters, trees, wires, awnings, and other pieces of urban infrastructure redefines those infrastructures as places for casting bread away ethically. And bread deposits draw some privately owned materials—like the stone wall or the window grate—into the public. Cast-off bread transforms the empty outsideness of these materials into inhabited publicness. But it also layers new uses of those materials onto old ones, thickening people's semiotic and physical experiences of the city.[28]

This is an example of how urban inhabitants can shape the experience of their landscape through small gestures even when, as we saw in the first three chapters, the built environment with which they interact to make those gestures is most often controlled by actors and processes that appear beyond their reach. Casting away bread outside is informal, and cast-off bread becomes infrastructural through the simple placement of an unwanted thing. Discards, again here, do not only *require* infrastructures in order to be managed. They can also *constitute* infrastructures because they themselves have the capacity to facilitate flows.

Bread left out constitutes an infrastructure for ethical self-fashioning by drawing elements of the existing built environment into a system for making bread visible, and therefore accessible, to passing beings. To be left out ethically, bread needs these existing urban elements to predate it. Bread constitutes an infrastructure, then, not through tampering with the built environment or through the construction of a new version of an older infrastructure, what Nikhil Anand (2015) calls "accretion," or layering, or through acts like graffiti or breakage. *Layering* may not fully capture what bread does because the word suggests the accretion of one infrastructure on top of another. Layers are distinct units placed in immediate proximity to one another, as when a person wears a sweater over a T-shirt. The sweater and T-shirt remain ontologically distinct while they touch. The Palestinian practice of casting bread away is more than a layering—it is total dependence. Acts of casting away bread rely on the stability of certain features of the built environment. They rely especially on the stability of those features' significations. Placing bread on a wall is ethical because the wall is a wall and not the ground. Wall, handle, tree, and grate define outsideness, off-the-groundness, as meaningful sites of nondisposal.

Casting off bread is not articulated as a political gesture. Bread left outside may appear as "domestication" of the occupied landscape or its reclamation. And the unceasing brutality of Israeli interventions on land and population, coupled with Authority ineffectiveness and neglect, would seem to suggest that Palestinians who use their cities in this way are offering a political response to that twin sense of invadedness and abandonment that characterizes hypo- and hypergovernance. But we misunderstand how practices like outdoor bread disposal work if we read them either as private or as overtly politicized claims to the city beyond-one's-reach, as gestures of possession or as proprietorship over spaces that government, for example, seeks to make public in particular ways.

When people leave bread out of doors, they use urban structures and materials in ways that are, rather, also symbiotic with the dominant usages of those structures and elements. The term *symbiotic relationship* usually refers to multiple animate organisms living together. Bread-as-infrastructure emerges from a symbiosis—a living together—among inanimate objects. That is a symbiosis of bread and the urban environment with the help of humans who may never meet.[29]

But if bread deposits are infrastructural, Mr. Badir's critique and Lina's discomfort show that bread infrastructure, at least for some, only approximates a solution to the ethical precarity of possessing unwanted bread. It is only an approximation of, or a gesture toward, bread's idealized reuse or donation. It approximates ethical practice the way Jenin's *rabish* market approximates Israeli citizens' experiences of governance and consumption without ever completely offering it.

Scholarship on refuse and human excrement often centers on cleaning and disposal, what Reno (e.g., 2015b) calls absential practices, despite broad consensus that the work of ordering matter is never actually done. *Management* and *maintenance* are more apt terms for thinking human interactions with disorderly and toxic materials, as humans constantly engage with waste in order to approximate cleanliness or a sense of control over their environment. The perpetual need to maintain spaces free of refuse and to engage with it means humans constantly engage in incomplete acts.

Casting away bread outdoors shows that there is another version of incompleteness in discarding that does not require human presence. Instead incompleteness inheres in the object's placement and remains with the object after the placer has left. The original act—for example, hanging the bread bag on a grate—gives the bread a status as a thing that remains in limbo. Bread out of doors reveals the possibility of partial and imperfect acts of object abandonment and the possibility of halfway, good-enough approaches to ethical dilemmas. The partialness and unknownness of the full cycle of the gesture, the noncompletion of a circle, is part of what makes the gesture imperfect in the eyes of Dr. Badir and Lina but is also what makes the gesture of casting away bread generative.

Cast-off bread's moral injunctions can be seen as counterhegemonic in that they implicitly critique the wastefulness of a capitalist consumer culture that many Palestinians worry characterizes West Bank society. Bread practices challenge the individualist ethos of post-Oslo Palestine by performing public gestures of consideration for others in need even if those gestures neither are based on, nor create, long-term relationships with those others.

Palestinians experience waste siege in relation to bread as an ethical precarity around its disposal. Out of that precarity emerge forms of aspired-to collectivity that both affirm the roots of the ethical precarity (individualism) and offer people a way to live with it. Palestinians work with and within that precarity to approximate ethical selves through the approximation of ethical praxis. They make cities into sites for forms of ethical living and the geographies that symbolize the anonymity and individualism that helped give birth to ethical precarity into livable sites. This suggests that, as existing forms of community are diminished or rearranged, nondiscursive forms of belonging to a collectivity may be emergent as supplements (Derrida 1998, 145) to existing forms.

This chapter has explored what happens to the micropractices of ethical living as the phantom state and its constituents assert autonomy vis-à-vis the aid industry that provides services and welfare for the occupied population in place of its occupier. In focusing on unwanted bread that should not be wasted, it has examined some of the material waste produced by those assertions of autonomy and the dilemmas with which that waste then burdens the people whose responsibility it is to dispose of it.

The following chapter turns to the experiences of the Authority officials who are held accountable for waste siege not only by local constituents like the Shuqba council but also by Israeli actors. Palestinian bureaucrats at the helm of the phantom state must answer for the waste flows into Israel from the West Bank's many accumulation sites. The chapter tacks back to those Palestinians who are arguably some of the most implicated in the politics of international aid—the aid from which leaving bread out of doors offers a temporary reprieve. It centers on their attempts to compel Israelis and donors to support construction of the most critical of waste infrastructures: sewage networks and treatment plants R. (George 2008). Consumed by the need to convince foreigners that Palestinians are, as a collective, worthy humanitarian subjects for the "gift" of funding for environmental projects, these actors face their own cognitive and ethical dilemmas. Their improvisations in navigating those dilemmas entail performances of deservingness through affirmations of willingness to participate in a *global* collectivity as environmental custodians who uphold elements of the very settler colonial framework they hope sewage infrastructures will help them escape.

Chapter 5

LEAKAGE

Sewage and Doublethink in a "Shared Environment"

PALESTINIAN SEWAGE SEEPS AND FLOWS INTO SPACES THAT ISRAELIS perceive as parts of the Israeli environment. The Oslo Accords continued the pre-Oslo arrangement whereby various Israeli actors are empowered to influence whether, when, and how Palestinians manage their sewage and freshwater (Selby 2003, 2013; Trottier 1999). Though these actors do not all agree with one another about what should happen to Palestinian sewage, they tend to "read" Palestinian waste flows in and through the West Bank as a form of political aggression against Israel. They read sewage as evidence that the Authority is unfit to govern and Palestinians are unfit for sovereignty. Some go so far as to view Palestinians' sewage as an unwelcome reciprocation for what they construe as Israel's gift of fresh water to occupied Palestinians.

A small group of Palestinian professionals with whom I spent time on the third floor of the Palestinian Water Authority (PWA) building felt incited to respond. They had been trying unsuccessfully to plug the leak, or at least to demonstrate their desire to do so, for twenty years. Their integrity was on the line. Despite their frustration with the way their occupiers perceived them, they felt compelled to show Israelis that they were willing to "cooperate" and that they shared Israelis' concern for the environment.

Blocked from building the wastewater networks and treatment plants they saw as necessary both for the population now and for the future state, they poured energy into complementary forms of labor that worked to counter Israeli readings of Palestinian wastes as signs of Palestinian malice and ineffectiveness. These forms of verbal and gestural labor (Elyachar 2011) can easily be dismissed as less significant than designing sewage plants or digging holes for pipes, but they allowed Palestinian professionals to make gestures of care toward the environment as defined by Israelis and donors, thereby also making gestures of desire to stop the hemorrhaging of the occupied population's sewage.

In mobilizing their speech and comportment to transmit messages to their Israeli interlocutors and to donors, these professionals had two short-term goals: one, to dissolve suspicions about the Palestinian government, and two, to establish infrastructural arrangements that, paradoxically, they also viewed as ethically and politically compromising but knew Israelis and donors perceived positively as material evidence of intent to normalize relations with Israel, and as material gestures to match their discursive and affective ones.

The speech and comportment I describe here were *aspirational* forms of what anthropologist Julia Elyachar (2010) calls "phatic labor." Drawing on Bronislaw Malinowski's (1936) concept of "phatic communion" as well as a Marxian understanding of labor, Elyachar (2010, 453) uses the term *phatic labor* to describe labor that "produces communicative channels that can potentially transmit not only language but also semiotic meaning and economic value." My interlocutors not only transmitted but aspired to elicit these two forms of value from *their* interlocutors in ways that parallel capitalist storytelling as David Pedersen (2013, 13) describes it. They attempted to commodify their words and affect, rendering them exchangeable for support and diminished suspicion. Yet there was no guarantee that commodification would work. This exchange, like that initiated by people who cast off their bread out of doors and like the Shuqba council's letters, could remain incomplete—an *offering*. The professionals' phatic labor thus constituted what Douglas Holmes (2014, 1) calls "communicative experiments." But these experiments are constrained. They are made of what he calls "communicative imperatives" (6) in that professionals' ways of speaking and relating to those with the power to stop their projects were obliged to remain within what was desired by, and legible to, the latter.

Professionals offered gestures as ways of expressing the Authority's good intentions vis-à-vis Israel through its intention to prevent pollution, in turn providing social capital that could translate into their own ability to build more necessary and desirable infrastructures in the future. This chapter argues that aspirational phatic labor was the *communicative* infrastructure necessary for building waste's *material* infrastructures.

Made under such imperfect conditions, however, gestures must always themselves be imperfect, compromised practices. They were a way of apologizing for Palestinian sewage flows for which the gesturers knew they were not responsible. In this sense, the gestures were irksome affirmations of an Israeli "environmental imaginary" of the West Bank they believed to be false. An "environmental imaginary" is a way of perceiving a landscape's natural features and their relationship to its inhabitants. Diana Davis (2011, 15) uses the term to describe how Anglo-European imperial powers "portrayed the Middle East and North Africa as being on the edge of ecological viability or as a degraded landscape facing imminent disaster." She argues that this imaginary allowed imperial powers—who blamed local inhabitants for degrading their own landscapes—to tell stories "that facilitated imperial goals in the name of 'improvement' and environmental 'protection'" (15).[1] Beyond the fact that gestures cannot replace actual infrastructures to plug real waste leaks, gestures of apology and good intent reify the very Israeli environmental imaginaries that justify Israeli practices undermining the Authority's ability to control Palestinian wastes. They do so by framing Palestinian sewage—wherever it is—as pollution to the Israeli environment. By assuming responsibility for Palestinian sewage flows, Palestinian professionals dissimulated their lack of sovereign control over Palestinian waste.

Yet this chapter also shows that, since the phatic labor sewage professionals performed was both strategically aimed at plugging the leaks and an expression of a way of thinking they held to be only partially true, its repetition suggests that efforts to build a state through environmental projects in this twenty-first-century settler colonial context entail a form of consciousness George Orwell (1949, 32) calls "doublethink." Doublethink demands that a subaltern state builder have the "power of holding two contradictory beliefs in one's mind simultaneously, and accepting both of them." It involves a "tampering with reality" by telling deliberate lies while simultaneously believing them.

HOLES IN THE WALL

A Tulkarem resident sits on a toilet. He flushes. What is flushed travels downward through a network of pipes. The first, vertical pipe from the toilet bowl down is narrow. It meets with a horizontal pipe underground. The horizontal pipe has a wider diameter. It is part of a network that collects sewage from about half of Tulkarem's urban population. Tulkarem is a Palestinian city of roughly sixty-three thousand residents on the very western edge of the northern West Bank. The network is angled downward at a slight diagonal following the sloping incline of Tulkarem's land from East to West. The horizontal pipes' diagonal flows follow the hill's incline. They transport feces, urine, personal care products, and detergents under and across the city by gravitational pull. The network of pipes comes to a single end point, joining underground at the lowest, western edge of the city. They are brought together by an end-pipe with an even larger diameter. The downward incline of the network and the joining of several horizontal pipes' full of sewage generate pressure in the end-pipe.

The mouth of the end-pipe opens into a shallow ravine. Sewage gushes out onto rocks, dirt, and scraggly plants. The center of Tulkarem is in Area A. As sewage flows westward through the network or ground, it traverses Area B. At the point where some of it shoots out of the end-pipe, the wastewater arrives in Area C, where some of Tulkarem's agricultural lands are located. At the western edge of Area C, the sewage-filled ravine meets the Wall.

Israel built the piece of the Wall at Tulkarem in 1994, during the earliest phase of the Wall's construction. Now the Wall's concrete T-wall slabs stand about twenty-six feet tall and border the entire western side of Tulkarem. Tulkarem's downward slope toward the slabs makes the Wall look even taller at its base. At certain times of day the Wall casts a shadow over much of the area around it.

The combination of the slope and Wall makes water pool, sometimes flooding adjacent buildings when it rains. I remember visiting Tulkarem for the first time in January 2004. We braced our umbrellas sideways against freezing rain. Boys in sweaters played in puddles at the Wall's edge. I remember wondering if their laughs reached the ears of soldiers hidden in a military watchtower in the Wall above them. I read an article four years later that described Tulkarem Refugee Camp, where I had celebrated my birthday on that first visit and children had sung "Happy Birthday." The article had reported that during heavy rain in winter, an old sewage line connected unofficially to the stormwater drainage caused floods of dirty water, especially in the area of the school.

At the point where the river of sewage meets the Wall, the concrete barrier has an unusual physical feature: a hole beneath it. The hole is where the ravine, which is below ground level, carves out the ground. The hole is square and several feet wide but hard to see. An iron grate—there to prevent Palestinians from passing through it and into Israel—attracts detritus of various shapes and sizes. When it picks up enough force by virtue of its volume, the sewage river rushes between the crevices of trash and through the grate.

On a hot and sunny Monday, April 26, 2010, I stood on an open piece of land in a part of central Israel called Emek Hefer, which is also the name of a regional council composed of forty-four small communities with a total population of about thirty-five thousand Israelis. I stood at Emek Hefer's easternmost edge where Emek Hefer and Tulkarem would meet if it weren't for the Wall that divides them.

I squinted against the sun to see the hole in Tulkarem's part of the Wall from its other side. I was flanked by Ayelet and Umbarto. Ayelet was an Israeli employee at Friends of the Earth Middle East (FOEME, now EcoPeace), an environmental NGO with offices in Tel Aviv, Bethlehem, and Amman. She and Umbarto were taking me on a private tour of Emek Hefer, part of what a brochure Ayelet wrote with another Israeli colleague calls "the neighbors' path." The brochure told me that she takes groups on tours of this area to "raise public awareness of shared water and environment concerns of the communities" on both sides of the Wall.

Ayelet saw herself as a progressive Israeli. On our drive to the site, she was candid about her worries about raising two children in Israel. Her son had just begun his army service. She saw her work with FOEME as an antidote to the version of Israeli nationalism he would learn in the army. She believed in peace, she said. "If we all just realize we are drinking from the same bowl, maybe we can manage to live together in peace." Knowing the work of FOEME, I understood "we" to encompass Israelis and Palestinians. EcoPeace is at the forefront of what its proponents refer to as the "environmental peace-building" movement, premised on the idea that recognition of a common dependency among Israelis and Palestinians "on natural resources and a healthy environment facilitates cooperation between societies and nations and can therefore foster the process of peacemaking in conflict regions" (EcoPeace n.d.). It proposes that ecological features of the West Bank and Israel constitute what some call a "shared environment."

The word *bowl* referred to the Mountain Aquifer, an underground system of rocks, soil, and openings that straddles Israel and the West Bank from below. Imagine a Venn Diagram underground. Most (80 percent) of the aquifer's *recharge* area, where rainwater refills the aquifer by percolating through porous rocks, is in the West Bank. Most (80 percent) of the aquifer's *storage* area, where water is held, is inside Israel. Israel has been using about 80 percent of the water the aquifer provides.[2] And the aquifer provides Palestinians with all of their water, save rainwater they are able to collect in cisterns. As Israel prohibits most Palestinians from drilling wells in the aquifer, however, Palestinians end up buying about 50 percent of their water—which Israel draws from the aquifer—from the Israeli national water company, called Mekorot.

The concept of a shared environment emerged as a moral and conceptual frame—as an environmental imaginary—for this situation in the early 1990s and has become an increasingly powerful fund-raising tool and rallying cry. EcoPeace has received prestigious international awards for its work on environmental peace building, helping the latter become a worldwide, multi-billion-dollar industry. EcoPeace has exported its expertise from what it calls the "good water neighbors" model in the Israeli-Palestinian context to other "conflict" contexts such as Bosnia Herzegovina, Kosovo, Sri Lanka, India, and Pakistan.

Ayelet, Umbarto, and I stood silently for a few seconds, listening to the rush of the water. The hole in the Wall emitted frothy brown water into a stream (figure 13). It stank of rotten eggs. Ayelet stood holding her hands in front of her, squinting with me. The banks of the stream were covered in low, green plants. We had just driven over to this spot from the Yad Hannah wastewater treatment plant, which Umbarto was managing. He broke the silence. "Tulkarem's sewage is not very saline," he said. The chemical makeup of Tulkarem's sewage, which travels one hundred yards to Yad Hannah and is channeled into treatment ponds, determines whether and how the sewage can be used once treated.

Umbarto was like many Israeli environment professionals I met: he spoke with pride about Israel's wastewater innovations, repeating the much-touted statistic that Israel reclaims over 80 percent of its sewage for use in irrigation—more than any other country. Treated sewage makes up about one-quarter of Israel's water demand (E. Harris 2015; Lipchin 2017; Rinat 2015; Shuval 1977, 1980). After days in the ponds, Tulkarem's wastewater is transferred by pipes and pumps to a reservoir a few miles northwest of the plant. There Tulkarem's filtered sewage mixes with treated wastewater from the Israeli cities of Netanya and Kfar-Yona and from several Emek Hefer villages.

The next stop on our tour was the reservoir's lookout point, marked in the pamphlet as number 4 on the neighbors' path. This time I was alone with Ayelet, a slender woman in her forties whose expressions animated her wrinkles while she spoke. She had brought me to the visitors' center, a glass building with large posters explaining how the reservoir works in Hebrew and English. The large, marble hall was air-conditioned. We pulled out our cardigans. I read that Afikay Emek Hefer is the company that owns the reservoir. It runs one of the largest water return enterprises in the world.

Granot Cooperative is an Israeli agricultural cooperative and purchasing organization. It is one of the largest agricultural cooperatives in the world, sometimes annually making up to 3.5 billion NIS ($1 billion) in revenue. Granot purchases treated wastewater from Afikay Emek Hefer and distributes it to farmers in Emek Hefer and other northern Israeli councils. In this way the reservoir provides Israeli farmers with over seven hundred million cubic feet of free or cheaply priced water for irrigation annually and is one of a handful of reservoirs allowing 80 percent of Emek Hefer's farms to be irrigated with recycled wastewater.

Much of the water goes to Israeli farmers who cultivate avocados, Ayelet reminded me, recapping what Umbarto had said with her own proud smile.

FIGURE 13. Sewage spilling out of the West Bank through a hole in the Wall into Emek Hefer, 2010. Photograph by the author.

Wastewater treated to a secondary degree, she explained, is appropriate for the hearty and relatively less sensitive avocado plant. Avocados absorb treated wastewater while filtering it before elements toxic to human health reach the fruit. Most of Israel's avocado exports end up in Europe. The rest of the avocados go to Israel, which is one of the largest avocado consumers in the world.

By comparison with low-lying Israeli areas proximate to it, the West Bank's mountainous topography facilitates this "cross-border" arrangement, as FOEME's pamphlet calls it. The topography means that gravity pulls fresh groundwater—and wastewater—downward from the West Bank into Israel (see figure 1). The Palestinian city of Nablus, for example, is located east of Tulkarem, deeper in the northern West Bank and further from Israel. It is nestled between two mountains at an elevation of around 1,800 feet above sea level. Tel Aviv, which lies about 17.4 miles southwest of Nablus, stands at about 16 feet above sea level. Sewage from Nablus, like sewage from Tulkarem, flows downhill in the Nablus River, across the Green Line and into Israel. There the Nablus River meets the Alexander River, which leads to the Mediterranean Sea.

"THE POLLUTER PAYS"

During the tour I learned that there is another hole in the Wall in Emek Hefer, not far from the one that separates it from Tulkarem. The second hole is for sewage from Nablus, which is home to several industries, including soap factories and olive mills. Industries make Nablus sewage saline. Umbarto and his coworkers capture Nablus's sewage in a separate pond at the Yad Hannah plant. Emek Hefer cannot use it for irrigation because of its salinity. Its operators reinsert the treated wastewater into the Nablus River in summer to replenish the riverbed with cleaner water, which flows into the Alexander River inside Israel. "The Nablus River is the only effluent that gives life to the Alexander River in hot summer months," Ayelet said, raising her thin, brown eyebrows. Sewage from occupied Nablus keeps an Israeli river running year-round.

For the past fifteen years, Israel has treated one-third of the sewage produced in West Bank Palestinian cities in "off-site" infrastructures like Had Hannah inside Israel. Israel treats the sewage in five wastewater treatment plants located, like Yad Hannah, across the Green Line and adjacent to the Wall. The Drom Hasharon plant borders Qalqilya; the Shoket plant borders Hebron; the Hagihon plant borders Bir Nabala, al-Ram, and al-'Eizariya; and Hagilboa borders Jenin. This allows Israeli agricultural cooperatives to provide treated Palestinian sewage from across the West Bank as free or cheap water for irrigating industrial Israeli farms while Israeli ecologists in organizations like EcoPeace pump some of the water into Israel's river systems.

Israel funds the five plants with millions of dollars, money it withholds from the Palestinian Authority's Ministry of Finance by citing what is called the "polluter pays" principle. Developed in late twentieth-century environmental international law, the "polluter pays" principle frames the party responsible for generating pollution as the party responsible for paying for the damage done to the natural environment (de Sadeleer 2015; Grossman 2009; OECD 2008). Between 1996 and around 2010, Israel had already withheld over $47.6 million from Authority coffers for construction of wastewater treatment plants and for operation and maintenance costs for sewage infrastructures located inside Israel treating wastewater originating from the West Bank (PNA 2010b, 5).

Meanwhile, citing environmental and security arguments or giving no explanation at all, Israeli government officials and activist groups have blocked the Authority from building its own sewage networks and treatment plants. The Oslo Accords transferred responsibility over Palestinians' sewage to the Authority, placing much of the planning for sewage networks, data gathering, regulation of Palestinian industries' wastewater emissions, and farmers' use of wastewater for irrigation in the hands of Palestinian professionals working in the PWA. Yet wastewater infrastructures for Palestinian communities remain under scrutiny and control by Israelis.

The Accords filed sewage under the Water Article, known as Article 40, which frames all water-related issues in the West Bank as issues over which the Israeli government has a right to intervene no matter whether they arise in Area A, B, or C and no matter whether or not the Authority is technically responsible for them.[3] Article 40's premise was that the West Bank is part of the Israeli environment even if Israel must now "share" it with a new Palestinian government.

The Water Article determined that all major Palestinian wastewater infrastructures in the West Bank must be approved by the Israeli government and established the Joint Water Committee (JWC), where Israeli and Palestinian officials evaluate and vote on West Bank wastewater project applications from both the Authority and Israeli settlements. JWC votes must be unanimous for a project to move forward. This means the JWC gives Israeli government officials the opportunity to veto or delay Palestinian water projects.[4] If a Palestinian project is proposed for Area C, as are most waste infrastructures like landfills and treatment plants, which must be far from residential areas, the project must also be approved by the Civil Administration. Both the JWC and the Civil Administration are connected to the central Israeli government in Tel Aviv, including the ministries of infrastructure, environment, and transportation, where Israeli officials receive copies of proposed Palestinian projects and exchange opinions about Palestinian designs. Both the JWC and the Civil Administration are lobbied by politicians, settler organizations, corporations, and NGOs inside Israel.

This institutional arrangement is informed by, and helps bolster, the idea that the environment into which Palestinian sewage flows is shared by Israel and that Israel therefore has a stake in how the sewage is managed. It also posits Palestinians as "polluters," at least potentially, of an environment that is never entirely theirs and for whose pollution they owe Israel, as true custodian of that environment, remuneration.

Between the early 1990s and the 2010s the PWA submitted applications to construct large-scale wastewater treatment plants for each major Palestinian city, doing its part to support this same framework that both constrains the Authority and offers it pathways to infrastructural development. The PWA applied to build twenty-one new wastewater treatment plants, to rehabilitate one plant, to reuse wastewater from one existing plant, and to construct eight new sewage collection networks in twenty-one locations across the West Bank. By 2010 only four of these thirty-one proposals had been approved (PNA 2010b, 6).

MANAGING A SEEPING TIME BOMB

I spent much of my time in Ramallah with the Palestinians designing Authority sewage projects. A group of engineers, lawyers, and accountants, they worked together at the PWA office in al-Bireh, where a decidedly dry, human-sized statue of a blue water drop welcomes visitors entering the ministry's ground floor.

I first met Tarek Suleiman upstairs in his brightly lit office. He sat behind a large metal desk with a formica surface. His small stature meant that, from certain angles, he looked as if he was buried behind the stacks of binders that surrounded him. Posters encouraging water conservation with large, crossed-out images of a dripping, old-fashioned water tap were tacked to his walls. He was not a politician, he started by telling me. He was an engineer. He held an MSc in Water Engineering and Sanitation and had spent twenty years on sewage. He had an unassuming presence that didn't seem to correspond to the magnitude of responsibilities he shouldered as director of wastewater planning in the PWA. Tarek was what people in Palestine refer to, in English, as a "professional." He took orders from politicians like Dr. Shaddad Attili, then Palestinian water minister, and the Palestinian prime minister's office. While politicians envisioned national strategies for water and wastewater and negotiated water allocation with Israelis officials, Tarek worked behind the scenes to bring Palestinian centers on line with sewage networks and to connect networks to treatment plants.

Tarek's goal was ambitious. His job was to get the entire would-be state's sewage collection and treatment system built from scratch. Only around 30 percent of Palestinian households were connected to a sewage network. No rural communities had networks. And only one semifunctioning plant treated any Palestinian sewage. Tarek and his colleagues had been trying to build wastewater infrastructures for Palestinian communities for two decades and had been largely unsuccessful. Ninety-eight percent of occupied Palestinians' sewage still spilled out of homes and factories and flowed, untreated, through neighborhoods and into valleys.

Raw sewage percolates through karstic carbonate rocks with high recharge rates and into the Mountain Aquifer. Karstic topographies are areas usually constituted when soluble rocks like limestone, dolomite, and gypsum dissolve from rain with acidic features in it. They are characterized by sinkholes and caves because they tend to drain water downwards easily (Popperl 2018). Rain causes fissures in the rocks as they dissolve. Palestinians' sewage percolates vertically downward, and, where the underground aquifer's passageways provide openings, it flows downhill and horizontally from the hills of the West Bank into the lowlands of Israel.

As chapter 3 demonstrated, the effects of constant sewage flows can be devastating for the Palestinian communities that Authority officials are charged with governing but whom they are unable or unwilling to help. Yet Tarek and his colleagues spent as much time consumed by thoughts about what Israelis thought about Palestinian sewage as about the experiences of Palestinian communities. When they thought about the diameter of sewage networks they wanted to build under a city like Nablus, for example, they also thought about whether Israeli soldiers, settlers, government officials, and environmental activists would agree to its dimensions. When they thought of drawing up designs for a wastewater treatment plant to filter contaminants out of sewage in hopes of reusing the water for irrigation on Palestinian farms, they also thought about whether employees in the Tel Aviv Israeli ministries of environment and infrastructure would think the designs would produce an effluent they considered clean enough. This kind of thinking constitutes another version of "doublethink," where the professionals had to always think doubly about who cared about Palestinian sewage.

Tarek and his colleagues read English and Arabic translations—and, if they could, the Hebrew originals—of articles in which Israeli officials and environmental activists accused them of environmental pollution. They read articles calling Palestinian sewage "political pollution" tantamount to terrorism. They read that members of the settler movement set on undermining the state-building project of which the Palestinian professionals were a part attributed Palestinian sewage to an Arab strategy of environmental destruction.

At PWA headquarters, they received letters from Israeli ministries in which they were informed that, to deal with Palestinian pollution, Israel had deducted millions of dollars from the taxes Israel collected on the Authority's behalf. As one Palestinian representative working in the United Nations Development Programme (UNDP) explained, "The letter the PWA employees receive reads like this: 'You have _____ million dollars. We deduct _____ on the Ministry's behalf, we deduct _____, and we deduct _____, for the cleaning of the pollution produced by your communities. Therefore you have _____ left. Take it.'" Tarek and his colleagues knew that Israelis in Israel and in settlements were daily calculating the volume of sewage Palestinians produced. Israelis like Umbarto were testing it for chemical components and debating how it should be dealt with, usually out of earshot of the Authority.

For Tarek and his colleagues, Palestinian sewage—and waste siege more broadly—was never just a Palestinian problem. It was always also an Israeli problem, and that fact became a problem for people like Tarek. Waste siege was not just a material and moral challenge for and among Palestinians; it was also a challenge to Palestinians because of what it meant to their occupiers that it "leaked."

The word *leak* indicates a condition of disrepair, incompleteness, or brokenness. A leak is a passage through a membrane that someone does not intend, whether that someone is the party who designed the membrane, the party who is meant to control the substance on the initial side of the boundary, or the party that is on the "receiving" side of the boundary. The Israeli actors about whom

Tarek and his colleagues were forced to think had different ideas of that membrane's location. For some, like Umbarto, it was the Green Line. When sewage crossed that line from the West Bank into Israel, it constituted an offense to the Israeli environment. For others, leakage emitted directly from Palestinians' bodies. From the moment when a Palestinian shat, the material excreted became a matter of Israeli concern. Article 40 of the Oslo Agreements framed Palestinian bodies as the origin of the leak: the open place in a boundary through which a dangerous substance passed. Tarek and his colleagues were keepers of that boundary.

For Tarek and his colleagues, the inability to contain flows of the occupied populations' sewage constituted a leak for three additional reasons. First, Palestinian sewage leaks translated into financial leaks for the would-be state's institutions because Israel deducted sewage-treatment funds from the Authority's budget. Second, sewage contaminated existing water resources upon which Palestinians relied. Third, without infrastructures, Palestinians lost their own sewage to gravity. Leakage prevented Tarek and the PWA from recycling the wastes for the Palestinian population. Wastewater treatment plants would allow the PWA to infuse the treated sewage into the Palestinian economy. For Tarek and his colleagues, Palestinians' treatment of their own wastewater was the only feasible method for generating water in the absence of a larger freshwater allocation by Israel. The other, much more expensive and complicated option, was desalination. It was complicated partly because Palestinians lacked exclusive control over any saltwater source, depending on agreement from Israel, Egypt, and Jordan for access to saltwater for desalination.[5]

The Authority had been trying to cope with its artificial rise in water scarcity—artificial because it was a result of Israeli restrictions on Palestinian water extraction—by reallocating water meant for agriculture to communities for drinking. Palestinians produced upwards of 2,472 cubic feet of wastewater annually. Treating that would allow farmers to use treated wastewater instead of water from the West Bank Aquifer, freeing up aquifer water for drinking. And it would make more water available for more lucrative crops requiring irrigation. Treating wastewater was a way of using Palestinian bodies to generate usable water as an alternative to a political settlement with Israel. Untreated Palestinian sewage flows into the West Bank landscape constituted a leak in the available fresh water that sustained the population.

In 2006, FOEME published a report titled *A Seeping Time Bomb: Pollution of the Mountain Aquifer by Sewage*. The report treats sewage as a "time bomb" because it is a threat to the Mountain Aquifer, "the largest and most significant groundwater reservoir in the region" (Tagar, Keinan, and Bromberg 2004, 6). For Tarek, the fact that almost all Palestinian sewage flowed out of Authority-controlled areas was also a time bomb. He was breathless as he invited me to sit for what would be over an hour during our first meeting in his office. His understated, generous demeanor encouraged a kind of respectful chaos around him. Young people peeked their heads into his doorway. Students from Birzeit and al-Quds universities often interned with him and shadowed him, he told me. While I was there, Nada, a Canadian-Palestinian master's student helping him write a report, stopped in to say hello.

The report Tarek and Nada were preparing was titled *Status of Wastewater Treatment Plant Projects in the West Bank*. It documented the life histories of the twenty-two projects. Tarek turned the screen of his desktop computer toward me to show me a table. It listed each project's "date of submission to JWC," the Joint Water Committee, in one column. The Authority had submitted sixteen of the listed wastewater projects for JWC approval. Some had been "pending approval" for months, others for up to fifteen years. If the JWC approved a project, twelve different departments in the Civil Administration had to agree as well. Some projects in Tarek's report were "Approved by JWC/Pending in Civil Administration." The rest, he said, were soon to be submitted.

Transferring a PDF of the report from his desktop onto my USB drive, Tarek explained that its purpose was to "try to prove the history of delays." He was wearing a suit jacket and button-down shirt. His sleeves were slightly too long. He pulled them back nervously as if he were going to jump out of the suit. With each day that passed without a network or plant being built, another several cubic feet of sewage spilled out into the ground. Raw sewage flooded Palestinian cities and homes. In 2008 the BBC ran a story about an eleven-day-old girl in Nablus. She had been bitten on the face by a rat carried into her house on one of the many occasions when "a filthy, stinking, brown deluge ha[d] swept up to the first floor of the house" (Franks 2008). Her thirty-three-year-old father owned a sweetshop. Her mother took care of her at home. They carried their daughter, her face bloodied from the bites, to the hospital, where she stayed for two days. At the time of the article's publication the doctors did not yet know if the bites would scar. While I was living in Jenin, a trickle of sewage ran along streets in winter.

Hay al-Basateen, the flat neighborhood where Jenin's exit pipe once connected to a functioning treatment plant, smelled perpetually of sewage. Friends with homes and businesses in this former watermelon field kept windows closed, preferring to pay the expense of using electric fans.

Over the next two years, Tarek became the Authority employee with whom I spent the most time. His desk was covered in binders and documents pending his signature. The more I saw him, the more I learned how urgently Tarek felt about his work. His breathlessness did not go away as the months passed. An urgency unfamiliar to me from my time in municipal offices in Shuqba, Jenin, Nablus, and al-Bireh shot through Tarek's daily schedule. He worked eighteen-hour days, six days a week. He couldn't leave emails unanswered; he was too impatient. He woke up every day to pray at 4:00 a.m. He went back to sleep and awoke again at 6:00 a.m. in time to be at work by 7:15 a.m. He was known among his colleagues, many of whom arrived around 8:30 a.m. and left around 2:00 p.m., for arranging meetings at annoyingly early and late hours.

A year into shadowing him, I accompanied Tarek on a trip to discuss a treatment plant for Nablus. We drove in his car. He was in an unusually foul mood. Germany was funding the plant. German representatives were attending the meeting. Not realizing how sensitive a subject it was, I asked what donors added to his work other than funds. "What I need is time!" he exclaimed, swerving to pass a car and kicking up dust around our open windows. "I don't need someone to tell me what to do. I *know* what to do!" he added, referring to the foreign consultants who often absorbed much of the foreign aid.[6]

Tarek's fast pace was an inverse correlate of the molasses-like pace of trying to get wastewater infrastructures built and then operational. No project was yet online. Another two decades of sewage had spilled into the landscape of the last remaining piece of territory that Palestinians could hope to call their own. Wastewater infrastructures anywhere in the world take time to build. And they tend to be built piecemeal, creating uneven geographies of sewage-related "development" (Anand 2017; Farmer 2017). But Tarek's travels abroad had shown him that projects in the Occupied Territory were particularly slow. The section below describes effort to mitigate slowness by turning to infrastructures Israelis were likely to view as environmentally friendly. To explain the need for approval, the section that follows depicts how Israelis framed the relationship between Palestinians' environmental friendliness, sewage, and politics.

CROSSING A QUESTIONABLE BOUNDARY TO
BUILD QUESTIONABLE INFRASTRUCTURES

In 2007 Authority officials had approached the UNDP to request support to build underground wastewater networks for three Palestinian villages. Like Tulkarem, the three villages, Baqa al-Sharqiyah, Habla, and Barta'a al-Sharqiyah, abut the Green Line demarcating the northern West Bank from Israel. Officials proposed to connect each village's underground grid to a sewage network in the Israeli town closest on the other side of the Green Line. The three West Bank communities had been disposing of sewage in mostly unlined cesspits that seeped into the ground. Untreated sewage also flowed into the Wadi Abu al-Nar River and from there into neighboring Israeli towns. Authority officials proposed that a wastewater treatment plant be operated inside the Israeli towns to catch and treat the sewage. The UNDP agreed to liaise between the Authority and the Israeli government and asked Japan for funding, receiving $6.2 million.

When I accompanied Tarek and Majdi, a water pricing expert, on a trip up to the three villages and two Israeli towns in June 2011, the project was in its planning stages. We met outside the PWA building next to the water drop statue. It was 7:00 a.m., only fifteen minutes before Tarek's usual arrival time, but Majdi was grumpy; it was about an hour and a half before his day began. We had to get an early start because part of the trip was in Israel and would involve crossing checkpoints. Samer, our Jerusalemite taxi driver, leaned against his white taxi smoking a cigarette, his body hiding Hebrew writing on the door. We needed a taxi because Authority cars are not permitted inside Israel. We needed a taxi licensed *in Israel* (i.e., not a Palestinian taxi) because Palestinian-plated cars are also prohibited from driving in Israel. Majdi and Tarek both had West Bank IDs and could not drive an Israeli-plated car.

The four of us piled into the taxi and headed northwest. Our first destination was Barta'a East, which falls in the West Bank but on the western, Israeli side of the Wall. In this sense it is the inverse of Kufr 'Aqab, a part of Jerusalem that is trapped on the eastern side of the Wall we encountered in chapter 3. It would take us three hours to reach the village, with much of the drive on Route 6 in Israel, which hugs the outer boundary of the West Bank to the Wall's west.

Ni'lin checkpoint separating the West Bank from Israel was the same checkpoint I had crossed with Jenin's *rabish* traders. Samer slowed and stopped at one of the turnstiles. A fresh-faced soldier approached the car on his side. It was strange to think that we were on official Authority business, on our way to meetings about a multi-million dollar, Japanese-funded project, some of which involved the Israeli government—the mayors of Baqa West and Barta'a West—and United Nations representatives, and that we were on a delegation to help provide sanitation to the would-be citizens of the would-be state, yet our small, white taxi bore no government markings. The soldier had no way of knowing our car from any other taxi transporting passengers on their way to a day at the beach.

The soldier tapped the glass for us to lower our windows. She took my passport and Tarek's and Majdi's thin green IDs. They unfolded crisp, white papers: special permits to enter Israel that they had obtained from the Civil Administration just two days before. She took her time scrutinizing them. She walked away, taking the papers. She returned a while later, her machine gun swinging by her side. Majdi smiled up at her through the front passenger window, addressing her in Hebrew. She smiled back, said something, and nodded while waving us through.

We exhaled. The highway seemed endless in front of us. Apropos of the UNDP "Project Fact Sheet" that Majdi had handed me when we had started driving, I mentioned that Tahkeem, a UNDP representative working on the project, had said it was going to be a model for future transboundary agreements between the Authority and Israel around water and wastewater. The project's aim, the sheet stated, was "to promote peace building through cross boundary cooperation in wastewater management in order to enhance the communities' wellbeing and security and to protect [sic] shared environment and natural resources." Majdi scoffed, delivering a biting response: "How are we going to do cross-boundary cooperation if we don't have boundaries, or we don't know them?" He was referring to the fact that Israel has never declared its borders and that the status of the West Bank as occupied territory means the Authority is not yet a sovereign state and also does not therefore yet have political boundaries—the kind of boundaries the fact sheet implied were being "crossed" by the project.

Though the Authority had initiated the project, Authority bureaucrats in charge of implementing their end of it were deeply ambivalent about it. They were glad the project would prevent three villages' worth of sewage from continuing to pollute their own agricultural areas. But the three villages together had a total of only roughly fifteen thousand inhabitants. They represented a tiny fraction of the Authority's much larger problem.

Clutching his copy of the fact sheet, Majdi made a lengthy and impassioned speech. Where they really needed wastewater treatment, West Bank Palestinians were not getting it. He reminded us that, according to FOEME research, all five streams that Palestinians in the West Bank had historically relied upon for drinking water and irrigation were now flowing with sewage. In Tulkarem, ten miles south of the Baqas, groundwater was people's only source of water. In areas close to Tulkarem and Qalqiliya, wells tapping into the aquifer had been closed for reaching levels of pollution above safe drinking standards (Reidy 2013). Palestinian universities reported that a large percentage of springs contained concentrations of coliform bacteria exceeding World Health Organization standards for drinking water.

Through the frame of environmental peace building that assumes two "sides," the project we were traveling to promote prioritized the outer margins of the West Bank, where the Palestinian population tended to be less densely located. The Authority's application to build a treatment plant for Tulkarem, a major city, had been pending JWC approval since 1995. The German development agency (KfW) had pledged 20 million euros to build it. But the delay had prevented their disbursal. This project between the three Palestinian villages and the Israeli towns would allow the status quo to continue. It would allow most occupied Palestinians' sewage to continue contaminating Palestinians' immediate surroundings and would do nothing to help Palestinians reuse their own wastewater. Israel would continue to control Palestinian sewage.

ISRAELI EYES ON PALESTINIAN SEWAGE

The project made sense for other reasons, however, some of which I understood from comments and conversations I observed while spending time with the Authority employees still working on the project four years after the initial proposal. Perhaps the most important reason was that the initiative was an opportunity for them to perform care for the environment in terms legible both to Israeli and to international actors.

About a month before I had first met Tarek and a year before our visit to the three villages, Israel had shut off the main water source for agriculture in Bardalah, a Jordan Valley village in the northeastern West Bank. It was vegetable harvesting season, and fruits were in bloom. Three thousand greenhouses in Bardalah required irrigation. The water cutoff threatened to destroy tens of thousands of citrus and palm trees, and with them the livelihoods of more than 1,900 village residents. Bardalah received its water from pipes that Israel controlled. Employees at Mekorot, Israel's water company, could turn the "tap" on and off at will without Palestinian involvement.[7] Nader Thawabteh, a Bardalah lawyer representing the village, and Fat'hi Ikdeirat, a campaign coordinator for Save the Jordan Valley, gave interviews implying that the cutoff constituted collective harassment of the community as well as a way to divert more water to Israeli settlements.

Prominent Palestinian and Israeli media outlets argued that the cutoff was Israeli "retaliation" for Palestinians' waste flows through and out of the West Bank. Journalists pointed to the fact that the water cutoff had come four days after Israeli infrastructure minister Uzi Landau had threatened to restrict West Bank Palestinians' water supply if no sewage treatment plants were installed there. "'They get clean water from us,'" he had said on Israeli Army Radio, "'and in return they give us sewage. This destroys nature, and I would say that this is the way that wicked people behave'" (Ma'an 2010).

Landau's statement was a boldfaced acknowledgment of Israel's power over Palestinians' relationship to their environment and bodies. It revealed that everything from the way Israelis represented Palestinians to whether Israel allowed them access to life-sustaining resources hinged on Palestinians' ability to control their own waste flows. As Israel's infrastructure minister, Landau knew a lot about Palestinian sewage. He would have seen Authority plans to build wastewater treatment plants and sewage networks connecting buildings to new plants in the West Bank.

And when a public statement like Landau's was launched into the ether it was the job of a handful of people on the PWA's third floor, including Tarek, to take special note. Tarek had opened a desk drawer and pulled out a paper a few minutes into our first meeting. It was an article about the Landau incident in Arabic. He handed it to me. "They're threatening to cut off our water if Palestinians don't stop polluting the aquifer," he said, shuffling a stack of papers around on his desk, clearly upset. In the course of our conversation I realized that, for him, any Israeli or foreign statement about flows of West Bank Palestinians' waste, and especially connections between flows and Palestinians' access to resources, was a matter of personal as well as professional concern. It was as if Landau had sent Tarek a personal, yet very public, letter.

Landau had been quoted in the *Jerusalem Post* as saying, "'It is infuriating that we give the Palestinians fresh water and yet they do not adequately treat their sewage and instead pollute our shared environment'" (Waldocks 2010). Tarek and his colleagues paid attention to several details about a statement like this. One was the fact that a major Israeli political figure was reminding them that their work was being watched. They paid attention to his use of the term *shared environment* and his characterization of Palestinians as "wicked people" and to the implicit depiction of Israelis as victims of Palestinian aggression. Landau was a major player in deciding whether Palestinian sanitary infrastructures were built. As an Israeli government official, he also had the ear of the international community.

Tarek felt his ability to do his job depended on what people like Landau thought of him and his colleagues as much as it did on what they thought of designs Tarek presented to them. Israelis most directly empowered to offer or to withhold approval were Civil Administration employees and Israeli ministry officials like Landau. But since Oslo other Israelis had also become increasingly empowered to intervene. For example, representatives and employees of the settlement Municipal Environmental Associations of Judea and Samaria, which we encountered in chapters 1 and 3, had been monitoring environmental issues in the West Bank since the mid-1990s. They spoke for settlement municipalities that sought the West Bank's total absorption into Israel.

I had numerous conversations with Avi, a leader of the Judea (southern West Bank) association, between 2011 and 2017. Avi said he spoke with the Civil Administration's environment department, which evaluated Palestinian wastewater projects, "every day." "We give each other assignments," he added, explaining daily collaboration between their offices. "They ask me to check if a truck they saw with waste in the West Bank has a license," for example. Avi was brought in as an environmental expert when Civil Administration committees met to evaluate Palestinian infrastructure proposals. He had the ear of central Israeli government officials and on environmental issues represented settlers to the Israeli parliament (Knesset), lobbying Israeli politicians. His association was able to stop construction of the proposed Authority-run landfill for Ramallah in Rammun, for example (Stamatopoulou-Robbins 2014). On the phone in 2017, Avi recalled that he had sat in meetings with Landau during the period when Landau threatened to cut off Palestinians' water. "In matters of wastewater,"

Avi told me, hinting that his association might have had something to do with Landau's statements, "[Landau] was a minister who was willing to hear what we had to say about it."

I asked Avi to introduce me to the Civil Administration's environment department in Beit El, a military base, a settlement, and the West Bank's Civil Administration headquarters. Though Beit El was walking distance from places where I spent time, such as the Authority's ministry of local government, I had no way of gaining access without an Israeli connection. Avi drove me over to Beit El one morning on his way to visit. He brought me to Assaf's office, where two metal desks were arranged in an L-shape cluttered by binders and loose papers, yellow Post-it notes, and an ancient-looking desktop computer. The binders looked familiar: they were environmental impact assessments of Palestinian proposals for infrastructures in Area C, including wastewater treatment plant projects Tarek and his colleagues had submitted.

Assaf read all environment-related Palestinian proposals. He was a clean-shaven thirty-something environmental engineer with decent English. He wore a kippah, a brimless cap worn by religious Jewish men. He occasionally looked down at my recorder but seemed comfortable, especially after stating that he didn't think our conversation about environmental standards was political. He spoke "technically," he said, recalling the word people used for Tarek. His office required the same standards in the West Bank as the Israeli government did in Israel. The reason: "Environmental issues have no borders. . . . The highest standards we need to have in Israel are the same standards here." That Assaf would have sent copies of Palestinian project proposals to Landau's office in Tel Aviv made management of West Bank Palestinian sewage a borderless practice, while applying Israeli standards to those projects crossed an implicit boundary in an effort to elevate the infrastructural standards of the colonized to the levels of the metropolis.

GIFTS AND REFUSALS

On the phone several years later, Avi called Landau "a very honest and good man." His words reminded me of language I had heard other Israelis use about people working on the environment. Among them was Sarah Ozacky-Lazar, who ran the joint Israeli-Palestinian Environment and Regional Sustainability Forum at the Van Leer Institute in Jerusalem between 2008 and 2012. Established in 1959, the Van Leer is a prominent research center for education, philosophy, society, and culture. When I spoke with Sarah at the Van Leer two months before the Landau incident, she told me that Beni Elbaz, director of the Civil Administration's environment department and Assaf's boss, "is a bureaucrat," meaning he was not an environmental expert like the people the Van Leer tended to train and host. "But," she said, "he has good intentions!" To explain, Sarah told a story from 2008. A group of environmental experts from Israel and Palestine had gone on a West Bank tour to observe Israeli construction waste dumping there. They caught an Israeli driver red-handed. "Beni took it seriously," she said. "He put huge signs at checkpoints. He caught drivers and fined them. Now he said this phenomenon is almost gone." She smacked her hand down on her desk, performing how impressed she was as she delivered the punch line. "He used to say: 'When it comes to the environment, I'll cooperate with everyone—*even Hamas!*"

For Sarah, Beni's willingness to cooperate showed the way forward for Israel/Palestine. It was the kind of approach inspiring her work at the Van Leer, which had a reputation among Israelis as a haven for voices critical of Israeli policy—for positions that complicated dominant political divisions. She believed the environment was "the most important field that Israelis and Palestinians can cooperate on, *despite politics*." Like many in the growing environmental peace-building movement of which she saw herself as a part, she believed the environment could unite people with different political positions.

Sarah contrasted Beni's willingness to be what she called nonpolitical with the Authority's behavior, offering an example of the latter's unwillingness to collaborate even with well-intentioned Israelis. "The [Fatah-dominated] Palestinian Authority won't let the Civil Administration work with the heads of Palestinian municipalities directly, since many of them are Hamas," she said. She hoped Palestinians would emulate approaches like Beni's.

Sarah was suggesting that Authority officials and the Israeli military were equal players on an equal playing field and that the former were not playing by the latter's civil rules. She was also indignant at what she saw as Palestinians' refusal of the Israeli gift of civility, their "willingness to cooperate." Authority refusal to allow Palestinian municipalities to work with the Israeli army appeared as an indigenous rejection of a state "gift," like the rejection of American and Canadian passports by indigenous North Americans. I use quotation marks around "gift" because, as Audra Simpson (2014) has demonstrated, such gifts are perceived as gifts only by the colonial state and its representatives.

Where waste's relationship to the environment was concerned, accepting the colonial state's "gift" of civility was twinned with being a good environmentalist and with being committed to seeing beyond political boundaries. Sarah collaborated with FOEME and was planning events on what she referred to as the "borderlessness" of the environment, her understanding of what that meant echoing Ayelet's at FOEME. For Sarah there were political borders. But in the words of an event poster she was preparing for later that year and echoing Assaf's formulation, "Environmental pollution respects no borders." To be an environmentalist was to assert borderlessness.

Deemphasizing political boundaries like the Green Line and managing the problem of borderless pollution demanded that those living in zones of pollution work together. The epiphany-like realization that environmental peace builders like Sarah and Ayelet liked to repeat they had had was that Israelis and Palestinians found themselves in that zone and should set reducing pollution together as a common goal. The next logical step seemed not to require explanation. Cooperation was a form of peace building. The more Israelis and Palestinians worked together, the closer the two peoples would be to solving the issues dividing them. To refuse to work together on environmental issues was, therefore, to reject an available path toward peace. With Palestinians' nontreatment of their sewage framed as an act causing immediate, physical harm to Israelis, Palestinians lacking intent to take care of the environment implied a lack of good intentions both toward Israel and toward peace.

It was this set of assumptions, and the presupposition that Palestinians might not have the *capacity* to cooperate, that framed my Palestinian interlocutors' efforts while engaging with Israelis. Avi's description of Landau contrasted with the words both he and Landau had used about Palestinians and their waste. In response to my asking about Israeli nuclear dumping in the West Bank, Avi scoffed, asserting forcefully that Palestinians suffered from an "eastern imagination." His words previewed an article that would be published nine days later in *Arutz Sheva*, an Israeli newspaper associated with the settler movement. The article was titled "Arab Imagination: Sewage Wars." It described what the author called "a 19-mile-long pool of sewage water stretching from the Arab city of Ramallah all the way to Israel's Modi'in Illit," a settlement. In addition to normalizing the presence of Modi'in settlement, the author used the word *imagination* to undermine Palestinian Information Center (PIC) employees' argument that Israeli occupation authorities were trying to "damage the Palestinian environment with wastewater of illegal settlements in the West Bank" (Sones 2017).

Prominent Israeli politicians had been connecting sewage and terrorism for years. In 1996, for example, Sallah Tarif, chairman of the Knesset's Interior and Environment Committee, told the *Jerusalem Post* that Palestinians' sewage was "political pollution. They are using sewage as ammunition," he said, calling "the damage to health from the untreated sewage" "potentially as damaging as terror attacks" (Jerusalem Post 1996). A few weeks after I spoke with Avi, *Arutz Sheva* published a series of articles on Palestinian sewage. One quoted Avi's colleague, who said Palestinians' sewage threatened settlers' health (Polon 2017). Another argued that "Israel has tried to help the PA [the Authority] solve the problem, but the PA refuses to cooperate with Israel," calling the PA's behavior part of an "Arab environmental destruction strategy" (Sones 2017).

For Israelis who subscribed to this framing, Palestinian reluctance to cooperate on the environment stood in contrast to Israeli willingness to "do" things. Avi and I discussed negotiations between the Authority and the Civil Administration around payment for Israeli settlers dumping wastes at al-Minya, the Authority-run landfill in Hebron that Avi's association monitored. He told me the two parties were coming to an agreement to allow settlers to pay the Authority for using the landfill through a third party—possibly a Palestinian company based in Jerusalem. Avi admitted he was surprised. "[Palestinians] surprise me every time because of their reluctance to do anything." By "do anything" Avi might have meant taking care of the environment or working with Israelis. Within the discourse that conflated environmental cooperation with "good intentions" toward peace, the distinction was inconsequential.

Equating environmentalism with peacefulness embroiled sewage in a system of gift exchange. Landau had commented seven years prior that "they get clean water from us and in return they give us sewage." He had framed Israeli extraction and sale to Palestinians of the water beneath the land they inhabited as an Israeli gift, and Palestinian sewage—the water produced after bodies and industries consumed fresh water—as that gift's unwelcome, "wicked" reciprocation. I raised this with Avi, who remembered the statements. "Yes," Avi said, his tone implying agreement. "[Palestinians] want more water. But more water will become wastewater. *That's why we won't give them more water*. Because the Mountain Aquifer is in danger." Avi's version of Landau's statement implied that a population was undeserving of more water if it did not control or mitigate the effects of water's transformation into waste.[8] Deserving water depended on control over water's outputs. Avi's comment signaled that he, too, was watching for signs of Palestinians' deservingness of water, signs that could include showing *good intentions* to control waste flows or control of the flows themselves.

GESTURES TOWARD THE "SHARED ENVIRONMENT"

Tarek, Majdi, Samer, and I arrived in Baqa West around midday. We pulled into a densely populated area. Majdi read out Hebrew from the building signs, showing off what he had learned in Israeli prison. "We're arriving in Baqa al-Gharbiyah [West]. In Israel," he said. "In the part that is occupied from the *Palestinian nation*," Tarek retorted, elbowing me. Turning over his left shoulder from the front passenger seat, Majdi responded with a phrase he had used several times that day: "You see how history is stronger than geography?" With the word *history*, Majdi invoked the historic presence and unity of Palestinian communities as they had lived in Ottoman and British Mandate Palestine, before Palestinians were exiled en masse and before the Green Line had been drawn, and affirmed Tarek's referral to Baqa West as territory seized from the Palestinian nation. It was a nod toward a sensibility many Palestinians share: the imperative to remember the national history and ongoing experience of exile.[9] It was also Majdi's way of issuing another refusal: the refusal to use the language of "sides" upon which the "transboundary" project they were implementing was premised.

We alighted in front of the Baqa West municipal building. Two high-carriage jeeps—one for a group of UNDP representatives and another for a group of Japanese representatives—were already parked. The donor representatives descended out of shiny, spacious vehicles with tinted windows and logos on their doors, hoods, and roofs (see figure 14). (The markings on the hood and roof were intended to protect international passengers from Israeli assault helicopters and planes.) The scene threw into pitiful relief the dusty white sedan with Hebrew writing on it from which Majdi, Tarek, and I descended, our bodies squished and faces squinting, small indignities on a continuum with territorial seizure and exile.

Yet as the day's meetings proceeded I saw that for Tarek and Majdi the project that brought them there was an attempt at reversing some of those indignities, if indirectly, imperfectly, and too slowly. For them the Baqa, Barta'a, and Habla wastewater proposal constituted a Palestinian gesture toward the environment as defined by Israeli actors. It might get them closer, they imagined, to building a state—or at least something resembling one—because it allowed them to appear fit to govern by allowing them to perform willingness to cooperate with Israel. And a gesture toward the environment qua Israel might open channels permitting wastewater treatment plants in Palestinian cities and stemming the tide of counterproposals—for example, from settlers—to capture more Palestinian sewage and divert it to Israeli settlements.

Avi had been close to convincing the Israeli government to construct wastewater treatment plants on the outskirts of Palestinian cities, in Area C. He had presented Landau with proposals for treating Palestinian sewage unilaterally—without the Authority's involvement or approval. "Landau is the only one who agreed for Israel to take over the wastewater treatment of the Palestinians if they don't do anything about it," he said. "Since water is subject to gravity . . . the sewage eventually comes to a point where you can catch it and treat it." If Palestinians within Areas A or B, where the Authority had some control, did not catch it in wastewater treatment plants, sewage would travel outside the Authority's jurisdiction into Area C.

FIGURE 14. Palestinian Authority–proposed sewage pipeline under construction to transport sewage from the West Bank Palestinian village of Baqa al-Sharqiyah to an Israeli plant in Baqa al-Gharbiyah, 2011. A photographer documents Authority officials, Japanese and UNDP representatives, and Israeli municipal engineers discussing the designs. Photograph by the author.

Israel had held elections before Landau could execute Avi's proposed plan. But as the idea of a shared environment had taken hold, the prospect of protecting the West Bank's environment across any type of political boundary, even if it were between Areas B and C, had gained appeal in Israeli and donor circles, circles upon whom Tarek and his colleagues relied for support.

The idea that Palestinians were "unwilling to cooperate" opened up room for maneuver for members of the Israeli settler movement, like Avi, who wished to take over management of Palestinian wastes. It made the idea of constructing Israeli-run plants at the edges of Palestinian cities appear commonsensical. Such plants would catch Palestinian waste closer to its place of production than those like Emek Hefer across the Green Line, ostensibly requiring shorter pipes and therefore less vulnerable infrastructures. They would protect groundwater resources from exposure to contamination while allowing settlers to turn Palestinian excrement into a resource for irrigation and groundwater rehabilitation projects such as river replenishment.

The Authority's proposed three villages' wastewater project could potentially delay the success of campaigns like Avi's by serving as a gesture of "willingness to cooperate" in several ways. For one, it was an Authority initiative, unlike Yad Hannah and the other four "off-site" plants, which Israel built unilaterally, and offered Israelis direct help. The three-village project proposed collecting Palestinian wastewater that flowed into Israel, creating a physical barrier between the sewage and the ground in the form of a network. The Israeli-run treatment plant to which the Authority proposed to channel sewage from Baqa East, Barta'a East, and Habla was in Baqa West. The plant did not have enough wastewater to function properly, so the Authority's proposal offered technical support for Baqa West municipality, which was concerned with maximizing the plant's efficiency. Second, the project gave Tarek and his colleagues a rare opportunity to call meetings with Israeli government officials, even if the latter were low in rank (relative to Tarek and Majdi) and even if they represented only Palestinian communities with Israeli citizenship, like Baqa West.

The Baqa West municipal headquarters was a modest, three-story, concrete building. The meeting took place on the second floor in a room occupied by two large white plastic tables surrounded by plastic chairs. Our group entered and scooted around the tables' perimeter to take seats. A rotund, white-haired man stepped in with a younger woman holding a clipboard. A Palestinian-Israeli municipal employee leaned over to inform Tarek and Majdi in Arabic that this was the mayor.

It was palpable, at least for those of us who had arrived from Ramallah, that we were meeting the mayor on terms that were rare because they were set by occupied Palestinians and approved by a UN agency and a powerful foreign government. We were there not to apply for permission but with a proposal in hand—an offering. Majdi and Tarek exchanged greetings in Arabic with Baqa West's municipal engineers delegated to work on building the piped connection between the three Palestinian villages and Baqa's treatment plant. Differences in their Arabic accents signaled decades of separation between this Palestinian community and those of the West Bank. The Japanese consul, who was fluent in classical Arabic, joined in with his own formal, stylized greetings as the Jewish Israeli mayor, who did not speak Arabic and was not from Baqa, looked on.

The meeting in Baqa was also rare because Tarek and Majdi's offer was unprecedented. Since the 1990s the Authority had been refusing to connect Palestinian waste infrastructures inside the West Bank with settlement infrastructures, one of Israel's conditions for approving Palestinian projects. If infrastructural work was to be national work, it could not legitimize settlements through material connectedness. That the proposal sought connection with Israeli infrastructures was thus a strong gesture of "cooperation."

The Authority-proposed project also offered Tarek and his colleagues the chance to engage Israelis in meetings under the watchful eyes of international donors (figure 14). Tarek was the person to whom international consultants were often assigned as outside advisers on what technologies to use to treat different types of wastewater. The Baqa project departed from these dynamics in offering him an opportunity to be the one reaching out to donors and in staging opportunities for him to show donors how he related to Israelis.

The meeting was conducted in heavily accented English. The Dutch UNDP representatives did not speak Arabic either. The mayor welcomed the group. He explained that although Israel usually held municipal and mayoral elections, the Israeli central government had appointed him four years earlier to govern the twenty-seven thousand Muslim and Christian Palestinian Israeli citizens of the Israeli city of Baqa, adding later that he had been appointed because "things were in chaos here." He didn't explain what kind of chaos, but his words carried the coded message that Arabs left alone yielded chaos. He said it as if it were a fact that anyone, including the Palestinians around the table, would believe. It was insulting, but no one said anything. Tarek and Majdi's goals lay elsewhere. They likely did not want to spoil a special opportunity.

The mayor continued in story format, notably as if he had been the one to think of the project. He described the two "sides" involved in the proposed sewage project. The Israeli "side" was narrow, he said, flanked by the Mediterranean Sea on one side and what he called the "Palestinian side" on the other. He called Baqa West a "border town." The words *side* and *border* suggested two geographical units mirroring one another across a line. He was projecting a geographical imaginary that understood separation of the West Bank from Israel to be separation of two discrete territories and conflated the Authority with the geographical territory of the West Bank as a whole.

This conflation was common, I discovered, and an important component of the incoherent environmental imaginary of a "shared environment." People used the term *PA* to describe both the Palestinian institutions that had a very partial authority to govern on pockets of noncontiguous land and to describe a territorially bounded geographical entity. The conflation was especially common among the Israeli environmentalists I encountered, including those familiar with Areas A, B, and C who knew the Authority as a set of institutions—ministries, police stations, budgets, and mandates—rather than a location.

This institutional-geographical conflation took the Green Line as a border between two sovereign states. It allowed people to describe sewage as flowing "from the Palestinian Authority into Israel," for instance. Thus Israeli newspapers decried "the state of the environment *in the Palestinian Authority*." One wrote, for instance, that "an ecological time bomb is ticking beyond the border. The bomb is located *inside the Palestinian Authority*" (Leshem 2002, italics mine). To grasp the absurdity of this conflation, imagine someone saying sewage flows "from the US State Department into Mexico" to refer to sewage traveling across the US-Mexico border. The false conflation has become such a problem among American journalists that in June 2013 the Library of Congress published instructions in its *Subject Headings Manual* instructing that the "Palestinian National Authority . . . represents a governmental entity, *not a geographic area*" (Library of Congress 2013, 3, italics mine).

The Baqa West mayor's words also omitted what Tarek, Majdi, and I had discussed in the car: the Authority's nominal jurisdiction over a fraction of the West Bank and Israeli sovereignty over the whole territory including its underground, which Israel controls all the way up to where a vertical pipe meets the base of a Palestinian's toilet. The mayor's formulation further elided that over four hundred thousand Israeli settlers also produce sewage in the West Bank, much of which flows westward into Israel or eastward into the Dead Sea. It conveniently omitted that it was because of the Authority's crippled authority that Majdi and Tarek were obliged to go to Israel to offer care for what Israelis perceived as their environment while Palestinian wastewater projects in Tulkarem, Nablus, Jenin, Hebron, and Salfit were stalled or canceled.

Yet the mayor was in fact assuming two contrasting spatial schemas. One conceived of a solid border between two distinct, coherent national wholes. That made Baqa West a "border town." The other ignored the border, instead looking at the problem of waste from below the earth's surface. "We know our sewage problems are not only *our* problems," he said. "Because we are sitting on a very big aquifer here. And if it is spoiled by the Israeli side, or by the Palestinian side, it doesn't matter! Because it will be spoiled! Because in the underground aquifer—they don't know borders!. . . . We are ready to connect the project . . . to the other side, the Palestinian side." In one breath, he presented sewage as straddling the border. In the next breath, he returned to the fiction of two symmetrical sides.

The Japanese consul's welcome followed: "I . . . see this as a sort of political, symbolic project to show that we can cooperate in order to have unity among two nations," he said. But the mayor interjected with a different interpretation: "As you understand, this is a very complicated region here. *Very* complicated. Where everything comes to politics! Instead, we should look at the physical problems. The physical problems are *physical problems—not politics*!" The mayor did not hide his dislike for the consul's comments. He objected to the use of the term *political*. The whole point of the project—and here we saw that Majdi, Tarek, and their colleagues had succeeded in presenting the project as cooperation around shared environmental concerns—was that it flew below the radar of politics by digging beneath the Wall.

Majdi, who had been holding his tongue, smiled as he waited for the mayor to finish. "Thank you very much for receiving us," he began. "We are working together with our neighbors on the other side—the Israeli side." He extended his chest in the mayor's direction and his head toward the Japanese consul, his physical contortion attempting the impossibility of orienting himself toward both men's perspectives. "We really understand your concern about our wastewater . . . coming from our side," he said. "We understand that some lessons can be learned from nature itself. We know that water and wastewater do not recognize any borders! And we hope that one day we can take lessons from nature." He paused, letting the room fall silent, then added, "We should say: 'Let us put our past away, very far away.' And we should focus strongly on the future."

Our wastewater. By referring to something called "our wastewater," Majdi gestured toward the notion that he was part of the "side" that formed Israel's other. Not only did this formulation echo the mayor's conflation between the Authority and the West Bank; it also implied Authority ownership over Palestinians' sewage. In this and other encounters like it, Authority waste professionals presented themselves as spokespersons of Palestinians' wastes as *national* wastes.

I use the term *national wastes* to refer to waste to which national markers are attributed. Elsewhere in the world, attribution of a national marker to waste usually refers to the territory in which waste is produced. Waste produced in Canada, for example, is deemed "Canadian waste." That makes statements like "x percent of Canadian municipal solid waste is sent to American landfills" make sense. Such a territorial designation erases differences among the legal statuses of the people actually producing the waste—for instance, the fact that some percentage of it is produced by residents of Canada who are citizens of other countries or are stateless.

To attribute ownership over occupied Palestinians' wastes to a set of Palestinian institutions lacking authority to control them is out of step with this logic that maps sovereign control over a territory and wastes' national designation. Rather, Palestinian sewage should be considered *Israeli waste*—a form of "imperial debris" (Stoler 2013). Yet Majdi, who in private would have agreed with my assertion in a heartbeat, chose at the meeting instead to act as if the Authority were sovereign over the West Bank, extending an apology, in bodily as well as verbal form, for its uncontrolled spillages.

Water and wastewater do not recognize borders. In the same breath, however, Majdi reiterated the framework of a shared environment the mayor had just put his weight behind, undermining the very notion of sovereignty he had just asserted. He appeared to follow the mayor's lead, presenting the project as an abstract good divorced from political interests and valued instead for its usefulness in fixing "physical problems." Majdi's repetition of the mayor's language contradicted statements Majdi had made privately in the car before the meeting. And the mayor's comments themselves held two logically opposing positions: one that saw borders and one that did not. Knowing them to be contradictory, Majdi seemed to comply with the mayor's proposed incoherence through Majdi's use of language as well as through his silences. His long midsection pressing against the edge of the table, Majdi nodded gratefully toward the mayor as if the mayor had just proposed a new idea.

In one sense Majdi was subscribing to the mayor's environmental imaginary. In another sense he was taking the bitter lemons he had been served and making lemonade. Majdi attested to his willingness to "take lessons from nature," speaking as if he had gone through the mental exercise of suspending recognition of the Green Line as an international border between two states. This entailed thinking "like the environment": like the aquifer straddling it from below and like sewage flowing across it. Yet he also professed a willingness to work with "our neighbors on the other side," recognizing the border quite clearly. Majdi was taking an opportunity to prove his good intentions and those of his colleagues toward solving the physical problems the mayor understood to be the project's target.

Reversing what in the car he had called the victory of history over geography, Majdi insinuated that "we" Palestinians should think less about the political (historical) past and think more about the ecological (geographical) future. And his insinuation did something. It allowed the conversation to flow smoothly. The mayor's face remained relaxed. Majdi's words did not provoke the same reaction as the consul's. That Majdi appeared willing to take responsibility over wastewater was part of what made that possible. The mayor nodded, leaning back in his chair. It seemed as though the Israeli and Palestinian officials at the table were on one side and the Japanese representatives were on the other. The Japanese consul cleared his throat, and the meeting proceeded with the mayor asking his secretary to bring coffee.

As the meeting's participants went over the project's technical updates with notable ease, I recalled something Majdi had said as we had driven out of Ni'lin checkpoint on our way up to Baqa that morning after he had spoken in Hebrew with the soldier. "Did you see what I did?" he had asked, excited. "I tell you that soldier is my friend! I said to her, 'How is your mother?' Like I know her mother. She said *'Biseder, udkhul'* [Okay, enter]. That's how we got through." The sewage project designs connecting West Bank and Israeli villages through what some of its proponents called a "bridge of sewage" and Majdi's way of carrying himself in the meeting constituted forms of aspirational phatic labor. Like his deployment of Hebrew and feigned interest in the soldier's mother at the checkpoint, they created an infrastructure of communicative channels that deferred possible tensions and facilitated a sense of agreement where one did not necessarily exist.

But the truth is that Tarek, Majdi, and their colleagues had no way of knowing why they were permitted to cross a checkpoint one day while another day they were turned back. They had no way of knowing why the Civil Administration rejected one of their applications to build a treatment plant while permitting a landfill for Ramallah. All they had was guesswork and messages into the ether like the one Landau had delivered. That made the phatic labor I witnessed in Baqa *aspirational,* much like the gesture of hanging bread on a window grate that aspires to be ethical practice. They saw how productive the idea of Israelis and Palestinians having common environmental concerns had been for Israelis and for organizations like FOEME and hoped to harness that productivity.

CONCLUSION

Discursive incoherencies like the one that Majdi mirrored from the mayor did not emerge only in the presence of Israelis, though they certainly seemed to facilitate smoother interactions with Israelis.[10] This is the sense in which Majdi and Tarek's aspirational affective labor spilled over into doublethink, where they seemed to believe in what they did and said even while they questioned it. Earlier that day, Majdi, Tarek, and I had also visited the town of Barta'a, which, like Baqa, had been split in two in 1948. Another "cross-boundary" sewage project was planned there. The mayor had hosted us, the UNDP, and Japanese representatives, on our own, without Israeli participants. Contrasting with the English-dominated Baqa meeting, the Barta'a meeting had been conducted in Arabic with sporadic English translations for some UNDP staff.

Tarek, less comfortable in English than Majdi, had been more vocal. Tarek had spent two years in an Israeli prison with Barta'a al-Sharqiyah's Palestinian mayor in the early 1990s. The two men shared a jovial, familiar, almost informal mode at the table. This seemed more like an "in-group" occasion despite the presence of several foreign donor agency representatives. Yet toward the end of the meeting Tarek made a rather formal statement, almost out of the blue, about Palestinians and Israelis being "neighbors" across "two sides" of a line. He addressed it to the donor representatives: "We are trying to improve the relationship between the two parties," he said. "We're in conflict with our neighbors here, and we think this sewage project can help." His assertion both echoed and followed a similar comment by Barta'a's mayor: "This is a peace project . . . of trust and peace between the two peoples. . . . We as Palestinians believe in peace. We are partners," the mayor had said.

Tarek's audience had nodded and smiled. They seemed to be receiving the message well. But it had quickly become apparent that, unlike Majdi and Tarek, most of the donor representatives present knew little about the project. They knew little about where sewage flowed, where the network would send it, how it would be treated, or what the area's political geography was like. They seemed to uphold the abstract idea of "crossing" as an unqualified good, while they knew little about where the physical lines to be crossed by the sewage were. One UNDP representative described only having been "briefed this morning." Both the Japanese consul and the UNDP representatives expressed confusion about their geographical location in Barta'a. "But now we are not on the West Bank side, are we?" one woman had asked, prompting the Barta'a mayor's assistants to produce fold-out maps.

On the one hand, this set of dynamics—acting neighborly, confusing border locations—suggests that all the day's meetings were characterized by a degree of superficiality. Participants appeared simply to be mirroring each other's gestures, as though no single speaker was the true generator of the doubled, contradictory language being used. Each meeting created a hall-of-mirrors effect in which the words *peace*, *borders*, *neighbors*, and, occasionally, *sewage* and *aquifer* seemed capable of bouncing back and forth to infinity. There was something about everything said that lacked traction. So superficial did these statements seem, in fact, that I neglected to write most of them down during the trip. Only because my voice recorder remained on most of the day was I able to return to them.

On the other hand, such visits take place up to three, four, and five times a week for dozens of Authority and municipal bureaucrats and Palestinian NGO and aid agency employees. Infrastructures are ushered through the permitting-and-funding pipeline by the repeated holding of such meetings. This suggests that the apparent superficiality does work to smooth out potentially contentious interactions among the bureaucrats and politicians involved (cf. Siegel 1997, 15–16). That work resonates with work performed by the "I" in Indonesia's lingua franca, Melayu, as described by James Siegel. Siegel writes that Melayu's "I" belongs to no one who uses it. This is because "one learned the lingua franca by imitating what the other said while the other was doing the same. . . . The lingua franca took shape in the middle, between the speakers. Eventually, they could comprehend each other." The superficiality of this incoherent environmental imaginary qua lingua franca appears to be necessary to management of Palestinian waste.

As a result, certain ways of framing waste problems—and the particular Israeli definitions of environmental care from which they derive—shape not only the daily experiences of the Palestinian waste professionals but also the waste-be-sieged present and infrastructural futures of an entire occupied population. They bolster Israeli government, military, and settler ideas of the West Bank as territory rightfully under Israeli control. In doing so, they shape the olfactory, tactile, and spatial experiences of Palestinians across the West Bank as they shape imaginative horizons and the parameters of everyday ethical practices at the levels of the kitchen and the street.

CONCLUSION

ON A THURSDAY IN APRIL AT ABOUT 7:00 P.M., I STOOD IN A BARELY lit parking lot with two friends from Ramallah. The sun was down, and no buildings were to be seen in any direction save a small kiosk. I knew Mustafa and Sawsan, members of a Palestinian *dabkeh* troupe based in al-Bireh, from dance classes I had taken at the Popular Arts Center, the troupe's headquarters.[1] Mustafa was in his late thirties, stout with a magnetic laugh. He managed a printing press during the day and in the evening led *dabkeh* practices at the center. He had four children and lived in al-ʿAmari refugee camp on the litter-strewn road between al-Bireh and Qalandiya checkpoint. Sawsan had worked at Jawwal, a major Palestinian telecommunications company, but she had just lost her job. Israel had again withheld millions of dollars in tax revenues from the Authority. The Authority, whose employees were breadwinners for about one-third of West Bank Palestinians, was suddenly unable to pay salaries. Businesses were sputtering and firing employees. Sawsan pulled her large, curlicue hair into a ponytail. On a whim she had asked me and Mustafa to take her out to help her feel better about being between jobs.

We stood in a stunning blackness. The stars were out. We pulled off sweatshirts and jackets. We had just driven an hour southeast from Ramallah, descending from Ramallah's mountains to the western coast of the Dead Sea, which sits 1,412 feet below sea level. We were at the lowest place on earth. The hot, dry breeze reminded us that the temperature in the parking lot was fifteen degrees warmer than Ramallah's. We held onto Mustafa's dusty white car to put on flip-flops.

The parking lot was outside the entrance of Biankini Beach, an Israeli-run beach resort on the part of the Dead Sea located in the West Bank. We had just encountered Biankini's guards: three Palestinian men from Jericho, a West Bank city about thirty minutes' drive from there. A dog with matted fur sat in front of a turnstile as a guard told us we could not enter. Biankini is one of three organized Dead Sea beaches still open to West Bank Palestinians, at the sea's northwesternmost edge. Biankini, Kalya, and Siesta beaches have infrastructures allowing for a comfortable stay, including cantinas, restaurants, and bathrooms. They have showers, which are crucial for washing off salt and mud crusts from the Dead Sea, as well as trash cans and bungalows for overnight stays. They have picnic tables and chairs, swimming pools, and lifeguards, and they are wheelchair accessible.

Palestinians are permitted to enter one more beach, called 'Ayn Fashkhah, which is part of an area Israel confiscated from the Palestinian town of Al-'Ubeidiya in 1969 (ARIJ 2010, 19). But 'Ayn Fashkhah lacks infrastructure and is harder to reach. To enter the water one traverses patches of slippery mud that can turn to a kind of quicksand, sucking feet and other objects into it. The largest, best-organized beachfront resort on the Dead Sea is south at Ein Gedi in Israel, and most West Bank Palestinians like Mustafa and Sawsan cannot obtain Israeli military permits they need to go there.

Yet even the Israeli managers of the West Bank's Biankini beach have potential customers vetted by local Palestinians. One of the guards we encountered was a thin man in shorts. We had approached the turnstile in front of the kiosk to pay the entry fee. We had stood clutching towels, staring at the sign of entry prices taped to the glass. The sign was in English, French, Spanish, German, and Hebrew. No Arabic. They offered day and overnight passes. Smoking a cigarette, the guard started a conversation with Mustafa. "Good evening," he said in Arabic, probably having seen the white, West Bank license plate on Mustafa's car. "Sorry," he continued. "You can't go in until 8:00 p.m. That's when the Jews leave." He seemed apologetic. Embarrassed, even. But he didn't explain further, leaving it to be understood that while Israelis—what he had meant by "Jews"—were using the beach, Palestinians could not.

The parking lot was full of other cars and buses, all with Israeli plates. We leaned against Mustafa's car. We pulled out phones, checking the time. At 8:00 p.m. a rush of sound emanated from behind the kiosk. Hundreds of men and boys burst through the turnstiles. They flooded the parking lot, gripping towels and large water bottles. They wore long swim trunks and many were bare-chested. Older men had long beards and a strand of long, wet hair on either side of their faces. Some clasped their heads to keep kippahs on. They all appeared to be Orthodox Jews. "It's a holiday," Mustafa said, referring to Passover. "They're probably on a special trip." Our car was closest to the kiosk, so we were the first sight the men encountered as they left the beach. Some looked surprised, others nervous, averting their eyes. They made staccato movements to stream around the car, avoiding collision with us. Pushing the men in front of them, older men grabbed boys by the hand to direct them away from our car and onto buses. We were silent, waiting for the rush to pass.

It took time for them to load onto the buses. It was 8:30 p.m. when we were able to approach the kiosk again to pay our fees. As we walked into the resort the guard yelled after us: "Remember, after 8:00 p.m. you can't enter the water. Just the upper tier is open!" The upper tier featured picnic tables and tent spaces. The Dead Sea's waters were in the distance past a gate and down a flight of stairs. I looked at my group, worried. Hadn't we come all the way here to swim in the Dead Sea? Mustafa and Sawsan smiled defiantly at each other and at me. "We're going in, don't worry. We'll just wait for the guards to sit," they whispered in Arabic.

Past the kiosk was a gift store, now closed, with posters of bath salts, jars of mud, and Moroccan imports. To our right small, criss-crossing paths cut through grassy areas with plastic chairs set up in haphazard formations. Strings with Israeli flags billowed above our heads. We passed signs for a Moroccan restaurant and a synagogue. Lit by white lampposts, we walked to the edge where a fence separated this upper tier from a big open blackness. The wind got gustier. We found an opening in the fence. Hunched over so as not to be seen, phones out to light our feet, we walked down a long, unlit flight of stairs that were grainy under our flip-flops. The stairs spilled out onto a small, muddy flat area. Black, motionless water stretched out before us. Spots of white on its oil-like surface reflected the lights from the plateau with the flags and chairs above.

The ground was sticky and slippery as I moved to grab three lounge chairs from a stack under a tarp at the edge of the mud. We set them beside one another. Opening our towels onto the chairs, we found the chairs' plastic surfaces wet. We didn't say anything, but we seemed to be thinking something similar: the wetness was from the chairs' previous users. In the thick blackness of the upper plateau's shadow, we couldn't see what they were wet with. It could be seawater, or water from the freshwater showers, or sweat. We lay down in a row. Our towels absorbed the chairs' moisture, transferring it to our backs and legs. We lay there, saying nothing.

Despite the Israeli state's best efforts to separate Israeli bodies from Palestinian bodies, our bodies mixed with droplets that had rolled off the bodies of people we had just encountered. Our sneaking into the sea constituted "leakage" through a boundary reminiscent of those erected during antimiscegenation campaigns, segregation, and apartheid. Because this was after the time for the Jews, management had turned the lights off. But lights from buildings on the beaches across the sea in Jordan (figure 15) winked at us in the quiet. We let the silence envelop us. It was a stolen moment outside unwritten regulations handed down to us by reluctant executors. It felt like a miracle to be alone at one of the most tourist-packed spots on earth.

Living in a Möbius strip means living both abandoned and controlled by a state that is not one's own. In this sense, Palestinians' status vis-à-vis the state resounds

FIGURE 15. A view of Jordan across the Dead Sea from a West Bank roadside, 2015. Photograph by Simone Popperl, 2015.

in the Syrian refugee camps beyond those lights as it resounds across the globe. It reverberates as much in the Palestinian refugee camps of Lebanon as it does in Dadaab, the world's largest refugee complex, in Kenya. It also echoes experiences in Flint, New Orleans, and Athens, Greece, in the slums of Rio de Janeiro and Mumbai, and in African cities where the urban poor are left to fend for themselves but where the harshness of the conditions in which they live is a direct result of policies of the states that appear to abandon them (Anand 2017; Allan 2013; Chalfin 2014; Comaroff and Comaroff 2006; de Boeck 2009; Mbembé 2001; Millar 2014; Penglase 2009; Simone 2004a; Von Schnitzler 2016). Understanding Palestinian experiences of infrastructural abandonment—which, among other things, yields uncomfortable and sometimes disastrous proximities to waste—is a way of understanding the nuances of abandonment in other parts of the world.

At the same time, in the West Bank, unlike many other places, there are pro-tostate actors who are kept from forming a state but who continue to try to do so and to perform state-like functions. In this sense the Authority's role is not so different from that of the guard at the kiosk. It creates a dynamic that does not correspond either to the Western liberal model of an all-seeing, surveillant state (Scott 1998) organized around controlling the forces of life or to the model of the abandoned slum or camp, where citizens' lives are rendered acutely precarious as corrupt governors confine their care to those who can pay for it.

By offering an ethnographic depiction of the experiences of Palestinian pro-tostate actors alongside those of the protocitizens they try to govern, this book has invited readers to consider a third model where life is shaped by the effects of state abandonment combined with governance by other, state-like actors. It also offers parallels with contexts that appear to manifest pure abandonment, such as the poor black parts of New Orleans during and after Hurricane Katrina, or Puerto Rico after Hurricane Maria, but that may exist in more of a gray zone than might initially appear to be the case—a zone that Palestinians call the "phantom state." And it offers an understanding of such places as spaces that may be governed by a conglomeration of nonprofit organizations, private companies, and individuals making collectivities that are rarely more than fleeting.

This book has suggested, in other words, that while abandonment—as the precondition for what we think of as "wastelands" in the empty sense of the term—may be a helpful analytic for critiquing state negligence, it may not be an adequate descriptor for how governance in these contexts both operates and is experienced.

Waste management is particularly helpful for making this doubleness visible, since it is one of the most necessary practices for modern life. Just as waste siege inundates spaces with waste, as if embodying earlier colonial representations of Palestine as an empty wasteland while also filling them in and filling them up, this book has revealed that abandonment (by the state) and absence (of a state of one's own) can actually be lived as *inundation*.

A few minutes later we headed down into the water single file. At knee-depth we sat down and let our bodies unfold like flowers blooming. We floated on our backs, faces up to the stars. I closed my eyes. My ears went underwater. The temperature of the third of my body outside the water enveloped the rest of me below. More boundaries melted away. I heard nothing and saw only blackness behind my eyelids. I hardly felt myself at all. As I kept my mouth closed to keep out the bitter saltiness, my nose was the only part of me still open to the air and alert. I drew in breaths of air foul with the odor of rotten eggs. Sulfur. Sewage. Deadness.

The magic stillness and end-of-the-worldness of this floating moment mixed with fragments of the time I had spent with Palestine's waste managers. The Dead Sea, I remembered them telling me, is the final resting place for about eight million gallons of sewage that daily stream down the hillsides of the West Bank. The sewage travels there over eighteen miles from Jerusalem. The Jerusalem sewage network opens out onto Wadi al-Nar and winds eastward and downhill, making the river of sewage whose stench opened this book. On its way, the river gathers more sewage from wastewater spilling from an open end-pipe in Bethlehem's sewage network. The sewage river emitted annually by roughly eight hundred thousand residents and millions of visitors is raw. It contains everything people in the two holy cities flush down their toilets and down their shower drains, including pharmaceuticals, hormones, detergents, and pathogens.

As the lowest place on earth, the Dead Sea is like a drain in a public shower. It gathers wastes away from two of the holiest places on earth so that they and their holiness can continue to exist. But the Dead Sea is shrinking. It loses an average of three feet per year to evaporation. Only sewage and effluent from fish ponds run into the Jordan River's channel. And the channel is the only moving body of water feeding the Dead Sea. Ever since the Jordan River's freshwaters were diverted in the 1960s, the sea stopped receiving enough water to keep its current size. As it shrinks, the ratio of waste dissolved into it increases, intensifying the Dead Sea's waste siege.

We can understand what is taking place on our planet in a similar way. The ratio of waste to the planet is growing. Waste production outpaces technologies to make waste go away. It surpasses efforts like large-scale recycling aimed to rescue refuse from abjectness. Humans have yet to invent a sewage treatment technology that can remove all contaminants from domestic and industrial wastewater. Even Israeli wastewater treatment plants, which Israeli companies export across the world, do not treat wastewater to a degree that returns it to potable levels. Most countries in the world, including the United States, continue to bury garbage underground. Many places that do not bury garbage export it by barge or plane, sending it elsewhere and sending emissions into the atmosphere. People in places that import others' waste or are dumpsites find ways of reassigning value to that waste. They separate damaged cars into parts, for example, selling some bits as scrap and others as replacement parts for cars. But something is always left over.

As excesses are inherent to the way we live, our planet has become a storage site for waste.[2] It is besieged by growing quantities of waste with no place to go.[3] As the siege grows, the proportion of resources upon which life depends relative to waste also shifts. There may be a fixed amount of water on earth, for example. But the form in which it is stored (e.g., as freshwater, saltwater, ice, clouds) changes, as do the locations where it is stored (e.g., in aquifers under the United States or in African lakes) and the extent to which it can accommodate life based on materials it contains (e.g., salt, nitrates). As a microcosm of this principle, the Dead Sea loses water to evaporations that carry the water far from a thirsty Palestine. A slightly larger microcosm is the West Bank. The absolute amount of water to which Palestinians have access in the West Bank aquifers has remained roughly the same over the past two decades. Meanwhile, the population increases, yielding a decreasing per capita water volume access as the volume of different types of wastes increases.

Palestinians' experience of a growing waste siege with decreasing access to potable water and space in which to live safely is metaphorical for the condition of a dying planet. It is also a metonym for the uneven way waste siege is distributed across different populations. The Israeli state limits Palestinians' access to water and intensifies Palestinians' proximities to waste while at the same time giving water to its citizens and removing waste from their midst.

Yet this book has also pointed to another, important feature of this story of shifting proportions. Commentators often speak of processes like the shrinking of the Dead Sea in terms of loss. Environmentalists ring the Dead Sea's death knell just as they lament the melting of polar ice caps and the death of the Great Barrier Reef. They are right insofar as the presence of those earthly features diminishes daily with devastating short- and long-term effects. But this book has argued that an accurate portrayal of what is changing demands we also think in terms of a *buildup* or an *accrual*. As some things diminish, others increase.

As waste accrues, waste siege develops as a kind of ecological system in which people dwell and that dwells within their bodies.[4] Ecologies are systems with interacting organisms. They involve the mixing of humans with nonhuman things. Waste siege ecologies include humans, infrastructures, waste, and land. Ecologies operate according to distributions and flows. They also operate through blockages. The constant trickle of sewage entering the Dead Sea meets the finitude of the sea as a dead end. But although the term *ecology* is frequently used in depoliticized ways, here I use it to capture the inescapable character of waste siege as well as the uneven distribution of dilemmas with which it burdens humans.[5] Like our bodies' contact with the water during our stolen moment in the Dead Sea, waste siege is an encounter. It is relational. But it is also a shifting milieu. Each improvisation to make life in that milieu more livable reconstitutes siege. Waste siege is ambient.[6] Even if it goes unnoticed or uncommented upon, like the smell of rotten eggs that enveloped us in the water, it forms part of the material and sensory surroundings shaping people's experiences of time and place. Waste siege is an ecology without harmony.[7] It causes damage while it generates and sometimes generates because it causes damage.

Robust discussions in anthropology and related disciplines over the past decades have raised questions about how nature is objectified and produced (Agrawal 2005; Braun and Castree 1998, 2001; Bird, 1987; Brosius 1999; Castree 1995; Darier 1999; Dove and Carpenter 2008; Eder 1996; Escobar 1999; Golinski 1998; Matthews 2011; Smith 1991; P. Townsend 2000; Tsing 2005; Walley 2004; West 2006, 2012). Some argue that nature and the environment are constituted through the work of the human imagination.[8] Some propose that the nature-society dichotomy is a false one imposed upon a world of hybrids (Haraway 1991; Latour 1987, 1993, 2011). Others emphasize the material "artificiality" of nature. They point to thousands of years of human impact on the planet, including on those features like soil and water popularly thought of as "nature." They point to the nature that grows in human-disturbed ecosystems like forests (Tsing 2015). Attention to the geological period currently being called the Anthropocene (H. Davis and Todd 2017; Dove 2013; Haraway 2015; Haraway et al. 2016; Kersten 2013; Latour 2017; Lorimer 2015; A. Moore 2016, 2018; Ogden et al. 2013; Whyte 2017) can be understood as the most recent example of this kind of human-impact thinking.

To many in the social sciences and humanities, questioning the naturalness of nature has become the starting point for discussing the pressing environmental issues of our time. Yet when it comes to thinking about the relationship between human-produced refuse and the spaces into which that refuse is emitted, commentaries on the uneven distribution of waste still portray the environment as a natural object into which "unnatural," human-produced substances are inserted (Bohme 2014; Bond 2013; Kuletz 1998; Newman 2016; Nixon 2011; Voyles 2015). Among the most iconic images of humans' effect on the environment in this vein are satellite images of the Great Pacific garbage patch. Visualized from space, the giant floating island of nonbiodegradable plastic discards between Hawaii and California is used to depict the massive unnatural blotch with which humans have defaced the earth.

We tend to think of waste in such contexts as lethal or toxic. Studies of waste as pollution—read as the cause of anthropogenic geological changes to the planet—(re)assert the separation of nature from society. Commentators highlight wastes' incompatibility with nature, positing that they are part of a hostile human take-over. In this spirit, scholars who focus on toxicity frequently end up reifying the distinctness of the ecosystem, environment, or nature exposed to toxicity, calling for an understanding of the natural properties (e.g., soil's porosity) that make certain areas more vulnerable to wastes. Where certain areas are more vulnerable, the argument goes, so are populations. This attributes to waste its own kind of agency, as in studies of climate refugees and climate-induced violence that highlight the environment's tendency to act "back" upon politics (H. Baer and Singer 2014; Barnes et al. 2013; Crate 2011; Dove 2013; Oliver-Smith 2009). Others highlight the human body as a site that condenses waste's damage to environments more broadly (Blanc 2016; Bullard 2000; Cordner 2016; Fleming and Johnson 2014; E. Grossman 2006; Kimura 2016; Kroll-Smith and Floyd 2000; Lerner 2010; Little 2014; Markowitz and Rosner 1994, 2013; Mikkelsen and Brown 1997; Murphy 2006; Pellow 2007; Reich 1991; Sze 2006; Troesken 2004). These analytical moves have bolstered attention to international and local environmental movements, increasingly twinning them with efforts to prevent war and even "terrorism."

Waste Siege has shown how waste and its management become political. But it has also argued that the people most affected by waste do not always articulate their dissatisfaction with the impact of waste in environmentalist terms, in contrast to the way other contemporary communities articulate waste-related suffering.[9] Nor, more surprisingly still, do the Palestinians featured in this ethnography always orient their energies toward those with the greatest capacity to change their conditions. The premise of this book is that that matters. Let us try not to take the environment as a category for granted. Let us instead ask a question that recently became more relevant for Americans watching the water crisis in Flint, Michigan: How, why, and to what effect do people organize themselves around "environmental" problems in the first place? By focusing on the materials most easily taken to be pollutants, this book has interrogated what constitutes some problems as environmental and others as something else entirely—or *in addition.* Out of their proximities to waste people make unexpected meaning. Other considerations—for instance commitments to ethical practice and anxieties about uncertain future political arrangements— can shape both the wastescape they live in and their attempts to change their conditions. And waste, for its part, can be less-than-toxic, more-than-toxic, or other-than-toxic in the conventional sense.

This book has thus pointed to the need for a more expansive understanding of waste and of the ecological. It has pointed to the need to reconceptualize waste as constitutive of waste siege but also as itself *an environment* rather than as a foreign object whose salient characteristic is that it has been forcibly and detrimentally inserted into "the environment."

Waste Siege offers a view of waste as ecology that presents waste neither as a backdrop nor as an acute, toxic *cause* of politics. Rather, waste convenes a set of interconnected dilemmas. The book has built upon recent efforts to challenge the idea that ecosystems are natural in the terms that evoke images of trees and oceans and on arguments for writing the "natural histories" of waste (e.g., Gabrys 2011; Schneider 2011; Tsing 2015). It has invited readers to think of waste both as a part of "the environment" and as an environment within which people make their lives. Neither what people refer to as the natural environment nor what they refer to as the built environment, waste constitutes and is a part of both. The institutions humans invent and transform to confront the dilemmas of waste siege also constitute part of the ecology of siege.

Some might call thinking of the planet in these terms "environmental aware-ness," arguing that having awareness is the first step toward doing something about it. Indeed, environmentalists, governments, and the institutions that fund them often privilege the ability to name an environmental problem as such, as we saw in chapter 5. To recognize a problem as environmental suggests the ability to recognize that damage is being done, to see the possibility of one's own culpability, and to see the need for a solution. This is one way in which debates have played out around anthropogenic climate change.

But ecologies are complex systems that can defy attempts at linear under-standings of causation. As Sawsan, Mustafa, and I floated, I decided not to ruin the moment by mentioning that one of the main ingredients in which we floated was sewage. I thought to myself that they had likely heard talk about pollution of this, yet another, Palestinian resource. No need to reiterate that now. Plus, they might understandably ask who was responsible for all the shit that floated in this sea. Was it the Jerusalem municipality? Was responsibility shared by the 65 percent of Jerusalem's 760,000 inhabitants who are Jewish-Israeli—who can vote in Israeli elections—and the 35 percent who are Christian and Muslim Pal-estinians—who cannot? To what extent was the Authority, under whose aegis Bethlehem municipality operates, responsible?

These are questions that strike at the heart of the infrastructural politics this book has sought to illuminate. In the growing literature on the Anthropocene, questions about the local, municipal scales of governance and the infrastructures that mediate them, so long important to scholars studying the state's relationship to population and territory, often give way to interest in the scales of international treaties, inequalities among states, and the philosophical and material relation-ship between the history of humanity as a species and the natural history of the planet (e.g., Chakrabarty 2012).[10] What lessons does the ethnography of a setting like the West Bank offer anthropologies of waste, of infrastructure, of the state, and now of the Anthropocene?

Inspired by the call of science and technology studies to "follow the thing"—in this case, waste—this book has imagined waste infrastructures as nodal points from which we can trace relationships among actors that might normally be thought of separately. To do this it has drawn on methodological propositions put forth in STS suggesting we think of infrastructure as a socio-technical assemblage that helps reveal how "modern societies cannot be described without recognizing them as having a fibrous, thread-like, wiry, stringy, ropy, capillary character that is never captured by the notions of levels, layers, territories, spheres, categories, structure, systems" (Latour 1996, 370). My goal has been to map the web of waste-managed networks that cut across and at the same time help produce divides between Palestinian, donor, Israeli, national, municipal, and communal and that give their shape to the ethical and political dilemmas of contemporary Palestinians.

Accordingly, this book has demonstrated that infrastructure's "strength does not come from concentration, purity and unity, but from dissemination, heterogeneity and the careful plaiting of weak ties" (Latour 1996, 370). Mapping the sewage flows, pipelines, gestures, consumption patterns, waste pileups, meetings, and passing comments involved in making waste infrastructures and making certain wastes infrastructural allowed me access to social worlds (and material networks) assembled, albeit ephemerally, under waste siege. Though these worlds have been largely overlooked in depictions of Palestine, select histories and sociological works on Palestine have taken similar paths before (e.g., Eyal 2006; Lockman 1996). Still, most observers of Palestine, as of other similar contexts, have tended to frame analyses through the geographic, institutional, or national units with which their interlocutors are conventionally associated. Palestine scholarship has been interested in bounded sociological units such as the village, the city, and class; in social groups such as peasants, workers, and women; and now in larger geographical units such as the West Bank, Israel, and Gaza. By following *things*, this book has examined how relations around infrastructure transcend, cross-cut, crystallize around, and even reshape these units, as we saw in Shuqba and in the streets where people cast off bread. This perspective reveals understudied forms of sociality, conditions through which Palestinians' expectations of government are shaped, and the unintended effects of infrastructural change.

Given that the daily practices of Palestinians improvising to manage waste are not adequately captured by prevailing, often rights-based, frameworks for understanding Palestinians' experiences of occupation, the perspective of waste siege compelled me to ask new questions about the spatial and institutional boundaries of Palestinian governance. How is the Authority's constituency constituted, and what forms of collectivity exist outside its interpellating call? To what extent can examining infrastructures-in-the-making, or failed or absent infrastructures, tell us something about the so-called political imaginaries (Star 1999, 380) of designers and managers?

Among other things, following infrastructure as a process, by following trash and sewage flows in real time, necessitated the reorientation of my ethnographic focus from the effects that an infrastructure's operation has had on the broader population (e.g., people's relative politicization, income, access to resources) to the experiences of its makers. My research thus challenged the assumption that the ethnonational, ideological, or institutional "authorship" of infrastructure—and the extent to which an infrastructure "embodies" a particular ideology—can be determined prior to understanding the practices that go into its design, establishment, and use.

Waste Siege has in other words highlighted the semiotic instability of waste and its infrastructures. In chapter 1 we saw how waste management became part of the Authority's modernizing, developmental path as it focused on technical advancement and on distinguishing the landscape it governed from those preceding it, periodizing the pre- and the post-Oslo periods. More recently, discourses around environmental security linked to climate change adaptation in Palestine have become entangled with discourses around the risk of political collapse (Stamatopoulou-Robbins 2018).[11] Waste management is now becoming a tactic for adapting to decreased water quantities due to global warming. Since the Authority envisions environmental securitization as part of gaining international recognition of state readiness, failing to manage waste can appear to threaten Authority breakdown. The braiding together of environmental protection and statecraft—as infrastructural development—that we saw in chapter 5 is becoming ever stronger.[12]

At the same time, the temporalities demanded by the management of each problem—environmental degradation and possible political collapse—differ in important ways. Environmental degradation to a point where the West Bank would become uninhabitable for humans, for example, is often imagined as so far off as to seem irrelevant to current governmental decisions. Like the temporal frame intensified by climate change, environmental protection can present those working on it with "a future beyond the grasp of historical sensibility" (Chakrabarty 2009, 197). Palestinians can imagine political collapse, on the other hand, as an event that could occur from one day to the next. Donors could stop funding the Authority, as they did after Hamas's victory in 2006 and before Sawsan was fired. The Israeli military could at any moment lay siege to Palestinian cities, reactivate checkpoints and roadblocks, stage mass arrests, kill thousands, and disarm the Authority police, as they do periodically in Gaza. The occupied population, for its part, could take up arms against the Authority for failing to protect them. In contexts like these, "in-between" temporalities like the landfill time we encountered in chapter 1 serve as a temporal compromise in which the ethics of waste accumulations are adjudicated.

In 2001, a handful of Israeli and Palestinian environmental professionals, including FOEME, drafted a proposal to clean up Wadi al-Nar and its basin. The proposal, which has yet to be implemented, has taken different iterations over the past eighteen years. The first proposed step is to remove sewage and solid waste from the valley. One goal would be to divert wastewater from five towns in the valley to a treatment plant that would be built in the same West Bank Palestinian town of al-'Ubeidiya southeast of Bethlehem whose lands Israel confiscated to develop the underserving beach of 'Ayn Fashkhah. Another would be to build a sewage pipeline extending from Jerusalem to al-'Ubeidiya. International donors would fund construction of the plant, which would be jointly owned and operated by Palestinians and Israelis: another move in the direction of so-called environmental peace building. The plant's managers would sell the treated wastewater for local agricultural use, and, the *New York Times* reported, under the heading "In a Polluted Stream, a Pathway to Peace," "Ubeidiya would get a modern landfill for its trash" (Wheelright 2013).

Like many other enthusiasts of the project, the *Times* article's author failed to mention that al-'Ubeidiya residents, whose trash currently goes to al-Minya landfill many miles away in Hebron, might not want a landfill. Nor did he mention that little would be "modern" about having a landfill. He also overlooked the ambiguities around whether a landfill would be beneficial for the agricultural town of ten thousand other than the fact that al-'Ubeidiya would likely need a landfill because the town would now have a wastewater plant. Treating the sewage of hundreds of thousands of people annually, the plant would produce large quantities of dewatered sludge in need of disposal. More wastes produced across the Wall would be buried deep in the West Bank.

Still floating, I continued taking in breaths of foul air. I remembered conversations with Tarek at the Palestinian Water Authority, which had applied for a wastewater treatment plant for Bethlehem in 1995 that Israel had rejected. A treatment plant would have captured the city's sewage, treated it, and made it available for local irrigation or for channeling cleaner water into Wadi al-Nar. But Israel had only approved a pipe network to connect Bethlehem's buildings to an underground collection system—without a treatment option. The network concentrated greater volumes of raw sewage at the output of the city where it opens onto Wadi al-Nar. The al-'Ubeidiya project's proponents, most of whom are Israeli and American, fail to mention that a plant in al-'Ubeidiya would mean Palestinians' forfeiting of plans to treat—and thereby capture and reuse—Bethlehem's wastewater in Bethlehem.

Authority officials have hesitated to sign onto the new Wadi al-Nar cleanup project, which, again, was spearheaded almost exclusively by non-Palestinians. The project's proponents have responded by denouncing what they call Palestinians' unwillingness to cooperate, publishing moralizing commentaries on the fact that Dr. Shaddad Attili, for example, who was the Authority's minister of water while I was conducting fieldwork, was wary about the implications of moving forward with it (Laster and Livney 2013, 235). The proponents of the Israeli plan to clean up Wadi al-Nar, which Israelis call the Kidron Valley, refer to it as an environmental project. To them there is no need to explain why Israeli government agencies and NGOs would be involved in cleaning up the West Bank. What is surprising to them is that Palestinians who see themselves as environmentalists would hesitate to get on board. To the project's proponents, sewage is a pollutant and the environment is the thing they are offering to save from it.

I remembered speaking with 'Itiraf at Bethlehem's Joint Service Council for Solid Waste Management. From his perspective, the most environmentally friendly plan would be for each city to treat its sewage on-site and to pump the treated water into Wadi al-Nar. Years of sewage flow have carved a deep crevice into the landscape. When it rains, the presence of sewage creates a buffer between the rain and porous earth. Rainwater moves along the sewage surface as runoff. If sewage were to stop flowing in the Wadi, the rainwater would permeate the earth, pulling contaminants from decades of waste caked at the bottom of the crevice down with it. Rain would lead to the rapid contamination of the aquifer below. If the current sewage stream were to be replaced with treated water, rainwater could continue to flow downward toward the Dead Sea, protecting the aquifer as it did so. "The solution," 'Itiraf had said to me one morning in his Bethlehem office, "is that you should treat the sewage, send it into the Wadi, and it will flush itself, by itself."

In 'Itiraf's analysis raw sewage is both a *problem* (it pollutes the Dead Sea) and a *solution* to another problem (contamination of the aquifer through pressure from rain). Sewage, if treated, becomes a technical fix. It becomes *infrastructural*.

And it can be what Dominique Laporte (2000) called "gold" not only for humans but also for environments in which it is embedded and of which, in the end, it is a constitutive part.

Seen as something that is always more than environmental pollution, but that becomes politicized as such, waste siege is not an end point but a beginning. The Dead Sea may be dying, but its economic and religious value continues to develop, perhaps all the more so because of its impending disappearance. For Mustafa and Sawsan, swimming in the Dead Sea at this moment—no matter what the waters contained—represented a personal salve and political achievement. Our presence in the Sea's stillness indexed movement where their movement was curtailed. Both had traveled the globe with their dance troupe, swimming off beaches in Morocco and France. Swimming here, an hour's drive from Ramallah, meant accessing the one Palestinian seafront left. The unique, unmistakable smell of this swim might have been contributing to the swelling of our hearts as we relished the fact that we had made it into the water despite the guard's prohibition. Waste siege is a place where life continues to be lived. It is a way to name the kind of living we do in the constantly changing ruins we have made.[13]

Notes

PREFACE

1. As shorthand but without implying the conflation of the two, I refer to the West Bank and Palestine interchangeably throughout. Where I use the term *Occupied Palestinian Territory* or *Occupied Territory*, I am referring to the West Bank and Gaza unless otherwise noted. If something pertains only to the West Bank or to Gaza but not to both, I make that clear through context.

2. On the adjacent question of how ethics is animated through the experience of emotional ties and affective attachments to nature, see Sivaramakrishnan (2015).

3. I use "Palestinian Authority" and "Authority" interchangeably.

4. A sample of discussions of nonhuman agency includes Bennett (2010); Callon, Law, and Rip (1986); Kohn (2013); Latour (1987, 1988, 1993, 2005, 2011). On how ontology debates have affected the study of waste, see S. Moore (2012); Reno (2015a). For exemplary materialist challenges to the view that dirt is a matter of classification, see Boscagli (2014); Bowler (1998); Edensor (2005); Gabrys (2011); Gabrys, Hawkins, and Michael (2013); Gordillo (2014); Jorgensen (2011); Lippert (2011); Magnani (2012); Molotch and Norén (2010); Nagle (2013).

5. See Lyons's (2016) related concept of "decomposition as life politics."

6. Much of the former work has focused on how Palestine can be productively compared with settler colonies like the United States, Canada, and Australia. On

settler colonialism in Palestine, see, e.g., Abdo and Yuval-Davis (1995); Hanafi (2009); Hilal (2015); Jabbour (1993); Lloyd (2012); Peteet (2005, 2017); Piterberg (2008); Puar (2013); Rouhana and Sabbagh-Khoury (2015); Salamanca et al. (2012); Shafir (1996); Shohat (1992); Yiftachel (1999); Zureik (1979). See also Wolfe (2006). Others focus on space to consider the analytical benefits of comparing Palestine's condition to that of apartheid South Africa: Bakan and Abu-Laban (2010); M. Bishara (2002); Carter (2007); U. Davis (2003); Dayan (2009); M. Marshall (1995); Peteet (2017); Yiftachel (2005); Zreik (2004). A growing group of scholars has also been showing how processes of neoliberalization and capital accumulation in Palestine are a part of and bolster parallel processes across the globe. See, e.g., Haddad (2016); Hanieh (2002, 2003, 2011, 2013); Raja Khalidi and Samour (2011); Merz (2012); Rabie (2014).

7. This book follows a long and important tradition in offering an ethnographic study of an aspect of quotidian Palestinian life. For early studies, see, e.g., Canaan (1927, 1935); Granqvist (1931, 1947). Ethnographic writing about Palestine burgeoned over the twentieth century. Naturally enough, much of the English-language scholarship since 1967 has attempted to give "voice" to various Palestinian subgroups—e.g., women, kinship groups, and peasants—or to examine the disciplinary and other logics of occupation. See, e.g., Cohen (1965); N. Gordon (2008); Moors (1995); Rothenberg (2004); Swedenburg (2003); Tamari (1981); Warnock (1990); Weizman (2007). Central to these accounts is the idea that Palestinian cultural and political formations are manifestations of either "coping" or "resistance" to occupation (Zureik 2003). Perhaps because the Occupied Palestinian Territory has also been characterized as an exception to the international order of states with centralized governance structures, it has been hard to see those Palestinian institutions of governance, bureaucracy, and infrastructure that operate, one could say, between these subgroups and occupation. It has been hard to see the quotidian in everyday life and its materialities without those being subsumed by politics with a capital P. This book seeks to reframe and thus to revalorize the existing scholarship. Three examples of recent ethnographic works that capture ordinary life under occupation are Allen (2008); A. Bishara (2013); Kelly (2008); Peteet (2017).

8. For compelling recent analyses of waste and war, see, e.g., al-Mohammad (2007); Rubaii (2018); Touhouliotis (2018).

9. American diplomat Dennis Ross argued, for example, that Hamas "provides services—clinics, after-school programs, food distribution centers—that the Palestinian Authority fails to offer" (Levitt 2006, ix). See also Mishal and Sela (2000, xxii).

INTRODUCTION

1. The film was directed by Fady Al-Ghorra and produced by LifeSource.

2. I have changed most people's names to pseudonyms throughout the text. I have kept real names where people asked me to do so or where people spoke with me in their official capacities.

3. I use *Israel/Palestine* to refer to the combination of Israel, the West Bank, and Gaza.

4. For a discussion of Palestinians who choose not to rebuild their homes after they are demolished and on the politics of memorializing camp architecture as refugee heritage, see Allan (2013); Feldman (2015b, 2016); Petti, Hilal, and Weizman (2013); Plascov (1981); Ramadan (2010); Schiff (1995); R. Sayigh (1993, 1995).

5. On Palestinians' experiences of UNRWA, see, e.g., Allan (2013); Feldman (2018); Gabiam (2012); Hanafi, Hilal, and Takkenberg (2014); Salam (1994); R. Sayigh (1993). For analysis of the category of the "Palestine refugee," see Akram (2002); Feldman (2012).

6. For another iteration of the question of how sovereignty and toxicity relate, see Langwick (2018).

7. Toxic dumping on the lands of indigenous peoples and in areas inhabited by the poor and the racially marginalized has been well documented. See, e.g., Auyero and Swiston (2009); P. Brown (1997); Bullard (2000); Checker (2005); Cole and Foster (2001); Lerner (2010); Little (2014); Lora-Wainwright (2013); Pellow (2002); Szasz (1994); Voyles (2015).

8. The name of the administration was changed from "Military" to "Civil" Administration in 1981.

9. Palestine's imports have recently increased at an annualized rate of 4.8 percent—for example, from $3.36 billion in 2011 to $4.95 billion in 2016 (Observatory of Economic Complexity n.d.). Thanks to Kareem Rabie for alerting me to this resource.

10. This book is one of the first book-length ethnographies that simultaneously examines everyday life both under and *within* the Palestinian Authority. It is the first study to tack back and forth between Authority employees' experiences governing and the experiences of the people they govern, and it is one of the first to focus on the Authority's infrastructural functions rather than those of its security services or economic visionaries. In this sense it echoes Ilana Feldman's (2008, 2015a) historical work on Gaza. For work on the Palestinian security services and repressive functions, see Farsakh (2012); Frisch (1997); Lia (1999); Ghanim (2008); Nossek and Rinnawi (2003); Parsons (2005); Tartir (2015b); Turner (2009); Zureik, Lyon, and Abu-Laban (2010). For important work on the Authority's economic poli-

cies, see Dana (2014, 2015b); Daoudi and Khalidi (2008); Haddad (2016); Raja Khalidi and Samour (2011); Tartir (2015a).

11. For another ethnography framed around dilemmas, see Hutchinson (1996).

12. Such studies contribute to discussions of Palestinian nationalism and resistance that have generally presented Palestinians as having a clear sense of the object they are resisting and of the reason for committing to the nationalist movement. Examples include Abufarha (2009); Rashid Khalidi (2006); Meari (2014); Peteet (1994); Tamari (1983). This ethnography takes as its starting point the observation that the period after the second intifada is characterized by what many are calling the collapse of the national movement. See, e.g., Allen (2013). With such a collapse comes murkiness around the goals of political action and indeed the parameters that make any act political.

13. On indeterminacy, see Csordas (1993); Fisch (2013); Hird (2013); Morgensen (2016); Samuels (2001); Weszkalnys (2015).

14. On wastes as indexical, see Reno (2015a). For a relevant consideration of indexicality, see Kohn (2013).

15. On environmental framing, see McKee (2018).

16. For a recent, related discussion of settler colonial capitalism and toxicity, see Murphy (2017).

17. See also Rashid Khalidi (2010, 101) and Meisels (2002).

18. Justification for land confiscation based on the idea that lands are being misused or underutilized is a familiar one in the colonial literature. For discussions of John Locke's argument on property in *Two Treatises*, see Arneil (1996); Barton (2002); Buchan (2001); d'Avignon (2016, 2017); de Hoop and Arora (2017); Goldstein (2013); McLaren, Buck, and Wright (2005); McNally (1990); Sreenivasan (1995); Tully (1980); Udi (2015); Van der Vossen (2015); Waldron (1988); Whitehead (2010, 2012); Wood (1984).

19. On nature reserves, see Tesdell (2013) and Benjamin et al. (2011).

20. Electricity, water, roads, and telecommunications remained largely controlled by Israel. For discussions of Israeli control over these and other fields of service provision, see, e.g., A. Bishara (2015); Dumper (1993); Diwan and Shaban (1999); R. Isaac (2013); Pullan et al. (2007); Salamanca (2011, 2014); Selby (2003, 2013); Selwyn (2001); Shah (1997); Trottier (1999, 2007); Yiftachel (2005). For a historical account of early Zionist and Israeli state control over electricity, see Shamir (2013).

21. Israel bombed and damaged hundreds of Palestinian Authority infrastructures during the second intifada. The most famous example was the military siege of Palestinian President Yasser Arafat's Ramallah compound in 2002.

22. The Accords did not provide for settler and NGO involvement, but both have increasingly gained the ear of Israeli government and military officials, thereby influencing the fates of Palestinian infrastructures indirectly.

23. Under international law, belligerent occupiers must further the development of the economy for the population whose territory they occupy and must protect the occupied population's health, institutions, and infrastructures (UNCTAD 2018).

24. For relevant discussions, see, e.g., Farsakh (2008, 2009); Feldman (2007b); Gabiam (2012); Hever (2007); Brynen (2000); Roy (1995); Le More (2005).

25. On effects of conditional aid, see, e.g., Bhungalia (2015); Escobar (1995); Fassin (2011); Ferguson (1990); Mosse (2005, 2013); Rossi (2004); Ticktin (2014).

26. On the politics of life under occupation, see N. Gordon (2008).

27. On the construction of water scarcity, see, e.g., Alatout (2008).

28. For important work documenting the occupation's effects on Palestinian incomes and employment rates and debt, see, e.g., Ajluni (2003); Brynen (2000); Diwan and Shaban (1999); El-Musa and El-Jaafari (1995); Farsakh (2002, 2005, 2009); Raja Khalidi and Taghdisi-Rad (2009); Roy (1998, 1999); Yusif Sayigh (1986); Tawil-Souri (2009).

29. Scholars often draw on historian Michel Foucault's concepts of discipline, governmentality, and biopower to emphasize the ways in which governance has operated through hygiene campaigns that echoed military sieges. Hygiene, like military siege, seeks to discipline a confined population, rendering bodies docile and creating self-regulating—and self-transforming—subjects. The logic of this disciplining sheds light on what counts as waste in different places and times, how it relates to power, what forms of waste disposal and revaluation are thinkable, and what forms fall outside that remit. See, e.g., W. Anderson (1995, 2007); C. Gupta (2002); Legg (2013); McFarlane (2008); Mills and Sen (2004); Pati and Harrison (2008); Rabinow (1989).

30. On state-like life under conditions of nonsovereignty, see Bonilla (2015); Navaro-Yashin (2012).

31. On Palestinian improvisation, see, e.g., Allen (2008); Peteet (2017, 136); Sbait (1993); Slyomovics (1998, 105).

32. On experimental meaning and urban experience, see, e.g., Larkin (2008); Mbembé and Nuttall (2004). To these depictions of improvisational life in the (post)colony *Waste Siege* contributes the idea that Palestinians embed conscious imperfection within improvisation. They are ambivalent about their improvisations as they put genuine energy into improvising, which implies that practice may not always be the perfect manifestation of belief or intent.

33. On waiting and the Palestinian condition, see, e.g., Dhillon and Yousef (2009); Hage (2009); Hammami (2001); Joronen (2017); Peteet (2017, 2018).

34. On consciously imperfect Palestinian governance in historical context, see Feldman (2005). On improvisation in postcolonial cities, see Chakrabarty (2012); Karlström (2003); Mbembé (1992); Obadare (2010); Robins, Cornwall, and Von Lieres (2008); Rai (2015); Silver (2014).

35. For a similar effort, see Graham and McFarlane (2015).

36. This point contrasts with the argument some make that infrastructures become visible only when they break down. See, e.g., Collier (2011); Elyachar (2010); Graham and Marvin (2001); Graham and McFarlane (2014); Graham and Thrift (2007); Larkin (2008, 2013); Schwenkel (2015); Star (1999).

37. I echo Filip de Boeck's (2012) argument for moving beyond flow as the main infrastructural paradigm. Infrastructures can also be blocking or deceleration devices, imposing their own spatial and temporal logics. See also Carse, Cons, and Middleton (n.d.); Starosielski (2015).

38. For commentary on the representational challenges of slow violence, see Nixon (2011).

39. Important English-language works documenting contemporary life and violence in Jenin include ethnographic writing (e.g., Abufarha 2009; Audeh 2002; Tabar 2007a, 2007b), novels (e.g., Abulhawa 2010), and documentaries such as *Jenin, Jenin* (Bakri 2002), *Arna's Children* (Mer Khamis and Danniel 2004) and *Heart of Jenin* (Geller and Vetter 2008).

40. There is no official or public agreement on who murdered Juliano. For insights into the incident, see Shatz (2013).

CHAPTER 1

1. Dina Zbidat helped translate this from the Hebrew.

2. In 2007 Fatah staged what many call a coup in the West Bank following Hamas's victory in the 2006 Palestinian legislative elections. With the help of the United States and Israel and other states, it flushed Hamas affiliates from West Bank Authority ministries. The Authority has not held legislative elections since 2006 (K. Brown 2010; Erlanger 2006; Hilal 2010; Jarbawi and Pearlman 2007; Koshy 2007; Schanzer 2008; Usher 2006; Wilson and Kessler 2006).

3. On PLO and Fatah-led attempts to homogenize the needs and demands of Palestinian refugees, see, e.g., Allan (2013). Also, neither the mayors nor the Author-

ity represent unified interests. The mayors, for example, represent political parties and families, and within the Authority different ministries advocate for different interests.

4. For relevant discussions of behaving "as if" a government or bureaucracy has authority or legitimacy, see, e.g., Navaro-Yashin (2012) and Wedeen (1999).

5. I thank Iyad Aburdeineh for giving me the landfill's coordinates.

6. On similar moves to centralized, national-scale infrastructure projects that enact scalar reconfigurations, enlarging the governmental gaze, see Swyngedouw (2015, 103).

7. On the politics of legibility and state ordering of "random" practices, see Nugent (2010); T. Mitchell (1991, 34–62); Scott (1998, 11–33).

8. In 2010 the Authority reported that "the total funding provided by foreign donors in support of the Palestinian SW [solid waste] sector has totaled $72.274 million since 1994" (PNA 2010a, 3).

9. See also World Bank (2016).

10. For a contrasting case, see Chatterjee (2010, 26–27).

11. On utopian infrastructures in colonies and postcolonies, see Coronil (1997); Günel (2019); Larkin (2008); T. Mitchell (2011b); Rubenstein (2010); A. Townsend (2013).

12. Exemplary works that discuss or assume the timelessness of infrastructures include Björkman (2015); D. Davis and Burke III (2011); Günel (2016); Larkin (2008); T. Marshall (2013); T. Mitchell (2002); Masco (2006); Nielsen and Pedersen (2015).

13. On construction of such categories in the context of the Red-Dead Canal project, see Havrelock (2017, 6). For a sample discussion by international policy makers and donors of the economic feasibility of introducing incinerators into other contexts, see UN Habitat (2010, 21). On customers and consumers of infrastructure, see also Anand (2017); Farmer (2017); Von Schnitzler (2016).

14. Researchers and governments have grown concerned over possible birth defects and health effects of living near landfill sites. Since the 1990s, research has proliferated on the health and environmental effects of landfills in Europe, Africa, the United States, and Asia (e.g., Assmuth and Strandberg 1993; Dolk et al. 1998; Dummer, Dickinson, and Parker 2003; Elliott et al. 2001; Triassi et al. 2015; Vrijheid 2000).

15. On landfills' effects on industry and consumption, see Gabrys, Hawkins, and Michael (2013); Liboiron (2013); Reno (2015b).

16. See COGAT (n.d.-b).

17. *Judea and Samaria* is the term the Israeli government and settler organizations use for the occupied West Bank. It connotes Jewish and Israeli entitlement to that land and denial of the West Bank's status as territory militarily occupied under international law.

18. Reno (2015b) describes the connection between Four Corners landfill and homes of the people whose trash the landfill consumes as one that generates a kind of object stasis. This suggests one way in which a landfill can act upon time: by making time appear to stand still. Here I suggest another way of thinking about the relationship between landfills and time that resembles what Akhil Gupta (2015) calls "suspension." The difference between Gupta's use of the term *suspension* to describe projects in the midst of being built and the Palestinian case is that Zahrat al-Finjan is complete and yet it creates suspension simultaneously. See also Rabinow (2007).

19. Vincent Ialenti (2014) develops the concepts of "deep time" and "the long now" to think about the relationship between radioactive wastes and temporality. See also Bloomfield and Vurdubakis (2005); Ialenti (2013); Kruse and Galison (2011); Shrader-Frechette (2005).

20. On similar disaggregations elsewhere, see Marres (2016).

21. On the politics and materialities of Dead Sea sinkholes, see Popperl (2018).

22. Checkpoints also "leak" onto local economies and people's experiences of space and time (Tawil-Souri 2011).

23. On "NGOization" of Palestine since Oslo, see Allen (2013); Da'na (2014); Dana (2015a); Hammami, Hilal, and Tamari (2001); Hanafi and Tabar (2005); Jad (2007); Merz (2012); Salem (2012). On privatization of various sectors of governance, see Haddad (2016); Rabie (2014); Raja Khalidi and Samour (2011).

24. On ethnic and national associations with infrastructures in colonial and postcolonial settings, see Larkin (2008).

25. Prepaid meters were also being tried out for potable water in the northern West Bank during my fieldwork. On the proliferation of prepaid meters elsewhere, see Von Schnitzler (2008).

26. In arguing that the context of an infrastructure activates it to become a political actor, I diverge from Latour's (2005) proposal that what he calls "context" is inconsequential. For critiques of Latour but from a Marxian perspective, see Kirsch and Mitchell (2004); Strathern (1996).

CHAPTER 2

1. On checkpoint economies, see Tawil-Souri (2009).

2. This contrasts with a sense of freedom or control, for example. On the relationship between consumption and freedom, see, e.g., Keller (2005); Nussbaum (1998); Rose (1999); Varman and Vikas (2007).

3. Whereas analyses of secondhand markets often present overconsumption of clothing in one place as what leads to a secondhand market in another place, I am interested in how secondhand markets in a place that receives secondhand goods from elsewhere function as a response to *local* consumption of unused clothing. I seek to valorize efforts to bring analysis of emerging economies in the Global South together with analyses of consumers and households (e.g., Gregson and Crang 2015).

4. My focus here parallels the critique offered by Reno and others of the things that matter to informal waste traders, many of which are often elided because of a focus on their poverty or destitution. For an overview of this literature, see Reno (2015a).

5. I was glad to have the chance to share with them hard copies of my article about the *rabish*. See Stamatopoulou-Robbins (2011).

6. For commentaries on Palestinian consumption after Oslo, see, e.g., Taraki (2008b) and Rabie (2014).

7. For comparable discussion on hosting in the Middle East, see Meneley (1996).

8. Taussig (1999, 72) argues that a public secret "greases and glues a society together."

9. On secondhand-market understandings beyond dominant-market or biosocial perspectives, see Halvorson (2015).

10. In the West Bank, the average annual income was $1,350 between 1994 and 2015. The Israeli average annual income has been roughly quadruple that over a similar period (Trading Economics n.d.).

11. Scholars and media tend to emphasize the poverty and economic inequalities that practices like these underscore (e.g., Brooks 2015; Gill 2009; Zimring 2005). On secondhand trade as a system based on different regimes of value, see Crang et al. (2013); Reno (2015a).

12. Hansen's book *Salaula* (2000, 2) offers a powerful corrective to the "passivity these observations attribute to the end of the commodity chain." See also Hansen (2004).

13. For a critical analysis of the problems with abundance in the context of water, see Barnes (2014).

14. On the corporeality of waste labor, see Norris (2012); Reno (2015a).

15. On sending used goods from one place to another because the people who send them cannot travel to the other place, see, e.g., Halvorson (2012).

16. This represents another, perhaps less expected experience of abandonment to add to the one scholars have documented among Palestinian refugees outside Palestine, who felt abandoned by the PLO after Oslo (Allan 2013).

17. On how borders can produce material fetishisms, see, e.g., Spyer (1998).

18. This contrasts with other contexts in which the ability of secondhand goods to forge positive relationships between givers and receivers (from the perspective of their receivers) is limited by signs of use visible on the goods. See, e.g., Halvorson (2015).

19. On durability, see Shevchenko (2002).

20. On authenticity and perceptions of counterfeits in consumption, see Crăciun (2009); Douglas (1979); Lin (2011); Nakassis (2013); Newell (2013); Vann (2006).

21. On temporal values of used goods, see Halvorson (2015); Miller (2009).

22. On secondhand clothing markets and/as service provision in an African context, see Hansen (2000).

23. Popular commentaries on the movement of secondhand clothing from the better-off to the less well-off—for example, from countries of the Global North to those of the South—frame it as a charity-based relation where, even if paid, charitable organizations appear as gift givers. Poor, local mediators selling or distributing secondhand objects to their own communities tend to be left out of the picture, mere conduits of a larger, North-South exchange.

24. On the related idea of people as infrastructure, see Simone (2004b). On people as key elements of *waste* infrastructures, see Reno (2015b).

25. On informal transboundary trade, see Roitman (2005).

26. Scholarship on postcolonial improvisations tends to elide questions about what improvisation makes possible beyond survival in the context of governmental neglect. An exception is Desai, McFarlane, and Graham (2015, 116).

27. For foundational work on market life in the Middle East and North Africa, see Geertz (1979).

28. My work provides further support for Lepawsky's (2012) argument that Basel-era thinking relies on overly simplistic geographical divisions.

CHAPTER 3

1. Anwar's experience is not an isolated incident (Hasson 2012).

2. On Kufr ʿAqab, see Hertz (2016).

3. A popular understanding of the originally medieval term *body politic* suggests it refers to people who come to appear as a single, coherent group. In addition to referring here to Palestinian communities as "bodies politic" in this sense, I draw on John Protevi's recent Deleuzian conceptualization of the term. In particular, I draw on Protevi's (2009, 33) argument that bodies politic involve the imbrication of "somatic and social systems."

4. On ungoverned or abandoned territories or fields of life, see Agamben (1998); Biehl (2005); Bonilla (2015); Clunan and Trinkunas (2010); Das and Poole (2004); Povinelli (2011). On territories characterized by infrastructural neglect, see, e.g., Anand (2017).

5. See also Elyachar (2012).

6. Thanks to Brian Boyd for helping with these dates.

7. In 2009, the Authority included the cave in its *Inventory of Cultural and Natural Heritage Sites of Potential Outstanding Universal Value in Palestine* (PNA 2009). Efforts have been ongoing since the early 2010s to designate Shuqba as a World Heritage Site with UNESCO (Borgia and Smith 2016; Boyd and Crossland 2000).

8. As of 2014, there were around 252 Israeli industrial facilities operating in the West Bank (ARIJ 2015, 121). The major industries in the Ramallah area include fiberglass and leather tanning from Halamish, rubber from Givout Hadasha, aluminum in Nili, fiberglass and plastic in Shilat, and aluminum, cement, plastic, and food canning in ʿAtarot (Qumsieh and Tushyeh 2000, 16).

9. This phrase inverts Marxist geographer David Harvey's expression "accumulation by dispossession." Harvey's expression describes how post-1970s neoliberal policies have worked to transfer wealth and access to it from the laboring classes to the capitalist class, leading to dispossession of the former and enrichment and empowerment of the latter. I reverse Harvey's expression to highlight the way material accumulations in some spaces—here not of wealth but of what is arguably its opposite—can lead to dispossession for the people who live and rely on those spaces (D. Harvey 2003; Swapna Banerjee-Guha 2010). See also the related concept of "dispossession by contamination" (Leifsen 2017) and West's (2016) work on dispossession and the environment.

10. Commercial-scale quarries began functioning in the West Bank in the 1970s (Qumsieh and Tushyeh 2000, 16). Between 80 and 94 percent of both Israeli and Palestinian-owned quarries in the West Bank send the stones they produce into Israel, providing roughly one-quarter of the quarry materials used in the Israeli economy. Their waste, however, remains in the West Bank. Israeli stone quarries and crushers had devoured 3,522 dunums of Palestinian private lands in the West Bank by 2015 (Mawqadi 2017).

11. For recent anthropological work on petitions in the Muslim world, see, e.g., Hull (2012).

12. On responsibility and the adjacent concept of "infrastructural violence," see Appel (2012b); on "chemical body burdens" as a maternal responsibility, see Mackendrick (2014); and on obligation and toxicity, see Fennell (2016).

13. On the principle of "good enough," see Tsing (2015, 255).

14. On matter-of-factness and political authority, see Weber (2013).

15. This is a riff on the famous "turtles all the way down" Indian story that Geertz (1973, 29) recounts to emphasize the bottomlessness of ethnographic truth-telling and its antidote, interpretation.

16. I say "local" here because, outside of Palestine (especially in Europe and North America), it is largely unheard of for Palestinians or for people who self-identify as advocates for Palestinian rights to refer to the occupation in the past tense.

17. In this sense the phantom state in some ways resembles Timothy Mitchell's (2006) "state effect." The "phantomness" I depict here also resonates with Michael Taussig's (1997, 87) depiction of the "strategic formlessness" and inventiveness of the "magic of the state." For Taussig, the magic of the state is "too familiar, yet beyond belief."

18. This is one way Wedeen (1999) describes legitimacy (and its absence) in Syria.

19. In her historical ethnography of governance in Gaza from 1917 to 1967, Ilana Feldman (2008, 17–18) argues that in Gaza the persistence of relatively stable rule relied on bureaucratic authority in the absence of legitimacy.

20. Here Markell is paraphrasing Hannah Arendt in her discussion of human finitude.

CHAPTER 4

1. It is not an exclusive one: casting off bread out of doors occurs in parts of Egypt and among Jewish communities in Israel, for example.

2. I use the term *out of doors* to refer to spaces that are not one's private property, whether a home, a business, a car, or one's own body. I prefer the term to *public space* because the spaces I refer to may or may not be property owned by the municipality, for example. I also prefer it because my argument is premised on the idea that public space is not a category or entity given in advance of the practices that produce it (Lefebvre 1991). On the production of the distinction between private and public spheres through waste, see Laporte (2000).

3. For comparative discussions of food waste as material culture, see D. Evans (2014). On the anthropology of food and eating, see Mintz and Du Bois (2002).

4. I thank my research assistant, Jamal, for pointing me to this nuance.

5. The concept of "sacred waste" has gained traction in literary studies, art theory, semiotics, religious studies, and anthropology. A sample selection of discussions includes C. Anderson (2010); Chidester (2014); Morrison (2008); Riccardi (n.d.); Stengs (2014).

6. Drawing primarily on Foucault's concept of discipline, there is a large literature in anthropology on the cultivation, formation, and technologies of the ethical self. See, e.g., Faubian (2011); Hawkins (2006); Lambek (2010); Rabinow (1996). The anthropology of Islam has been particularly focused on self-cultivation. See, e.g., Hirschkind (2006); Mahmood (2005). For a critique of self-cultivation as a trope in the anthropology of Islam, see Mittermaier (2012). On acts of cultivating ethical and spiritual selves—including through authentications of faith—through engagement with sacred trash, see Riccardi (n.d.). On care for bread elsewhere in the Middle East, see Barnes and Taher (forthcoming).

7. For important critiques of Mauss's essay and how it has been taken up, see, e.g., Graeber (2001); Godelier (1999); Parry (1986, 1989); Sahlins (1972); Weiner (1992).

8. If we borrow Mauss's (1990, 11–12) interpretation of gift circulation among the Maori, we have recipients B and C receiving at the same time, where each receives *because* the other receives.

9. On recycling as an ideology whose attendant infrastructures help individuals feel they are "doing their part" to prevent global waste, see Liboiron (2010).

10. Notable exceptions include works on public health and sanitation in the nineteenth and twentieth centuries such as Sufian (2007) and works that focus on domestic life, such as Granqvist (1931); Moors (1995); Seikaly (2016).

11. On other shifts in ecological relations around changes in consumer waste in the Middle East, see, e.g., Furniss (2010, 2012, 2016).

12. On cynicism and anomie in Palestine, see Allen (2013).

13. On the impacts of aid to occupied Palestinians, see Hanafi and Tabar (2005); Le More (2005); Roy (1995); Farsakh (2016); Villanger (2007).

14. Many camp residents view food and other forms of aid from UNWRA as a political right and as a sign of recognition of their liminal status as refugees. On the politics of being a recipient of "handouts" in a Palestinian refugee camp as well as the politics of infrastructure and aid in Palestinian refugee camps, see Allan (2013); Feldman (2018). See also Petti, Hilal, and Weizman (2013); Stamatopoulou-Robbins (2011).

15. Exceptions include arrangements between hosts of large weddings and mosques. Excess bread and other food left over from the wedding can be brought to a mosque for redistribution to the poor.

16. This resonates with what Laporte (2000) found in sixteenth-century France, where edicts demanding that Paris residents keep their excrement at home and release it at newly regulated times, eventually leading to the creation of water closets inside houses, led to the "privatization" of shit and to the domestication of its odor.

17. *Shrāk* and *ṭabūn* bread are now associated with Palestinian heritage, and consuming them has become a symbol of respect and conservation of that heritage. See Abou Jalal (2015).

18. On the way that cement mediates sociality in Palestinian refugee camps, see Abourahme (2015).

19. This is why, for Sahlins (1972, 169), the gift is an analogue for what the state is for Hobbes.

20. Graffiti can often be a form of signature. But it can also be purposefully anonymous. On the relationship between graffiti and anonymity, see E. Butler (2006); Gonos, Mulkern, and Poushinsky (1976); Palmer (1997); Peteet (1996); Rodriguez and Clair (1999).

21. Godelier (1999, 11) argues that, for Mauss, "To give is voluntarily to transfer something that belongs to you to someone who you think cannot refuse to accept it." Graeber (2001, 224) also argues that "to give a gift is to transfer something without any immediate return, or guarantee that there will ever be one."

22. As UNRWA has faced major budget cuts over the past few decades, its preconditions for distributing aid have become more strict. The categories of people eligible for aid have become narrower.

23. Though what is formed in Palestine around bread is not exactly a public, I note that the ambiguity of a public's content is also important to the Habermasian understanding of a public (Habermas 1989).

24. How such "vernacular" socialities emerge outside the usual state and national rubrics has garnered renewed attention (e.g., Sand 2011).

25. Scholars have recently expanded their understandings of modes of address for publics to include ways that do not depend on participation in rational exchanges of speech or text—for example, through the public sharing of intimacies or through affect (Kunreuther 2014). See also Berlant (1997, 2008); Cody (2011); Habermas (1989); Warner (2002).

26. On the related concept of "infrastructural publics," see Collier, Mizes, and von Schnitzler (2016).

27. Scholars have argued that the problems wastes produce can create a social cohesion by constituting communities of class-based taste and disgust (Anand 2012); W. Anderson (1995, 2007); Argyrou (1997); Laporte (2000); Otter (2008). They can do so by serving as the terrain upon which claims to rights to "sanitation," to live separately from excrement, and to produce waste in private, are made (Appadurai 2001; Chalfin 2014; Hawkins 2004). Analyses of acts like the communal cleanup of Zucotti Park during Occupy Wall Street's occupation and that of Tahrir Square during Egypt's "Arab Spring," like the communal cleanups of West Bank and Gazan Palestinian cities during and after the two intifadas, are emblematic of this view (e.g., Winegar 2011, 2016). These analyses often suggest that those who clean public space together make conscious decisions to sweep streets and to pick up trash collectively as a way of producing cohesion. Or they imply that solidarities preexisted acts of cleaning and that acts of cleaning therefore reflect those solidarities.

28. On infrastructural layerings, see, e.g., Larkin (2008); Lefebvre (1991); Graham and Marvin (1996); Anand (2015). On the meanings of Palestinian practices of burning the Israeli Apartheid Wall, see A. Bishara (2013, 233–58).

29. This complicates arguments that present "unintended usages" of infrastructures as forms either of "resistance" or of an "undermining" of the authority of experts or of other political actors who designed or manage those infrastructures (e.g., Larkin 2008).

CHAPTER 5

1. For a critique of the "imaginariness" of environmental imaginaries, see T. Mitchell (2011a).

2. Water under the West Bank makes up about 60 percent of Israel's water sources (e.g., El-Fadel et al. 2001; Libiszewski 1995).

3. The fact that this includes wastewater projects like underground urban sewage networks and treatment plants makes wastewater infrastructures different from solid waste infrastructures like landfills, which require Israeli permits only if they are in Area C.

4. For example, it met only once between 2011 and 2013 and did not approve any projects (Reidy 2013).

5. The Red-Dead Canal project between Israel, the Authority, and Jordan is one current example (Al-Omari, Salman, and Karablieh 2014; Havrelock 2017).

6. For critiques of the international aid industry in Palestine and channeling of funds to foreign consultants, see Hattem (2014a); Le More (2008).

7. West Bank Palestinians purchase roughly fifty million cubic meters per year of water from Mekorot, which obtains the water by drilling wells in the West Bank, selling the water beneath Palestinians' feet back to them.

8. On shit's constant return, see Laporte (2000).

9. On collective memory after the *nakba*, see, e.g., Abdo and Lentin (2002); Collins (2004); R. Davis (2010); Kassem (2011); Khalili (2005); Nur (2008); Saʿdi and Abu-Lughod (2007); Siddiq (1995); Slyomovics (1998). On pressures on Palestinians to remember in particular ways, see Allan (2013).

10. On mediation, networks, and municipal government in Israel and in early Zionist statecraft, see Eyal (2006, 38–39).

CONCLUSION

1. Also spelled *dabkah, dabki, debka*, and *dabke, dabkeh* is a popular dance form danced by Arabs in Palestine, Lebanon, Jordan, and Syria. For scholarly work on Palestinian dabkeh, see Al-Awwad (1983); Kanaaneh et al. (2013); H. Hamdan (1996); Ladkani (2005); Van Aken (2006).

2. This point echoes Gille's (2007) idea that something is always left out of waste regimes and that abject materials therefore end up "biting back."

3. This is a point researchers and activists have also made in a variety of ways (e.g., Humes 2012).

4. On dwelling and the sensory, see Bachelard (1964).

5. On the making of "social ecologies"—for example, in and after empire—see Stoler (2006).

6. For an interesting parallel analysis of the ambience of sound, see, e.g., Feld and Brenneis (2004).

7. For an overview of research that argues for consideration of nonequilibrium ecologies, see Zimmerer (2000).

8. Growing interest among Middle East scholars in environmental issues has yielded important work on the role of imagination in giving meaning to landscapes there. See, e.g., D. Davis and Burke III (2011); Guarasci (2015); McKee (2016).

9. Waste is an emerging topic for scholars interested in environmentalisms and in humans' relationships to the environment. Scholars have looked at environmental crises produced by human-produced waste or leaks—for example, from nuclear disasters (e.g., Auyero and Swiston 2009; Fortun 2001; Kimura 2016; Murphy 2006; Newman 2016; Petryna 2003). And they have examined how some communities are disproportionately affected by the "slow violence" (Nixon 2011) of toxic materials and pollution. Many of these studies have documented important moments when slow violence gives rise to movements for environmental justice (e.g., Cole and Foster 2001; Mohai, Pellow, and Roberts 2009; Oliver-Smith 1996; Pellow 2002, 2007; Rootes and Leonard 2010).

10. An exception is the work of Ogden et al. (2013).

11. See also Limbert (2001, 37) and Rudiak-Gould (2014).

12. Concerns about climate change are also tethered to statecraft in that Palestine-based experts argue that the Israeli occupation makes Palestinians unnaturally more vulnerable to climate change (e.g., Mason, Zeitoun, and Mimi 2012).

13. I draw here on Tsing's (2015) account of the forms of life made possible out of the ruins of industrial capitalism.

References

Abdel-Qader, Selma, and Tanya Lee Roberts-Davis. 2018. "Toxic Occupation: Leveraging the Basel Convention in Palestine." *Journal of Palestine Studies* 47 (2): 28–43. https://doi.org/10.1525/jps.2018.47.2.28.

Abdo, Nahla, and Ronit Lentin, eds. 2002. *Women and the Politics of Military Confrontation: Palestinian and Israeli Gendered Narratives of Dislocation*. New York: Berghan Books.

Abdo, Nahla, and Nira Yuval-Davis. 1995. "Palestine, Israel and the Zionist Settler Project." In *Unsettling Settler Societies: Articulations of Gender, Race, Ethnicity and Class*, edited by Daiva Stasiulis and Nira Yuval-Davis, 291–322. London: Sage Publications.

Abou Jalal, Rasha. 2015. "Demand Rises for Traditional Gazan Bread." *Al-Monitor*, December 15. http://www.al-monitor.com/pulse/tr/originals/2015/12/gaza-palestinian-traditional-bread.amp.html.

Abourahme, Nasser. 2015. "Assembling and Spilling-Over: Towards an 'Ethnography of Cement' in a Palestinian Refugee Camp." *International Journal of Urban and Regional Research* 39 (2): 200–217. https://doi.org/10.1111/1468-2427.12155.

Abu El-Haj, Nadia. 2001. *Facts on the Ground: Archaeological Practice and Territorial Self-Fashioning in Israeli Society*. Chicago: University of Chicago Press.

Abufarha, Nasser. 2009. *The Making of a Human Bomb: An Ethnography of Palestinian Resistance*. Durham, NC: Duke University Press.

Abulhawa, Susan. 2010. *Mornings in Jenin*. London: Bloomsbury Press.

Adam, Barbara. 1998. *Timescapes of Modernity: The Environment and Invisible Hazards*. London: Routledge.

Agamben, Giorgio. 1998. *Homo Sacer: Sovereign Power and Bare Life*. Translated by Daniel Heller-Roazen. Stanford, CA: Stanford University Press.

Agrawal, Arun. 2005. *Environmentality: Technologies of Government and the Making of Subjects*. Durham, NC: Duke University Press.

Ahmad, Amal. 2014. "The Customs Union and Israel's No-State Solution." *Al-Shabaka*, November 26. https://al-shabaka.org/briefs/the-customs-union-and-israels-no -state-solution/.

Ajluni, Salem. 2003. "The Palestinian Economy and the Second Intifada." *Journal of Palestine Studies* 32 (3): 64–73.

Akahane, Keiichi, Makoto Akashi, Masaki Matsumoto, Hiroshi Yasuda, Nobuyuki Miya-hara, Shigekazu Fukuda, Kazuki Iwaoka, Shunsuke Yonai, and Akifumi Fukumura. 2012. "The Fukushima Nuclear Power Plant Accident and Exposures in the Environment." *Environmentalist* 32 (2): 136–43.

Akram, Susan M. 2002. "Palestinian Refugees and Their Legal Status: Rights, Politics, and Implications for a Just Solution." *Journal of Palestine Studies* 31 (3): 36–51.

Al-Aref, Aref. 2013. *Al-Nakba: Nakbat Bayt al-Maqdis wal-Firdaws al-Mafqud* [The *nakba*: The *nakba* of Jerusalem and the lost paradise, 1947–1949]. 3 vols. Beirut: Institute for Palestine Studies.

Alatout, Samer. 2006. "Towards a Bio-Territorial Conception of Power: Territory, Population, and Environmental Narratives in Palestine and Israel." *Political Geography* 25 (6): 601–21.

———. 2008. "'States' of Scarcity: Water, Space, and Identity Politics in Israel, 1948–59." *Environment and Planning D: Society and Space* 26 (6): 959–82.

Al-Awwad, Suhad. 1983. *Al-Dabkeh* [The Dabkeh]. In *Dirisat fi al-fulklur al-Filistini* [Studies in Palestinian Folklore], 100–103. Amman, Jordan: Palestine Liberation Organization, Department of Media and Culture.

Al-Haq. 2016. "Environmental Rights Case Succeeds in Holding Israel Accountable for Illegal Hazardous Waste Dumping in Palestine." August 25. http://www.alhaq .org/advocacy/topics/housing-land-and-natural-resources/1066–environmental -rights-case-succeeds-in-holding-israel-accountable-for-illegal-hazardous-waste -dumping-in-palestine.

Alkhalil, Suleiman, and Issam Qasem. 2009. "The Impact of Israeli Industrial Zone on Environmental and Human Health in Tulkarm City." Paper presented at the

Second International Conference on the Palestinian Environment, An-Najah National University, Nablus, Palestine, October 13–14. https://pdfs.semanticscholar .org/3517/e951c07490c2ed98a0563b872152ebcf9b5a.pdf.

Al-Khatib, Issam, and Rula Abu Safieh. 2003. "OPT: Solid Waste Management in Emergency: A Case Study from Ramallah and Al-Bireh Municipalities." Institute of Community and Public Health, Birzeit University, January 5. http://reliefweb .int/report/israel/opt-solid-waste-management-emergency-case-study-ramallah -and-al-bireh-municipalities.

Al-Khazendar, Sami. 1997. *Jordan and the Palestine Question: The Role of Islamic and Left Forces in Foreign Policy-Making.* Reading, Berkshire: Ithaca Press.

Allan, Diana. 2013. *Refugees of the Revolution: Experiences of Palestinian Exile.* Stanford, CA: Stanford University Press.

Allen, Lori. 2008. "Getting by the Occupation: How Violence Became Normal during the Second Palestinian Intifada." *Cultural Anthropology* 23 (3): 453–87.

———. 2013. *The Rise and Fall of Human Rights: Cynicism and Politics in Occupied Palestine.* Stanford, CA: Stanford University Press.

Al-Mohammad, Hayder. 2007. "Ordure and Disorder: The Case of Basra and the Anthropology of Excrement." *Anthropology of the Middle East* 2 (2): 1–23.

Al-Omari, Abbas, Amer Salman, and Emad Karablieh. 2014."The Red Dead Canal Project: An Adaptation Option to Climate Change in Jordan." *Desalination and Water Treatment* 52 (13–15): 2833–40.

Anand, Nikhil. 2012. "Municipal Disconnect: On Abject Water and its Urban Infrastructures." *Ethnography* 13 (4): 487-509.

———. 2015. "Accretion." *Cultural Anthropology* website, Fieldsights, Editors' Forum, Theorizing the Contemporary, Infrastructure Toolbox Series, September 24. https://culanth.org/fieldsights/accretion.

———. 2017. *Hydraulic City: Water and the Infrastructures of Citizenship in Mumbai.* Durham, NC: Duke University Press.

Anderson, Christopher Todd. 2010. "Sacred Waste: Ecology, Spirit, and the American Garbage Poem." *Interdisciplinary Studies in Literature and the Environment* 17 (1): 35–60.

Anderson, Warwick. 1995. "Excremental Colonialism: Public Health and the Poetics of Pollution." *Critical Inquiry* 21 (3): 640–69.

———. 2007. *Colonial Pathologies: American Tropical Medicine, Race, and Hygiene in the Philippines.* Quezon City: Ateneo de Manila University Press.

Angell, Elizabeth. 2014. "Assembling Disaster: Earthquakes and Urban Politics in Istanbul." *City* 18 (6): 667–78.

Appadurai, Arjun, ed. 1988. *The Social Life of Things: Commodities in Cultural Perspective*. Cambridge: Cambridge University Press.

———. 1996. *Modernity at Large: Cultural Dimensions of Globalization*. Minneapolis: University of Minnesota Press.

———. 2001. "Deep Democracy: Urban Governmentality and the Horizon of Politics." *Environment and Urbanization* 13 (2): 23–43.

Appel, Hannah C. 2012a. "Offshore Work: Oil, Modularity, and the How of Capitalism in Equatorial Guinea." *American Ethnologist* 39 (4): 692–709.

———. 2012b. "Walls and White Elephants: Oil Extraction, Responsibility, and Infrastructural Violence in Equatorial Guinea." *Ethnography* 13 (4): 439–65.

Appel, Hannah C., Arthur Mason, and Michael Watts, eds. 2015. *Subterranean Estates: Life Worlds of Oil and Gas*. Ithaca, NY: Cornell University Press.

Argyrou, Vassos. 1997. "'Keep Cyprus Clean': Littering, Pollution, and Otherness." *Cultural Anthropology* 12 (2): 159–78.

ARIJ (Applied Research Institute of Jerusalem). 2006. "The Israeli Fever of House Demolition Continues in Shuqba." Eye on Palestine, March 2. http://poica.org/2006/03/the-israeli-fever-of-house-demolition-continues-in-shuqba-village/.

———. 2010. "Al 'Ubeidiya Town Profile." http://vprofile.arij.org/bethlehem/pdfs/VP/Al%20'Ubeidiya_tp_en.pdf.

———. 2012. "Shuqba Village Profile." http://vprofile.arij.org/ramallah/pdfs/vprofile/Shuqba_vp_en.pdf.

———. 2015. *The Status of Environment in the State of Palestine, 2015*. Bethlehem, Palestine: ARIJ. https://www.arij.org/files/arijadmin/2016/SOER_2015_final.pdf.

———. 2016. "Israeli Stone Quarries and Crushers Are Founded on Palestinian Private Lands and Do Continuously Expand." Eye on Palestine, January 8. http://poica.org/2016/01/israeli-stone-quarries-and-crushers-are-founded-on-palestinian-private-lands-and-do-continuously-expand/.

Arneil, Barbara. 1996. *John Locke and America: The Defence of English Colonialism*. Oxford: Clarendon Press.

Arnold, David. 2016. *Toxic Histories: Poison and Pollution in Modern India*. Cambridge: Cambridge University Press.

Arnould-Bloomfield, Elisabeth. 2016. "Sacrifice." In *Georges Bataille: Key Concepts*, edited by Mark Hewson and Marcus Coelen, 99–111. New York: Routledge.

Asher, Kiran. 2009. *Black and Green: Afro-Colombians, Development, and Nature in the Pacific Lowlands*. Durham, NC: Duke University Press.

Assmuth, T. W., and T. Strandberg. 1993. "Ground Water Contamination at Finnish Landfills." *Water, Air, and Soil Pollution* 69 (1–2): 179–99.

Audeh, Ida. 2002. "Narratives of Siege: Eye-Witness Testimonies from Jenin, Bethlehem and Nablus." *Journal of Palestine Studies* 31 (4): 13–34. https://doi.org/10.1525/jps.2002.31.4.13.

Austin, J. L. 1962. *How to Do Things with Words*. 2nd ed. Edited by J. O. Urmson and Marina Sbisá. Cambridge, MA: Harvard University Press.

———. 1970. *Philosophical Papers*. Edited by J. Urmson and G. Warnock. Oxford: Oxford University Press.

Auyero, Javier, and Deborah Swistun. 2007. "Confused Because Exposed: Towards an Ethnography of Environmental Suffering." *Ethnography* 8 (2): 123–44.

———. 2008. "The Social Production of Toxic Uncertainty." *American Sociological Review* 73: 357–79.

———. 2009. *Flammable: Environmental Suffering in an Argentine Shantytown*. Oxford: Oxford University Press.

Babül, Elif M. 2017. *Bureaucratic Intimacies: Translating Human Rights in Turkey*. Stanford, CA: Stanford University Press.

Bachelard, Gaston. 1964. *The Poetics of Space*. Translated by Maria Jolas. New York: Orion Press.

Baer, Gabriel. 1978. "The Economic and Social Position of the Village-Mukhtar in Palestine." In *The Palestinians and the Middle East Conflict*, edited by Gabriel Ben-Dor, 101–18. Ramat Gan: Turtledove.

Baer, Hans, and Merrill Singer. 2014. *The Anthropology of Climate Change: An Integrated Critical Perspective*. London: Routledge.

Bakan, Abigail B., and Yasmeen Abu-Laban. 2010. "Israel/Palestine, South Africa and the 'One-State Solution': The Case for an Apartheid Analysis." *Politikon* 37 (2–3): 331–51.

Bakri, Mohamed. 2002. *Jenin, Jenin*. Videorecording. Directed by Mohamed Bakri. Seattle, WA: Arab Film Distribution.

Banerjee-Guha, Swapna, ed. 2010. *Accumulation by Dispossession: Transformative Cities in the New Global Order*. New Delhi: Sage Publications.

Barkey, Karen. 1994. *Bandits and Bureaucrats: The Ottoman Route to State Centralization*. Ithaca, NY: Cornell University Press.

Barnes, Jessica. 2014. *Cultivating the Nile: The Everyday Politics of Water in Egypt*. Durham, NC: Duke University Press.

Barnes, Jessica, Michael Dove, Myanna Lahsen, Andrew Mathews, Pamela McElwee, Roderick McIntosh, Frances Moore et al. 2013. "Contribution of Anthropology to the Study of Climate Change." *Nature Climate Change* 3 (6): 541–44.

Barnes, Jessica, and Mariam Taher. Forthcoming. "Care and Conveyance: Buying Baladi Bread in Cairo." Cultural Anthropology.

Baroud, Ramzy. 2006. *The Second Palestinian Intifada: A Chronicle of a People's Struggle.* London: Pluto Press.

Bartlett, Eva. 2013. "The Siege Is Rubbish." Inter Press Service, March 31. http://www.ipsnews.net/2013/03/the-siege-is-rubbish/.

Barton, Gregory Allen. 2002. *Empire Forestry and the Origins of Environmentalism.* Cambridge: Cambridge University Press.

Bataille, Georges. 1988. *The Accursed Share: An Essay on General Economy.* Translated by Robert Hurley. New York: Zone Books.

———. 1997. "Sacrifice, the Festival, and the Principles of the Sacred World." In *The Bataille Reader,* edited by Fred Botting and Scott Wilson, 210–20. Oxford: Blackwell.

Bauman, Zygmunt. 2004. *Wasted Lives: Modernity and Its Outcasts.* Cambridge: Polity Press.

Bear, Laura, and Nayanika Mathur. 2015. "Remaking the Public Good: A New Anthropology of Bureaucracy." *Cambridge Journal of Anthropology* 33 (1): 18–34.

Benjamin, Jesse, M. B. Levy, S. Kershnar, and M. Sahibzada, eds. 2011. *Greenwashing Apartheid: The Jewish National Fund's Environmental Cover Up.* JNF eBook No. 4. http://stopthejnf.org/documents/JNFeBookVol4.pdf.

Bennett, Jane. 2010. *Vibrant Matter: A Political Ecology of Things.* Durham, NC: Duke University Press.

Berlant, Lauren. 1997. *The Queen of America Goes to Washington City: Essays on Sex and Citizenship.* Durham, NC: Duke University Press.

———. 2008. *The Female Complaint: The Unfinished Business of Sentimentality in American Culture.* Durham, NC: Duke University Press.

Bernasconi, Robert. 1990. "Rousseau and the Supplement to the Social Contract: Deconstruction and the Possibility of Democracy." *Cardozo Law Review* 11 (5–6): 1539–64.

Bhungalia, Lisa. 2015. "Managing Violence: Aid, Counterinsurgency, and the Humanitarian Present in Palestine." *Environment and Planning A* 47 (11): 2308–23.

Biehl, João. 2005. *Vita: Life in a Zone of Social Abandonment.* Berkeley: University of California Press.

Bimkom. 2008. *The Prohibited Zone: Israeli Planning Policy in the Palestinian Villages in Area C.* Jerusalem: BIMKOM. http://bimkom.org/eng/wp-content/uploads /ProhibitedZone.pdf.

Bird, Elizabeth Ann R. 1987. "The Social Construction of Nature: Theoretical Approaches to the History of Environmental Problems." *Environmental Review* 11: 255–64.

Bishara, Amahl. 2013. *Back Stories: U.S. News Production and Palestinian Politics.* Stanford, CA: Stanford University Press.

———. 2015. "Driving while Palestinian in Israel and the West Bank: The Politics of Disorientation and the Routes of a Subaltern Knowledge." *American Ethnologist* 42 (1): 33–54.

Bishara, Marwan. 2002. *Palestine/Israel: Peace or Apartheid Occupation, Terrorism, and the Future.* London: Zed Books.

Björkman, Lisa. 2015. *Pipe Politics, Contested Waters: Embedded Infrastructures of Millennial Mumbai.* Durham, NC: Duke University Press.

Blanc, Paul David. 2016. *Fake Silk: The Lethal History of Viscose Rayon.* New Haven, CT: Yale University Press.

Bloomfield, Brian, and Theo Vurdubakis. 2005. "The Secret of Yucca Mountain: Reflections on an Object in Extremis." *Environment and Planning: Society and Space* 23 (5): 735–56.

Bocco, Riccardo. 2009. "UNRWA and the Palestinian Refugees: A History within History." *Refugee Survey Quarterly* 28 (2–3): 229–52.

Bohme, Susanna Rankin. 2014. *Toxic Injustice: A Transnational History of Exposure and Struggle.* Berkeley: University of California Press.

Bond, David. 2013. "Governing Disaster: The Political Life of the Environment during the BP Oil Spill." *Cultural Anthropology* 28 (4): 694–715.

Bonilla, Yarimar. 2015. *Nonsovereign Futures: French Caribbean Politics in the Wake of Disenchantment.* Chicago: University of Chicago Press.

Borgia, Valentina, and Pamela Jane Smith. 2016. "No Country for Archaeologists: Shuqba Cave, an Illustration of the Grave Situation of Palestinian Archaeology." *Archaeological Review from Cambridge* 31 (1): 14–37.

Borneman, John. 1997. "State, Territory, and National Identity Formation in the Two Berlins, 1945–1995." In *Culture, Power, Place: Explorations in Critical Anthropology*, edited by Akhil Gupta and James Ferguson, 93–117. Durham, NC: Duke University Press.

Boscagli, Maurizia. 2014. *Stuff Theory: Everyday Objects, Radical Materialism.* New York: Bloomsbury.

Bowler, Ian R. 1998. "Recycling Urban Waste on Farmland: An Actor-Network Interpretation." *Applied Geography* 19 (1): 29–43.

Boyd, Brian, and Zoë Crossland. 2000. "New Fieldwork in Shuqba Cave and in Wadi en-Natuf, Western Judea." *Antiquity* 74 (286): 755–56.

Braun, Bruce, and Noel Castree. 1998. *Remaking Reality: Nature at the Millenium.* London: Routledge.

———, eds. 2001. *Social Nature: Theory, Practice and Politics.* Oxford: Blackwell.

Brickman, Ronald, Sheila Jasanoff, and Thomas Ilgen. 1985. *Controlling Chemicals: The Politics of Regulation in Europe and the United States.* Ithaca, NY: Cornell University Press.

Brooks, Andrew. 2015. *Clothing Poverty: The Hidden World of Fast Fashion and Second-Hand Clothes.* London: Zed Books.

Brosius, Peter J. 1999. "Anthropological Engagements with Environmentalism." *Current Anthropology* 40 (3): 277–308.

Broswimmer, Franz. 2002. *Ecocide: A Short History of the Mass Extinction of Species.* London: Pluto Press.

Brown, Kate. 2016. "The Last Sink: The Human Body as the Ultimate Radioactive Storage Site." In "Out of Sight, Out of Mind: The Politics and Culture of Waste," edited by Christof Mauch, special issue, *RCC Perspectives: Transformations in Environment and Society*, no. 1: 41–47.

Brown, Nathan J. 2003. *Palestinian Politics after the Oslo Accords: Resuming Arab Palestine.* Berkeley: University of California Press.

———. 2010. "The Hamas-Fatah Conflict: Shallow but Wide." *Fletcher Forum of World Affairs* 34 (2): 35–51.

Brown, Phil. 1997. *No Safe Place: Toxic Waste, Leukemia, and Community Action.* Berkeley: University of California Press.

———. 2007. *Toxic Exposures: Contested Illnesses and the Environmental Health Movement.* New York: Columbia University Press.

Brynen, Rex. 1995. "The Neopatrimonial Dimension of Palestinian Politics." *Journal of Palestine Studies* 25 (1): 23–36. https://doi.org/doi:10.2307/2538102.

———. 2000. *A Very Political Economy: Peacebuilding and Foreign Aid in the West Bank and Gaza.* Washington, DC: United States Institute of Peace Press.

B'Tselem. 2017a. *Made in Israel: Exploiting Palestinian Land for Treatment of Israeli Waste*. Jerusalem: B'Tselem.

———. 2017b. "The Separation Barrier." November 11. https://www.btselem.org /separation_barrier.

Buch, Elana. 2015. "Anthropology of Aging and Care." *Annual Review of Anthropology* 44 (1): 277–93.

Buchan, Bruce. 2001. "Subjecting the Natives: Aborigines, Property and Possession under Early Colonial Rule." *Social Analysis: The International Journal of Social and Cultural Practice* 45 (2): 143–62.

Bullard, Robert D. 2000. *Dumping in Dixie: Race, Class, and Environmental Quality.* Vol. 3. Boulder, CO: Westview Press.

Burrow-Goldhahn, Amber. 2008. "Spaces of Chernobyl: Emptiness and Fullness, Absence and Presence." PhD diss., University College London.

Butler, Ella. 2006. *The Anthropology of Anonymity: Toilet Graffiti at the University of Melbourne*. Melbourne: School of Anthropology, Geography and Environmental Studies, University of Melbourne.

Butler, Judith. 1997. *The Psychic Life of Power: Theories in Subjection*. Stanford, CA: Stanford University Press.

———. 2009. *Frames of War: When Is Life Grievable?* New York: Verso.

Callon, Michel, John Law, and Arie Rip, eds. 1986. *Mapping the Dynamics of Science and Technology: Sociology of Science in the Real World*. Basingstoke: Macmillan.

Canaan, Taufik. 1927. *Mohammedan Saints and Sanctuaries in Palestine*. Vol. 5. London: Luzac; Jerusalem: Ariel Publishing House.

———. 1935. "The Curse in Palestinian Folklore." *Journal of the Palestine Oriental Society* 15: 235–79.

Carse, Ashley, Jason Cons, and Townsend Middleton, eds. 2018. "Chokepoints." *Limn* 10. https://limn.it/issues/chokepoints/.

Carter, Jimmy. 2007. *Palestine Peace Not Apartheid*. New York: Simon and Schuster.

Castree, Noel. 1995. "The Nature of Produced Nature." *Antipode* 27 (1): 12–48.

Chakrabarty, Dipesh. 2009. "The Climate of History: Four Theses." *Critical Inquiry* 35 (2): 197–222.

———. 2012. "Postcolonial Studies and the Challenge of Climate Change." *New Literary History* 43 (1): 1–18.

Chalfin, Brenda. 2014. "Public Things, Excremental Politics, and the Infrastructure of Bare Life in Ghana's City of Tema." *American Ethnologist* 41 (1): 92–109.

Challand, Benoît. 2008. "A Naḥḍa of Charitable Organizations? Health Service Provision and the Politics of Aid in Palestine." *International Journal of Middle East Studies* 40 (2): 227–47.

Chatterjee, Partha. 2010. *Empire and Nation: Selected Essays*. New York: Columbia University Press.

Checker, Melissa. 2005. *Environmental Racism and the Search for Justice in a Southern Town*. New York: New York University Press.

Chidester, David. 2014. "The Accidental, Ambivalent, and Useless Sacred." *Material Religion: The Journal of Objects, Art and Belief* 10 (2): 239–40.

Choy, Timothy. 2011. *Ecologies of Comparison: An Ethnography of Endangerment in Hong Kong*. Durham, NC: Duke University Press.

Clunan, Anne, and Harold A. Trinkunas, eds. 2010. *Ungoverned Spaces: Alternatives to State Authority in an Era of Softened Sovereignty*. Stanford, CA: Stanford University Press.

Cody, Francis. 2011. "Publics and Politics." *Annual Review of Anthropology* 40:37–52.

COGAT (Coordination of Government Activities in the Territories). 2017a. "The David Unit: Working to Prevent Waste Smuggling to Judea and Samaria." May 29. http://www.cogat.mod.gov.il/en/Our_Activities/Pages/CA-David-Unit.aspx.

———. 2017b. "Pollution? Not on Our Watch: Protecting the Environment in Judea and Samaria." February 26. http://www.cogat.mod.gov.il/en/Our_Activities/Pages/charcoal-production-enviroment-26.2.17.aspx.

———. n.d.-a. "Environmental Protection." Accessed April 5, 2017. http://www.cogat.mod.gov.il/en/Judea_and_Samaria/Pages/JSEnviromentSection.aspx.

———. n.d.-b. "Infrastructure." Accessed August 25, 2017. http://www.cogat.mod.gov.il/en/Judea_and_Samaria/Pages/JSInfrastructureSection.aspx.

Cohen, Abner. 1965. *Arab Border-Villages in Israel: A Study of Continuity and Change in Social Organization*. Manchester: Manchester University Press.

Cole, Luke W., and Sheila R. Foster. 2001. *From the Ground Up: Environmental Racism and the Rise of the Environmental Justice Movement*. New York: New York University Press.

Collier, Stephen J. 2011. *Post-Soviet Social: Neoliberalism, Social Modernity, Biopolitics*. Princeton, NJ: Princeton University Press.

Collier, Stephen J., James Christopher Mizes, and Antina von Schnitzler. 2016. "Preface: Public Infrastructure/Infrastructural Publics." *Limn* 7: 2–7. https://limn.it/issues/public-infrastructuresinfrastructural-publics/.

Collins, John. 2004. *Occupied by Memory: The Intifada Generation and the Palestinian State of Emergency*. New York: New York University Press.

Comaroff, Jean, and John Comaroff, eds. 2006. *Law and Disorder in the Postcolony.* Chicago: University of Chicago Press.

Cordner, Alissa. 2016. *Toxic Safety: Flame Retardants, Chemical Controversies, and Environmental Health.* New York: Columbia University Press.

Coronil, Fernando. 1997. *The Magical State: Nature, Money, and Modernity in Venezuela.* Chicago: University of Chicago Press.

Crăciun, Magdalena. 2009. "Trading in Fake Brands, Self-Creating as an Individual." In *Anthropology and the Individual: A Material Culture Perspective*, edited by Daniel Miller, 25–36. Oxford: Berg.

Cram, Shannon. 2011. "Escaping S-102: Waste, Illness, and the Politics of Not Knowing." *International Journal of Science in Society* 2 (1): 243–52. https://doi .org/10.18848/1836-6236/CGP/v02i01/51509.

Crang, Mike, Nicky Gregson, Farid Ahamed, Raihana Ferdous, and Nasreen Akhter. 2012. "Death, the Phoenix and Pandora: Transforming Things and Values in Bangladesh." In *Economies of Recycling: Global Transformations of Materials, Values and Social Relations*, edited by Catherine Alexander and Joshua Reno, 59–75. London: Zed Books.

Crang, Mike, Alex Hughes, Nicky Gregson, Farid Ahamed, and Lucy Norris. 2013. "Rethinking Governance and Value in Commodity Chains through Global Recycling Networks." *Transactions Institute of British Geographers* 38 (1): 12–24.

Crate, Susan A. 2011. "Climate and Culture: Anthropology in the Era of Contemporary Climate Change." *Annual Review of Anthropology* 40:175–94.

Cronon, William. 2003. *Changes in the Land: Indians, Colonists, and the Ecology of New England.* New York: Hill and Wang.

Csordas, Thomas J. 1993. "Somatic Modes of Attention." *Cultural Anthropology* 8 (2): 135–56.

Dalakoglou, Dimitris, and Penelope Harvey, eds. 2016. *Roads and Anthropology: Ethnography, Infrastructures, (Im) Mobility.* London: Routledge.

Da'na, Tariq. *See also* Dana, Tariq. 2014. "Disconnecting Civil Society from Its Historical Extension: NGOs and Neoliberalism in Palestine." In *Human Rights, Human Security, National Security: The Intersection*, edited by Saul Takahashi, 117–38. Denver, CO: Praeger Security International.

Dana, Tariq. *See also* Da'na, Tariq. 2014. "The Palestinian Capitalists That Have Gone Too Far." Al-Shabaka: The Palestinian Policy Network, January Policy Brief, January 14. https://al-shabaka.org/briefs/palestinian-capitalists-have-gone-too-far/.

———. 2015a. "The Structural Transformation of Palestinian Civil Society: Key

Paradigm Shifts." Middle East Critique 24 (2): 191–210. http://dx.doi.org/10.1080 /19436149.2015.1017968.

———. 2015b. "The Symbiosis between Palestinian 'Fayyadism' and Israeli 'Economic Peace': The Political Economy of Capitalist Peace in the Context of Colonisation." *Conflict, Security and Development* 15 (5): 455–77.

Daoudi, Hanna, and Raja Khalidi. 2008. "The Palestinian War-Torn Economy: Aid, Development and State Formation." *A Contrario* 5 (1): 23–36.

Darier, Éric, ed. 1999. *Discourses of the Environment*. Oxford: Blackwell.

Das, Veena, and Deborah Poole, eds. 2004. *Anthropology in the Margins of the State.* Santa Fe, NM: School of American Research Press.

Das, Veena, and Shalini Randeria. 2015. "Politics of the Urban Poor: Aesthetics, Ethics, Volatility." Precarity, An Introduction to Supplement 11. *Current Anthropology* 56 (S11): S3–S14.

d'Avignon, Robyn. 2016. "Subterranean Histories: Making 'Artisanal' Miners on the West African Sahel." PhD diss., University of Michigan.

———. 2017. "Minerals." *Somatosphere*, December 11. http://somatosphere.net/2017/12/ minerals.html.

Davis, Diana K. 2011. "Introduction: Imperialism, Orientalism, and the Environment in the Middle East." In *Environmental Imaginaries of the Middle East and North Africa*, edited by Diana K. Davis and Edmund Burke III, 1–22. Athens: Ohio University Press.

Davis, Diana K., and Edmund Burke III, eds. 2011. *Environmental Imaginaries of the Middle East and North Africa*. Athens: Ohio University Press.

Davis, Heather, and Zoe Todd. 2017. "On the Importance of a Date, or, Decolonizing the Anthropocene." *ACME* 16 (4): 761–80.

Davis, Rochelle. 2010. *Palestinian Village Histories: Geographies of the Displaced*. Stanford, CA: Stanford University Press.

Davis, Uri. 2003. *Apartheid Israel: Possibilities for the Struggle Within*. London: Zed Books.

Dayan, Hilla. 2009. "Regimes of Separation: Israel/Palestine and the Shadow of Apartheid." In *The Power of Inclusive Exclusion: Anatomy of Israeli Rule in the Occupied Palestinian Territories*, edited by Adi Ophir, Michal Givoni, and Sari Hanafi, 281–322. New York: Zone Books.

de Boeck, Filip. 2009. "At Risk, as Risk: Abandonment and Care in a World of Spiritual Insecurity." In *The Devil's Children: From Spirit Possession to Witchcraft—New Allegations that Affect Children*, edited by Jean La Fontaine, 129–50. Farnham: Ashgate.

———. 2011. "Inhabiting Ocular Ground: Kinshasa's Future in the Light of Congo's Spectral Urban Politics." *Cultural Anthropology* 26 (2): 263–86.

———. 2012. "Infrastructure: Commentary from Filip De Boeck." Curated Collections, *Cultural Anthropology Online*, November 26. http://www.academia .edu/4670577/De_Boeck_F._2012_._Infrastructure_Commentary_from_Filip_De _Boeck._Contributions_from_Urban_Africa_towards_an_Anthropology_of _Infrastructure.

de Hoop, Evelien, and Saurabh Arora. 2017. "Material Meanings: 'Waste' as a Performative Category of Land in Colonial India." *Journal of Historical Geography* 55: 82–92.

Derrida, Jacques. 1998. *Of Grammatology*. Baltimore: Johns Hopkins University Press.

de Sadeleer, Nicolas. 2015. "Polluter Pays Principle." In *Essential Concepts of Global Environmental Governance*, edited by Jean-Frédéric Morin and Amandine Orsini, 155. New York: Routledge.

Desai, Renu, Colin McFarlane, and Stephen Graham. 2015. "The Politics of Open Defecation: Informality, Body and Infrastructure in Mumbai." *Antipode* 47 (1): 98–120.

Deutsch, Judith. 2011. "JNF Greenwash." In *Greenwashing Apartheid: The Jewish National Fund's Environmental Cover Up*, JNF eBook 4, edited by Jesse Benjamin, M. B. Levy, S. Kershnar, and M. Sahibzada. http://stopthejnf.org/documents/JN FeBookVol4.pdf.

Dhillon, Navtej, and Tarik Yousef. 2009. *Generation in Waiting*. Washington, DC: Brookings Institution Press.

Dillon, Lindsey. 2014. "Race, Waste, and Space: Brownfield Redevelopment and Environmental Justice at the Hunters Point Shipyard." *Antipode* 46 (5): 1205–21.

Diwan, Ishac, and Radwan A. Shaban, eds. 1999. *Development under Adversity: The Palestinian Economy in Transition*. Washington, DC: World Bank Publications.

Dolk, Helen, Martine Vrijheid, Ben Armstrong, Lenore Abramsky, Fabrizio Bianchi, Ester Garne, Vera Nelen, et al. 1998. "Risk of Congenital Anomalies near Hazardous-Waste Landfill Sites in Europe: The EUROHAZCON Study." *Lancet* 352 (9126): 423–27.

Douglas, Mary. 1979. *The World of Goods: Towards an Anthropology of Consumption*. New York: Basic Books.

———. 2005. *Purity and Danger: An Analysis of Concepts of Pollution and Taboo*. London: Routledge Classics.

Doumani, Beshara. 1995. *Rediscovering Palestine: Merchants and Peasants in Jabal Nablus, 1700–1900*. Berkeley: University of California Press.

Dove, Michael R., ed. 2013. *The Anthropology of Climate Change: An Historical Reader.* Hoboken, NJ: John Wiley and Sons.

Dove, Michael R., and Carol Carpenter, eds. 2008. *Environmental Anthropology: An Historical Reader.* Boston: Blackwell.

Dummer, Trevor J. B., Heather O. Dickinson, and Louise Parker. 2003. "Adverse Pregnancy Outcomes near Landfill Sites in Cumbria, Northwest England, 1950–1993." *Archives of Environmental Health: An International Journal* 58 (11): 692–98.

Dumper, Michael. 1993. "Jerusalem's Infrastructure: Is Annexation Irreversible?" *Journal of Palestine Studies* 22 (3): 78–95.

Dunia al-Watan. 2014. *Makab Zahrat al-Finjan mostawdi lamukhalafat al-mustawtanat al-sina'iyeh* [Zahrat al-Finjan landfill is storage for wastes from industrial settlements]. July 5. https://www.alwatanvoice.com/arabic/news/2014/07/05/562222 .html.

EcoPeace Middle East. n.d. "Environmental Peacebuilding." Accessed August 29, 2017. http://ecopeaceme.org/ecopeace/environmental-peacebuilding/.

Edensor, Tim. 2005. *Industrial Ruins: Space, Aesthetics and Materiality.* London: Berg.

Eder, Klaus. 1996. *The Social Construction of Nature.* London: Sage Publications.

El-Fadel, Mutasem, Rola Quba'a, Nisrine El-Hougeiri, Zaher Hashisho, and Dima Jamali. 2001. "The Israeli Palestinian Mountain Aquifer: A Case Study in Ground Water Conflict Resolution." *Journal of Natural Resources and Life Sciences Education* 30: 50–61.

Elkins, Caroline, and Susan Pederson, eds. 2005. *Settler Colonialism in the Twentieth Century: Projects, Practices and Legacy.* New York: Routledge.

Elliott, Paul, David Briggs, Sara Morris, Cornelis de Hoogh, Christopher Hurt, Tina Kold Jensen, Ian Maitland, Sylvia Richardson, Jon Wakefield, and Lars Jarup. 2001. "Risk of Adverse Birth Outcomes in Populations Living near Landfill Sites." *British Medical Journal* 323 (7309): 363–68.

El-Musa, Sharif S., and Mahmud El-Jaafari. 1995. "Power and Trade: The Israeli-Palestinian Economic Protocol." *Journal of Palestine Studies* 24 (2): 14–32.

Elyachar, Julia. 2010. "Phatic Labor, Infrastructure, and the Question of Empowerment in Cairo." *American Ethnologist* 37 (3): 452–64.

———. 2011. "The Political Economy of Movement and Gesture in Cairo." *Journal of the Royal Anthropological Institute* 17:82–99.

———. 2012. "Next Practices: Knowledge, Infrastructure, and Public Goods at the Bottom of the Pyramid." *Public Culture* 24 (1): 109–29.

Environmental Resources Management. 2000. *West Bank and Gaza—Environment and Solid Waste Project: Environmental Assessment, Phase 2.* Vol. 4: *Jenin Governorate Environmental Assessment.* London: Environmental Resources Management. http://documents.worldbank.org/curated/en/941301468779420663/Jenin-Governorate-environmental-assessment.

Erlanger, Steven. 2006. "Palestinian Landslide: The Elections; Hamas Routs Ruling Faction, Casting Pall on Peace Process." *New York Times*, January 27. http://query.nytimes.com/gst/fullpage.html?res=9E01EFDB113FF934A15752C0A9609C8B63&pagewanted=all.

Escobar, Arturo. 1995. *Encountering Development: The Making and Unmaking of the Third World.* Princeton, NJ: Princeton University Press.

———. 1999. "After Nature: Steps to an Anti-essentialist Political Ecology." *Current Anthropology* 40:1–30.

Evans, David. 2014. *Food Waste: Home Consumption, Material Culture and Everyday Life.* London: Bloomsbury.

Evans, Ivan. 1997. *Bureaucracy and Race: Native Administration in South Africa.* Berkeley: University of California Press.

Eyal, Gil. 2006. *The Disenchantment of the Orient: Expertise in Arab Affairs and the Israeli State.* Stanford, CA: Stanford University Press.

Farmer, Tessa. 2017. "Willing to Pay: Competing Paradigms about Resistance to Paying for Water Services in Cairo, Egypt." *Middle East Law and Governance* 9 (1): 3–19.

Farmer, Tessa, and Jessica Barnes. 2018. "Environment and Society in the Middle East and North Africa: Introduction." *International Journal of Middle East Studies* 50 (3): 375–82.

Farsakh, Leila. 2002. "Palestinian Labor Flows to the Israeli Economy: A Finished Story?" *Journal of Palestine Studies* 32 (1): 13–27.

———. 2005. *Palestinian Labour Migration to Israel: Labour, Land and Occupation.* London: Routledge.

———. 2008. "The Political Economy of Israeli Occupation: What Is Colonial about It?" *MIT Electronic Journal of Middle East Studies* 8 (Spring): 1–14. http://www.ism-italia.org/wp-content/uploads/EJOMES2008Spring-The-Political-Economy-of-Israeli-Occupation-What-is-Colonial-about-It-by-Leila-Farsach.pdf.

———. 2009. "From Domination to Destruction: The Palestinian Economy under the Israeli Occupation." In *The Power of Inclusive Exclusion: Anatomy of Israeli Rule in the Occupied Palestinian Territories*, edited by Adi Ophir, Michal Givoni, and Sari Hanafi, 379–402. New York: Zone Books.

———. 2012. "Democracy Promotion in Palestine: Aid and the 'De-democratization' of the West Bank and Gaza." In *Rethinking Development under Occupation*, edited by Linda Tabar. Birzeit, West Bank: Center for Development Studies, University of Birzeit. http://rosaluxemburg.ps/wp-content/uploads/2015/03/Leila-Farsakh.pdf.

———. 2016. "Undermining Democracy in Palestine: The Politics of International Aid since Oslo." *Journal of Palestine Studies* 45 (4): 48–63. https://doi.org/10.1525/jps.2016.45.4.48.

Fassin, Didier. 2011. *Humanitarian Reason: A Moral History of the Present*. Berkeley: University of California Press.

Faubian, James. 2011. *An Anthropology of Ethics*. Cambridge: Cambridge University Press.

Feld, Steven, and Donald Brenneis. 2004. "Doing Anthropology in Sound." *American Ethnologist* 31 (4): 461–74.

Feldman, Ilana. 2005. "Government without Expertise? Competence, Capacity, and Civil-Service Practice in Gaza, 1917–67." *International Journal of Middle East Studies* 37 (4): 485–507.

———. 2007a. "Difficult Distinctions: Refugee Law, Humanitarian Practice, and the Identification of People in Gaza." *Cultural Anthropology* 22 (1): 129–69.

———. 2007b. "The Quaker Way: Ethical Labor and Humanitarian Relief." *American Ethnologist* 34 (4): 689–705.

———. 2008. *Governing Gaza: Bureaucracy, Authority, and the Work of Rule, 1917–1967*. Durham, NC: Duke University Press.

———. 2012. "The Challenge of Categories: UNRWA and the Definition of a 'Palestine Refugee.'" *Journal of Refugee Studies* 25 (3): 387–406.

———. 2015a. *Police Encounters: Security and Surveillance in Gaza under Egyptian Rule*. Stanford, CA: Stanford University Press.

———. 2015b. "What Is a Camp? Legitimate Refugee Lives in Spaces of Long-Term Displacement." *Geoforum* 66: 244–52. http://dx.doi.org/10.1016/j.geoforum.2014.11.014.

———. 2016. "Punctuated Humanitarianism: Palestinian Life between the Catastrophic and the Cruddy." *International Journal of Middle East Studies* 48 (2): 372–76.

———. 2017. "Humanitarian Care and the Ends of Life: The Politics of Aging and Dying in a Palestinian Refugee Camp." *Cultural Anthropology* 32 (1): 42–67.

———. 2018. *Life Lived in Relief: Humanitarian Predicaments and Palestinian Refugee Politics*. Berkeley: University of California Press.

Fendel, Hillel. 2014. "Garbage Smuggling to Judea/Samaria-Down 99%." *Arutz Sheva*, August 24. http://www.israelnationalnews.com/News/News.aspx/184350.

Fennell, Catherine. 2016. "The Family Toxic: Triaging Obligation in Post-welfare Chicago." *South Atlantic Quarterly* 115 (1): 9–32.

Ferguson, James. 1990. *The Anti-politics Machine: "Development," Depoliticization, and Bureaucratic Power in Lesotho*. Cambridge: Cambridge University Press.

Figueroa, Pablo M. 2013. "Risk Communication Surrounding the Fukushima Nuclear Disaster: An Anthropological Approach." *Asia Europe Journal* 11 (1): 53–64.

Fisch, Michael. 2013. "Tokyo's Commuter Train Suicides and the Society of Emergence." *Cultural Anthropology* 28 (2): 320–43. https://doi.org/10.1111/cuan.12006.

Fleming, James Rodger, and Ann Johnson. 2014. *Toxic Airs: Body, Place, Planet in Historical Perspective*. Pittsburgh, PA: University of Pittsburgh Press.

Franks, Tim. 2008. "Jerusalem Diary: Monday 11 February." BBC News, February 11. http://news.bbc.co.uk/2/hi/middle_east/7238454.stm.

Fortun, Kim. 2001. *Advocacy after Bhopal: Environmentalism, Disaster, New Global Orders*. Chicago: University of Chicago Press.

Foucault, Michel. 2008. *The Birth of Biopolitics: Lectures at the College de France, 1978–79*. Translated by Graham Burchell. New York: Palgrave Macmillan.

Fox, Julia. 1999. "Mountaintop Removal in West Virginia: An Environmental Sacrifice Zone." *Organization and Environment* 12 (2): 163–83.

Fredericks, Rosalind. 2014. "Vital Infrastructures of Trash in Dakar." *Comparative Studies of South Asia, Africa and the Middle East* 34 (3): 532–48.

———. 2018. *Garbage Citizenship: Vital Infrastructures of Labor in Dakar, Senegal*. Durham, NC: Duke University Press.

Frisch, Hillel. 1997. "Modern Absolutist or Neopatriarchal State Building? Customary Law, Extended Families, and the Palestinian Authority." *International Journal of Middle East Studies* 29 (3): 341–58.

Furniss, Jamie. 2010. "Private Sector Reform of Solid Waste Management in Egypt." In *Participation for What: Social Change or Social Control?*, edited by A. A. C. Georgina, M. Gómez, P. Goulart, and R. Namara, 99–138. The Hague: Hivos, Oxfam-Novib, and ISS Publications.

———. 2012. "What Did Neoliberalism Change for Waste? Foreign Waste Collection Companies in Cairo." *Anthropology News* 53 (8): 10–11.

———. 2015. "Alternative Framings of Transnational Waste Flows: Reflections Based on the Egypt–China PET Plastic Trade." *Area* 47: 24–30. https://doi.org/doi:10.1111/area.12160.

————. 2016. "Postrevolutionary Land Encroachments in Cairo: Rhizomatic Urban Space Making and the Line of Flight from Illegality." *Singapore Journal of Tropical Geography* 37: 310–29.

Gabiam, Nell. 2012. "When 'Humanitarianism' Becomes 'Development': The Politics of International Aid in Syria's Palestinian Refugee Camps." *American Anthropologist* 114 (1): 95–107.

Gabrys, Jennifer. 2011. *Digital Rubbish: A Natural History of Electronics*. Ann Arbor: University of Michigan Press.

Gabrys, Jennifer, Gay Hawkins, and Mike Michael, eds. 2013. *Accumulation: The Material Politics of Plastic*. London: Routledge.

Gandy, Matthew. 2013. "Marginalia: Aesthetics, Ecology, and Urban Wastelands." *Annals of the Association of American Geographers* 1036: 1301–16.

Geertz, Clifford. 1973. *The Interpretation of Cultures: Selected Essays*. New York: Basic Books.

————. 1979. "Suq: The Bazaar Economy in *Sefrou*." In *Meaning and Order in Moroccan Society: Three Essays in Cultural Analysis*, by Clifford Geertz, Hildred Geertz, and Lawrence Rosen, 123–313. Cambridge: Cambridge University Press.

Geller, Lior, and Marcus Vetter, dirs. 2008. *Heart of Jenin*. Film. Eikon Südwest.

George, Alan. 1979. "'Making the Desert Bloom': A Myth Examined." *Journal of Palestine Studies* 8 (2): 88–100.

George, Rose. 2008. *The Big Necessity: The Unmentionable World of Human Waste and Why It Matters*. New York: Metropolitan Books.

Gerber, Haim. 1994. *State, Society, and Law in Islam: Ottoman Law in Comparative Perspective*. Albany: SUNY Press.

Ghanim, Honaida. 2008. "Thanatopolitics: The Case of the Colonial Occupation in Palestine." In *Thinking Palestine*, edited by Ronit Lentin, 65–81. New York: Zed Books.

Gill, Kaveri. 2009. *Of Poverty and Plastic: Scavenging and Scrap Trading Entrepreneurs in India's Urban Informal Economy*. New Delhi: Oxford University Press.

Gille, Zsuzsa. 2007. *From the Cult of Waste to the Trash Heap of History: The Politics of Waste in Socialist and Postsocialist Hungary*. Bloomington: Indiana University Press.

————. 2010. "Actor Networks, Modes of Production, and Waste Regimes: Reassembling the Macrosocial." *Environment and Planning* 42 (5): 1049–64.

Godelier, Maurice. 1999. *The Enigma of the Gift*. Chicago: University of Chicago Press.

Goldstein, Jesse. 2013. "Terra Economica: Waste and the Production of Enclosed Nature." *Antipode* 412: 357–75.

Golinski, Jan. 1998. *Making Natural Knowledge: Constructivism and the History of Science*. New York: Cambridge University Press.

Gonos, George, Virginia Mulkern, and Nicholas Poushinsky. 1976. "Anonymous Expression: A Structural View of Graffiti." *Journal of American Folklore* 89 (351): 40–48.

Gordillo, Gordon. 2014. *Rubble: The Afterlife of Destruction*. Durham, NC: Duke University Press.

Gordon, Beverly. 2006. *The Saturated World: Aesthetic Meaning, Intimate Objects, Women's Lives, 1890–1940*. Knoxville: University of Tennessee Press.

Gordon, Neve. 2008. *Israel's Occupation*. Berkeley: University of California Press.

Goumopoulos, Christos, and Achilles Kameas. 2009. "Ambient Ecologies in Smart Homes." *Computer Journal* 52 (8): 922–37.

Graeber, David. 2001. *Toward an Anthropological Theory of Value: The False Coin of Our Own Dreams*. New York: Palgrave.

———. 2012. "Afterword." In *Economies of Recycling: The Global Transformation of Materials, Values and Social Relations*, edited by Catherine Alexander and Joshua Reno, 277–90. Chicago: University of Chicago Press.

Graham, Stephen, ed. 2010. *Disrupted Cities: When Infrastructure Fails*. New York: Routledge.

Graham, Stephen, and Simon Marvin. 1996. *Telecommunications and the City: Electronic Spaces, Urban Places*. London: Routledge.

———. 2001. *Splintering Urbanism: Networked Infrastructures, Technological Mobilities and the Urban Condition*. London: Routledge.

Graham, Stephen, and Colin McFarlane, eds. 2014. *Infrastructural Lives: Urban Infrastructure in Context*. London: Routledge.

Graham, Stephen, and Nigel Thrift. 2007. "Out of Order: Understanding Repair and Maintenance." *Theory, Culture and Society* 24 (3): 1–25.

Granqvist, Hilma. 1931. *Marriage Conditions in a Palestinian Village*. Helsingfors, Finland: [Akademische Buchhandlung].

———. 1947. *Birth and Childhood among the Arabs: Studies in a Muhammadan Village in Palestine*. Helsingfors, Finland: Söderström.

Greenhouse, Carol, Elizabeth Mertz, and Kay Warren, eds. 2002. *Ethnography in Unstable Places: Everyday Lives in Contexts of Dramatic Political Change*. Durham, NC: Duke University Press.

Gregory, Derek. 2004. *The Colonial Present: Afghanistan, Palestine, Iraq*. Malden, MA: Blackwell.

Gregson, Nicky. 2007. *Living with Things: Accommodation, Ridding, Dwelling.* Oxford: Sean Kingston.

Gregson, Nicky, and Mike Crang. 2010. "Materiality and Waste: Inorganic Vitality in a Networked World." *Environment and Planning A* 42: 1026–32.

———. 2015. "From Waste to Resource: The Trade in Wastes and Global Recycling Economies." *Annual Review of Environment and Resources* 40 (1): 151–76.

Gregson, Nicky, Mike Crang, F. Ahamed, N. Akhter, and R. Ferdous. 2009. "Following Things of Rubbish Value: End-of-Life Ships, 'Chock-Chocky' Furniture and the Bangladesh Middle Class Consumers." *Geoforum* 41 (6): 846–54.

Grossman, Elizabeth. 2006. *High Tech Trash: Digital Devices, Hidden Toxics, and Human Health.* Washington, DC: Shearwater Books.

Grossman, Margaret Rosso. 2009. *Agriculture and the Polluter Pays Principle.* London: British Institute of International and Comparative Law.

Guarasci, Bridget L. 2015. "The National Park: Reviving Eden in Iraq's Marshes." *Arab Studies Journal* 23 (1): 128–53.

———. 2018. "The Architecture of Environment: Building Houses along the Great Rift Valley in Jordan." *International Journal of Middle East Studies* 50 (3): 513–36.

Günel, Gökçe. 2016. "The Infinity of Water: Climate Change Adaptation in the Arabian Peninsula." *Public Culture* 28 (2): 291–315. https://doi.org/10.1215/08992363-3427463.

———. 2019. *Spaceship in the Desert: Energy, Climate Change, and Urban Design in Abu Dhabi.* Durham, NC: Duke University Press.

Gupta, Akhil. 1995. "Blurred Boundaries: The Discourse of Corruption, the Culture of Politics, and the Imagined State." *American Ethnologist* 22 (2): 375–402.

———. 2012. *Red Tape: Bureaucracy, Structural Violence, and Poverty in India.* Durham, NC: Duke University Press.

———. 2015. "Suspension." *Cultural Anthropology* website, Fieldsights, Editors' Forum, Theorizing the Contemporary, Infrastructure Toolbox series. https://culanth.org/fieldsights/722-suspension.

Gupta, Charu. 2002. *Sexuality, Obscenity, Community: Women, Muslims, and the Hindu Public in Colonial India.* New York: Palgrave.

Habermas, Jürgen. 1989. *The Structural Transformation of the Public Sphere: An Inquiry into a Category of Bourgeois Society, Polity.* Cambridge: Cambridge University Press.

Habiby, Emile. 1985. *The Secret Life of Saeed: The Pessoptimist.* London: Zed Books.

Haddad, Toufic. 2016. *Palestine Ltd.: Neoliberalism and Nationalism in the Occupied Territory.* London: I. B. Tauris.

Hage, Ghassan, ed. 2009. *Waiting*. Melbourne: Melbourne University Publishing.

Hajjar, Lisa. 2005. *Courting Conflict: The Israeli Military Court System in the West Bank and Gaza*. Berkeley: University of California Press.

Haklai, Oded. 2007. "Religious-Nationalist Mobilization and State Penetration: Lessons from Jewish Settlers' Activism in Israel and the West Bank." *Comparative Political Studies* 40 (6): 713–39.

Hall, Stuart. 1988. "The Toad in the Garden: Thatcherism among the Theorists." In *Marxism and the Interpretation of Culture*, edited by Cary Nelson and Lawrence Grossberg, 35–74. Urbana: University of Illinois Press.

Halvorson, Britt. 2012. "'No Junk for Jesus': Redemptive Economies and Value Conversions in Lutheran Medical Aid." In *Economies of Recycling: Global Transformations of Materials, Values and Social Relations*, edited by Catherine Alexander and Joshua Reno, 207–33. London: Zed Books.

———. 2015. "The Value of Time and the Temporality of Value in Socialities of Waste," *Discard Studies*, September 21. https://discardstudies.com/2015/09/21/the-value-of-time-and-the-temporality-of-value-in-socialities-of-waste/.

Hamdan, Ayat. 2010. *Foreign Aid and the Molding of the Palestinian Space*. Palestine: Bisan Centre for Research and Development.

Hamdan, H. 1996. *Al-Dabkah al-Shabiyyah al-Filistiniyyah bi-'l-Sawt al-Hadir wa-Anin al-Madi* [Palestinian Popular *Dabkeh* in the Present Voice and the Moan of the Past]. *At-Turath wa-'l Mujtama* 27: 39–64.

Hammami, Rema. 2001. "Waiting for Godot at Qalandya: Reflections on Queues and Inequality." *Jerusalem Quarterly* 13: 8–16.

Hammami, Rema, Jamil Hilal, and Salim Tamari, eds. 2001. "Civil Society in Palestine: 'Case Studies.'" EUI Working Paper RSC No. 2001/36. European University Institute, Florence, Italy. http://cadmus.eui.eu/bitstream/handle/1814/1745/RSCAS_2001_36.pdf?sequence=1&isAllowed=y.

Hanafi, Sari. 2009. "Spacio-cide: Colonial Politics, Invisibility and Rezoning in Palestinian Territory." *Contemporary Arab Affairs* 2 (1): 106–21.

Hanafi, Sari, Leila Hilal, and Lex Takkenberg, eds. 2014. *UNRWA and Palestinian Refugees: From Relief and Works to Human Development*. London: Routledge.

Hanafi, Sari, and Linda Tabar. 2005. *The Emergence of a Palestinian Globalized Elite: Donors, International Organizations, and Local NGOs*. Jerusalem: Institute of Jerusalem Studies.

Hanieh, Adam. 2002. "Class, Economy, and the Second Intifada." *Monthly Review* 54 (5): 29–42.

———. 2003. "From State-Led Growth to Globalization: The Evolution of Israeli Capitalism." *Journal of Palestine Studies* 32 (4): 5–21.

———. 2011. *Capitalism and Class in the Gulf Arab States*. New York: Palgrave Macmillan.

———. 2013. *Lineages of Revolt: Issues of Contemporary Capitalism in the Middle East.* Chicago: Haymarket Books.

Hansen, Karen Tranberg. 2000. *Salaula: The World of Secondhand Clothing and Zambia.* Chicago: Chicago University Press.

———. 2004. "Helping or Hindering? Controversies around the International Second -Hand Clothing Trade." *Anthropology Today* 20 (4): 3–9.

Haraway, Donna. 1991. *Simians, Cyborgs, and Women: The Reinvention of Nature*. New York: Routledge.

———. 2015. "Anthropocene, Capitalocene, Plantationocene, Chthulucene: Making Kin." *Environmental Humanities* 6 (1): 159–65.

Haraway, Donna, Noboru Ishikawa, Scott F. Gilbert, Kenneth Olwig, Anna L. Tsing, and Nils Bubandt. 2016. "Anthropologists Are Talking about the Anthropocene." *Ethnos* 81 (3): 535–64.

Harker, Christopher. 2014. "The Only Way Is Up? Ordinary Topologies of Ramallah." *International Journal of Urban and Regional Research* 38: 318–35.

Harris, Emily. 2015. "Israel Bets on Recycled Water to Meet Its Growing Thirst." NPR, June 21. http://www.npr.org/sections/parallels/2015/06/21/415795367/israel-bets -on-recycled-water-to-meet-its-growing-thirst.

Harris, Leila. 2011. "Salts, Soils, and (Un)Sustainabilities? Analyzing Narratives of Environmental Change in Southeastern Turkey." In *Environmental Imaginaries of the Middle East and North Africa*, edited by Diana K. Davis and Edmund Burke III, 47–66. Athens: Ohio University Press.

Harvey, David. 2003. *The New Imperialism*. Oxford: Oxford University Press.

Harvey, Penelope. 2012. "The Topological Quality of Infrastructural Relation: An Ethnographic Approach." *Theory, Culture and Society* 29 (4–5): 76–92.

———. 2017. "Waste Futures: Infrastructures and Political Experimentation in Southern Peru." *Ethnos* 82 (4): 672–89. https://doi.org/10.1080/00141844.2015.1108351.

Harvey, Penny [Penelope], and Hannah Knox. 2015. *Roads: An Anthropology of Infrastructure and Expertise*. Ithaca, NY: Cornell University Press.

Hass, Amira. 2014. "UN Report: 300,000 Palestinians Live in Area C of West Bank." *Ha'aretz*, March 5. https://www.haaretz.com/.premium-un-300k-palestinians -live-in-area-c-1.5329286.

Hasson, Nir. 2012. "For East Jerusalem Palestinians, Taking Out the Trash Is More Than a Chore." *Ha'aretz*, March 8. http://www.haaretz.com/for-east-jerusalem-palestinians -taking-out-the-trash-is-more-than-a-chore-1.417209.

Hattem, Ben. 2014a. "Controversial Landfill Prompts West Bank Showdown." *Daily Beast*, February 2. http://www.thedailybeast.com/articles/2014/02/02/controversial -landfill-prompts-west-bank-showdown.html.

———. 2014b. "Palestine's Other Land War." *Middle East Eye*, September 18. http:// www.middleeasteye.net/in-depth/features/palestine-s-other-land-war-1213915354 #block-disqus-disqus-comments.

Havrelock, Rachel. 2017. "The Dead End Canal." Paper presented at the Third Annual Meeting of the "Water Boundaries" Group, "Topographies of Citizenship" sympo- sium, Centre for Research in the Arts, Social Sciences and Humanities (CRASSH), University of Cambridge, March.

Hawk, Byron. 2018. *Resounding the Rhetorical: Composition as a Quasi-object.* Pittsburgh, PA: University of Pittsburgh Press.

Hawkins, Gay. 2004. "Shit in Public." *Australian Humanities Review* 32:33–47.

———. 2006. *The Ethics of Waste: How We Relate to Rubbish.* Lanham, MD: Rowman and Littlefield.

Hawkins, Gay, and Stephen Muecke. 2003. "Introduction: Cultural Economies of Waste." In *Culture and Waste: The Creation and Destruction of Value*, edited by Gay Hawkins and Stephen Muecke, ix–xvii. Lanham, MD: Rowman and Lit- tlefield.

Herskovitz, Yaakov. 2015. "Settlers versus Pioneers: The Deconstruction of the Settler in Assaf Gavron's *The Hilltop.*" *Shofar: An Interdisciplinary Journal of Jewish Studies* 33 (4): 173–89.

Hertz, Neil. 2016. "Kufr Aqab and the 'Cleansing' of Jerusalem." *Politics/Letters*, November 25. http://politicsslashletters.org/2016/11/kufr-aqab/.

Herzfeld, Michael. 1992. *The Social Production of Indifference: Exploring the Symbolic Roots of Western Bureaucracy.* New York: Berg.

———. 2016. *Cultural Intimacy: Social Poetics and the Real Life of States, Societies and Institutions.* London: Routledge.

Hever, Shir. 2006. *Foreign Aid to Palestine/Israel.* Jerusalem: Alternative Information Center.

———. 2007. *Political Economy of Aid to Palestinians under Occupation.* Jerusalem: Alternative Information Center.

———. 2015. "How Much International Aid to Palestinians Ends Up in the Israeli Economy?" Aid Watch, September. http://www.aidwatch.ps/sites/default/files /resource-field_media/InternationalAidToPalestiniansFeedsTheIsraeliEconomy .pdf.

Hilal, Jamil. 2010. "The Polarization of the Palestinian Political Field." *Journal of Palestine Studies* 39 (3): 24–39.

———. 2015. "Rethinking Palestine: Settler-Colonialism, Neo-liberalism and Individualism in the West Bank and Gaza Strip." *Contemporary Arab Affairs* 8 (3): 351–62.

Hird, Myra J. 2013. "Is Waste Indeterminacy Useful? A Response to Zsuzsa Gille." *Social Epistemology Review and Reply Collective* 2 (6) 28–33.

Hirschkind, Charles. 2006. *The Ethical Soundscape: Cassette Sermons and Islamic Counterpublics.* New York: Columbia University Press.

Hoffman, Danny. 2017. "Toxicity." *Somatosphere*, October 16. http://somatosphere .net/2017/10/toxicity.html.

Holmes, Douglas. 2014. *Economy of Words: Communicative Imperatives in Central Banks.* Chicago: University of Chicago Press.

Hoover, Elizabeth. 2017. *The River Is in Us: Fighting Toxics in a Mohawk Community.* Minneapolis: University of Minnesota Press.

Humes, Edward. 2012. *Garbology: Our Dirty Love Affair with Trash.* New York: Avery.

Hull, Matthew S. 2012. *Government of Paper: The Materiality of Bureaucracy in Urban Pakistan.* Berkeley: University of California Press.

Hutchinson, Sharon. 1996. *Nuer Dilemmas: Coping with Money, War, and the State.* Berkeley: University of California Press.

Ialenti, Vincent. 2013. "Nuclear Energy's Long Now: Intransigent Wastes and Radioactive Greens." *Suomen Antropologi: The Journal of the Finnish Anthropological Society* 38 (3): 61–65.

———. 2014. "Adjudicating Deep Time: Revisiting the United States' High-Level Nuclear Waste Repository Project at Yucca Mountain." *Science and Technology Studies* 2 (27): 27–48.

Isaac, Jad. 2007. "Israeli Violations against the Palestinian Environment." Applied Research Institute–Jerusalem, Bethlehem. http://www.arij.org/files/admin /2007/Israeli%20Violations%20against%20the%20Palestinian%20 Environment.pdf.

Isaac, Rami. 2013. "Palestine Tourism under Occupation." In *Tourism and War*, edited by Richard Butler and Wantanee Suntikul, 143–58. London: Routledge.

Isotalo, Riina. 1997. "Yesterday's Outsiders, Today's Returnees: Transnational Processes and Cultural Encounters in the West Bank." In *Under the Olive Tree: Reconsidering Mediterranean Politics and Culture*, edited by Aini Linjakumpu and Kirsti Virtanen, 163–84. Tampere: Tampere Peace Research Institute.

Israeli Ministry of Environmental Protection. n.d. "Landfilling." Accessed November 27, 2018. http://www.sviva.gov.il/English/env_topics/Solid_Waste/landfilling /Pages/default.aspx.

Issacharoff, Avi. 2015. "In Jenin, Once the 'Suicide Bomber Capital,' a Fragile Transformation." *Times of Israel*, April 25. http://www.timesofisrael.com/in-jenin-once -the-suicide-bomber-capital-a-fragile-transformation/.

Jabbour, Elias. 1993. *Sulha: Palestinian Traditional Peacemaking Process*. Edited by Thomas C. Cook Jr. Montreat, NC: House of Hope Publications.

Jad, Islah. 2007. "The NGO-ization of Arab Women's Movements." In *Feminisms in Development: Contradictions, Contestations and Challenges*, edited by Andrea Cornwall, Elizabeth Harrison, and Ann Whitehead, 177–90. London: Zed Books.

James, William. 1929. *The Varieties of Religious Experience: A Study in Human Nature*. New York: Longmans, Green.

Jarbawi, Ali, and Wendy Pearlman. 2007. "Struggle in a Post-charisma Transition: Rethinking Palestinian Politics after Arafat." *Journal of Palestine Studies* 36 (4): 6–21.

Jasanoff, Sheila, Gerald E. Markle, James C. Peterson, and Trevor Pinch, eds. 2001. *Handbook of Science and Technology Studies*. Thousand Oaks, CA: Sage Publications.

Jayaraman, Nityanand. 2008. "Garbage as a Metaphor." *Agenda* 13: 10–14.

Jerusalem Post. 1996. "Sewage from Autonomous Areas Is Threatening Israel's Aquifers." *Jerusalem Post*, December 14.

Johnston, Barbara Rose, ed. 2007. *Half-Lives and Half-Truths: Confronting the Radioactive Legacies of the Cold War*. Santa Fe, NM: School for Advanced Research Press.

Jones, Toby Craig. 2010. *Desert Kingdom: How Oil and Water Forged Modern Saudi Arabia*. Cambridge, MA: Harvard University Press.

Jorgensen, Finn Arne. 2011. *Making a Green Machine: The Infrastructure of Beverage Container Recycling*. New Brunswick, NJ: Rutgers University Press.

Joronen, Mikko. 2017. "Spaces of Waiting: Politics of Precarious Recognition in the Occupied West Bank." *Environment and Planning D: Society and Space* 35 (6): 994–1011.

Joseph, Gilbert Michael, and Daniel Nugent, eds. 1994. *Everyday Forms of State Formation: Revolution and the Negotiation of Rule in Modern Mexico*. Durham, NC: Duke University Press.

Kanaaneh, Moslih, Stig-Magnus Thorsén, Heather Bursheh, and David A. McDonald, eds. 2013. *Palestinian Music and Song: Expression and Resistance since 1900.* Bloomington: Indiana University Press.

Karlström, Mikael. 2003. "On the Aesthetics and Dialogics of Power in the Postcolony." *Africa* 73 (1): 57–76.

Kassem, Fatma. 2011. *Palestinian Women: Narrative Histories and Gendered Memory.* London: Zed Books.

Keating, Michael, Anne Le More, and Robert Lowe, eds. 2006. *Aid, Diplomacy and Facts on the Ground: The Case of Palestine.* London: Chatham House.

Kedar, Alexandre, Ahmad Amara, and Oren Yiftachel. 2018. *Emptied Lands: A Legal Geography of Bedouin Rights in the Negev.* Stanford, CA: Stanford University Press.

Keenan, Thomas, and Eyal Weizman. 2012. *Mengele's Skull: The Advent of a Forensic Aesthetics.* Berlin: Sternberg Press.

Keller, Margit. 2005. "Freedom Calling: Telephony, Mobility and Consumption in Post-socialist Estonia." *European Journal of Cultural Studies* 8 (2): 217–38.

Kelly, Tobias. 2008. "The Attractions of Accountancy: Living an Ordinary Life during the Second Palestinian Intifada." *Ethnography* 9 (3): 351–76.

Kendon, Adam. 1983. "The Study of Gesture: Some Remarks on Its History." In *Semiotics 1981,* edited by John N. Deely and Margot D. Lenhart, 153–64. Boston: Springer.

———. 2004. *Visible Action as Utterance.* Cambridge: Cambridge University Press.

Kersten, Jens. 2013. "The Enjoyment of Complexity: A New Political Anthropology for the Anthropocene?" *RCC Perspectives* 3: 39–56.

Khalidi, Raja, and Sobhi Samour. 2011. "Neoliberalism as Liberation: The Statehood Program and the Remaking of the Palestinian National Movement." *Journal of Palestine Studies* 40 (2): 6–25.

Khalidi, Raja, and Sahar Taghdisi-Rad. 2009. "The Economic Dimensions of Prolonged Occupation: Continuity and Change in Israeli Policy towards the Palestinian Economy." UN Conference on Trade and Development, Globalization and Development Strategies, August, UNCTAD/GDS/2009/2. https://unctad.org/en/Docs/gds20092_en.pdf.

Khalidi, Rashid. 2006. *The Iron Cage: The Story of the Palestinian Struggle for Statehood.* Boston: Beacon Press.

———. 2010. *Palestinian Identity: The Construction of Modern National Consciousness.* New York: Columbia University Press.

Khalili, Laleh. 2005. "Places of Memory and Mourning: Palestinian Commemoration in the Refugee Camps of Lebanon." *Comparative Studies of South Asia, Africa and the Middle East* 25 (1): 30–45.

Khan, Mushtaq Husain, George Giacaman, and Inge Amundsen, eds. 2004. *State Formation in Palestine: Viability and Governance during a Social Transformation.* London: Routledge.

Kimura, Aya Hirata. 2016. *Radiation Brain Moms and Citizen Scientists: The Gender Politics of Food Contamination after Fukushima.* Durham, NC: Duke University Press.

Kirsch, Scott, and Don Mitchell. 2004. "The Nature of Things: Dead Labor, Nonhuman Actors, and the Persistence of Marxism." *Antipode* 36 (4): 687–705.

Kohn, Eduardo. 2013. *How Forests Think: Toward an Anthropology beyond the Human.* Berkeley: University of California Press.

Koshy, Ninan. 2007. "Palestine's New Partition." *Economic and Political Weekly*, July 14, 2871–73.

Kristeva, Julia. 1982. *Powers of Horror: An Essay on Abjection.* New York: Columbia University Press.

Kroll-Smith, Stephen, and H. Hugh Floyd. 2000. *Bodies in Protest: Environmental Illness and the Struggle over Medical Knowledge.* New York: New York University Press.

Kruse, Jamie, and Peter Galison. 2011. "Waste-Wilderness: A Conversation with Peter L. Galison." *Friends of the Pleistocene* (blog), March 31. https://fopnews.wordpress.com/2011/03/31/galison/.

Kuletz, Valerie. 1998. *The Tainted Desert: Environmental Ruin in the American West.* New York: Routledge.

Kunreuther, Laura. 2014. *Voicing Subjects: Public Intimacy and Mediation in Kathmandu.* Berkeley: University of California Press.

Ladkani, Jennifer Lee. 2005. "Dabke Music and Dance and the Palestinian Refugee Experience: On the Outside Looking In." PhD diss., Florida State University.

Lambek, Michael, ed. 2010. *Ordinary Ethics: Anthropology, Language, and Action.* New York: Fordham University Press.

Langwick, Stacey Ann. 2018. "A Politics of Habitability: Plants, Healing, and Sovereignty in a Toxic World." *Cultural Anthropology* 33 (3): 415–43.

Laporte, Dominique. 2000. *History of Shit.* Cambridge, MA: MIT Press.

Larkin, Brian. 2008. *Signal and Noise: Media, Infrastructure, and Urban Culture in Nigeria.* Durham, NC: Duke University Press.

———. 2013. "The Politics and Poetics of Infrastructure." *Annual Review of Anthropology* 42: 327–43.

Lasensky, Scott. 2004. "Paying for Peace: The Oslo Process and the Limits of American Foreign Aid." *Middle East Journal* 58 (2): 210–34.

Laster, Richard, and Dan Livney. 2013. "Basin Management in the Context of Israel and the Palestine Authority." In *Water Policy in Israel: Context, Issues and Options*, edited by Nir Becker, 227–42. New York, Springer.

Latour, Bruno. 1987. *Science in Action: How to Follow Scientists and Engineers through Society*. Cambridge, MA: Harvard University Press.

———. 1988. *The Pasteurization of France*. Cambridge, MA: Harvard University Press.

———. 1993. *We Have Never Been Modern*. Translated by Catherine Porter. Cambridge, MA: Harvard University Press.

———. 1996. "On Actor-Network Theory: A Few Clarifications." *Soziale Welt* 47 (4): 369–81.

———. 2005. *Reassembling the Social: An Introduction to Actor-Network-Theory*. Oxford: Oxford University Press.

———. 2011. *Politics of Nature: How to Bring the Sciences into Democracy*. Translated by Catherine Porter. Cambridge, MA: Harvard University Press.

———. 2017. "Anthropology at the Time of the Anthropocene: A Personal View of What Is to Be Studied." In *The Anthropology of Sustainability*, edited by Marc Brightman and Jerome Lewis, 35–49. New York: Palgrave Macmillan.

Lazaroff, Tova. 2016a. "Lawmakers Call for a Report on Palestinian Police Activity in Area C." *Jerusalem Post*, August 17. http://www.jpost.com/Arab-Israeli -Conflict/Lawmakers-call-for-a-report-on-Palestinian-police-activity-in-Area -C-464292.

———. 2016b. "PA Security Forces Fire Shots in Air at Palestinians in Area C." *Jerusalem Post*, August 10. http://www.jpost.com/Arab-Israeli-Conflict/PA-security-forces -fire-in-air-due-to-planned-Area-C-landfill-squabble-463712.

Lefebvre, Henri. 1991. *The Production of Space*. Translated by Donald Nicholson-Smith. Oxford: Blackwell.

Legg, Stephen. 2013. "Planning Social Hygiene: From Contamination to Contagion in Interwar India." In *Imperial Contagions: Medicine, Hygiene, and Cultures of Planning in Asia*, edited by Robert Peckham and David M. Pomfret, 105–22. Hong Kong: Hong Kong University Press.

Leifsen, Esben. 2017. "Wasteland by Design: Dispossession by Contamination and the Struggle for Water Justice in the Ecuadorian Amazon." *Extractive Industries and Society* 4 (2): 344–51.

Le More, Anne. 2005. "Killing with Kindness: Funding the Demise of a Palestinian State." *International Affairs* 81 (5): 981–99.

———. 2008. *International Assistance to the Palestinians after Oslo: Political Guilt, Wasted Money*. London: Routledge.

Lepawsky, Josh. 2012. "Legal Geographies of E-Waste Legislation in Canada and the US: Jurisdiction, Responsibility and the Taboo of Production." *Geoforum* 43 (6): 1194–1206.

———. 2015. "The Changing Geography of Global Trade in Electronic Discards: Time to Rethink the E-waste Problem." *Geographical Journal* 181 (2): 147–59.

Lepawsky, Josh, and Charles Mather. 2011. "From Beginnings and Endings to Boundaries and Edges: Rethinking Circulation and Exchange through Electronic Waste." *Area* 43 (3): 242–49.

Lepawsky, Josh, and Chris McNabb. 2010. "Mapping International Flows of Electronic Waste." *Canadian Geographer* 54 (2): 177–95.

Lerner, Steve. 2010. *Sacrifice Zones: The Front Lines of Toxic Chemical Exposure in the United States*. Cambridge, MA: MIT Press.

Leshem, Guy. 2002. "The Ecological Disaster Posed by the Palestinian Authority." *Israel behind the News: Israel Resource Review*, March 26, reprinted from *Yedi'ot Ahronot*, March 22. http://www.israelbehindthenews.com/bin/content.cgi?ID=1389&q=1.

Lévi-Strauss, Claude. 1966. *The Savage Mind*. Chicago: Chicago University Press.

———. 1969. *The Raw and the Cooked*. Translated by John and Doreen Weightman. Chicago: University of Chicago.

Levitt, Matthew. 2006. *Hamas: Politics, Charity, and Terrorism in the Service of Jihad*. New Haven, CT: Yale University Press.

Li, Darryl, and Yehezkel Lein. 2006. *Act of Vengeance: Israel's Bombing of the Gaza Power Plant and Its Effects*. Status Report. Jerusalem: B'Tselem.

Lia, Brynjar. 1999. *A Police Force without a State: A History of the Palestinian Security Forces in the West Bank and Gaza*. New York: Garnet.

Libiszewski, Stephan. 1995. "Water Disputes in the Jordan Basin Region and Their Role in the Resolution of the Arab-Israeli Conflict." ENCOP Occasional Paper 13, Center for Security Policy and Conflict Research, Swiss Peace Foundation, Zurich. http://www.mideastweb.org/Mew_water95.pdf.

Liboiron, Max. 2010. "Recycling as a Crisis of Meaning." *eTOPIA: Canadian Journal of Cultural Studies* 4: 1–9.

———. 2013. "Modern Waste as Strategy." *Lo Squaderno: Explorations in Space and Society* 29: 9–12.

————. 2014. "Against Awareness, for Scale: Garbage Is Infrastructure, Not Behavior." *Discard Studies* (blog), January 23. https://discardstudies.com/2014/01/23/against-awareness-for-scale-garbage-is-infrastructure-not-behavior/.

Library of Congress. 2013. "Jerusalem, Gaza Strip, Golan Heights, West Bank, and Palestine." H-980, Subject Headings Manual, June 2013. http://www.loc.gov/aba/publications/FreeSHM/H0980.pdf.

Limbert, Mandana. 2001. "The Senses of Water in an Omani Town." *Social Text* 19 (3): 35–55.

Lin, Yi-Chieh Jessica. 2011. *Fake Stuff: China and the Rise of Counterfeit Goods*. New York: Routledge.

Lipchin, Clive. 2017. "Israel Is First in Wastewater Reuse, but Palestinians Are Last." *Jerusalem Post*, February 19. http://www.jpost.com/Opinion/Israel-is-first-in-wastewater-reuse-but-Palestinians-are-last-482025.

Lippert, Ingmar. 2011. "Sustaining Waste: Sociological Perspectives on Recycling a Hybrid Object." In *Implementing Environmental and Resource Management*, edited by Michael Schmidt, Vincent Onyango, and Dmytro Palekhov, 283–305. Berlin: Springer.

Little, Peter. C. 2014. *Toxic Town: IBM, Pollution, and Industrial Risks*. New York: New York University Press.

Lloyd, David. 2012. "Settler Colonialism and the State of Exception: The Example of Palestine/Israel." *Settler Colonial Studies* 2 (1): 59–80.

Lockman, Zachary. 1996. *Comrades and Enemies: Arab and Jewish Workers in Palestine, 1906–1948*. Berkeley: University of California Press.

Lora-Wainwright, Anna. 2013. *Fighting for Breath: Living Morally and Dying of Cancer in a Chinese Village*. Honolulu: University of Hawaii Press.

Lorimer, Jamie. 2015. *Wildlife in the Anthropocene: Conservation after Nature*. Minneapolis: University of Minnesota Press.

Lubbad, Ismail. 2007. "Demographic Profile of Palestinian migration." Working paper, Center of Forced Migration and Refugee Studies, American University, Cairo. https://pdfs.semanticscholar.org/dcbe/febc3e449d41992280ca098780a691c3030a.pdf.

Lyons, Kristina Marie. 2016. "Decomposition as Life Politics: Soils, Selva, and Small Farmers under the Gun of the U.S.-Colombia War on Drugs." *Cultural Anthropology* 31 (1): 55–80.

Ma'an News Agency. 2010. "Report: Israel Shuts Off Water to Jordan Valley Farms." *Ma'an News Agency*, April 11. http://www.maannews.com/Content.aspx?id=275681.

Maček, Ivana. 2009. *Sarajevo under Siege: Anthropology in Wartime*. Philadelphia: University of Pennsylvania Press.

Mackendrick, Norah. 2014. "More Work for Mother: Chemical Body Burdens as a Maternal Responsibility." *Gender and Society* 28 (5): 705–28.

Magnani, Natalia. 2012. "Nonhuman Actors, Hybrid Networks, and Conflicts over Municipal Waste Incinerators." *Organization and Environment* 25 (2): 131–45.

Mahmood, Saba. 2005. *The Politics of Piety: The Islamic Revival and the Feminist Subject*. Princeton, NJ: Princeton University Press.

Maidhof, Callie. 2013. "Settlement Secularism." *Middle East Report*, no. 269 (Winter): 30–34.

———. 2016. "A House, a Yard, and a Security Fence: Israel's Secular Settlers in the West Bank." PhD diss., University of California, Berkeley.

Mains, Daniel. 2012. "Blackouts and Progress: Privatization, Infrastructure, and a Developmentalist State in Jimma, Ethiopia." *Cultural Anthropology* 27 (1): 3–27.

Majer, Hans Georg. 1984. *Das Osmanische "Registerbuch der Beschwerden" (Şiˋkāyet defterˈ) vom Jahre 1675: Einleitung, Reproduktion des Textes, Geographische Indices*. Vienna: Österreichischen Akademie der Wissenschaften.

Makdisi, Saree. 2008. *Palestine Inside Out: An Everyday Occupation*. New York: W. W. Norton.

Maliki, Majdi, and Yasser Shalabi. 2000. *Internal Migration and Returnees in the West Bank and Gaza Strip*. Ramallah: Palestine Economic Policy Research Institute.

Malinowski, Bronislaw. 1936. "The Problem of Meaning in Primitive Languages." In *The Meaning of Meaning*, edited by C. K. Ogden and I. A. Richards, 296–336. London: Kegan Paul.

Markell, Patchen. 2009. *Bound by Recognition*. Princeton, NJ: Princeton University Press.

Markowitz, Gerald, and David Rosner. 1994. *Deadly Dust: Silicosis and the Politics of Occupational Disease in Twentieth-Century America*. Princeton, NJ: Princeton University Press.

———. 2013. *Lead Wars: The Politics of Science and the Fate of America's Children*. Berkeley: University of California Press.

Marres, Noortje. 2016. *Material Participation: Technology, the Environment and Everyday Publics*. New York: Palgrave Macmillan.

Marshall, Mark. 1995. "Rethinking the Palestine Question: The Apartheid Paradigm." *Journal of Palestine Studies* 25 (1): 15–22.

Marshall, Tim. 2013. *Planning Major Infrastructure: A Critical Analysis*. New York: Routledge.

Martin, Aryn, Natasha Myers, and Ana Viseu. 2015. "The Politics of Care in Technoscience." *Social Studies of Science* 45 (5): 625–41.

Martinez-Alier, Joan. 2003. *The Environmentalism of the Poor: A Study of Ecological Conflicts and Valuation*. Northampton, MA: Edward Elgar.

Masco, Joseph. 2004. "Nuclear Technoaesthetics: Sensory Politics from Trinity to the Virtual Bomb in Los Alamos." *American Ethnologist* 31 (3): 1–25.

———. 2006. *The Nuclear Borderlands: The Manhattan Project in Post–Cold War New Mexico*. Princeton, NJ: Princeton University Press.

———. 2010. "Bad Weather: On Planetary Crisis." *Social Studies of Science* 40 (1): 7–40.

Mason, Michael, Mark Zeitoun, and Ziad Mimi. 2012. "Compounding Vulnerability: Impacts of Climate Change on Palestinians in Gaza and the West Bank." *Journal of Palestine Studies* 41 (3): 38–53.

Matthews, Andrew S. 2011. *Instituting Nature: Authority, Expertise, and Power in Mexican Forests*. Cambridge, MA: MIT Press.

———. 2015. "Imagining Forest Futures and Climate Change: The Mexican State as Insurance Broker and Storyteller." In *Climate Cultures: Anthropological Perspectives on Climate Change*, edited by Jessica Barnes and Michael R. Dove, 109–220. New Haven, CT: Yale University Press.

Mauss, Marcel. 1990. *The Gift: The Form and Reason for Exchange in Archaic Societies*. Translated by W. D. Halls. New York: W. W. Norton.

Mawqadi, Ola. 2017. "Feature: Israel's Quarries Plunder Palestinian Natural Resources." Wafa, November 26. http://english.wafa.ps/page.aspx?id=G39g3ra 95387540919aG39g3r.

Mbembé, Achille. 1992. "The Banality of Power and the Aesthetics of Vulgarity in the Postcolony." *Public Culture* 4 (2): 1–30.

———. 2001. *On the Postcolony*. Berkeley: University of California Press.

Mbembé, Achille, and Sarah Nuttall. 2004. "Writing the World from an African Metropolis." *Public Culture* 16 (3): 347–72.

McClintock, Anne. 2013. *Imperial Leather: Race, Gender, and Sexuality in the Colonial Contest*. London: Routledge.

McElwee, Pamela. 2015. "From Conservation and Development to Climate Change: Anthropological Engagements with REDD+ in Vietnam." In *Climate Cultures: Anthropological Perspectives on Climate Change*, edited by Jessica Barnes and Michael R. Dove, 82–106. New Haven, CT: Yale University Press.

McFarlane, Colin. 2008. "Governing the Contaminated City: Infrastructure and Sanitation in Colonial and Post-colonial Bombay." *International Journal of Urban and Regional Research* 32 (2): 415–35.

McKee, Emily. 2016. *Dwelling in Conflict: Negev Landscapes and the Boundaries of Belonging.* Stanford, CA: Stanford University Press.

———. 2018. "Environmental Framing and Its Limits: Campaigns in Palestine and Israel." *International Journal of Middle East Studies* 50 (3): 449–70. https://doi.org/doi:10.1017/S0020743818000806.

McLaren, John, Andrew Richard Buck, and Nancy E. Wright, eds. 2005. *Despotic Dominion: Property Rights in British Settler Societies.* Vancouver: University of British Columbia Press.

McNally, David. 1990. *Political Economy and the Rise of Capitalism.* Berkeley: University of California Press.

Meari, Lena. 2014. "Sumud: A Palestinian Philosophy of Confrontation in Colonial Prisons." *South Atlantic Quarterly* 113 (3): 547–78.

Meisels, Tamar. 2002. "'A Land without a People': An Evaluation of Nations' Efficiency-Based Territorial Claims." *Political Studies* 50 (5): 959–73.

Melosi, Martin V. 2004. *Garbage in the Cities: Refuse Reform and the Environment.* Pittsburgh, PA: University of Pittsburgh Press.

Meneley, Anne. 1996. *Tournaments of Value: Sociability and Hierarchy in a Yemeni Town.* Stanford, CA: Stanford University Press.

Mer Khamis, Juliano, and Danniel Danniel, dirs. 2004. *Arna's Children.* DVD. Tel Aviv: Trabelsi Productions.

Merz, Sibille. 2012. "'Missionaries of the New Era': Neoliberalism and NGOs in Palestine." *Race and Class* 54 (1): 50–66.

Messick, Brinkley. 1996. *The Calligraphic State: Textual Domination and History in a Muslim Society.* Berkeley: University of California Press.

Mikhail, Alan. 2011. *Nature and Empire in Ottoman Egypt: An Environmental History.* Cambridge: Cambridge University Press.

———. 2013a. *The Animal in Ottoman Egypt.* Oxford: Oxford University Press.

———, ed. 2013b. *Water on Sand: Environmental Histories of the Middle East and North Africa.* Oxford: Oxford University Press.

Mikkelsen, Edwin J., and Phil Brown. 1997. *No Safe Place: Toxic Waste, Leukemia, and Community Action.* Berkeley: University of California Press.

Millar, Kathleen. 2014. "The Precarious Present: Wageless Labor and Disrupted Life in Rio de Janeiro, Brazil." *Cultural Anthropology* 29 (1): 32–53.

Miller, Daniel. 2005. *A Theory of Shopping*. Cambridge: Polity Press.

———. 2009. "Buying Time." In *Time, Consumption and Everyday Life: Practice, Materiality and Culture*, edited by Elizabeth Shove, Frank Trentmann, and Richard Wilk, 157–70. Oxford: Berg.

Mills, James H., and Satadru Sen, eds. 2004. *Confronting the Body: The Politics of Physicality in Colonial and Post-colonial India*. London: Anthem Press.

Minter, Adam. 2013. *Junkyard Planet: Travels in the Billion Dollar Trash Trade*. London: Bloomsbury.

Mintz, Sidney W., and Christine M. Du Bois. 2002. "The Anthropology of Food and Eating." *Annual Review of Anthropology* 31 (1): 99–119.

Mishal, Shaul, and Avraham Sela. 2000. *The Palestinian Hamas: Vision, Violence, and Coexistence*. New York: Columbia University Press.

Mitchell, Jerry, Deborah Thomas, and Susan Cutter. 1999. "Dumping in Dixie Revisited: The Evolution of Environmental Injustices in South Carolina." *Social Science Quarterly* 80 (2): 229–43.

Mitchell, Timothy. 1991. *Colonising Egypt*. Berkeley: University of California Press.

———. 2002. *Rule of Experts: Egypt, Techno-Politics, Modernity*. Berkeley: University of California Press.

———. 2006. "Society, Economy and the State Effect." In *The Anthropology of the State: A Reader*, edited by Aradhana Sharma and Akhil Gupta, 169–86. Oxford: Blackwell.

———. 2011a. "Afterword." In *Environmental Imaginaries of the Middle East and North Africa*, edited by Diana K. Davis and Edmund Burke III, 265–73. Athens: Ohio University Press.

———. 2011b. *Carbon Democracy: Political Power in the Time of Oil*. London: Verso.

Mittermaier, Amira. 2012. "Dreams from Elsewhere: Muslim Subjectivities beyond the Trope of Self-Cultivation." *Journal of the Royal Anthropological Institute* 18 (2): 247–65.

Mohai, Paul, David Pellow, and J. Timmons Roberts. 2009. "Environmental Justice." *Annual Review of Environment and Resources* 34: 405–30.

Mol, Annemarie, Ingunn Moser, and Jeannette Pols. 2010. "Care: Putting Practice into Theory." In *Care in Practice: On Tinkering in Clinics, Homes, and Farms*, edited by Annemarie Mol, Ingunn Moser, and Jeannette Pols, 7–26. Bielefeld: Transcript.

Molotch, Harvey L., and Laura Norén. 2010. *Toilet: Public Restrooms and the Politics of Sharing*. New York: New York University Press.

Moore, Amelia. 2016. "Anthropocene Anthropology: Reconceptualizing Contemporary Global Change." *Journal of the Royal Anthropological Institute* 22 (1): 27–46.

———. 2018. "Selling Anthropocene Space: Situated Adventures in Sustainable Tourism." *Journal of Sustainable Tourism*: 2–16.

Moore, Sarah A. 2012. "Garbage Matters: Concepts in New Geographies of Waste." *Progress in Human Geography* 36 (6): 780–99.

Moors, Annelies. 1995. *Women, Property and Islam: Palestinian Experiences, 1920–1990*. Cambridge: Cambridge University Press.

Morgensen, Scott L. 2016. "Encountering Indeterminacy: Colonial Contexts and Queer Imagining." *Cultural Anthropology* 31 (4): 607–16. https://doi.org/10.14506/ca31.4.09.

Morrison, Susan. 2008. *Excrement in the Late Middle Ages: Sacred Filth and Chaucer's Fecopoetics*. New York: Palgrave Macmillan.

Mosse, David. 2005. *Cultivating Development: An Ethnography of Aid Policy and Practice*. Ann Arbor, MI: Pluto Press.

———. 2013. "The Anthropology of International Development." *Annual Review of Anthropology* 42: 227–46.

Murphy, Michelle. 2006. *Sick Building Syndrome: Environmental Politics, Technoscience, and Women Workers*. Durham, NC: Duke University Press.

———. 2017. "Alterlife and Decolonial Chemical Relations." *Cultural Anthropology* 32 (4): 494–503.

Musleh, Reem, and Rita Giacaman. 2001. "The Problems of Solid Waste on the West Bank since September 28th, 2000." Report, Institute of Community and Public Health, Birzeit University.

Myers, Garth Andrew. 2005. *Disposable Cities: Garbage, Governance and Sustainable Development in Urban Africa*. Aldershot: Ashgate.

Nagle, Robin. 2013. *Picking Up: On the Streets and behind the Trucks with the Sanitation Workers of New York City*. New York: Farrar, Straus and Giroux.

Nakassis, Constantine V. 2013. "Brands and Their Surfeits." *Cultural Anthropology* 28 (1): 111–26.

Nash, Linda Loraine. 2006. *Inescapable Ecologies: A History of Environment, Disease, and Knowledge*. Berkeley: University of California Press.

Navaro-Yashin, Yael. 2012. *The Make-Believe Space: Affective Geography in a Postwar Polity*. Durham, NC: Duke University Press.

Negt, Oskar. 2006. "The Production of Counter-publics and the Counter-publics of Production: An Interview with Oskar Negt." Interviewed by Monika Krause. *European Journal of Social Theory* 9 (1): 119–28.

Newell, Sasha. 2013. "Brands as Masks: Public Secrecy and the Counterfeit in Côte d'Ivoire." *Journal of the Royal Anthropological Institute* 19 (1): 138–54.

Newman, Richard. 2016. *Love Canal: A Toxic History from Colonial Times to the Present.* New York: Oxford University Press.

Neyland, Daniel, and Elena Simakova. 2012. "Managing Electronic Waste: A Study of Market Failure." *New Technology, Work and Employment* 27 (1): 36–51.

Nielsen, Morten, and Morten Axel Pedersen. 2015. "Infrastructural Imaginaries: Collapsed Futures in Mozambique and Mongolia." In *Reflections on Imagination: Human Capacity and Ethnographic Method*, edited by Mark Harris and Nigel Rapport, 237–62. Surrey: Ashgate.

Nissim, Ilan, Tal Shohat, and Yossi Inbar. 2005. "From Dumping to Sanitary Landfills: Solid Waste Management in Israel." *Waste Management* 25 (3): 323–27.

Nixon, Rob. 2011. *Slow Violence and the Environmentalism of the Poor.* Cambridge, MA: Harvard University Press.

Norris, Lucy. 2012. "Shoddy Rags and Relief Blankets: Perceptions of Textile Recycling in North India." In *Economies of Recycling: The Global Transformation of Materials, Values and Social Relations*, edited by Catherine Alexander and Joshua Reno, 35–58. London: Zed Books.

Nossek, Hillel, and Khalil Rinnawi. 2003. "Censorship and Freedom of the Press under Changing Political Regimes: Palestinian Media from Israeli Occupation to the Palestinian Authority." *Gazette* (Leiden, Netherlands) 65 (2): 183–202.

Nucho, Joanne. 2016. *Everyday Sectarianism in Urban Lebanon: Infrastructures, Public Services, and Power.* Princeton, NJ: Princeton University Press.

Nugent, David. 1997. *Modernity at the Edge of Empire: State, Individual, and Nation in the Northern Peruvian Andes, 1885–1935.* Stanford, CA: Stanford University Press.

———. 2010. "Domestication, Legibility, and Efficacy: Toward a Reflexive Understanding of the Social Sciences." *Identities: Global Studies in Culture and Power* 17 (1): 72–81.

Nur, Masalha. 2008. "Remembering the Palestinian Nakba: Commemoration, Oral History and Narratives of Memory." *Holy Land Studies* 7 (2): 123–56.

Nussbaum, Martha. 1998. "The Good as Discipline, the Good as Freedom." In *Ethics of Consumption: The Good Life, Justice, and Global Stewardship*, edited by David A. Crocker and Toby Linden, 312–41. Lanham, MD: Rowman and Littlefield.

Obadare, Ebenezer. 2010. "State of Travesty: Jokes and the Logic of Socio-cultural Improvisation in Africa." *Critical African Studies* 2 (4): 92–112.

Observatory of Economic Complexity, MIT Media Lab. n.d. "Imports 2016." Accessed November 29, 2018. https://atlas.media.mit.edu/en/profile/country/pse/#Imports.

Ochs, Juliana. 2011. *Security and Suspicion: An Ethnography of Everyday Life in Israel.* Philadelphia: University of Pennsylvania Press.

OECD (Organisation for Economic Co-operation and Development). 2008. *The Polluter Pays Principle.* Paris: OECD Publishing.

Ogawa, Akihiro. 2014. "The Right to Evacuation: The Self-Determined Future of Post-Fukushima Japan." *Inter-Asia Cultural Studies* 15 (4): 648–58.

Ogden, Laura, Nik Heynen, Ulrich Oslender, Paige West, Karim-Aly Kassam, and Paul Robbins. 2013. "Global Assemblages, Resilience, and Earth Stewardship in the Anthropocene." *Frontiers in Ecology and the Environment* 11 (7): 341–47.

Oliver-Smith, Anthony. 1996. "Anthropological Research on Hazards and Disasters." *Annual Review of Anthropology* 25 (1): 303–28.

———. 2009. "Climate Change and Population Displacement: Disasters and Diasporas in the Twenty-First Century." In *Anthropology and Climate Change: From Encounters to Actions*, edited by Susan Crate and Mark Nuttal, 116–36. Walnut Creek, CA: Left Coast Press.

Omar, Dina. 2013. "Trashing Four Generations of Palestinian Inheritance." *Al-Shabaka*, June 4. https://al-shabaka.org/node/618.

Ophir, Adi, Michal Givoni, and Sari Hanafi, eds. 2009. *The Power of Inclusive Exclusion: Anatomy of Israeli Rule in the Occupied Palestinian Territories.* Cambridge, MA: MIT Press.

O'Reilly, Jessica. 2017. *The Technocratic Antarctic: An Ethnography of Scientific Expertise and Environmental Governance.* Ithaca, NY: Cornell University Press.

Ortner, Sherry. 2006. *Anthropology and Social Theory: Culture, Power, and the Acting Subject.* Durham, NC: Duke University Press.

Orwell, George. 1949. *Nineteen Eighty-Four.* London: Martin Secker and Warburg.

Otter, Christopher. 2008. *The Victorian Eye: A Political History of Light and Vision in Britain, 1800–1910.* Chicago: University of Chicago Press.

Palmer, Daniel. 1997. "In the Anonymity of a Murmur: Graffiti and the Construction of the Past at the Fremantle Prison." *Studies in Western Australian History* 17: 104–15.

Papadopoulou, Elizabeth, Sarah Gallacher, Nick K. Taylor, and M. Howard Williams. 2012. "A Personal Smart Space Approach to Realising Ambient Ecologies." *Pervasive and Mobile Computing* 8 (4): 485–99.

Pappe, Ilan. 2006. *The Ethnic Cleansing of Palestine.* Oxford: Oneworld.

Parkhill, Karen A., Nick F. Pidgeon, Karen L. Henwood, Peter Simmons, and Dan Venables. 2009. "From the Familiar to the Extraordinary: Local Residents' Perceptions of Risk when Living with Nuclear Power in the UK." *Transactions of the Institute of British Geographers* 35 (1): 39–58.

Parry, Jonathan. 1986. "The Gift, the Indian Gift and the 'Indian Gift.'" *Man*, n.s., 21 (3): 453–73.

———. 1989. "On the Moral Perils of Exchange." In *Money and the Morality of Exchange*, edited by Maurice Bloch and Jonathan Parry, 64–93. Cambridge: Cambridge University Press.

Parsons, Nigel. 2005. *The Politics of the Palestinian Authority: From Oslo to al-Aqsa.* London: Routledge.

Pasternak, Shiri. 2014. "Occupy(ed) Canada: The Political Economy of Indigenous Dispossession." In *The Winter We Danced: Voices from the Past, the Future, and the Idle No More Movement*, edited by the Kino-nda-niimi Collective, 40–43. Winnipeg: ARP Books.

Pateman, Carol, and Charles Mills. 2007. *Contract and Dominion.* Cambridge: Polity Press.

Pati, Biswamoy, and Mark Harrison, eds. 2008. *The Social History of Health and Medicine in Colonial India.* London: Routledge.

Peace Now. n.d. "Data." Accessed November 20, 2018. peacenow.org.

Pedersen, David. 2013. *American Value: Migrants, Money, and Meaning in El Salvador and the United States.* Chicago: University of Chicago Press.

Pellow, David Naguib. 2002. *Garbage Wars: The Struggle for Environmental Justice in Chicago.* Cambridge, MA: MIT Press.

———. 2007. *Resisting Global Toxics: Transnational Movements for Environmental Justice.* Cambridge, MA: MIT Press.

Penglase, Ben. 2009. "States of Insecurity: Everyday Emergencies, Public Secrets, and Drug Trafficker Power in a Brazilian Favela." *PoLAR: Political and Legal Anthropology Review* 32 (1): 47–63.

Peteet, Julie. 1994. "Male Gender and Rituals of Resistance in the Palestinian Intifada: A Cultural Politics of Violence." *American Ethnologist* 21 (1): 31–49.

———. 1996. "The Writing on the Walls: The Graffiti of the Intifada." *Cultural Anthropology* 11 (2): 139–59.

———. 2005. *Landscape of Hope and Despair: Palestinian Refugee Camps.* Philadelphia: University of Pennsylvania Press.

———. 2017. *Space and Mobility in Palestine.* Bloomington: Indiana University Press.

———. 2018. "Closure's Temporality: The Cultural Politics of Time and Waiting." *South Atlantic Quarterly* 117 (1): 43–64.

Petryna, Adriana. 2003. *Life Exposed: Biological Citizens after Chernobyl.* Princeton, NJ: Princeton University Press.

Petti, Alessandro, Sandi Hilal, and Eyal Weizman. 2013. *Architecture after Revolution*. Berlin: Sternberg Press.

Pinker, Annabel. 2015. "Papering over the Gaps: Documents, Infrastructure and Political Experimentation in Highland Peru." *Cambridge Journal of Anthropology* 33 (1): 97–112.

Piterberg, Gabriel. 2008. *The Returns of Zionism: Myths, Politics and Scholarship in Israel*. London: Verso.

Plascov, Avi. 1981. *The Palestinian Refugees in Jordan, 1948–1957*. London: F. Cass.

PNA (Palestinian National Authority). 2010a. *Palestinian National Strategy for Solid Waste Management*. Ramallah: Palestinian National Authority.

———. 2010b. "Status of Wastewater Treatment Plant Projects in the West Bank: An Internal Working Document." Ramallah.

PNA (Palestinian National Authority), Ministry of Local Government. 2013. "The Preparatory Survey (Basic Design) on the Project for the Improvement of Solid Waste Management in the West Bank, Palestine: Final Report." February. Japan International Cooperation Agency and NJS Consultants Co. http://open_jicareport .jica.go.jp/pdf/12111258_01.pdf.

PNA (Palestinian National Authority), Ministry of Tourism and Antiquities. 2009. *Inventory of Cultural and Natural Heritage Sites of Potential Outstanding Universal Value in Palestine*, edited by Hamdan Taha. Ramallah: Department of Antiquities and Cultural Heritage.

Polon, Tal. 2017. "19–Mile Long Sewage Pool from Ramallah Reaches Modiin Illit: Massive Sewage Overflows from Ramallah Threaten Jewish Town." *Arutz Sheva*, May 14. http://www.israelnationalnews.com/News/News.aspx/229614.

Pontin, Benjamin, Vito De Lucia, and Jesus Gamero Rus. 2015. *Environmental Injustice in Occupied Palestinian Territory*. Ramallah: Al-Haq Organization.

Popperl, Simone. 2018. "Geologies of Erasure: Sinkholes, Science, and Settler Colonialism at the Dead Sea." *International Journal of Middle East Studies* 50 (3): 427–48.

Povinelli, Elizabeth A. 2011. *Economies of Abandonment: Social Belonging and Endurance in Late Liberalism*. Durham, NC: Duke University Press.

Protevi, John. 2009. *Political Affect: Connecting the Social and the Somatic*. Minneapolis: University of Minnesota Press.

Puar, Jasbir. 2013. "Rethinking Homonationalism." *International Journal of Middle East Studies* 45 (2): 336–39.

Pullan, Wendy, Philipp Misselwitz, Rami Nasrallah, and Haim Yacobi. 2007. "Jerusalem's Road 1: An Inner City Frontier?" *City* 11 (2): 176–98.

Purdy, Jedediah S. 2011. "Afterword: An American Sacrifice Zone." In *Mountains of Injustice: Social and Environmental Justice in Appalachia*, edited by Michele Morrone and Geoffrey L. Buckley, 181–84. Athens: Ohio University Press.

Qumsieh, Violet. *See also* Qumsiyeh, Violet. 1998. "The Environmental Impact of Jewish Settlements in the West Bank." *Palestine-Israel Journal of Politics, Economics and Culture* 5 (1). http://www.arij.org/files/admin/1998/1998%20The%20Environmental%20Impact%20of%20Jewish%20Settlements%20in%20the%20West%20Bank.pdf

Qumsiyeh, Violet, and Yousef Tushyeh. 2000. "Assessment of the Impact of Israeli Industries on the West Bank Environment." In *Industrial Liquid Waste: Impact on the Environment and Public Health, Proceedings of the Workshop entitled "Industrial Waste Water in Palestine—Impact on Environment and Public Health," December 11, 1997*, edited by Maisoun Filfil and Issam al-Khatib, 13–28. Birzeit: Institute of Community and Public Health Environmental Health Unit, Birzeit University.

Rabie, Kareem. 2014. "Palestine Is Throwing a Party and the Whole World Is Invited: Private Development and State Building in the Contemporary West Bank." PhD diss., City University of New York.

Rabinow, Paul. 1989. *French Modern: Norms and Forms of the Social Environment*. Cambridge, MA: MIT Press.

———. 1996. *Essays on the Anthropology of Reason*. Princeton, NJ: Princeton University Press.

———. 2007. *Marking Time: On the Anthropology of the Contemporary*. Princeton, NJ: Princeton University Press.

Radford, Tom. 2010. "The Sacrifice Zone: Living in the Shadow of the Tar Sands." In *Alberta Encore: People, Places and Poetry from Legacy Magazine*, edited by Barbara Dacks, 43–47. Edmonton: Alberta Ltd.

Rai, Amit S. 2015. "The Affect of Jugaad: Frugal Innovation and Postcolonial Practice in India's Mobile Phone Ecology." *Environment and Planning D: Society and Space* 33 (6): 985–1002.

Ramadan, Adam. 2010. "In the Ruins of Nahr al-Barid: Understanding the Meaning of the Camp." *Journal of Palestine Studies* 40 (1): 49–62.

Rathje, William, and Cullen Murphy. 2001. *Rubbish! The Archaeology of Garbage*. Tuscon: University of Arizona Press.

Reich, Michael. 1991. *Toxic Politics: Responding to Chemical Disasters*. Ithaca, NY: Cornell University Press.

Reid, Anna. 2011. *Leningrad: The Epic Siege of World War II, 1941–1944*. New York: Walker.

Reidy, Eric. 2013. "Palestinians Thirst for Water Treatment Plant." *Al-Jazeera*, December 21. http://www.aljazeera.com/indepth/features/2013/12/palestinians-thirst-water -treatment-plant-2013121612171192492.html.

Reno, Joshua. 2011. "Beyond Risk: Emplacement and the Production of Environmental Evidence." *American Ethnologist* 38 (3): 516–30.

———. 2015a. "Waste and Waste Management." *Annual Review of Anthropology* 44: 557–72.

———. 2015b. *Waste Away: Working and Living with a North American Landfill*. Berkeley: University of California Press.

———. 2016. "The Life and Times of Landfills." *Journal of Ecological Anthropology* 18 (1): 1–7. https://scholarcommons.usf.edu/cgi/viewcontent.cgi?referer=https:// www.google.com/&httpsredir=1&article=1197&context=jea.

Riccardi, Sarah A. n.d. "Sacred Waste." In *Discard Studies Compendium*, edited by Max Liboiron, Michele Acuto, and Robin Nagle. Accessed January 23, 2017. https:// discardstudies.com/discard-studies-compendium/#Sacredwaste.

Rinat, Zafrir. 2015. "Israeli Wastewater Policy Continues to Pay Off." *Ha'aretz*, March 23. http://www.haaretz.com/israel-news/science/.premium-1.648332.

Roberts, Elizabeth F. S. 2017. "What Gets Inside: Violent Entanglements and Toxic Boundaries in Mexico City." *Cultural Anthropology* 32 (4): 592–619.

Robins, Steven, Andrea Cornwall, and Bettina Von Lieres. 2008. "Rethinking 'Citizenship' in the PostColony." *Third World Quarterly* 29 (6): 1069–86.

Rodinson, Maxime. 1973. *Israel: A Settler-Colonial State?* Translated by David Thorstad. London: Pathfinder Press.

Rodriguez, Amardo, and Robin Patric Clair. 1999. "Graffiti as Communication: Exploring the Discursive Tensions of Anonymous Texts." *Southern Communication Journal* 65 (1): 1–15.

Roitman, Janet. 2005. *Fiscal Disobedience: An Anthropology of Economic Regulation in Central Africa*. Princeton, NJ: Princeton University Press.

Romero, Adam. 2016. "'From Oil Well to Farm': Industrial Waste, Shell Oil, and the Petrochemical Turn (1927–1947)." *Agricultural History* 90 (1): 70–93.

Rootes, Christopher, and Liam Leonard, eds. 2010. *Environmental Movements and Waste Infrastructure*. London: Routledge.

Rose, Nikolas. 1999. *The Powers of Freedom: Reframing Political Thought*. Cambridge: Cambridge University Press.

Rossi, Benedetta. 2004. "Order and Disjuncture: Theoretical Shifts in the Anthropology of Aid and Development." *Current Anthropology* 45 (4): 556–60.

Rothenberg, Celia. 2004. *Spirits of Palestine: Gender, Society, and the Stories of the Jinn.* Lanham, MD: Lexington Books.

Rouhana, Nadim N., and Areej Sabbagh-Khoury. 2015. "Settler-Colonial Citizenship: Conceptualizing the Relationship between Israel and Its Palestinian Citizens." *Settler Colonial Studies* 5 (3): 205–25.

Rousseau, Jean-Jacques. 1999. *Discourse on the Origin and Foundation of Inequality among Men.* Translated by Franklin Philip. Oxford: Oxford University Press.

———. 2000. *Confessions.* Translated by Angela Scholar. Oxford: Oxford University Press.

Roy, Sara M. 1995. *The Gaza Strip: The Political Economy of De-development.* Washington, DC: Institute for Palestine Studies.

———. 1998. "The Palestinian Economy after Oslo." *Current History* 97 (615): 19–25.

———. 1999. "De-development Revisited: Palestinian Economy and Society since Oslo." *Journal of Palestine Studies* 28 (3): 64–82.

Rubaii, Kali. 2016. "Concrete and Liveability in Occupied Palestine." *Engagement* (blog), September 20. https://aesengagement.wordpress.com/2016/09/20/concrete-and-livability-in-occupied-palestine/.

———. 2018. "Counterinsurgency and the Ethical Life of Material Things in Iraq's Anbar Province." PhD diss., University of California, Santa Cruz.

Rubenstein, Michael. 2010. *Public Works: Infrastructure, Irish Modernism, and the Postcolonial.* Notre Dame: University of Notre Dame Press.

Rudiak-Gould, Peter. 2014. "Climate Change and Accusation: Global Warming and Local Blame in a Small Island State." *Current Anthropology* 55 (4): 365–86.

Ryan, Simon. 2002. "Inscribing the Emptiness: Cartography, Exploration and the Construction of Australia." In *De-scribing Empire: Post-colonialism and Textuality,* edited by Chris Tiffin and Alan Lawson, 115–30. London: Routledge.

Sa'di, Ahmad, and Lila Abu-Lughod, eds. 2007. *Nakba: Palestine, 1948, and the Claims of Memory.* New York: Columbia University Press.

Sahlins, Marshall. 1972. *Stone Age Economics.* New York: Aldine de Gruyter.

Salam, Nawaf A. 1994. "Between Repatriation and Resettlement: Palestinian Refugees in Lebanon." *Journal of Palestine Studies* 24 (1): 18–27.

Salamanca, Omar Jabary. 2011. "Unplug and Play: Manufacturing Collapse in Gaza." *Human Geography* 4 (1): 22–37.

———. 2014. "Hooked on Electricity: The Charged Political Economy of Electrification in the Palestinian West Bank." Working paper presented at the symposium "Political Economy and Economy of the Political," Brown University.

Salamanca, Omar Jabary, Mezna Qato, Kareem Rabie, and Sobhi Samour. 2012. "Past Is Present: Settler Colonialism in Palestine." *Settler Colonial Studies* 2 (1): 1–8.

Salem, Walid. 2012. "Civil Society in Palestine: Approaches, Historical Context and the Role of the NGOs." *Palestine-Israel Journal of Politics, Economics, and Culture* 18 (2–3): 17–23.

Samuels, David. 2001. "Indeterminacy and History in Britton Goode's Western Apache Placenames: Ambiguous Identity on the San Carlos Apache Reservation." *American Ethnologist* 28 (2): 277–302.

Sand, Jordan. 2011. *Tokyo Vernacular: Common Spaces, Local Histories, Found Objects.* Berkeley: University of California Press.

Sayigh, Rosemary. 1993. *Too Many Enemies: The Palestinian Experience in Lebanon.* London: Zed Books.

———. 1995. "Palestinians in Lebanon: Harsh Present, Uncertain Future." *Journal of Palestine Studies* 25 (1): 37–53.

———. 2007. *The Palestinians: From Peasants to Revolutionaries.* New York: Zed Books.

Sayigh, Yezid. 2007. "Inducing a Failed State in Palestine." *Survival* 49 (3): 7–39.

Sayigh, Yusif A. 1986. "The Palestinian Economy under Occupation: Dependency and Pauperization." *Journal of Palestine Studies* 15 (4): 46–67.

Sbait, Ḍirghām Ḥ. 1993. "Debate in the Improvised-Sung Poetry of the Palestinians." *Asian Folklore Studies* 52 (1): 93–117.

Scaramelli, Caterina. 2013. "Making Sense of Water Quality: Multispecies Encounters on the Mystic River." *Worldviews: Global Religions, Culture, and Ecology* 17 (2): 150–60.

Schanzer, Jonathan. 2008. *Hamas vs. Fatah: The Struggle for Palestine.* New York: Palgrave Macmillan.

Schiff, Benjamin N. 1995. *Refugees unto the Third Generation: UN Aid to Palestinians.* Syracuse, NY: Syracuse University Press.

Schneider, Daniel. 2011. *Hybrid Nature: Sewage Treatment and the Contradictions of the Industrial Ecosystem.* Cambridge, MA: MIT Press.

Schulz, Helena Lindholm. 1999. *The Reconstruction of Palestinian Nationalism: Between Revolution and Statehood.* Manchester: Manchester University Press.

Schwenkel, Christina. 2015. "Spectacular Infrastructure and Its Breakdown in Socialist Vietnam." *American Ethnologist* 42 (3): 520–34.

Scott, James. 1998. *Seeing Like a State: How Certain Schemes to Improve the Human Condition Have Failed*. New Haven, CT: Yale University Press.

Seikaly, Sherene. 2016. *Men of Capital: Scarcity and Economy in Mandate Palestine*. Stanford, CA: Stanford University Press.

Selby, Jan. 2003. "Dressing Up Domination as 'Cooperation': The Case of Israeli-Palestinian Water Relations." *Review of International Studies* 29 (1): 121–38.

———. 2013. "Cooperation, Domination and Colonisation: The Israeli-Palestinian Joint Water Committee." *Water Alternatives* 6 (1): 1–24.

Selwyn, Tom. 2001. "Landscapes of Separation: Reflections on the Symbolism of Bypass Roads in Palestine." In *Contested Landscapes*, edited by Barbara Bender and Margot Winer, 225–40. Oxford: Berg.

Shafir, Gershon. 1989. *Land, Labor and the Origins of the Israeli-Palestinian Conflict, 1882–1914*. Cambridge: Cambridge University Press.

———. 1996. "Zionism and Colonialism: A Comparative Approach." In *Israel in Comparative Perspective: Challenging the Conventional Wisdom*, edited by Michael N. Barnett, 227–42. Albany: State University of New York Press.

Shah, Samira. 1997. "On the Road to Apartheid: The Bypass Road Network in the West Bank." *Columbia Human Rights Law Review* 29: 221–60.

Shamir, Ronen. 2013. *Current Flow: The Electrification of Palestine*. Stanford, CA: Stanford University Press.

Shapira, Anita. 1999. *Land and Power: The Zionist Resort to Force 1881–1948*. Translated by William Templer. Stanford, CA: Stanford University Press.

Shapiro, Nicholas. 2015. "Attuning to the Chemosphere: Domestic Formaldehyde, Bodily Reasoning, and the Chemical Sublime." *Cultural Anthropology* 30 (3): 368–93.

Shatz, Adam. 2013. "The Life and Death of Juliano Mer Khamis." *London Review of Books* 35 (22): 3–11.

Shevchenko, Olga. 2002. "'In Case of Fire Emergency': Consumption, Security and the Meaning of Durables in a Transforming Society." *Journal of Consumer Culture* 2 (2): 147–70.

Shohat, Ella. 1992. "Notes on the 'Post-colonial.'" *Social Text* 31/32: 99–113.

Shrader-Frechette, Kristin. 2005. "Mortgaging the Future: Dumping Ethics with Nuclear Waste." *Science and Engineering Ethics* 11 (4): 518–20.

Shuval, Hillel, ed. 1977. *Water Renovation and Reuse*. New York: Academic Press.

———, ed. 1980. *Water Quality Management under Conditions of Scarcity: Israel as a Case Study*. New York: Academic Press.

Siddiq, Muhammad. 1995. "On Ropes of Memory: Narrating the Palestinian Refugees."
In *Mistrusting Refugees*, edited by Valentine Daniel and John C. Knudsen, 87–101.
Berkeley: University of California Press.

Siegel, James. 1997. *Fetish, Recognition, Revolution*. Princeton, NJ: Princeton University
Press.

Silver, Jonathan. 2014. "Incremental Infrastructures: Material Improvisation and Social Collaboration across Post-colonial Accra." *Urban Geography* 35 (6): 788–804.

Simmons, Kristen. 2017. "Settler Atmospherics." *Cultural Anthropology* website, Fieldsights, Member Voices, November 20. https://culanth.org/fieldsights/1221–settler
-atmospherics.

Simone, AbdouMaliq. 2004a. *For the City Yet to Come: Changing African Life in Four
Cities*. Durham, NC: Duke University Press.

———. 2004b. "People as Infrastructure: Intersecting Fragments in Johannesburg."
Public Culture 16 (3): 407–29.

Simpson, Audra. 2014. *Mohawk Interruptus: Political Life across the Borders of Settler
States*. Durham, NC: Duke University Press.

Sivaramakrishnan, Kalyanakrishnan. 2015. "Ethics of Nature in Indian Environmental
History: A Review Article." *Modern Asian Studies* 49 (4): 1261–310.

Slyomovics, Susan. 1998. *The Object of Memory: Arab and Jew Narrate the Palestinian
Village*. Philadelphia: University of Pennsylvania Press.

Smith, Neil. 1991. "The Production of Nature." In *Uneven Development: Nature, Capital
and the Production of Space*, 34–65. Oxford: Blackwell.

Sones, Mordechai. 2017. "Arab Imagination: Sewage Wars." *Arutz Sheva*, May 15. http://
www.israelnationalnews.com/News/News.aspx/229685.

Sowers, Jeannie. "Remapping the Nation, Critiquing the State Environmental Narratives and Desert Land Reclamation in Egypt." In *Environmental Imaginaries of
the Middle East and North Africa*, edited by Diana K. Davis and Edmund Burke
III, 22–46. Athens: Ohio University Press.

Spyer, Patricia. 1998. *Border Fetishisms: Material Objects in Unstable Spaces*. New York:
Routledge.

Sreenivasan, Gopal. 1995. *The Limits of Lockean Rights in Property*. Oxford: Oxford
University Press.

Stamatopoulou-Robbins, Sophia. 2008. "The Hamas Effect: A Summary," *Anthropology
News*, November, 54.

———. 2011. "In Colonial Shoes: Notes on the Material Afterlife in Post-Oslo Palestine."
Jerusalem Quarterly 48: 54–77.

————. 2014. "Occupational Hazards." *Comparative Studies of South Asia, Africa and the Middle East* 34 (3): 476–96.

————. 2018. "An Uncertain Climate in Risky Times: How Occupation Became Like the Rain in Post-Oslo Palestine." *International Journal of Middle East Studies* 50 (3): 383–404.

Star, Susan Leigh. 1999. "The Ethnography of Infrastructure." *American Behavioral Scientist* 43 (3): 377–91.

Starosielski, Nicole. 2015. *The Undersea Network*. Durham, NC: Duke University Press.

Steiner, Christopher B. 2001. "Rights of Passage: On the Liminal Identity of Art in the Border Zone." In *The Empire of Things: Regimes of Value and Material Culture*, edited by Fred Myers, 207–32. Santa Fe, NM: School for Advanced Research Press.

Stengs, Irene. 2014. "Sacred Waste." *Material Religion: The Journal of Objects, Art and Belief* 10 (2): 235–38.

Stern, Samuel M. 1964. "Petitions from the Ayyūbid Period." *Bulletin of the School of Oriental and African Studies* 27 (1): 1–32.

Stoler, Ann Laura. 2006. Preface to *Haunted by Empire: Geographies of Intimacy in North American History*, edited by Ann Stoler. Durham, NC: Duke University Press.

————, ed. 2013. *Imperial Debris: On Ruins and Ruination*. Durham, NC: Duke University Press.

Strasser, Susan. 2000. *Waste and Want: A Social History of Trash*. New York: Holt.

Strathern, Marilyn. 1996. "Cutting the Network." *Journal of the Royal Anthropological Institute* 2 (3): 517–35.

Sufian, Sandra. 2007. *Healing the Land and the Nation: Malaria and the Zionist Project in Mandatory Palestine, 1920–1947*. Chicago: University of Chicago Press.

Swedenburg, Ted. 2003. *Memories of Revolt: The 1936–39 Rebellion and the Palestinian National Past*. Durham, NC: Duke University Press.

Swyngedouw, Erik. 2015. *Liquid Power: Water and Contested Modernities in Spain*. Cambridge, MA: MIT Press.

Szasz, Andrew. 1994. *Toxic Waste and the Movement for Environmental Justice*. Minneapolis: University of Minnesota Press.

Sze, Julie. 2006. *Noxious New York: The Racial Politics of Urban Health and Environmental Justice*. Cambridge, MA: MIT Press.

Tabar, Linda. 2007a. "Memory, Agency, Counter-narrative: Testimonies from Jenin Refugee Camp." *Critical Arts: South-North Cultural and Media Studies* 21 (1): 6–31.

———. 2007b. "The Rise of Localized Popular Resistance Formations: Jenin Camp and the Future of Palestinian Political Activism." In *Between the Lines: Israel, the Palestinians, and the U.S. "War on Terror,"* edited by Tikva Honig-Parnass and Toufic Haddad, 167–72. Chicago: Haymarket Books.

Tagar, Zecharya, Tamar Keinan, and Gidon Bromberg. 2004. *A Seeping Time Bomb: Pollution of the Mountain Aquifer by Sewage.* Tel Aviv: Friends of the Earth Middle East.

Taghdisi-Rad, Sahar. 2011. *The Political Economy of Aid in Palestine: Relief from Conflict or Development Delayed?* New York: Routledge.

Tahal Engineering Consultants Ltd. 1987. *Tokhnit-Av le-Siluk Psolet Mutzaka be-Ezor Yehuda ve-Shomron* [Master-plan for the disposal of solid waste in the Judea and Samaria region]. Tel-Aviv: Civil Administration of Judea and Samaria, Department of Environmental Engineering.

Tal, Alon. 2002. *Pollution in a Promised Land: An Environmental History of Israel.* Berkeley: University of California Press.

Tamari, Salim. 1981. "Building Other People's Homes: The Palestinian Peasant's Household and Work in Israel." *Journal of Palestine Studies* 11 (1): 31–66.

———. 1983. "In League with Zion: Israel's Search for a Native Pillar." *Journal of Palestine Studies* 12 (4): 41–56.

Tanigawa, Koichi, Yoshio Hosoi, Nobuyuki Hirohashi, Yasumasa Iwasaki, and Kenji Kamiya. 2012. "Loss of Life after Evacuation: Lessons Learned from the Fukushima Accident." *Lancet* 379 (9819): 889–91.

Taraki, Lisa. 2008a. "Enclave Metropolis: The Paradoxical Case of Ramallah/Al-Bireh." *Journal of Palestine Studies* 37 (4): 6–20.

———. 2008b. "Urban Modernity on the Periphery: A New Middle Class Reinvents the Palestinian City." *Social Text* 26 (2): 61–81.

Tartir, Ala'a. 2015a. "Contentious Economics in Occupied Palestine." In *Contentious Politics in the Middle East*, edited by Gerges Fawaz, 469–99. New York: Palgrave Macmillan US.

———. 2015b. "Securitised Development and Palestinian Authoritarianism under Fayyadism." *Conflict, Security and Development* 15 (5): 479–502.

Taussig, Michael T. 1997. *The Magic of the State.* New York: Routledge.

———. 1999. *Defacement: Public Secrecy and the Labor of the Negative.* Stanford, CA: Stanford University Press.

———. 2010. *The Devil and Commodity Fetishism in South America.* Chapel Hill: University of North Carolina Press.

———. 2016. "Viscerality, Faith, and Skepticism: Another Theory of Magic." *HAU: Journal of Ethnographic Theory* 6 (3): 453–83.

Tawil-Souri, Helga. 2009. "New Palestinian Centers: An Ethnography of the Checkpoint Economy." *International Journal of Cultural Studies* 12 (3): 217–35.

———. 2011. "Qalandia Checkpoint as Space and Nonplace." *Space and Culture* 14 (1): 4–26.

Tesdell, Omar. 2013. "Shadow Spaces: Territory, Sovereignty, and the Question of Palestinian Cultivation." PhD diss., University of Minnesota.

———. 2015. "Territoriality and the Technics of Drylands Science in Palestine and North America." *International Journal of Middle East Studies* 47 (3): 570–73.

———. 2017. "Wild Wheat to Productive Drylands: Global Scientific Practice and the Agroecological Remaking of Palestine." *Geoforum* 78: 43–51.

Thomas, Peter. 2014. "Railways." In *The Routledge Handbook of Mobilities*, edited by Peter Adey, David Bissell, Kevin Hannam, Peter Merriman, and Mimi Sheller, 214–24. London: Routledge.

Ticktin, Miriam. 2011. *Casualties of Care: Immigration and the Politics of Humanitarianism in France.* Berkeley: University of California Press.

———. 2014. "Transnational Humanitarianism." *Annual Review of Anthropology* 43: 273–89.

Touhouliotis, Vasiliki. 2018. "Weak Seed and a Poisoned Land: Slow Violence and the Toxic Infrastructures of War in South Lebanon." *Environmental Humanities* 10 (1): 86–106.

Tousignant, Noémi. 2018. *Edges of Exposure: Toxicology and the Problem of Capacity in Postcolonial Senegal.* Durham, NC: Duke University Press.

Townsend, Anthony M. 2013. *Smart Cities: Big Data, Civic Hackers, and the Quest for a New Utopia.* New York: W. W. Norton.

Townsend, Patricia. 2000. *Environmental Anthropology: From Pigs to Policies.* Long Grove, IL: Waveland Press.

Trading Economics. n.d. "Palestine GDP per Capita." Accessed March 13, 2017. http://www.tradingeconomics.com/palestine/gdp-per-capita.

Triassi, Maria, Rossella Alfano, Maddalena Illario, Antonio Nardone, Oreste Caporale, and Paolo Montuori. 2015. "Environmental Pollution from Illegal Waste Disposal and Health Effects: A Review on the 'Triangle of Death.'" *International Journal of Environmental Research and Public Health* 12 (2): 1216–36.

Troesken, Werner. 2004. *Water, Race, and Disease.* Cambridge, MA: MIT Press.

Trottier, Julie. 1999. *Hydropolitics in the West Bank and Gaza Strip*. Jerusalem: Palestinian Academic Society for the Study of International Affairs.

———. 2007. "A Wall, Water and Power: The Israeli 'Separation Fence.'" *Review of International Studies* 33 (1): 105–27.

Trouillot, Michel-Rolph. 2003. *Global Transformations*. New York: Palgrave Macmillan.

Tsing, Anna Lowenhaupt. 2005. *Friction: An Ethnography of Global Connection*. Princeton, NJ: Princeton University Press.

———. 2015. *The Mushroom at the End of the World: On the Possibility of Life in Capitalist Ruins*. Princeton, NJ: Princeton University Press.

Tully, James. 1980. *A Discourse on Property: John Locke and His Adversaries*. Cambridge: Cambridge University Press.

Turner, Mandy. 2009. "The Power of 'Shock and Awe': The Palestinian Authority and the Road to Reform." *International Peacekeeping* 16 (4): 562–77.

Udi, Juliana. 2015. "Locke on Territorial Rights." *Review of Politics* 77: 191–215.

UNCTAD (United Nations Conference on Trade and Development). 2018. *The Economic Costs of the Israeli Occupation for the Palestinian People and Their Human Right to Development: Legal Dimensions*. UNCTAD/GDS/APP/2017/2. New York: United Nations. https://unctad.org/en/PublicationsLibrary/gdsapp2017d2_en.pdf.

UN Habitat. 2010. *Solid Waste Management in the World: Water and Sanitation in the World's Cities*. London: Earthscan.

Usher, Graham. 2006. "The Democratic Resistance: Hamas, Fatah, and the Palestinian Elections." *Journal of Palestine Studies* 35 (3): 20–36.

Van Aken, Mauro. 2006. "Dancing Belonging: Contesting Dabkeh in the Jordan Valley, Jordan." *Journal of Ethnic and Migration Studies* 32 (2): 203–22.

Van der Vossen, Bas. 2015. "Locke on Territorial Rights." *Political Studies* 63: 713–28.

Vann, Elizabeth F. 2006. "The Limits of Authenticity in Vietnamese Consumer Markets." *American Anthropologist* 108 (2): 286–96.

Varman, Rohit, and Ram Manohar Vikas. 2007. "Freedom and Consumption: Toward Conceptualizing Systemic Constraints for Subaltern Consumers in a Capitalist Society." *Consumption Markets and Culture* 10: 117–31.

Vetter, Marcus, and Leon Geller, dirs. 2008. *The Heart of Jenin*. Videorecording. Germany: Arsenal Film.

Villanger, Espen. 2007. "Arab Foreign Aid: Disbursement Patterns, Aid Policies and Motives." *Forum for Development Studies* 34 (2): 223–56.

Von Schnitzler, Antina. 2008. "Citizenship Prepaid: Water, Calculability, and Techno-Politics in South Africa." *Journal of South African Studies* 34 (4): 899–917.

———. 2016. *Democracy's Infrastructure: Techno-Politics and Protest after Apartheid.* Princeton, NJ: Princeton University Press.

Voyles, Traci Brynne. 2015. *Wastelanding: Legacies of Uranium Mining in Navajo Country.* Minneapolis: University of Minnesota Press.

Vrijheid, Martine. 2000. "Health Effects of Residence near Hazardous Waste Landfill Sites: A Review of Epidemiologic Literature." *Environmental Health Perspectives* 108 (S1): 101–12.

Waldocks, Ehud Zion. 2010. "Palestinians Do Not Adequately Treat Their Sewage." *Jerusalem Post*, April 7. http://www.jpost.com/Health-and-Sci-Tech/Science-And-Environment/Palestinians-do-not-adequately-treat-their-sewage.

Waldron, Jeremy. 1988. *The Right to Private Property.* Oxford: Clarendon Press.

Walley, Christine. 2004. *Rough Waters: Nature and Development in an East African Marine Park.* Princeton, NJ: Princeton University Press.

Warner, Michael. 2002. "Publics and Counterpublics." *Public Culture* 14 (1): 49–90.

Warnock, Kitty. 1990. *Land before Honour: Palestinian Women in the Occupied Territories.* Basingstoke: Macmillan.

Weber, Max. 1958. "The Three Types of Legitimate Rule." Translated by Hans Gerth. *Berkeley Publications in Society and Institutions* 4 (1): 1–11.

———. 2013. *From Max Weber: Essays in Sociology.* New York: Routledge.

Wedeen, Lisa. 1999. *Ambiguities of Domination: Politics, Rhetoric, and Symbols in Contemporary Syria.* Chicago: University of Chicago Press.

———. 2003. "Seeing Like a Citizen, Acting Like a State: Exemplary Events in Unified Yemen." *Comparative Studies in Society and History* 45: 680–713.

Weiner, Annette B. 1992. *Inalienable Possessions: The Paradox of Keeping-While-Giving.* Berkeley: University of California Press.

Weiss, Hadas. 2009. "Ideology and Practice in the West Bank Settlement Movement." PhD diss., University of Chicago.

Weizman, Eyal. 2007. *Hollow Land: Israel's Architecture of Occupation.* London: Verso.

———. 2017. *Forensic Architecture: Violence at the Threshold of Detectability.* New York: Zone Books.

West, Paige. 2006. *Conservation Is Our Government Now: The Politics of Ecology in Papua New Guinea.* Durham, NC: Duke University Press.

———. 2012. *From Modern Production to Imagined Primitive: The Social World of Coffee from Papua New Guinea*. Durham, NC: Duke University Press.

———. 2016. *Dispossession and the Environment: Rhetoric and Inequality in Papua New Guinea*. New York: Columbia University Press.

Weszkalnys, Gisa. 2015. "Geology, Potentiality, Speculation: On the Indeterminacy of First Oil." *Cultural Anthropology* 30 (4): 611–39. https://culanth.org/articles/794 -geology-potentiality-speculation-on-the.

Wheelright, Jeff. 2013. "In a Polluted Stream, a Pathway to Peace." *New York Times*, October 9. http://www.nytimes.com/2013/10/10/opinion/in-a-polluted-stream-a -pathway-to-peace.html.

Whitehead, Judy. 2010. "John Locke and the Governance of India's Landscape: The Category of Wasteland in Colonial Revenue and Forest Legislation." *Economic and Political Weekly* 45 (50): 83–93.

———. 2012. "John Locke, Accumulation by Dispossession and the Governance of Colonial India." *Journal of Contemporary Asia* 42 (1): 1–21.

Whitington, Jerome. 2016. "What Does Climate Change Demand of Anthropology?" *PoLAR: Political and Legal Anthropology Review* 39 (1): 7–15.

Whyte, Kyle Powys. 2017. "Our Ancestors' Dystopia Now: Indigenous Conservation and the Anthropocene." In *The Routledge Companion to the Environmental Humanities*, edited by Ursula K. Heise, Jon Christensen, and Michelle Niemann, 206–15. New York: Routledge.

Wildeman, Jeremy, and Alaa Tartir. 2014. "Unwilling to Change, Determined to Fail: Donor Aid in Occupied Palestine in the Aftermath of the Arab Uprisings." *Mediterranean Politics* 19 (3): 431–49.

Wilson, Scott, and Glenn Kessler. 2006. "US Funds Enter Fray in Palestinian Elections." *Washington Post*, January 22. http://www.washingtonpost.com/wp-dyn/content /article/2006/01/21/AR2006012101431.html.

Winegar, Jessica. 2011. "Taking Out the Trash: Youth Clean Up Egypt after Mubarak." *Middle East Report* 259:32–35.

———. 2016. "A Civilized Revolution: Aesthetics and Political Action in Egypt." *American Ethnologist* 43 (4): 609–22.

Wolfe, Patrick. 2006. "Settler Colonialism and the Elimination of the Native." *Journal of Genocide Research* 8 (4): 387–409.

———. 2016. *Traces of History: Elementary Structures of Race*. London: Verso.

Wong, Edward. 2018. "U.S. to End Funding to U.N. Agency That Helps Palestinian Refugees." *New York Times*, August 31. https://www.nytimes.com/2018/08/31/us/politics/trump-unrwa-palestinians.html.

Wood, Neal. 1984. *John Locke and Agrarian Capitalism*. Berkeley: University of California Press.

World Bank. 1993. *Developing the Occupied Territories: An Investment in Peace*. Vol. 5. *Infrastructure*. Washington, DC: World Bank. https://www.un.org/unispal/document/developing-the-occupied-territories-an-investment-in-peace-vol-v-infrastructure-world-bank-report/.

———. 2013. *West Bank and Gaza: Solid Waste Management*. Public-Private Partnership Stories. Washington, DC: World Bank Group. http://documents.worldbank.org/curated/en/558191467999717075/West-Bank-and-Gaza-Solid-Waste-Management.

———. 2016. "Working amid Fragility: Delivering Results in Essential Services in Palestine." February 17. World Bank website. http://www.worldbank.org/en/news/feature/2016/02/17/working-amid-fragility-delivering-results-in-essential-services-in-palestine.

Yesh Din (Volunteers for Human Rights). 2009a. "Petition" [English translation]. Yesh Din (Volunteers for Human Rights), et al. v. Commander of the IDF Forces in the West Bank, et al., 1–38. https://s3–eu-west-1.amazonaws.com/files.yesh-din.org/%D7%A2%D7%AA%D7%99%D7%A8%D7%95%D7%AA/%D7%9E%D7%97%D7%A6%D7%91%D7%95%D7%AA/Quarries+Petition+English.pdf.

———. 2009b. "Petition to Halt Israeli Quarry and Mining Activities in the West Bank." March 9. https://www.yesh-din.org/en/petition-to-halt-all-israeli-quarry-and-mining-activities-in-the-west-bank-hcj-216409–yesh-din-volunteers-for-human-rights-v-the-commander-of-the-idf-forces-in-the-west-bank/.

———. 2011. "Ruling" [English unofficial translation]. December 26. Israeli High Court of Justice, HCJ 2164/09, 1–20. https://s3–eu-west-1.amazonaws.com/files.yesh-din.org/%D7%A2%D7%AA%D7%99%D7%A8%D7%95%D7%AA/%D7%9E%D7%97%D7%A6%D7%91%D7%95%D7%AA/HCJ+2164–09+Judgement+%5BYD+Quarries+case%5D.pdf.

Yiftachel, Oren. 1998. "Democracy or Ethnocracy: Territory and Settler Politics in Israel/Palestine." *Middle East Report* 207: 8–13.

———. 1999. "'Ethnocracy': The Politics of Judaizing Israel/Palestine." *Constellations* 6 (3): 364–90.

———. 2005. "Neither Two States nor One: The Disengagement and 'Creeping Apartheid.' in Israel/Palestine." *Arab World Geographer/Le géographe du monde arabe* 8 (3): 125–29.

Zanotti, Jim. 2016. "U.S. Foreign Aid to the Palestinians." Congressional Research Service, Prepared for Members and Committees of Congress, December 16. https://fas.org/sgp/crs/mideast/RS22967.pdf.

Zimmerer, Karl. 2000. The Reworking of Conservation Geographies: Nonequilibrium Landscapes and Nature-Society Hybrids. *Annals of the Association of American Geographers* 90 (2): 356–69.

Zimring, Carl. 2005. *Cash for Your Trash: Scrap Recycling in America*. New Brunswick, NJ: Rutgers University Press.

Zreik, Raef. 2004. "Palestine, Apartheid, and the Rights Discourse." *Journal of Palestine Studies* 34 (1): 68–80.

Zureik, Elia. 1979. *The Palestinians in Israel: A Study in Internal Colonialism*. London: Routledge.

———. 2003. "Theoretical and Methodological Considerations for the Study of Palestinian Society." *Comparative Studies of South Asia, Africa and the Middle East* 23 (1): 152–62.

Zureik, Elia, David Lyon, and Yasmeen Abu-Laban, eds. 2010. *Surveillance and Control in Israel/Palestine: Population, Territory and Power*. London: Routledge.